Bellewaarde
June 1915

Bellewaarde
June 1915

By Carole McEntee-Taylor

Foreword by Peter Doyle
Introduction by Martin Clift

Hat Badges and other Illustrations by Dawn Monks
http://www.dawnmonksillustrations.co.uk/

Pen & Sword
MILITARY

First published in Great Britain in 2014 by
Pen & Sword History
an imprint of
Pen & Sword Books Ltd
47 Church Street
Barnsley
South Yorkshire
S70 2AS

Copyright © Carole McEntee-Taylor 2014

ISBN 978 1 78340 052 2

The right of Carole McEntee-Taylor to be identified as the Author of this Work has been asserted by her in accordance with the Copyright, Designs and Patents Act 1988.

A CIP catalogue record for this book is available from the British Library

All rights reserved. No part of this book may be reproduced or transmitted in any form or by any means, electronic or mechanical including photocopying, recording or by any information storage and retrieval system, without permission from the Publisher in writing.

Typeset in Ehrhardt by
Mac Style Ltd, Bridlington, East Yorkshire
Printed and bound in the UK by CPI Group (UK) Ltd, Croydon, CR0 4YY

Pen & Sword Books Ltd incorporates the imprints of Pen & Sword Archaeology, Atlas, Aviation, Battleground, Discovery, Family History, History, Maritime, Military, Naval, Politics, Railways, Select, Transport, True Crime, and Fiction, Frontline Books, Leo Cooper, Praetorian Press, Seaforth Publishing and Wharncliffe.

For a complete list of Pen & Sword titles please contact
PEN & SWORD BOOKS LIMITED
47 Church Street, Barnsley, South Yorkshire, S70 2AS, England
E-mail: enquiries@pen-and-sword.co.uk
Website: www.pen-and-sword.co.uk

Bellewaarde, June 1915

Commander in Chief Sir John French would later sum up the day in this despatch:

'On 16th June an attack was carried out by the 5th Corps on the Bellewaarde Ridge, east of Ypres. The enemy's front line was captured, many of his dead and wounded being found in the trenches. The troops, pressing forward, gained ground as far East as the Bellewaarde Lake, but found themselves unable to maintain this advanced position. They were, however, successful in securing and consolidating the ground won during the first part of the attack, on a front of a thousand yards, including the advanced portion of the enemy's salient north of the Ypres–Menin Road. During this action the fire of the artillery was most effective, the prisoners testifying to its destructiveness and accuracy. It also prevented the delivery of counter attacks, which were paralysed at the outset. Over two hundred prisoners were taken, besides some machine-guns, trench material and gas apparatus. Holding attacks by the neighbouring 2nd and 6th Corps were successful in helping the main attack, whilst the 36th French Corps cooperated very usefully with artillery fire on Pilkem. Near Hill 60 the 10th Infantry Brigade made four bombing attacks, gaining and occupying about fifty yards of trench.'

Contents

Acknowledgements ix
Foreword x
Introduction xii
Prologue xv

Part One: The Protagonists

Chapter 1	The Allies	3
Chapter 2	The Germans	11
Chapter 3	438th (1/1st Cheshire) Field Company RE	20
Chapter 4	1st Battalion Northumberland Fusiliers	22
Chapter 5	4th Battalion Royal Fusiliers	36
Chapter 6	1/10th The (King's) Liverpool Regiment	42
Chapter 7	1st Battalion Lincolnshire Regiment	56
Chapter 8	1st Battalion West Yorkshire Regiment	61
Chapter 9	1st Battalion Royal Scots Fusiliers	66
Chapter 10	3rd Battalion Worcestershire Regiment	70
Chapter 11	2nd Battalion South Lancashire Regiment	78
Chapter 12	1/4th Battalion South Lancashire Regiment	83
Chapter 13	1st Battalion Wiltshire Regiment	85
Chapter 14	1/4th Battalion Gordon Highlanders – 8th Brigade	90
Chapter 15	2nd Battalion Royal Irish Rifles	99
Chapter 16	Army Service Corps	106
Chapter 17	1st Battalion Honourable Artillery Company	108
Chapter 18	Queen's Westminster Rifles	113
Chapter 19	42nd Brigade 14th (Light Division)	121
Chapter 20	Preparations	126

Part Two: The Battle		133
Chapter 21	The Battle Begins	135
Chapter 22	Early Success	148
Chapter 23	The Attack Falters	161
Chapter 24	The Tide Turns	169
Chapter 25	A Desperate Situation	177
Chapter 26	Gas and Counter-Attack	184
Chapter 27	The Battle Ends	190
Part Three: Summing Up		195
Chapter 28	The Aftermath	197
Chapter 29	The British	206
Chapter 30	The Germans	213
Chapter 31	Conclusion	219
Appendix A	The Fallen – The British	221
Appendix B	The Fallen German	313
Index		341

Acknowledgements

First and foremost I would like to thank Martin Clift as without him this book would not have been written. I offered to write it because of the obvious passion and dedication that he had invested in ensuring the men of Bellewaarde were not forgotten. Writing the book is intended to enhance his work by bringing the story of Bellewaarde June 1915 to a much wider audience. Although much of the information prior and after the battle stems from my independent research, the chapters about the battle itself use information, letters and personal recollections from the website that Martin has spent several years painstakingly researching and collecting.

I would also like to offer my grateful thanks to Clive McPherson of the Combined Services Museum Maldon for reading the manuscript and correcting any errors relating to military terminology, Robert Flemming, Information and Community Outreach Curator, National Army Museum, for helping me with regimental seniority and author Jack Sheldon and military historian Rob Shäfer for translating large tracts of German text for me. A special thanks to Dawn Monks for her wonderful illustrations. If you'd like to see more of Dawn's work please visit her website http://www.dawnmonksillustrations.co.uk/

I would also like to thank everyone who has given permission for their material to be included and I hope they enjoy the book.

And not least I would like to thank my husband David for his continuing help, support and encouragement.

Foreword

Bellewaarde. To any casual visitor to the battlefields of the old Western Front, travelling eastwards along the old Menin Road, and slowly rising up the low slopes that were so troublesome to the British High Command, Bellewaarde is obscure. Today marred by a theme park that does brisk business in the summer months, in 1915 things were very different. Here was the British frontline, manned by Britain's Regular Army, who had survived the desperate winter of 1914, and the 'Saturday night soldiers' of the Territorial Force who had taken the 'Imperial Service Commitment' to serve overseas. Visitors, perhaps stopping at the Hooge Crater Museum, or the preserved trenches at Hill 62 – Sanctuary Wood – are all the more likely to pass on along the road to explore the front line as it was in 1917.

But for me, Bellewaarde makes a special connection. West of the theme park is a small piece of battlefield terrain marked now by a monument to the Royal Engineers tunnellers who died in later actions. But in the small copse nearby, stands a stone to the Liverpool Scottish, one of the territorial Battalions of the King's Liverpool Regiment. Under the headline 'Another local "Scot" falls', and a photograph of a handsome young man wearing the diced glengarry of the Liverpool Scottish, the *Birkenhead News* recorded the loss of the son of Mr and Mrs Black, of Neptune Street, Birkenhead, 'killed in the charge with his regiment at Hooge on 16 July'. William Black was my grandmother's fiancée. A railwayman, he was 20 when killed. Ultimately, my grandmother, Gertrude Moore, married another man – my grandfather, Arthur Doyle – but William was never forgotten. Like so many others, his body was never found; but his line on the Menin Gate is picked out by my family on every visit to this sacred memorial.

The *Official History* describes Bellewaarde as a 'minor action', its function, like so many others, to act as a diversion for an attack at Givenchy to the south, and to capture the marginally high ground at Hooge. It was also to 'straighten the line', impossible to comprehend as a kind of 'trench house-keeping exercise', but actually essential to reduce the possibility of increased observation and deadly crossfire. So it was that the Battle of Bellewaarde was fought, by men of the regulars and territorials, facing stiff resistance from the Germans arraigned in front of them. And in this rush forward, William Black was killed, and a family memory stored for future generations.

In her carefully researched account of the battle, Carole McEntee-Taylor describes the action, one of many 'minor operations' that came to be fought as part of the British offensive spirit while serving on the Western Front. Examining the battle from both sides, Carole gives a detailed understanding of the course of the action – and records the loss of the men, British and German during the fateful day.

Reading this account, pause a while at Bellewaarde, when next making the journey eastwards out of Ypres, along the old Menin Road.

Peter Doyle
London

Introduction

I remember as a child being curious about old photographs and on many occasions I would visit our Beautility sideboard and pull out the chocolate biscuit tin where the family photographs were kept. I spent hour upon hour looking at images of my mother and father, grandparents, aunts and uncles and those of my sisters and I that clearly we were not happy having taken of us. All would be replaced only to be pulled out again a few months later.

I was brought up in what can only be described as a very strict family unit and I never asked too many questions as it would usually be seen as impolite, so when we were staying with family I just did not discuss the family history. I do remember however at my grandmother's house a circular bronze plaque was placed on the hall table and I could not resist looking at it. There was a name, 'Austin Frank Broughton' and the words 'He died for freedom and honour.' I thought this a curious object and not knowing what it was I dismissed it from my mind, easily done at ten years of age.

Many years later I was employed by a company as a Training Manager and in late 1996 was given a laptop which would make my job easier, or so they said. I had only used the type of computer that had light green letters and numbers on a dark green screen, so when I discovered that I would have no training on the Windows 95 innovation with a 1.3 GB hard-drive to store masses of information on I almost gave it back, but I was glad that I didn't. To help me learn these new skills I thought I would purchase some software, something that would force me to repeat the same task time and again. Looking on the shelves of the store I came across the only item that looked as though it would help and be interesting. The item was a family history programme and I didn't know it then, but this would set me on a journey that is as interesting today as it was then.

The years of research conducted in dusty archives were really enjoyable and I would recommend getting your hands dirty with the real documents. All the information was carefully added to my computer. The programme also allowed me to add images of my family; the photographs I enjoyed looking at so long ago. There always will be those ancestors of whom there is little or no information and one of those was my great uncle, Austin Frank Broughton. I started to ask questions of the family, but sadly his brothers and sisters had passed away and my mother and her siblings only knew scant information. My uncle showed me a bronze plaque that had been neatly placed in a glass-covered frame and mounted on a wall. When I looked closely I saw that it was the same plaque from my grandmother's hall table. My uncle explained that Austin had died at Ypres in 1915, but as the family didn't talk about those things he knew little else. However, he did show me a small image of Austin in his uniform. Well the age of the high speed internet had arrived and I was certain I would find something, but I could find nothing and to be honest I didn't really know where to start.

A few years later a friend of mine who was interested in the First World War managed to get hold of some details from Austin's medal index card, but explained that all other records were lost during the Second World War. I found this quite annoying. How can there be so little information? I now had the bit between my teeth and I was determined to crack this conundrum.

In 2007 I found a First World War forum which was dedicated to the battlefields of Ypres and I asked questions about my great uncle. The first snippets came through regarding his regiment, 1st Battalion Northumberland Fusiliers, information from the pages of the regimental diary, Bellewaarde, 16 June 1915. I couldn't believe what I was reading. A part of the diary gave details of the casualties and there before me was my great uncle's name, recorded as wounded. I read about what he and his chums went through that day and I was astonished at the carnage.

I went on to look for details of all the men and regiments, British and German, so that I could piece together what had happened that day, and after eighteen months' research I decided to take it a stage further and created the website 'The Battle of Bellewaarde'. This was something I wanted to do so that I could share what I had found and make it easier for those who wished to research soldiers who fought there. I hoped my small contribution would help to ensure those men would never be forgotten.

I started to think more about how to get more visitors to the Bellewaarde website and decided to use social networking and set about creating a 'Bellewaarde Group' on Facebook. This action started to improve the volume of viewers to the main site.

I decided to visit Bellewaarde to see the battlefield and so on 16 June 2012 I stood at the edge of Railway Wood, the same place my ancestor fell. I was the first member of his family to visit in ninety-seven years. I looked around at the quiet fields and felt an emotion like nothing before. I thought of how many mothers, wives and children were left grieving for loved ones lost in a field only a half mile square; those who would never return. The shame was that they had no way of knowing where their men lay. It was then I decided that a memorial should be placed there on the field where so many had fallen. At the inauguration of the Menin Gate in 1927, Field Marshal Herbert Plummer said of the dead: 'They are not missing – they are here'. I now wanted to ensure that this could be said of those who fell on 16 June 1915 at Bellewaarde.

A battlefield memorial will be unveiled on the centenary of the battle on 16 June 2015. The cost of this memorial and the subsequent maintenance will be met by charitable funds. To donate please visit The Battle of Bellewaarde website at www.bellewaarde1915.co.uk and click the 'donate' button.

One evening I received a message from Carole McEntee-Taylor asking if it would be OK to write a book about the battle. She had viewed the website and social media page regarding my idea of a memorial and thought that this was an excellent idea for her to get involved with. We met and discussed how this could be done. I was flattered that she liked my work and regarded the cause worthy of her talent, but it was more than that. Carole explained that her royalties from the sale of the book would go directly to the memorial fund. This kind of selfless generosity is rare and it is a gift that I humbly accepted on behalf of the men, British and German who fought and fell on 16 June 1915.

Martin Clift

Prologue

16 June 1915

It was 2am and dawn was slowly breaking over Bellewaarde. It was exceptionally quiet; the troops of 3rd Division were situated on the western edge of Railway Wood and shrouded in a thick mist which reduced visibility and gave the illusion of safety. Private 21660, Patrick Joseph Carpenter, waited patiently for the order to fire. Born in 1878 in St Andrews, Dublin, Patrick had joined the Army on 9 August 1897 and enlisted in the Field Artillery. When war started in August 1914, Patrick had been posted to the 5th Division Ammunition Column as a driver and by 19 August he was on his way to Mons. His war had begun.

After the retreat from Mons Patrick had fought at Marne, Aisne and Ypres. By 1915 he was no stranger to battle and one of the few remaining members of the original British Army, most of whom had been killed or wounded in the first few months of the war. He had now been posted to the 23rd Battery, part of 40th Brigade, who, in turn, were part of the 3rd Division.

Across the few yards of no man's land, the German troops of Reserve Infantry Regiment (RIR) 248 and 246 were also blanketed in the thick, damp mist. It swirled round their trenches, deadening sound and reinforcing the illusion that all was secure. RIR 246 HQ had just received a report that the enemy was strikingly quiet and Gefreiter Wilhelm Schmid of RIR 248, a member of the Germans' highly prized Machine Gun Company, huddled deeper into his great coat, his eyes closed as he dreamed of those he loved back home. Schmid was to be killed in action on 16 June.

Compared to the destruction and devastation of the Second Battle of Ypres which had finished on 25 May 1915 with an estimated loss of 59,000 British troops, 10,000 French troops and 35,000 German troops (the difference in numbers is believed to be because of the use of chlorine gas by the Germans) the front had been relatively quiet. Well, quiet enough to allow the Germans to bring up RIR 248 to relieve Reserve-Jäger-Battalion 26 between 6 June and 8 June. But the silence was as deceptive as the delusion of safety. The seemingly protective blanket of the mist hid a growing tension.

Although the frontline fighting had reduced considerably over the past few weeks, skirmishes, sniping and intermittent shelling had continued. Men were still dying at an average rate of 300 a day along the length of the front, a front that was not as secure as it could be.

The end of the Battle of Ypres had left a salient protruding into the British front lines. At the southern point of the salient lay the battered, ruined remains of Hooge. German trenches ran between the Menin Road and the Ypres-Roulers railway and south of the railway was the eastern edge of Railway Wood, also held by the Germans. The British front line ran from opposite Hooge, along the Menin Road to east of Birr Cross Road. It then turned sharply northwards, skirting the eastern edges of Cambridge Road. When it reached the angle formed by the road and the railway line it followed the railway line eastwards for some 300 yards and then turned sharply north-west.

The Germans also held Bellewaarde Ridge, which was situated on the eastern side of the lake. This enabled them to overlook most of the ground east of Ypres, presenting a continual threat to the British front line. But not for much longer.

V Corps, under the command of Lieutenant General Sir E. Allenby, had devised a plan which aimed to take the ridge. This would deprive the enemy of its observation post and at the same time would straighten out the line between Hooge and Railway Wood. It was to be a minor operation that would also provide an effective diversion to the main attack planned to take place on the same day at Givenchy. This minor operation at Bellewaarde was due to begin at 2.50 am, a mere fifty minutes away.

The minutes ticked away, daylight gradually increased and so did the mist. The assault had been entrusted to the 9th and 7th Brigades of 3rd Division, under the command of Major General J.A.L. Haldane. Early the previous afternoon, the men from these Brigades had marched from their billets using two separate routes. Under cover of darkness they had relieved 8th Brigade and were already formed up in four lines.

In addition to the 9th and 7th Brigade, General Plumer of the 2nd Army Group had seconded No 6 Squadron, Royal Flying Corps, and No 2 Group, Honourable Artillery Company (HAC), to V Corps for the attack.

The HAC, who only had a limited amount of ammunition, were now waiting in their assembly trench at the apex of the triangle forming the Ypres salient. They had marched in columns of four straight down the Menin Road the previous night during a lull in the shelling.

The 9th Infantry Brigade, left column, consisting of the 1st Royal Scots Fusiliers, the 1st Northumberland Fusiliers, and the 10th (Scottish) Battalion the King's Liverpool Regiment (Liverpool Scottish) were spread from the north-west corner of Railway Wood almost down to the Menin Gate. In the Fire and Assembly Trenches on the east of Cambridge Road the 4th Royal Fusiliers, 1st Royal Scots Fusiliers and the 1st Northumberland Fusiliers waited. In the second line, occupying the Cambridge Road trench, were the 1st Lincolns, two sections of the Cheshire Field Company R.E. and the Liverpool Scottish.

Meanwhile the 7th Brigade had taken up their position in the Assembly Trenches west of Cambridge Road. 1 Battalion and 4 Battalion were positioned in the Assembly Trenches on the south side of the Menin Road and a Motor Machine Gun Battery had been set up on the south side of the Menin Road.

Each infantryman was loaded down with two extra bandoliers, one day's ration as well as his iron ration, two empty sandbags and a waterproof sheet. Each battalion was issued with 400 hand grenades and 150 wire cutters while two of the battalions had shovels on their backs. Having arrived at the Assembly Trenches after their march through the Belgian countryside, the men settled down and waited for their orders. They hoped that the enemy were unaware of their presence and the planned offensive, but as the trenches were overlooked they knew this was probably unlikely.

And they were right. Across the small expanse of no man's land the Germans knew that an attack was imminent.

Reserve-Infanterie-Regiment Nr. 246

'On 14 June 1915 an aerial photograph was received by the regiment. Clearly visible on it was the fact that south of the Menin – Ypres road between Hooge and 3rd Borne and east and west of the track between Eierwäldchen [Egg Copse – Railway Wood] the enemy had dug a complex of trenches (a so-called trench honeycomb) with four parallel lines of trenches arranged one behind the other. It was estimated that six battalions could be assembled within them ready to launch a quick succession of assaulting waves. The regiment realized at once that an attack was imminent and had the artillery increase its rate of firing. Stocks of ammunition and hand grenades were increased. In the main battle trench the firing points along the parapet were completed. The gunners of the machine gun platoon tested their weapons and inspected their ammunition. The artillery was briefed in fullest detail and kept completely up to date with the results of all observations.'[1]

Although the 2.00 am report had suggested all was quiet, the Germans did not relax their guard. Then, at 3.00 am (The German Reserve Infantry Regimental diary states it was quiet at 3.00 am. This would be 2.00 am British summer time) the artillery observation officer and the officer commanding 11th Company reported simultaneously.

Reserve-Infanterie-Regiment Nr. 246

'The enemy have opened gaps [in their wire] ready to assault. Noise and movement can be clearly detected in the enemy trenches. Strangely the enemy artillery is completely silent.'[2]

---

1. Extract from Leutnant der Reserve Louis Orgeldinger *Das Württembergische Reserve-Infanterie-Regiment Nr. 246* (1931) Stuttgart, 97–107. Translation © Dr Jack Sheldon 2012.
2. Translation courtesy of Dr Jack Sheldon ©2012.

This information was immediately passed to the artillery by the Regimental Adjutant and light and heavy artillery fire began to rain down on the British infantry positions. But the intensity of the fire soon died away and a heavy, tension-filled silence resumed.

Back in the British lines the men huddled down as they sheltered from the brief, but intense German bombardment. As the firing died away they stood up, dusted themselves down, stretchered away the few casualties and resumed their positions by the front trench wall and waited. The time for the assault grew ever closer and the men prepared to go over the top. As the seconds ticked away the silence was broken only by the muttered sound of prayers and the gentle rustling of the bandoliers on khaki as men crossed themselves and asked for God's protection. At 2.50 am (although some British Regimental diaries report it as 2.30 am) the planned bombardment began. After the silence the onslaught seemed even more deafening than it usually did as more than 200 British guns competed with each other to pound the enemy and their defences to dust. As the air around them filled with acrid corrosive smoke and their ears felt as if they would burst, the German artillery began to retaliate. The cacophony of sound increased as shells burst all around them. The explosions sent dust and debris into the trenches and created giant depressions in the already fractured ground. The men on both sides crouched down, heads bent as they instinctively sought to protect themselves from the onslaught. By the end of the day more than 4,000 men would be casualties in a field approximately half a mile square. It was 16 June 1915 and the First Battle of Bellewaarde had just begun.

Part One

The Protagonists

Chapter 1

The Allies

At the end of the First Battle of Ypres on 25 May 1915 the opposing armies settled in to a period of general trench warfare. Both French and British armies set about improving their defences while preparing for the next offensive. Although the volume of shelling had reduced, sniping and machine gun fire continued unabated, albeit in a more organized and systematic way. Ammunition was so short on the British side that Sir John French had no option but to order the First Army to restrict its operations to those that would not use too much ammunition or too many troops.

The Germans now held the whole of Bellewaarde Ridge and their front line was well established to the north of the Menin Road. From their positions overlooking the town they continued to bombard Ypres, gradually destroying the drainage,

Field Marshal Sir Edmund Henry Hynman Allenby, 1st Viscount Allenby.

buildings and other infrastructure. This eventually led to the decision to evacuate the civilians.

But, despite its deserted appearance during the daylight hours, Ypres was far from empty. It was actually occupied by thousands of allied soldiers, horses and waggons, mostly moving about under cover of darkness. With the civilians gone their possessions became easy prey to looting by the occupying troops.

Although this was strictly forbidden by the army most soldiers could see little wrong in helping themselves to items that were likely to disappear in the next German bombardment anyway. Many of the first scavengers managed to find expensive wines and cigars in cellars conveniently exposed by the shelling. The more enterprising of these even managed to remove enough wine to earn a little extra by selling it on to local wine merchants. Other items were buried, the intention being to recover them later, if the soldier survived.

This practice was not just restricted to junior ranks. Although the officers did not encourage theft they were unlikely to complain if a much needed table or armchair appeared at HQ or in a dug out on the front line. But unless their duties took them into Ypres, most ordinary frontline soldiers did not have the opportunity to look for souvenirs. The town was strictly out of bounds when off duty and on the way to and from the front it was a dangerous place to be.

General Joffre, Chief of French General Staff, was insistent the BEF took over a bigger share of the front. Although much of it was quiet the French were responsible for over 400 miles of the 475 miles from Switzerland to the sea.

However, he objected to the BEF relieving his troops near the coast, at Ypres and either side of the Belgian army at Nieuport, because the front there was too intimately connected with the defence of the fortress at Dunkirk. It was finally agreed that the British would take over the whole of the Ypres salient, a change that was completed on 7 and 8 June.

But this still did not satisfy the French who wanted the BEF to evacuate the Ypres salient so the troops could be used to relieve the six divisions of General de Castelnau's army between Hebuterne and Chaulnes. This was a front of twenty-one miles that was separated from the British right near Bethune by a thirty mile section held by the French Tenth Army.

Sir John French, Chief of Staff of the British Army and Commander of the BEF, wrote a strongly worded letter to the War Office on 11 June pointing out the damage that would be done to British and Belgian morale if this withdrawal went ahead. He also raised concerns that such a move would shorten the German line considerably more than the British line. This would free up enemy forces and thus leave the BEF open to a new offensive. But these were not his only concerns. He also objected strongly to a number of British divisions being included in the French line. He added that if this was to go ahead it would need eight British Divisions rather than six French Divisions because the French had more guns and more ammunition and therefore did not need as many men to hold the front line.

In 1914, the total size of the British Army was 710,000 but this included the Territorial Army and the reservists. There were only 247,000 regular personnel, of whom 13,000 were officers. The BEF was only 80,000 strong and consisted of six infantry divisions and one cavalry division.

Pre-war planning in Britain had seriously underestimated casualty rates. Planners had assumed there would be about forty per cent casualties over six months and between sixty-five to seventy per cent over twelve months. In reality the BEF had experienced over sixty per cent casualties in just the first three months.

They had also seriously underestimated how much ammunition would be needed for the war. There were only 1,000 shells per 18-pounder gun, with 300 shells in reserve and only 500 shells were produced over the first six months. As the gun had the ability to fire four shells per minute this meant the entire allotment of shells for six months would only allow for seven to eight hours of sustained fire support.

John Denton Pinkstone French

French became known as the Earl of Ypres in 1922. Born in Ripple Vale, Kent, in 1852, he joined the Royal Navy in 1866 as a naval cadet on HMS *Britannia* but he did not enjoy the Navy so in 1870 he resigned, intending to join the army instead. After spending some time in the Militia he was given a commission in the 8th Hussars in 1874. A few weeks later he transferred to the 19th Hussars. He became a Captain in 1880 and by 1883 he had been promoted to Major.

He served in the Sudan Campaign of 1884–1885 as a member of the party attached to Sir Herbert Stewart's column. This column was part of the forces sent to relieve General Gordon and he was present at the actions of Abu Klea, Gubat and Metammah. French distinguished himself in these battles and, by the time he returned to England, he had been promoted to a Brevet Lieutenant Colonel and Second in Command of the 19th Hussars. In 1889 he became the Commander of the Regiment. In 1891 the Regiment went to India with French in command. In 1892, having served the required period in command, he became staff officer to General Sir George Luck, Inspector-General of Cavalry in India. After General Sir George Luck transferred to the War Department both he and French returned to England. In 1895 French was appointed AAG for Cavalry.

In 1897 French took command of the newly formed 2nd Cavalry Brigade at Aldershot and, after the outbreak of the Boer War in 1899 he was given command of the mounted troops in Natal under Sir George White. As in the Sudan French distinguished himself. He successfully dislodged the Boers from their stronghold at Elandslaate and held Cape Colony while other British commanders suffered defeats and setbacks. January 1900 saw General Roberts advancing northwards to break the siege of Kimberley. French's orders were to turn the left flank of General Kronje's army. This would bring about the retreat of the Boers from Magersfontein and leave the way open to relieve the siege at Kimberley. On 11 February 1900 French's cavalry and mounted infantry forced the River Riet and by 15 February he entered Kimberley. He carried on to seize Koedoesrand Drift and then took part in the successful defeat of General Kronje's Boer forces at Paadeberg. He followed this with further successes at Poplar Grove and Driefontein against De Wet and Delarey. As the advance continued toward Johannesburg with Pretoria falling on 5 June, French played a major role in the Battle of Diamond Hill on 11 June and the subsequent pursuit of General Botha's forces.

French's reward was to be promoted to Major-General and he received the KCB. He went on to capture Middleburg and Barberton in the Eastern Transvaal and assumed control of Johannesburg District in November 1900. He remained here until June 1901 when he was transferred to the Cape. Here he commanded the forces south of the Orange River until the signing of the Treaty of Vereeniging in May 1902 which bought an end to the war. In August 1902 French returned to England to take up the Aldershot Command. He was promoted to Lieutenant General and awarded a KCMG. In November 1907 he was promoted again, this time to full General and made a GCVO. In December he was appointed Inspector General of the Forces.

As the BEF attempted to confront this new environment, senior military leaders faced massive managerial problems stemming from the rapidly growing size of the British Army. By 1917, there would be 1.5 million soldiers in fifty-six divisions assigned to Western Front, and the staff officer requirements of 1917 alone matched the entire officer cadre of 1914.

John Denton Pinkstone French was appointed Chief of Staff of the British Army in 1911 and Chief of the Imperial General Staff from 1912–1913. In 1913 he was promoted to Field Marshal. In April 1914 he resigned as Chief of the Imperial General Staff because the Cabinet would not back him over his decision not to use cavalry forces at Curragh against Ulster during the Irish Home Rule Crisis.

In the years leading up to the Great War the British Army was very much a product of the Field Marshal's leadership. French was also considered by many to be the driving force behind most of its tactical progress. By the time the war started it was a modern fully equipped army, mainly due to his efforts. It was, therefore, a foregone conclusion that he would be given command of the British Expeditionary Forces (BEF) in August 1914.

However he was soon at odds with Lord Kitchener and Sir Douglas Haig. The Cabinet and French wanted the BEF deployed to Belgium rather than Amiens. Kitchener and Haig both argued that deploying the BEF to Amiens would place it in the ideal position to deliver a vigorous counter-attack when they knew the route of the German advance. Kitchener argued that placing the BEF at Mons would be a big mistake as the Belgium Army would not be able to hold this position against the Germans. Trying to reinforce them would just lead to the BEF having to abandon both the position and much of their supplies.

Kitchener was proved right as the BEF were soon forced to abandon Mons and Le Cateau, in danger of being flanked when the Belgium Army failed. While the battle was on going, French gave a series of hasty orders to abandon positions and equipment. These were largely ignored by General Sir Horace Smith-Dorrien, his subordinate in charge of II Corps. Instead Smith-Dorrien defended Le Cateau vigorously which gave the troops time to reorganize and make a fighting withdrawal. This refusal to obey orders caused a massive rift between the two men and would lead to Smith-Dorrien being relieved of his command several months later.[3]

After the disaster at Mons French became increasingly indecisive and seemed more concerned with preserving his troops than fighting the enemy. At one point he had even suggested moving the BEF back to the channel ports rather than aid the French. It took an emergency visit in September 1914, from the then Secretary of War, Kitchener, to strengthen his resolve. As the main armies dug in towards

---

3. This happened after he advocated a tactical withdrawal away from the German front lines after the first use of poison gas. Several days later French ordered an almost identical withdrawal on the advice of General Sir Herbert Plumer.

the end of 1914 and trench warfare began, French remained in command and in December he had received the Order of Merit.

The BEF consisted of a GHQ and a number of Corps. By late 1914 the size of the army was so great that the decision was taken to sub divide the forces into two separate armies, each commanded by a Lieutenant General.

The Second Army was formed in France on 26 December 1914 and initially came under the command of Sir Horace Smith-Dorrien. After Smith-Dorrien resigned it fell under the command of Sir Herbert Plumer. By March 1915 these armies became officially defined as composing of an Army HQ, at least two Corps,

Lieutenant General Sir E. Allenby

Allenby was the son of Hynman and Catherine Anne Allenby (nee Cane) and was educated at Haileybury College. He had tried initially to enter the Indian Civil Service but, after failing the entrance exam in 1880 he sat the exam for the Royal Military College in Sandhurst. On 10 May 1882 he was commissioned as a Lieutenant in the 6th (Inniskilling) Dragoons. He joined his regiment in South Africa later that year. After serving at the Cavalry Depot in Canterbury he was promoted to Captain on 10 January 1888 and then returned to South Africa.

Allenby came back to Great Britain in 1890 and sat the entry exam for the Staff College at Camberley. Although he failed he re-sat the exam the following year and this time passed. At the same time Captain Douglas Haig of the 7th Hussars also entered the Staff College and the two men became rivals. Although Haig was a better rider Allenby was more popular and was made Master of the Draghounds. He was promoted to Major on 19 May 1897 and then posted to the 3rd Cavalry Brigade. He served in Ireland as the Brigade Major in March 1898.

When the Boer War broke out Allenby returned to his Regiment and landed in Cape Town, South Africa later that year. He took part in several actions in 1900 including Colesberg on 11 January, Klip Drift on 15 February and Dronfied Ridge on 16 February. He was also involved in actions at Zand River on 10 May, Kalkheuval Pass on 2 June, Barberton on 12 September and Tevreden on 16 October when Jan Smuts, the Boer General was defeated. On New Year's Day 1901 he was promoted to Lieutenant Colonel, followed swiftly by further promotion to local Colonel on 29 April. He became a Lieutenant Colonel on 2 August 1902 and a Brevet Colonel on 22 August 1902.

Back home in 1902 Allenby became the Commanding Officer of 5th Royal Irish Lancers in Colchester and was promoted to the temporary rank of Brigadier on 19 October 1905. He assumed command of the 4th Cavalry Brigade in 1906, was promoted to Major General on 10 September 1909 and was appointed Inspector General of Cavalry in 1910. As he grew older he had a tendency to bellow at his subordinates and was known for his explosive outbursts of rage which, combined with his powerful physical stature, led to the nickname of 'The Bull'.

At the outbreak of the Great War the BEF contained one Cavalry Division which was commanded by Allenby who distinguished himself when his unit covered the retreat after the Battle of Mons. His reward was to be made commander of the Cavalry Corps when the army was expanded and divided into two.

with various units attached as Army Troops. Each Army HQ, which consisted of thirty-one officers and 106 other ranks, reported up to GHQ. The Corps were not permanently attached to an Army and neither were the Divisions below them. These Army troops varied greatly and from day to day and although the number of Corps under each Army was two it could be increased if conditions demanded it. In addition to the two Corps, Army HQ also had supply troops, tactical units and strategic firepower, including artillery, engineers, transport, medical, machine guns, veterinary, labour and mounted troops.

Both Army and Corps HQs remained fixed in one place whilst Divisions were moved around with control passing from one Army to another as the fighting demanded. The Second Army HQ had its Headquarters in Hazebrouck in France.

Commanded by Lieutenant-General Sir E. Allenby, V Corps had its HQ in Poperinghe.

There were two Divisions in II Corps, the 3rd and the 5th and other attached troops were the 2nd Army HQ Signal Company, RE (E (Air Line) Section and M, O and P (Cable) Sections), No 2 Bridging Train RE, C Squadron North Irish Horse, 1st Battalion Cameron Highlanders and A Section, No 19 Field Ambulance RAMC.

The units of 3rd Division, based in Southern Command in England, arrived in France at the beginning of the war to join the BEF and remained on the Western Front throughout. As part of II Corps they had all arrived in France by 16 August 1914 and had gone straight to Mons. Positioned along the Mons-Conde Canal they took more than 3,000 casualties, but also won the first three VCs of the war.

Following the retreat from Mons they fought on the Aisne before moving up to French Flanders in October 1914. Here they fought south of Armentieres. During this fighting on 14 October Major General Hubert I. W. Hamilton was killed, the first Divisional Commander to be killed in the war.

Major General Mackenzie took over, but he was invalided home within ten days. The CRA, Brigadier-General Wing temporarily assumed command and the Division moved 20 miles north to the Ypres salient before trench warfare set in.

On 21 November Major-General James Aylmer Lowthorpe Haldane was appointed Commander.

Haldane was considered to be a tireless and resolute Commander, giving equal priority to tactical drive, administration and the well-being of his soldiers who were now spending four days on the front line followed by four days in billets. Although the Division endured the same hardships of the trenches as everyone else, he insisted on comfortable rest areas when the battalions were out of the line.

The fighting over the next few weeks was so ferocious that between mid-October and the end of November 1914 the Division as a whole had suffered 8,355 casualties.

During Haldane's command the 3rd Division became renowned for its reliability and was often used to reinforce or take over vulnerable sectors and to retake lost ground. Haldane was heard to say several times that the Germans often boasted

> **Major General James Alymer Lowthorpe Haldane**
>
> Haldane was born on 17 November 1862 and was a cousin of the War Secretary, Aylmer Haldane. In 1882, at the age of twenty, he was commissioned into the Gordon Highlanders and became part of the Waziristan Field Force between 1894 and 1895. (Waziristan is a mountainous region bordering Afghanistan in the northwest of Pakistan and covers some 11,585km (4,473 square miles). It is populated by ethnic Pashtuns). In 1895 he took part in the Chitral Expedition, a military expedition sent to relieve the fort at Chitral which was under siege after a local coup in which a British force of around 400 men was besieged until relieved by two expeditions from Gilgit and Peshawar. On 18 February 1896, Haldane was promoted to Lieutenant and a year later was promoted to Captain. He spent the next two years trying to quell the Afridis rebellion in the Tirah Campaign, an Indian Frontier War*.
>
> In 1898 Haldane became aide-de-camp to the Commander in Chief East Indies until the Second Boer War. Whilst he was a prisoner in Pretoria he planned the escape for which Winston Churchill was to become famous. Although he failed to escape at the same time he succeeded in doing so later. He was awarded the DSO on 20 May 1898 and promoted to Major in 1902, followed swiftly to Brevet Lieutenant-Colonel on 24 July of the same year. Promotions continued to follow, first to Brevet Colonel in March 1906, Substantive Colonel in November 1906 and temporary Brigadier-General on 1 October 1909. In 1910 he became Commander of the 10th Brigade, part of 4th Division. He continued to command them during the Retreat from Mons and the fighting following the retreat.

that once the 3rd Division left the area they would be able to retake the trenches they had lost.

Despite the harsh conditions 3rd Division soon settled into trench warfare and by 21 January 1915 they had achieved several successes. The divisional cyclist company had been trained as specialist bombing teams, experiments with trench mortars and grenades had proved successful and they had developed a visual signalling system by which the infantry could direct artillery fire onto the enemy trenches. Sappers had also been attached to infantry strong points to ensure damage to trenches could quickly be repaired.

In early 1915 the 3rd Division moved up to the Ypres salient and took over the trenches opposite the Messines Ridge, St Eloi and The Bluff. From here they moved up to the Menin Road sector at Hooge and Bellewaarde.

In June 1915 3rd Division consisted of four Brigades: 7th, 8th, 9th and 76th, Divisional Troops, Divisional Mounted Troops (C Sqn South Irish Horse and 3rd

---

* For sixteen years the Afridi tribe had received a subsidy from the government of British India for safeguarding the Khyber Pass and the government had maintained a local regiment stationed in the Pass that was composed entirely of Afridis. However the local tribesmen rose up and captured all the posts in the Khyber held by their own countrymen, and attacked the forts on the Samana Range near the city of Peshawar.

Company Army Cyclist Corps), Divisional Artillery (XXIII Brigade, Royal Field Artillery, X1 Brigade Field Artillery, XLI Brigade Royal Field Artillery, XXX (Howitzer) Brigade Royal Field Artillery, 3rd Divisional Ammunition Column), and the Royal Army Medical Corps: 4A Sanitary Section, 7th Field Ambulance, 8th Field Ambulance, 9th Field Ambulance.

The 7th Brigade consisted of 3rd Battalion Worcestershire Regiment, 2nd Battalion South Lancashire Regiment, 1st Battalion Wiltshire Regiment, 1st Battalion Honourable Artillery Company, 1/4th Battalion South Lancashire Regiment, 2nd Battalion The Royal Irish Rifles, Mortar Batteries RFA, 438th (1/1st Cheshire) Field Company, 9th Field Ambulance and 4A Sanitary Section. Brigade HQ was in some old fortified gun emplacements under the ancient ramparts of the town in Ypres. Several items had been salvaged from the ruins of the town including tables, beds and carpets and it was considered to be very comfortable.

The 8th Brigade consisted of 2nd Battalion the Royal Scots, 4th Battalion the Middlesex Regiment, 1st Battalion the Gordon Highlanders and the 2nd Battalion, the Suffolk Regiment.

The 9th Brigade consisted of 1st Battalion The Northumberland Fusiliers, 4th Battalion Royal Fusiliers, 1st Battalion The Lincolnshire Regiment, 1st Battalion Royal Scots Fusiliers, 1/10th Battalion the King's (Liverpool Regiment), West Yorkshire Regiment. It was commanded by Brigadier-General, F.C. Shaw.

Divisional Troops consisted of 3rd Divisional Motor Ambulance Workshop Unit, 4A Sanitary Section, and the 7th, 8th and 9th Field Ambulance.

With the loss of so much of the regular army during the Retreat from Mons there was a massive drive for the recruitment of volunteers. Army Order No 324 issued on 21 August 1914 authorized the formation of six new Divisions. Formed from volunteers it was initially numbered 8th (Light) Division but as more regular army units became available to create a Division it was renumbered the 14th (Light) Division. Despite having no equipment or arms of any kind the recruits were judged to be ready by May 1915 but their deployment to France was delayed because of a lack of rifle and artillery ammunition. They served on the Western Front throughout the war.

In 1915 the 14th Division consisted of 41st Brigade, 42nd Brigade, 43rd Brigade, Divisional Troops, Divisional Mounted Troops, Divisional Artillery, Royal Engineers and Royal Medical Corps and other Divisional Troops.

42nd Brigade was commanded by Brigadier General C. J. Markham and consisted of 5th Battalion the Oxford and Buckinghamshire Light Infantry, the 5th King's Shropshire Light Infantry, 9th Battalion the Rifle Brigade and the 9th Battalion The Kings Royal Rifle Corps.

Chapter 2

The Germans

In 1914 every German male was liable for military service for a total of twenty-seven years. This period started at the end of their seventeenth year and lasted until the end of their forty-fifth year. The individual would be called up aged twenty and then serve for two years with the Colours, (three years in the Cavalry) followed by four or five years as a Reserve. He was then transferred to the 1st Battalion of the Landwehr for five years and then to the 2nd Battalion of the Landsturm where he stayed until forty-five years old. The 1st Battalion of the Landsturm consisted of those aged between seventeen and twenty waiting for call up. There was also an Ersatz Reserve for those who were physically fit but not called up for National Service for some reason or other. A large number of those who were shot down by the rapid, accurate rifle fire of the BEF at Mons were Ersatz Reservists as were those during the First Battle of Ypres.

For recruiting and mobilization purposes Germany was divided into twenty-four Army Corps Districts. Each district provided a complete Army Corps of two Divisions plus supporting arms and services. The districts were numbered I-XXI plus I – III Bavarian. There was also a Guard Corps which recruited from Prussia and Alsace and Lorraine. Although composition of the Army Corps varied a typical one would consist of two infantry Divisions, a rifle (Jaeger) Battalion, a Pioneer Battalion, four batteries of heavy artillery, a bridging train, signals (telephone, telegraph and wireless), a flying detachment and an airship detachment, ammunition and supply columns, transport columns, field hospitals, field batteries and remount depots. The total strength was around 44,000 of all ranks.

The German basic Infantry Regiment unit was more like a British brigade. It had three battalions numbered I-III whereas the British version had varying numbers of battalions. Like the British each Battalion Section had machine guns of six guns or two per battalion, but the Germans grouped their guns into a company, something the British wouldn't do until much later in 1915.

There were two regiments in a brigade and two brigades to a division which equalled twelve battalions, again the same as the British. German Divisional Artillery had seventy-two guns compared to Britain's seventy-six and the number of machine guns was the same. The strength of a German Division was 17,600 all ranks compared to the British 18,073.

The British began reducing the strength of their Divisions in early 1918 due to a manpower shortage. The Germans began the process much earlier, in March

1915. But they used the reduced numbers to form new Divisions of three Infantry Regiments: nine Battalions and a reduction in artillery to one Regiment: thirty-six guns. The strength of these was 12,500. By 1917 this was the standard throughout the German army.

The Germans started the war with a standing army of fifty Divisions. By February 1915 that had risen to 105, by August 1815 it was 170 and by the end of 1916 was 203. The total at the end of 1917 was 241.

Thanks to conscription the German peacetime army stood at 900,000 men with four million trained reserves and the potential to double that to nearly ten million. The strength of the army lay in its infantry of which there were seventy-eight Divisions and 110,000 well trained officers and its Cavalry of over 100,000 men. Although its artillery was not as good as that of the British 18-pounder and French 75mm 'soixante–quinze' it had over 3,000 medium and heavy guns and mortars with calibres of 150mm, 210mm, 305mm and 420mm and their ammunition was very good quality.

The Schlieffen Plan relied on the German 8th Army to contain any threat on the Russian Front while the other five German Armies would crash through Belgium, capture Brussels, then swing west and south into France via Lille. With its right flank on the Channel coast it would cut through the Somme and Amiens and pass round Paris before encircling it and taking it from behind. The whole operation was expected to take forty days and speed was of the essence.

The first stumbling block came at Liege where the fortress garrison that guarded the River Meuse and all routes to Brussels was commanded by General Gerard Leman. The Belgians fought courageously and, while taking heavy casualties, managed to halt the Germans. This shocked the Germans who were unable to believe their superior forces had been stopped by, what they considered to be, inferior opposition. The Schlieffen Plan had hit its first hurdle.

However, eventually the heavy Krupp 420mm and Austrian supplied Skoda 305mm guns defeated Leman and the Schlieffen Plan was back on again. France immediately mobilized to protect its borders, confident that it too had an unbeatable plan to ensure a swift victory over their old enemy.

Unfortunately Plan XVII was based on a rather naïve belief that the French spirit would be enough to defeat the Germans. It began by stating that, 'Whatever the circumstances, it is the Commander in Chief's intention to advance, all forces united, to the attack of the German armies.'

The French army was more equipped for a colonial war, its infantry still wearing blue tunics and red trousers as they had done nearly 100 years ago. Many French officers considered it to be their fashionable duty to wear white gloves and carry a sword rather than a revolver and they lacked sufficient numbers of medium and heavy artillery.

The first part of the French plan was to retake Alsace and Lorraine, lost as part of the Franco-Prussian war, and initially they appeared to succeed. However it was not long before the Germans counter attacked with ruthless efficiency, their heavy artillery wiping out whole regiments of infantry and cavalry, over 300,000 men, who presented an easy target in their blue tunics and red trousers.

On 20 August General von Kluck's 1st Army entered Brussels and in the south General von Bulow's 2nd Army entered Namur. By 22 August they were heading for Mons putting them on a collision course for the BEF who were dug in just south of Mons. To start with the 1st Army were bought to an abrupt halt by the speed and accuracy of the British rifle fire, but then the BEF began to withdraw. The French were in total confusion and the 500,000 men of the three German Armies on the right wing were speeding towards Paris. In the east at Tannenburg the Russian 1st and 2nd Armies had been heavily defeated alleviating the threat to Germany's eastern border.

As the BEF and the French continued to withdraw General George's 'Papa' Joffe decided to strengthen his left wing to prevent Kluck's 1st Army outflanking the BEF and the French 4th and 5th Armies. All sides were completely exhausted. The Germans had been fighting and marching since Liege with little respite and they allowed a gap to open up between their 1st and 2nd Armies.

Alarmed by the gap Bulow asked for help from von Kluck. Bulow then halted his advance and swung back towards Paris and the River Marne while Kluck's 1st Army swung south east towards Bulow's 2nd Army and the River Marne. In doing so he exposed his right flank to the front line of General Maunory's 6th Army. By 11 September the German 1st and 2nd Armies had fallen back and the soldiers were exhausted and disillusioned. The Schlieffen Plan had unravelled completely and they did not have a Plan B.

But the pursuit of the Germans by the BEF and the French was much too slow and too cautious and they were held up by brave German rearguard actions and the demolition of bridges. By 13 September both sides were digging in and then the 'Race to the Sea' began as both sides tried to outflank each other as their armies headed northwards.

Leutn Eduard Haussler.

Erich Georg Anton Sebastian von Falkenhayn

Erich Georg Anton Sebastian von Falkenhayn was born to impoverished, but aristocratic parents in Graudenz, West Prussia on 11 September 1861. He joined the army in 1880 as a Second Lieutenant, aged nineteen. After leaving the Academy of War in Berlin as a Major, he served as a military instructor to the Chinese Army in 1899. He was a member of the German General Staff, under Count von Waldersee, in 1900 during the Boxer Rebellion and he saw action when the Allies marched to relieve Peking. He continued to serve in the German General Staff on his return to Germany and in 1911 he commanded the 4th Regiment of Guards. He was a favourite of Wilhelm II as he had been one of the young Crown Prince's military instructors and in 1912 he was appointed Chief of Staff of the 4th Army Corps.

In 1913 he was promoted to Prussian Minister of War. He clashed frequently with Helmuth von Moltke, the Chief of Staff, but, on 14 September 1914, after the defeat at Marne, the Kaiser, Wilhelm II, dismissed Moltke and replaced him with Falkenhayn. For the next five months he held both Prussian Minister of War and Chief of Staff. He was a cautious, highly intelligent man, but often indecisive and aloof. He was well suited to trench warfare and also inclined towards defensive rather than offensive operations. He also considered that the Western Front was the most important area of battle which bought him into conflict with von Hindenburg and Ludendorff, the heroes of the east.

The German 4th Army was commanded by Generalfeldmarschall Albrecht, Duke of Württemberg.

Generalfeldmarschall Albrecht, Duke of Württemberg

Albrecht, Duke of Württemberg was born on 23 December 1865. He was the eldest child of Duke Philipp of Württemberg and Arch Duchess Maria Theresa of Austria and great grandson of Frederick II Eugene, Duke of Württemberg. At the beginning of the Great War Duke Albrecht commanded the German 4th Army and he led them to victory in the Battle of the Ardennes in August 1914. The 4th Army also saw action in the First Battle of the Marne. In October they were transferred to Flanders where Duke Albrecht commanded them during the Battle of the Yser. He also commanded the German forces during the Second Battle of Ypres, where poison gas was used on a large scale for the first time.

The German 4th Army on 22 April 1915 is listed as consisting of XXIII Reserve Corps, XXVI Reserve Corps, XXVII Reserve Corps, XV Corps (132 Infantry Regiment) and the Heavy Artillery of XXIII, XXVI and XXVII Reserve Corps – formed from Saxon and Württemberg units and was commanded by Generalleutnant Adolf von Carlowitz from 25 August 1914 until 27 October 1914 when it came under the command of General der Artillerie Richard von Schubert.

Soldier Reserve Infanterie Regiment Nr 246 By kind permission of John Beech.

Gefreiter from Reserve Infanterie Regiment Nr 246 Munsingen October 1914 By kind permission of John Beech.

Hans Karl Adolph von Carlowitz

Von Carlowitz was born on 25 March 1858 in Riesa Sachsen (Saxony) to Georg von Carlowitz, a courthouse officer and his wife Ida (nee von Könneritz). After he completed his Abitur he began studying law at Leipzig University. However, after a couple of years he decided to join the Saxon Infantry having previously served as a volunteer with the 8th Infantry Regiment for a year.

He served in several general staff positions within the Saxon Army at both Division and Corps level and also with the Prussian General Staff in Berlin. He replaced von Hausen as Saxony's War Minister in May 1914 and was then called on to head the newly formed XXVII Reserve Corps (Sächsisch-Württembergische Reservekorps). This command did not last long as, although he returned to the field after a heart ailment in October 1914, it was only as an Infantry Division Commander. His replacement was Louis Theodor Richard von Schubert.

Louis Theodor Richard von Schubert

Von Schubert was born 19 April 1850 in Posen (Poznan) Poland. He had begun his military career as a Lieutenant in 1868 in a field artillery regiment. He earned the Iron Cross in the Franco-Prussian War of 1870–1871 and in 1902 he was promoted to Lieutenant General and served as Military Governor in Ulm Fortress. He was promoted to General of Artillery in 1907 and as Inspector General of Field Artillery from 1907–1911 he successfully campaigned for the increased use of field artillery as a tactical weapon.

When the war started in August 1914 he was attached to General Heeringen's 7th Army in command of the XIV Reserve Corps (Karlsruhe). One month later he transferred to take command of the 8th Army on the Eastern Front. However within days he came into conflict with General Francois, Commander of 8th Army's 1 Corps, over strategy and two weeks later he returned to Flanders to take command of XXVII Reserve Corps.

There were two divisions in XXVIII Corps, the 53rd Reserve Division and the 54th Reserve Division, both formed in September 1914 as part of the new wave of divisions set up at the start of the war.

Like most pre-First World War divisions, the 54th Reserve Division was originally organized as a square division. The main body was composed of four regimental elements. As tactical purposes could often require a regiment to be split

An infantryman Württembergisches Reserve Infantry Regiment 246 By kind permission of John Beech.

Schellhorn

Leutn. d. L. im Ref.-Inf.-Regt. 246, gefallen bei Gehöft Bellewaarde am 16. Juni 1915

Leutn Karl Schellhorn.

into separate battalions the natural division was to bind two regiments together to form a brigade. When seen on an organizational chart or lined up in the field these brigades typically form a square, hence the name.

A square division would advance with either two brigades in line or one in front of the other. One regiment would be forward while the other would remain in reserve, ready to engage the enemy once the first regiment made contact.

The nature of positional warfare meant regiments would advance in a line to cover as much of the sector as possible. They would often form their own reserves with one or two battalions forward while the rest remained in reserve. The strength of Square Divisions was approximately 17,500.

This formation would gradually change during the war to become triangular. In a triangular division the infantry would be organized into three regiments. These would either be directly controlled by division HQ or would come under a single brigade command. These triangular divisions were smaller which not only allowed more divisions to be formed, it was also considered more suited for this type of positional warfare in the First World War.

The 54th Reserve Division was formed from the men of Wurttemberg with the addition of one Infantry Battalion and one Battalion of Chasseurs from Saxony.

On 10 September the 54th Reserve Division consisted of the following: 107th Reserve Infantry Brigade (245th Reserve Infantry Regiment; 246th Reserve Infantry Regiment)[4] and 108th Reserve Infantry Brigade (247th Reserve Infantry Regiment; 248th Reserve Infantry Regiment).[5] The Reserve Infantry Regiments consisted of three battalions but only had a machine gun platoon (of two machine guns) rather than a machine gun company (of six machine guns).

The 26th Reserve Jaeger Battalion, like other Reserve Jäger Battalions did not have a machine gun company when they were formed, although some were provided with a machine gun platoon.

The 54th Reserve Artillery Regiment[6] like other Reserve Field Artillery Regiments consisted of three abteilungen (two guns and one howitzer) of three batteries each, but each battery had just four guns, rather than the six which the Active Regiments had or the Reserve Regiments had when they were formed. There were also Reserve Cavalry Detachments which were much smaller than the Reserve Cavalry Regiments. Thus when XXVII Reserve Corps mobilized it consisted of twenty-six infantry battalions, ten machine gun platoons (twenty machine guns),

---

4. 107 Reserve-Infanterie-Brigade: Königlich Sächsisches Reserve-Infanterie-Regiment Nr. 245; Königlich Württembergisches Reserve-Infanterie-Regiment Nr. 246; Königlich Sächsisches Reserve-Jäger-Bataillon Nr. 26.
5. 108.Reserve-Infanterie-Brigade: Königlich Württembergisches Reserve-Infanterie-Regiment Nr. 247; Königlich Württembergisches Reserve-Infanterie-Regiment Nr. 248.
6. Königlich Württembergische Reserve-Kavallerie-Abteilung Nr. 54; Königlich Württembergisches und Königlich Sächsisches Reserve-Feldartillerie-Regiment Nr. 54 (the I. Abteilung was Saxon; the II. and III. Abteilungen were from Württemberg); Königlich Sächsische Reserve-Pionier-Kompanie Nr. 54.

two cavalry detachments, eighteen field artillery batteries (seventy-two guns) and two pioneer companies. They trained at Muensingen Camp and arrived in the line in October 1914. Here they were assigned to the German 4th Army where they participated in the Race to the Sea and The Battle of the Yser which took place in October 1914 between the towns on Nieuwpoort and Diksmuide along a thirty-five-kilometre-long stretch of the Yser River and Yperlee canal in Belgium. The front line was held by a large Belgian force which succeeded in halting the German advance, though only after heavy losses. After two months of defeats and retreats, the battle of Yser finally halted the invasion that gave Germans control of over ninety-five per cent of Belgian territory.

The division then remained in the trenches along the Yser until April 1915, when it entered the Second Battle of Ypres. After the battle the division remained in the line along the Yser into 1916.

There were two Reserve Infantry brigades in 54th Division: 107th and 108th. Reserve Infantry Brigade 107 had two Reserve Infantry Regiments – 245 and 246; 108th Reserve Infantry Brigade had two Reserve Infantry Regiments 247 and 248.

It also consisted of 26th Reserve Jaeger Battalion, 54th Reserve Field Artillery Regiment, 54th Reserve Cavalry Detachment and 54th Reserve Pioneer Company.

Colonel D. Baron von Roschman was Colonel in charge of Reserve Infanterie Regiment 246 and was situated in Stuttgart. Other officers were Major Baumann (WR Gren 119), Maj (Rtd) Baron Varnbuler und Hemmingen; Major Von Der Holzhausen.

Reserve Infanterie Regiment 248 (54th Reserve Division – 108th Reserve Infantry Brigade – XXVII Corps – 4th Army) was situated in Ludwigsburg and was commanded by Colonel (Rtd) Baron von Hill; Major von Lutzow; Major (Rtd) Burgundy; Major Jordan. Between 21 October and 28 November they took severe casualties losing thirty-two officers and 1,395 men.

Unter-Elsässisches Infanterie-Regiment Nr. 132 (39th Division – 61 Infantry Brigade – XV Corps – 4th Army) were a regiment from Alsace and their Regimental HQ was in Strasburg, and was part of the XV Corps area.

They were placed into the 61st Brigade of the 39th Infantry Division, a mostly Prussian formation. The 39th Division also consisted of 82nd Brigade: Infantry Regiments 171 and 172, 8th Jaeger Battalion, 14th Jaeger Battalion, fourteen Dragoon Guards (Cavalry), 39 Brigade: eighty Regiments (Artillery), Engineers, two and 3 Field Company, one Pioneer Battalion Number 15. At the beginning of the war the 39th Division formed part of the 7th Army and fought in the Pass of Bonhomme.

In 1914 they fought in the Battle of the Frontiers, the Race to the Sea and the Battle of the Yser. They were in the Ypres area prior to the start of the Second battle of Ypres. At the end of October they became part of the 6th Army under the Crown Prince of Bavaria, of which 15th Corps formed the Right wing, north of Lille, until the summer of 1915. Before the attacks of 1915 it was attached to the 4th Army under the Duke of Wurttemberg, south of Ypres.

A German Regiment was the equivalent of a British three Battalion brigade. The Regiment was commanded by a Colonel and there were three Battalions all

Burry

Leutn. d. R. i. Ref.-Inf.-Reg. 246 (Gymnasiallehrer), gef. a. 16. Juni 1915 bei Gehöft Bellewaarde

Soldier Reserve Infanterie Regiment Nr 246 and friends By kind permission of John Beech.

Leutn Adolf Burry.

commanded by a Major. Battalion 1 had Companies 1, 2, 3 and 4. Battalion 2 had Companies 5, 6, 7 and 8. Battalion 3 had Companies 9, 10, 11, and 12. Each Company had five officers and fifty-nine other ranks comprising three platoons (Zug) of four Sections (Kamradenschaffeten) of two Gruppen of eight men. The Machine Gun Company was 13 Company and comprised two Officers, ninety-five other ranks and six Maxim Machine Guns.

By the spring of 1915 thousands of new British and French troops were pouring into northern France and Flanders, but both sides were suffering from the loss of experienced men and officers. The Germans found a solution to their lack of trained officers by using a cadre of twenty-five per cent experienced veteran soldiers in each new Division. This was to give the Germans a significant edge over their opponents on the Western Front. The Germans also led the way in the artillery war with their medium and heavy guns and 150mm howitzers causing real damage to the British and the French. To make matters worse the British not only suffered from a lack of heavy artillery pieces, they also had insufficient ammunition, some of which was faulty.

The Second Battle of Ypres ended on 25 May and in the last days of the battle the Germans gained the Bellewaarde Ridge. On 2 June they ejected the British from Hooge Chateau and the next day they took over the Chateau and the half finished strong point being created by the British when they lost the position.

Chapter 3

438th (1/1st Cheshire) Field Company RE

The Regiments in Order of Seniority[7]

Corps and army troops RE were formed during the war but did not have any sort of fixed organization. At Divisional level companies would be grouped into Divisional RE under a Lieutenant-Colonel. There were no engineer regiments i.e. the equivalent to infantry battalions.

The basic unit was a company under the command of a Major and they were either Regular, Special Reserve or Territorial Force (TF).

The Regular Companies were numbered from 1–59 with some gaps and included several different types of unit. There were twenty-seven Fortress Companies, stationed around the Empire, whose primary duty was to work with Royal Garrison Artillery to protect the coast. There were also two railway companies, two coast companies, three survey companies, communications companies and two bridging trains in Britain. There were only sixteen Field Companies, four of which were abroad. The existing thirteen were reorganized into twelve Field Companies, two companies for each of the six Divisions of the BEF. In addition there were five troops, one for each of the Cavalry Brigades. Men were transferred from the RE Training Depot at Aldershot (mounted men), the RE Reserve Battalion and Depot Companies at Chatham (dismounted men). These troops were consolidated in Squadrons for the mounted Divisions once war was declared.

The Special Reserve Companies were part of the two regiments of the former Militia: the Royal Monmouthshire RE and The Royal Anglesey RE. Each of these had three companies, either railway companies or siege companies. They had a unique numbering system i.e.: 1st Siege Coy, R Mon RE and they retained this during the war.

There were three different kinds of company in the Territorial Force. Two Field Companies were allocated to each of the fourteen Infantry Divisions. They were known by their geographical designation rather than their number egg: 1/1st (Cheshire) Field Company RE. In addition there were eighteen units of Fortress

---

7. I found this very confusing as there seemed to be several variations. My thanks to Robert Flemming, Information and Community Outreach Curator National Army Museum for all his valuable help. www.nam.ac.uk.

Engineers for coastal defence and the London Electrical Engineers and the Tyne Electrical Engineers who also manned searchlights for coastal defence.

But it was soon obvious that there were not enough Field Companies so the Regular units on overseas Garrison duty were replaced by Territorial units and recalled home. On arrival they were formed into new regular Divisions. In September 1914 urgent recommendations came from GHQ in France for three Field Companies per Division. This had been previously recommended in 1912 but had not been implemented. Arrangements were now made for eight Territorial Field Companies to fill the places in the first eight Divisions. 1/1st Cheshire RE formed up in Birkenhead and initially embodied with the 53rd (Welsh) Division until they joined the 3rd Division on 22 December 1914.

The TF had now doubled from fourteen Divisions (twenty-eight Companies) to twenty-eight Divisions (fifty-six Companies).[8] The number of new Army divisions being formed soon reached thirty and as each new army was formed their Field Company was numbered from sixty-one upwards in sequence from the regular companies.

438th (1/1st Cheshire) Field Company, The Royal Engineers joined 3rd Division on 22 of December 1914. They took part in the Winter Operations of 1914–15, The First Attack on Bellewaarde and the Actions at Hooge.

---

8. In 1917 the complex names and numbering system was replaced by a single system beginning with 400 after all the new army units.

Chapter 4
1st Battalion Northumberland Fusiliers

The 1st Battalion Northumberland Fusiliers returned from India to Portsmouth in the autumn of 1913 and Lieutenant Colonel H.S. Ainslie took over command. They were now reorganized from eight companies to four and the Adjutant, Captain W. N. Herbert, began preparing the Battalion Mobilisation Scheme. During May and June 1914 they were camped near Wool in Dorset and began training in the new four company organization for the first time. Back in England after several years abroad most members of the Battalion had their minds fixed firmly on thoughts of enjoying the English summer and the assassination of an Austrian Archduke and events in Europe seemed distant and irrelevant. But once the gravity of the situation became apparent, no time was wasted in preparing to call up the army reserve. Thus, once the order to mobilize was given at 6.00pm on 4 August, the Battalion were ahead of schedule. Two days later the first draft of the 420 reservists from the Depot arrived at Cambridge Barracks, followed by a further draft of 221 men later that evening. One of those reservists was Sergeant Alfred Hobday[9], a well-known Tottenham Hotspur player. The annual Army Horse Census, often treated as a bit of a farce by local farmers and horse owners, ensured that horses identified for mobilization purposes were in the transport lines of Cambridge Barracks by the 7th.

However, the Battalion was not completely ready. The terms of infantry service had been altered after the end of the South African War to three years with the Colours and nine with the reserve. The expectation was that the reservists would be ready and trained, but the reality was somewhat different. The policy was to first call up those reservists who had been civilians for the longest period. This meant many had been civilians for nearly nine years. Furthermore, training had changed considerably during those years. An urgent call went out to the Depot for 100 picked fully trained reservists to replace the twenty-five least trained men from each company. They achieved this by picking men who had only just left the Battalion on its return from India.

---

9. Alfred made twenty-four appearances for Tottenham Hotspur for their second XI in the South Eastern League, Middlesex Professional Cup and friendly matches. He also made one first team appearance in the London FA Challenge Cup semi-final against Arsenal at Stamford Bridge. He played at full back in the 2–1 victory.

Pte Rowley. Kind permission Mick Rowley.

As they waited for their orders to depart they were struck by the indifferent attitude of the public. As the searchlights on the foreshore swept the Solent for signs of invasion the public carried on enjoying their day trips and August holidays at the seaside. When they did finally march to the station on 13 August there were no cheering crowds, only a few relatives. It could have been a normal change of location, an impression reinforced by the signs on the Southampton trains which read 'Woking'. The more experienced men compared their departure to that in 1899 when they had gone to fight in South Africa. Then the streets had been full of cheering crowds wishing them well.

Southampton was just as quiet and they boarded the SS *Norman* with little fanfare. In fact many of their relatives had no idea they had left the country. But this was deliberate policy to keep troop movements as quiet as possible and it succeeded. Remarkably the German General Staff was almost entirely ignorant of the movements and location of the BEF.

The Battalion arrived in Le Havre at 3.00 am on 14 August and disembarked two hours later. As they began the six-mile march to Epremesnil the lack of training became apparent. The mist had now cleared and the sun was beating down on the long, steep, sandy road. Many of the reservists had been working in factories and had not marched for years; others had not eaten or were suffering from the effects of their inoculations for enteric. It wasn't just the men who were unable to cope, the horses also struggled to adapt to their new role. This meant the transport with their supplies failed to turn up until late afternoon leaving the men in the merciless sun with no rations or shade.

As the thunderstorm broke over the camp later that night the dry parched field turned almost immediately into a quagmire of sticky glutinous mud. The following night they marched back to Havre to entrain for the front. The rain had finally ceased, but the dreadful conditions of the ground and roads severely hampered all movement in the pitch black of the cloud filled night. It took three and three quarter hours to cover three and a half miles. The Battalion struggled painfully behind its transport as the horses bucked and jibbed with their unaccustomed tasks and both the water carts turned over in a narrow lane. Fortunately, on their arrival at the station, everything proceeded so smoothly they boarded the train an hour and a half ahead of schedule.

LT Dalbiac.

At the station they were joined by two interpreters, Soldat Simon and Soldat Steinhardt of 114e Infanterie. Both were wearing the old-fashioned French uniforms of heavy blue coats and red pantaloons and carried large knapsacks. They appeared quite intimidating until the men found out that they had no idea how to handle their Lebel rifles or the wicked looking bayonets. Simon was the head of a leading Jewellery firm in Paris while Steinhardt was a lawyer. Both were exempt from normal service because of their usefulness as interpreters.

The Battalion marched to meet 3rd Division which was assembling at Noyelles. On 21 August the Division left, heading east to meet the advancing German forces. After a long dreary march of twelve-and-a-half miles they arrived in La Longueville where they rested for the night. The following day they set out with 9th Brigade towards Mons.

Responsibility for a very extensive front was down to 3rd Division and 9th Brigade had been allocated the left section. This extended six miles westwards along the line of the Conde Canal from Nimy, due north of Mons, to the bridge of Mariette. The 4th Battalion Royal Fusiliers were on the right, the 1st Battalion Royal Scots Fusiliers in the centre and B and C Companies of the 1st Battalion Northumberland Fusiliers were to the left of Jemappes, excluding the town itself, to Mariette which was included. The rest of the 1st Battalion would be held in reserve with the 1st Battalion Lincolnshire Regiment, at Cuesmes, a suburb of Mons. The front held by the 3rd Division was divided in two. The area to the right was mainly agricultural with fields, farms and small villages. But the area allocated to the 9th Brigade, southwest of Mons and south of the canal, was a densely populated tangle of mining villages.

Companies B and C were under the command of Major Yatman and branched left once they reached the mining village of Genly and quickly made their way to their position on the left of the line. They would now come under the direct orders of 9th Brigade while the remainder made their way to Cuesmes. Battalion HQ was set up in a house on the square in Cure while the villagers made the troops welcome. The men noticed that although they were greeted just as warmly in Belgium as they had been in France, the greeting in France had come from children and older women. In Belgium it was young men who cheered them on. At this time there were many back in England who had not joined up so the men took little notice.

Cpl James Mavin. Kind permission of the descendants of James Mavin.

Finally, after marching for miles on cobblestones, their feet sore, their packs overflowing with gifts of chocolate, cigarettes and cigars, Major Yatman's men reached Quaregnon. This was the main street leading to the bridge of Mariette, the left flank of the division. The only verbal orders Major Yatman received were that if he came under heavy attack he should hold his position for as long as possible, that he would not be relieved and to use his discretion as to when he should withdraw.

At some later point in the day these orders were amended to state that mounted troops, cavalry and cyclists, would relieve any infantry outposts and that the infantry should retire to Ciply station in the event of a heavy frontal assault. Major Yatman never received these orders.

There were five bridges in the 9th Brigade front line, one of which was the Mariette Bridge. The canal here was 60ft wide and there was also a flood aqueduct on the Quaregnon side which was 15ft wide and very deep. They were separated by a 45ft-wide bank along which ran the southern tow path of the canal. The bridges across the canal were connected by a path and on either side there were two houses, one of which was the bridgekeeper's cottage. The task of holding the bridges was given to B Company while C Company were positioned to their right to defend the line of the

Cpt H. R. Sandilands.　　　　　　　　Alfred Hobday, Tottenham Hotspurs.

canal. They were still putting the defences together when Major Yatman was called to the station. Here he received a strange phone call from someone purporting to be a British agent who informed him that several German units were in the vicinity of Bois de Baudour, some four miles to the north. He was still giving his report when he was cut off abruptly. Yatman passed on the message to HQ, but was never to find out the identity of the man or whether he had survived.

The German attack began on the right of the 9th Brigade north of Mons on a bright sunny Sunday morning. The assault spread rapidly westwards along the canal but at the Mariette Bridge all was calm. Then suddenly the men at the bridgekeeper's cottage spotted German infantry in the main street. They immediately opened fire inflicting heavy casualties, but the survivors were able to take the houses north of the railway. Sergeant Panter and his men withdrew without loss and then found themselves under sporadic artillery fire. Fortunately this passed over the canal, landing mainly in the area around the railway station. However, Yatman had now lost contact with the troops of 5th Division. He had been in contact through a signaller sited on top of a gasometer, but the shelling had dislodged him leaving Yatman without any contact with the left flank. As noon approached the artillery bombardment gradually ceased but the infantry were still reluctant to advance and stalemate ensued. Although the situation on the right and centre of 9th Brigade's front line was becoming critical Yatman was totally unaware of this.

At around 3.00pm the enemy were spotted beginning another assault, but just as Captain St John's men opened fire, several little girls ran across the street and he immediately called a cease fire. The children ran backwards and forwards

1913–1914 Season, Tottenham Hotspurs.

three times across the street crying in fear before disappearing. Although it had only taken a few moments it was enough time for the Germans to cut the wire entanglements and take control of the coal sheds. Under covering fire they were able to bring up a field gun and they began pounding the British positions. At the same time 2nd Lt Boyd reported that hostile infantry and artillery were gathering opposite his position on the southern banks of the canal. But because they had no contact with the rest of 9th Brigade they still had no idea how serious their position was.

At 4.00 pm Yatman gave the order to withdraw, something he would probably have done a full hour earlier if he'd been in contact with the rest of the Brigade. Scarcely had he given the order when Lieutenant Wright of the 57th Field Company RE arrived to blow up the bridges. He also gave them the alarming news that the Germans had already crossed the canal and they were in danger of being flanked on both sides.

Unfortunately Lieutenant Wright had only been given leads for the main bridge and the nearer aqueduct had not been taken into consideration. Undaunted he lowered himself under the main bridge and made it under fire to the central bank where he searched unsuccessfully for the leads. Despite being awarded the Victoria Cross for his heroic actions he was forced to abandon the task, leaving the bridges intact. By now the garrison of the Brigade had already withdrawn leaving behind Captain St John and CQMS Lewis to provide what covering fire they could. Eventually, together with Lieutenant Wright and the other engineers, they too withdrew. Shortly afterwards a cyclist delivered the Brigade orders and the survivors of A and B Companies made their way back to Frameries. Once there they were ordered to take up defensive positions.

The withdrawal from the canal had opened up a dangerous gap between the inner flanks of the 3rd and 5th Divisions. To plug this the 5th Infantry Brigade was bought forward from 2nd Division, 1 Corps and occupied Pataurages on the west flank while the 2nd Worcester Regiment took up positions on the right of this brigade linking with the left flank of the 5th Division.

Despite the exhausting day there was no rest for the men of the 1st Battalion and B and C Companies dug trenches while A Company spent the night constructing barricades at the crossroads. There were no rations but fortunately the local bakery kept a supply of bread coming which took the edge off their hunger.

Frameries was alive with civilians who should have been confined to their homes to reduce the activity of spies in the vicinity, but no order had been given. Several rather suspicious people were seen during the night of the 23/24 August, but little could be done about them. The peace held until first light when the German bombardment began. Shells fell along the entire length of 9th Brigade's frontline trenches and with perfect accuracy on several houses within twenty yards of A Company's main barricade. Casualties began to mount and because the Regimental medical officers were forward with the troops the hospital further back began to struggle to cope with the increasing numbers of wounded.

An elderly Belgian lady appeared by A Company's barricade and demanded to be allowed through so she could speak to Doctor ***** who lived a short distance away. Despite the increasing danger from shells and the imminent threat of rifle fire she refused to budge, even when she was told they would go and get the doctor for her. Eventually she was given a megaphone through which she shouted. The doctor appeared and was almost immediately hit by a shell landing on a roof opposite. He disappeared back in his house only for her to call him again. Eventually, after the third time, he and his black bag made it to the shelter of the barricade and she directed him to the hospital.

The sporadic artillery fire continued for two hours, but any infantry attack was held in check by the British field guns to the south west of the village. It was now past 8.00 am and the troops in Frameries were holding their own, however they had no idea of the serious position they were in and that GHQ had long since ordered their withdrawal.

At 8.40 pm on the night of 23 August Sir John French had given orders from GHQ, at Le Cateau, thirty miles from Frameries, that they were to hold any ground that had been taken and drive back the enemy. This order had been transmitted to 9th Infantry Brigade from 3rd Division at 1.39 am on 24 August reaching the Battalions around 2.39 am. However, two hours prior to this order being transmitted by 3rd Division, news had reached GHQ that the French 5th Army on the right of the BEF was falling back. This left General Sir John French with no option but to order a withdrawal, which he did at 1 am. The orders did

Cpt L.V. Bagshaw.   Lieut E Dorman-Smith. Kind permission of Paul H. Collier.

not reach 3rd Division until several hours later and it was not until 6.30 am that they ordered the withdrawal of 7th and 8th Infantry Brigades. 9th and 5th Infantry Brigades were to hold Frameries until further orders. 5th Brigade had been lent to II Corps by I Corps and as such should have come under II Corps' orders. But instead I Corps ordered their withdrawal which was carried out so swiftly that it happened before B and C Companies had received similar orders and this left them dangerously exposed.

It was not until 9.30 am that the 1st Battalion were ordered to withdraw and act as rear guard to the Brigade. (There was some confusion as to who was the rear guard as both the Lincolnshire Regiment and the Northumberland Fusiliers thought they were.) The orders came not a moment too soon as within minutes German infantry appeared in the main street 100 yards to the north of A Company's central barricade. A brief fire fight ensued which killed two and dispersed the rest. The men of A Company continued to fire at snipers and keep the rest contained while the remainder of B and C Companies completed their withdrawal back to the safety of A company's barricade and then back to the relative safety of the southern outskirts of Frameries. Recorded casualties were light with three other ranks killed and two officers and thirty other ranks wounded. But these figures do not include the wounded who had been abandoned in the Convent when the order to withdraw had been received.

Thus began the Retreat from Mons and while the 3rd Division as a whole continued to withdraw, the 9th Brigade was ordered to remain at Sars La Bruyere to cover the right flank of the 5th Division. Eventually at 4.00 pm they were able to retire but although it was only seven miles to Bavay the men were totally exhausted, thirsty, hungry and suffering the effects of heat, lack of sleep and prolonged artillery bombardment. As they tramped wearily southwest they were passed by a group of mounted officers. One of these was the Corps Commander, Sir Horace Smith-Dorrien, who stopped and spoke to the men, something that helped to raise morale considerably.

Just after sunset they reached Bavay. But the town was congested with troops arriving from all directions and the men were ordered to march another couple of miles to Bermeries. It was dark when they arrived in the field assigned to them and the heat of the day had given way to a cold night. But, to the relief of the hungry exhausted men, the Quartermaster had hot meals ready for them after which most fell asleep on the bare ground.

By 5 September what remained of the BEF had retired to south of the Marne and Grand Morin rivers. The exhausted men of the 1st Battalion had hoped to remain in Chartres for a few days but orders arrived directing them to march to Lumigny on 6 September. They did not encounter any Germans, but as they continued on the advance over the next few days they found ample evidence of their occupation and hurried retreat. All telegraph wires had been cut, ransacked houses were strewn with empty bottles and they passed numbers of abandoned wagons and equipment.

Orders arrived on 14 September to cross the Aisne and push five miles northwards to the high ground and seize it. Up until that day casualties in the Battalion had been relatively light. Following these orders six Officers were killed and a further four were wounded. Other ranks casualties were 22 killed and 136 wounded. On 20 September they were relieved by the 8th Brigade and some troops from the 16th Brigade, temporarily attached to the 3rd Division from the recently arrived 6th Division.

They reached Estaires by 30 October expecting ten days' rest, but this was short lived. The Germans had launched an offensive at Ypres with the objective of taking the Messines-Wytschaete Ridge

Cpt Roddam.

Lt Roddam.

and the commanding position at Kemmel. The idea was to cut off the allied troops in and north of Ypres and drive them back to the coast. The heaviest attack was against the southern portion of the salient which was held by the Cavalry Corps. The British were thrust back west of Zandvoorte and in the south they fell back on Wytschaete where they struggled to contain the overwhelming numbers. The nearest troops were 9th Brigade who were still resting after the heavy fighting at Neuve Chapelle.

On 31 October Brigadier General Shaw set out from Estaires with the 1st Battalion and the 1st Lincolnshire in support. Initially the men thought they were just moving to better billets further back from the front, but they soon learnt the truth. They marched twelve miles to Lindenhoek, two and a half miles southwest of Wytschaete, and then in the evening they moved to billets in Kemmel.

At 1.45 am urgent orders arrived for them to support the cavalry at Wytschaete and in fifteen minutes they had formed up and were marching towards the Kemmel-Wytschaete Road with the 1st Lincolnshire in the lead.

The night was dark but the sky was lit by fires in burning houses and in the distance they could hear the continuing rattle of musketry fire and the crash of bursting shells. The noise of cartridges exploding on a nearby burning limber made the fighting sound much closer.

On arrival at 4th Cavalry Brigade HQ Brigadier General Shaw was told that the cavalry trenches had been overrun and the enemy were now occupying part of the village. A counter-attack to recover the lost positions was ordered for 4.30 am with the 1st Lincolnshire on the right, two Companies of the 1st Northumberland Fusiliers on the left and the remainder of the 1st Northumberland Fusiliers in support.

The ground they were to cross was supposed to be open but instead it was enclosed with barbed wire entanglements and there were very few wire cutters available. On the left, X Company found themselves confronted by a wood which spread to the north-west outskirts of the village and although W Company had a clearer line of advance between the edge of the wood and the road they came under heavy rifle and machine gun fire and subsequently lost contact with the 1st Lincolnshire.

Captain St John of X Company crossed the road to speak to Captain Fletcher of W Company but could not find him. Instead he found lines of wounded men. It was obvious that the counter-attack had failed. The objective to take back Kemmel Hill had cost the 1st Northumberland Fusiliers five officers and ninety-three other ranks – thirty per cent of the men present. The 1st Lincolnshire had lost eight officers and 293 other ranks. By 6 November only four officers of the twenty-six who had sailed with the Battalion remained and the total strength of the Battalion was a little over 200. This decreased to 170 in total by 16 November. At the same time 9th Brigade's total strength had diminished to 1,385 which equalled less than 300 per battalion.

A hard frost set in and the French took over the Ypres salient. The 1st Northumberland Fusiliers were finally relieved on the night of 20 November and they marched by Ypres and Dickebusch to Westoutre for six days of well-deserved rest.

The next day the first draft of reinforcements arrived, five officers and 295 other ranks. One of these was Fusilier James Howard Bodsworth

L/Cpl Austin Broughton. Kind permission of Martin Clift.

(he survived the battle and eventually transferred to the 2nd Garrison Battalion Northumberland Fusiliers. It's likely he spent the rest of the war in India as there was a large POW camp there. He died in Surrey in 1957). This was followed five days later by another two officers and eleven other ranks.

To combat the bitter cold they had finally been issued with leather jerkins and given instructions on how to use charcoal braziers in the trenches. They used their time watching demonstrations of bombing throwing, overhauling their rifles and having musketry practice. By 27 November they were back on the front line carrying out a five day tour of the Kemmel front. The weather was freezing with occasional rain and they were subject to continuous sniping from the enemy.

The Battalion, now up to its fighting strength of 772 men, were lucky enough to spend Christmas in billets at Locre where they all enjoyed half a pound of plum pudding.

Another draft of fifty men joined the Battalion on 6 January 1915 and one of the new arrivals was Lieutenant Corporal Austin Frank Broughton.[10] Austin had joined the army on his seventeenth birthday in April 1913, possibly against his mother's wishes. But his older brother William was already in the 3rd Battalion the Rifle Brigade and, enjoying the life, encouraged his younger brother to do the same.

On 17 February 1915 they marched with 9th Brigade from Dickebusch to Ypres where they were billeted in the Cavalry Barracks. Six days later they took over the trenches on the south of the canal in 28th Division's sector. They were not impressed by what they found.

Trenches P, R, S and N were all overlooked by German trenches. N trench was thigh deep in mud, the parapet was not bullet proof and the trench was isolated from the others. The trenches were not deep enough so the parapets had to be built up with sand bags. The nights were so bright that little wiring could be done and work outside N trench was impossible and as it contained little more than liquid mud nothing could be done to improve it with sandbags. Approaches to the trenches were flat and open and there were no communication trenches because of the waterlogged ground. The Battalion took many casualties when working outside the trenches. There was only one thin-line trench with no supporting trenches and the area was crowded with unburied dead and discarded material.

Because the communication cables were unprotected they were constantly being cut. Until the wire was mended orderlies were used to take messages. Struggling through thick mud, while running the gauntlet of snipers, meant a messenger could take two hours to cover 600 yards. The Battalion suffered heavy casualties

---

10. Lance Corporal Austin Frank Broughton is Martin Clift's great uncle. Martin's determination to research into what happened to him led to the website http://www.bellewaarde1915.co.uk/ and ultimately to this book being written.

Lt Fearnley-Whittingstall, St George's Gazette, 31 August 1916.

Pte James Miller. Kind permission of Jeff Jefferson.

during this time from bombs, snipers and artillery and in three short tours lost 45 killed and 164 wounded.

Ypres itself was damaged, but not yet the ruin it would become. Civilians still carried on trading. Members of the Battalion arriving in February and March noted the balcony above the infantry barracks filled with troops watching the Liverpool Scottish sounding the Retreat on penny whistles and tin cans. The air was filled with chatter and laughter and only the distant continuous desultory artillery fire reminded them that the war was so close.

After dark everything changed. The artillery died down only to be replaced by the ceaseless rattle of musketry fire in the not too distant trenches. Above them the Very lights from the opposing lines in the south, east and north lit the sky.

On 4 April the Battalion and 9th Brigade re-joined 3rd Division which now occupied the sector in the southern quarter of the Ypres salient. On 22 April a curious smell was noticed and the men in the trenches complained their eyes were smarting. At the time 3rd Division thought the gas shell had been used on their front but it was later confirmed as being on the St Julien front. The British were totally unprepared for this and one of the more desperate suggestions was for the men to soak their woollen caps or scarves in urine and use them as respirators.

Their relief was cancelled and nights were spent constructing a rear switch line in case of the complete collapse of the Ypres salient. They remained on the St

Eloi until 26 May and were then withdrawn to Ouderdon. By 6 June they were bivouacked at a farm near Ouderdon in reserve. In the seven months since the beginning of the First Battle of Ypres the Battalion had taken over 600 casualties yet not seen a single German face to face.

Chapter 5

4th Battalion Royal Fusiliers

The 4th Battalion Royal Fusiliers were based in Parkhurst at the beginning of the war and had mobilized by 8 August. Under the command of Brigadier-General N R McMahon DSO they sailed for Le Havre on 13 August arriving to a rapturous reception from the French soldiers on the quay. The 4th Battalion whistled the Marseillaise in gratitude and then began singing 'Hold your hand out you naughty boy'. This was sung with such fervour that the French soldiers thought it was the British National Anthem and removed their headgear and bowed respectfully.

The weather was extremely hot and the Battalion had 734 Reservists. The steep climb up to the rest camp at Harfleur after a seven-mile march was just too much and ninety-seven men fell out. Unfortunately they had moved so quickly that there were no tents for them so they settled down in the orchards in the open. As the evening arrived the sun disappeared and a thunderstorm broke over the camp and drenched the men through to their skin. The rain continued in torrents until 16 August when they entrained for the Division concentration area at Noyelles.

After several days travelling they arrived at Mons to an enthusiastic welcome from the townspeople who loaded them with presents of eggs, fruit, tobacco and even handkerchiefs.

The Royal Fusiliers were the right hand battalion of 9th Brigade and so were positioned along the western face of the canal bend in charge of all the crossings up to and including Nimy Bridge. The posts they occupied covering Ghlin, just south of Bois de Ghlin, and the Bois Brule had no field of

Lt Brian Douglas Warde. Kind permission of John Hamblin.

fire leaving them open to a surprise enemy attack. On their right were the 1st Middlesex who were defending the eastern face of the canal. Opposite them were the left Corps of the First German Army. This meant each of the two battalions were facing two regiments of three battalions each of the 18th Jaeger Division.

North of Nimy was Y Company with its left a little north of Lock 6 and its right joining with the 4th Middlesex. Two platoons held Nimy Bridge and the other two platoons and company HQ were entrenched at the railway bridge and on the canal bank to the left of it.

Meanwhile, Z Company held positions around Lock 6 and the Ghlin-Mons Bridge. The other two Companies were in support at Nimy Station (X Company) and in reserve (W Company) north of Mons. This left two Companies to face six German Battalions.

The twenty-mile march to Mons was tiring and as soon as they arrived they were put to work trying to make the Ghlin position defensible after which they were withdrawn to the canal line. The railway bridge was blocked by turning cable drums on their side.

By the time morning arrived on 23 August the men were exhausted having worked all night. They could hear the Germans moving about north of the canal in the dark and early in the morning a Cavalry patrol consisting of an officer and six men suddenly appeared on the Nimy Road. As they galloped straight towards the bridge the Royal Fusiliers opened fire shooting four of the men and the officer. The officer was captured and the two uninjured men escaped. The officer was Lieutenant Juergen von Arnim, son of the Commander of IV Army Corps.

Despite overnight reconnaissance the Germans appeared to have little idea of how many British were in front of them. At 10am they appeared above the skyline barely 1,000 yards away and the Fusiliers opened fire. The survivors hurriedly withdrew and their artillery began shelling the Battalion before making a second attempt. There was no British artillery to respond so the German guns continued to fire on them.

As the battle continued they received the order to be ready to withdraw within ten minutes. Because of this the ammunition that had earlier been distributed among the trenches was put into carts ready to be moved. This caused a severe shortage later in the battle. The German artillery gradually worked its way round and came up behind Y Company; Z Company only suffered from sporadic rifle fire and periodic bursts of shrapnel, but they had earlier sunk the boats and fired the barges in case of retreat and could do nothing to help.

The position in this section of the canal was becoming desperate. In the machine-gun position the space was so tight that when a member of the machine gun crew was hit he had to be removed before another could take his place. The approach from the trench to the machine gun was across open ground and whenever the gun stopped Lieutenant Maurice Dease went to see why. He repeated this several times and even when wounded twice he continued, insisting on remaining on duty all the time one of his crew could fire. The third wound proved fatal and he was awarded a posthumous VC.

Both guns had now ceased firing and Private Godley went forward under heavy fire and brought the gun back into action. But not for long as the gun was hit, the water jackets completely riddled with bullets and he was wounded and captured. He was given a VC whilst a POW.

At 1.40 pm they received the order to retire; Y Company had already suffered seventy-five casualties and the Germans were within 200 yards of their position. By the time they had withdrawn they had suffered a further 150 casualties.

By 5 September the Retreat from Mons was complete and the Royal Fusiliers arrived in Chartres to take up a defensive position south of La Haute Maison. Having spent much of the retreat as rear guard they were pleased to be the advance guard into the Battle of Marne. On 9 September the battalion crossed the Marne unopposed and the next day they came into contact with the enemy at Veuilly.

Sgt John Harvey. Kind permission of Mick Harvey.

It was cold and raining and the report said the German rear guard were breakfasting about two miles ahead. Despite being exhausted one platoon immediately went forward with another as reinforcement. In the engagement that followed five men were killed and thirty-one wounded, but the German rear guard was quickly overcome with the help of the Royal Scots Fusiliers. They captured 600 prisoners and the machine gun that had caused Y Company so many casualties.

On 13 September the Battle of the Aisne began. The Battalion reached Vailly only to find that all the bridges had been blown up and the only way across was by means of a narrow plank which wobbled precariously as they crossed. Their aim was to take up a position on the left of Rouge Maison Farm but it was pitch black and raining when they arrived. Meanwhile X and Z Companies pushed on reaching the Maison Rouge Spur at midnight, leaving the other two companies occupying a hollow in the road. There was no cover and all four companies spent a very wet night in the open.

Although the following morning was wet and foggy it was soon obvious that they had gone too far forward. They were so close to the enemy they could even hear them talking. The two forward companies tried to extend their line towards the left and W and Y companies were sent to support them. However, W Company had only moved a short distance when they discovered a German trench about 300 yards on their right. They sent a patrol forward which was immediately fired on and the Battalion on their right began to withdraw leaving their right flank open to enfilade fire from machine guns causing heavy casualties. The whole area was now under rifle and machine gun fire and by the end of the day they had taken 204 casualties.

Two platoons of X Company were still occupying the Maison Rouge Spur, clinging to their positions despite two German assaults. Lack of further assaults on the next three days allowed them to strengthen their positions, but on 19

September a heavy bombardment began and they took even more casualties, 5 officers and 300 men wounded or killed, before being relieved by the Lincolns at 5.00 pm. The Battalion rested at Courcelles where two reinforcement drafts arrived bringing the Battalion almost back up to full strength.

By the end of the second week in October the battalion was in Flanders and moving towards Vieille Chapelle as divisional reserve. On 15 October they fought and defeated the German Cavalry at Pont Du Hem. They continued forward to the Rue d'Enfer. Here they encountered some light resistance from the Germans which they easily overcame.

On 17 October they arrived at Aubers, which had been evacuated during the night but they were stopped by the presence of German Cavalry advancing from Fromelles. The advance came to a complete halt the following day and they spent the whole day strengthening their defences under heavy bombardment from German artillery.

The following night a platoon was sent to help the Royal Irish in Pilly leaving the Royal Fusiliers holding the line from the Pilly Road to the west side of Herlies. At 7.00 am on 20 October the Germans began shelling the town with such ferocity that it was quickly reduced to ruins, the only building that remained was the convent behind the church.

Fierce fighting continued and eventually they were withdrawn the next day although the Germans continued to shell the town long after they had gone. The battalion had suffered 155 casualties, either killed or wounded. The next day they received orders to move a further four miles back. However, because they were not given any transport, they had to abandon most of their ammunition and rations before the night march. At this point they were further east than any British troops would be for the next four years, but were unable to maintain it because of the strength of the enemy.

On 6 November the exhausted battalion took over the 6th Cavalry Brigade positions, on the south of the Ypres-Menin Road, east of Hooge. Having fought their way slowly along the heavily congested roads around Ypres they had only just arrived in position when the 1st Battle of Ypres began.

The Germans began shelling the Zouaves[11] on 7 November forcing them to leave their trenches. The shelling continued all day and several attacks were beaten back but eventually the Zouaves were forced to withdraw leaving the Fusiliers' left flank exposed. The Germans broke into the wood on their left, an assault that was immediately counter attacked by half of Y Company and two officers. Although they succeeded in reaching the German trenches both officers and sixty-two men were killed. But the counter-attack and another assault by the West Ridings had succeeded in restoring the line.

---

11. Zouave was the name of some light infantry regiments in the French Army, normally those who had served in French North Africa between 1831 and 1962.

On 11 November the Germans made their last attempt to break through to the coast. The day was dull and misty and at 6.30 am the Germans began shelling the front trenches with such ferocity that they were blown to pieces and many men were killed or buried. After two-and-a-half hours the shelling stopped and twelve battalions of the Guard Division attacked.

The Royal Fusiliers were attacked by the 4th (Queen Augusta's) Guard Grenadiers and although they repelled the first attack the Germans came back again. This time the men were forced from their trenches causing panic among the support troops further back who were mostly newly drafted reservists who had only arrived the day before.

A counter-attack on both sides of the Ypres–Menin Road by the Sussex and Scots Fusiliers managed to drive the Germans back and partially restore the line but the survivors of the Royal Fusiliers were scattered and disorganized. Only two officers and fifty men could be found. The fighting died down over night only to resume again the next morning and the remainder of the Fusiliers, now 100 men, were again forward supporting the Scots Fusiliers and Lincolns. The fighting continued for the next two days as the weather deteriorated from rain to heavy snow. But the German advance had been halted and 16 November they went into divisional reserve.

By 20 November the weather had deteriorated still further and the freezing conditions began to affect the men's feet. Another draft of 300 special reservists arrived and the companies were reorganized. On 27 November they were sent to the trenches at Kemmel. For a battalion who had been wiped out twice this was the last straw. Morale was very low and many of the men were suffering badly from nerves. The trenches were permanently water logged and many of the men had bad feet. However, after three days in the trenches the battalion began to settle down again and on the night of 30 November they marched to billets at Westoutre. In four months they had lost 1,900 NCOs and men and 50 officers.

Early in January 1915 Lieutenant Colonel Campbell took over command of the 4th Battalion. By now the men were really suffering from the cold and the terrible conditions in the trenches. The rest area in Ouderdom offered little respite as the huts weren't rainproof and the camp was a sea of mud. They were also under constant attack from enemy snipers losing no less than fifty-eight men within forty-eight hours to hostile fire on 23 February.

On 24 May the Germans delivered the first gas attack. It was a perfect summer day and the light north-easterly breeze carried the poisonous fumes across the British lines between Shell-Trap Farm, north of the St Julien Road, and Bellewaarde Lake. The surprise gained the enemy a considerable advantage and while the men were searching for their respirators the bombardment began. Although not in the direct line of fire the 4th Battalion suffered the effects five miles away at Dickebusch, many men suffering from sore eyes.

At the end of May the Germans were left in possession of Bellewaarde Lake and the 3rd Division was given the task of straightening out the line. 9th Brigade was given the task of storming Bellewaarde Farm Ridge.

By 1.30 am on 16 June the 4th Battalion Royal Fusiliers had moved into position east of Cambridge Road trench and were waiting for the orders to advance. They were on the right of 9th Brigade front.

Chapter 6

1/10th The (King's) Liverpool Regiment

On 27 January 1900, in response to the wave of patriotic feeling caused by the Boer War, a letter appeared in the daily press that suggested raising a volunteer corps of young Scotsmen in Liverpool on similar lines to the London Scottish. By 30 April the authority of the War Office was granted and the Battalion was called the 8th (Scottish) Volunteer Battalion, The King's Liverpool Regiment.

In January 1914 their Honourable Colonel, Lord Strathcona died but, on 13 June the Marquis of Tullibardine, Duke of Athol, became the Honourable Colonel. He was a popular choice, having seen service in South Africa with his own regiment, the Scottish Horse.

Despite the fact that France, Russia and Germany were already mobilizing, the Regiment carried on to Hornby for their annual training on 2 August. They arrived late in the afternoon and at 2.00 am the following morning received orders to return to Liverpool immediately. On arrival at Fraser Street the men were addressed by Colonel Nicholl and then sent home with instructions to be prepared to report to HQ at a moment's notice. On the following day the Territorial force was mobilized.

2nd Lieut John Christian Barber. By kind permission of Ben Muse.

The first three days were spent in issuing equipment, drawing stores, having medical inspections and collecting horses. Unfortunately Captain Harrison, the Transport Officer, found such a magnificent selection of horses that a Regular Battalion, billeted in St George's Hall, requisitioned them all and he had to start again.

On 8 August, 600 men reported to Fraser Street and were billeted in the Shakespeare Theatre. The next day they received their Embodiment Grant of £5 and their ten-shilling kit allowance and were issued with ball ammunition.

Unknown Liverpool Scottish. By kind permission of First World War Tommies Not Forgotten Post Cards from the period.

Companies A to F were billeted in the Stadium while G and H were in the Theatre. The owners of the Stadium placed the private boxes at the disposal of the Commanding Officer to be used as an Officers' Mess and boxing matches and concerts were organized each night to entertain the men.

As well as route marches and parades the Battalion also worked in the docks unloading frozen meat until 13 August when they, and the remainder of the South Lancashire Brigade, entrained for Edinburgh. Here they camped in King's Park, close to Holyrood Palace. The next few weeks were spent in training until, on 10 October, they moved to Tunbridge Wells where they were billeted in schools and empty houses. Finally, on 27 October they received the orders they had been waiting for. They were to embark on 30 October. However the last 300 men who had not been able to take their musketry course were to be left behind. The Battalion were also rather bemused to have all their rifles taken away and to be issued with new ones they would not have any opportunity to try out before embarkation. They entrained for Southampton on 1 November and boarded the *SS Maidan* late that afternoon. Also on the *SS Maidan* were the Queen Westminster Rifles, one of London's leading Territorial Units.

The Battalion landed at Havre at 8.00 am on 3 November and spent that night under canvas on the high ground above the town. The following day they entrained for St Omer in cattle trucks with forty men and six horses to a waggon. It was a journey of some 200 miles and took 27 hours as the train stopped for a considerable time at each station. They finally reached St Omer at 9.45 pm on 5 November and, after a long wait in the pouring rain, marched three miles to billets in Blendecques where they dug trenches and practised various types of attacks. The weather was atrocious and there were no facilities for drying clothes, but, despite this, only twenty men had to be left behind when they received their orders to move.

On 19 November they received orders to move forward the following day to Hazebrouck and then on to Bailleul. They spent the night being issued with new boots and tunics which they should have received earlier but that had not arrived until the last minute.

Marching to Hazebrouck the next day was a nightmare as the roads were frozen solid. The rear company struggled to keep the transport on the road and some of the men had bad falls, exacerbated by the weight of the full packs and rifles. There was no room when they arrived and they had to forage into the surrounding

Captain Noel Godfrey Chavasse. By kind permission of Liverpool Scottish Museum Trust.

Unknown Liverpool Scottish. By kind permission of First World War Tommies Not Forgotten Post Cards from the period.

countryside to find shelter in farm buildings. It was not until midnight that they were all housed.

The march to Bailleul was easier and they found good quality billets in the town. Here they remained until 23 November when they received orders that they would be joining a regular Brigade on 25 November, the 9th Brigade. This necessitated some reordering of the Battalion. Now A and B Company became one company, so too did C and D etc. However there was then some debate as to what to call these new company formations as to revert to A, B etc. might cause confusion. For a while they were known as 1, 2, 3, but subsequently became V, X, Y and Z.

The Battalion formed up on the morning of 25 November in a field near Bailleul and were addressed by General Sir H. Smith Dorien who expressed his opinion that if the British and French armies pinned down the enemy in the west during the winter the Russians could push through to Berlin in the spring. Thus the war would be over by the summer. Most of the men were astonished to hear that the General Staff thought it was going to last that long.

Their first sight of the Brigade was a shock. Many of the men had beards, their clothes were muddy and stained and several were wearing cap comforters rather than the regulation flat caps. But despite their unkempt appearance their rifles were spotless.

The battalion received their orders to move to the trenches at Kemmel on the evening of 27 November and to find 150 rifles for the front line, 100 as supports and two platoons as local reserves. There was considerable argument as to who should man the front lines. Captain Anderson claimed that his old Company, B Company, had won the Battalion Efficiency Shield, but Captain Twentyman claimed seniority and he won the day. Minus one platoon, Y Company had the honour of being the first into the front line; the remainder were detailed as support with one platoon of V Company. Two platoons of Z Company were local reserve.

The siting of the British trenches was quite haphazard, often the line on which a counter-attack had been held. There was little regard to field of fire or even to the direction of the enemy. Although the Germans had been halted they had managed to seize what little high ground there was. Many of the Kemmel trenches were open to enfilade fire from both rifle and artillery while in other parts the enemy trenches could not be seen at all. The front line was often not continuous. Support trenches did not exist and there were no strong points or defended areas to serve as rallying points or to hold up an attack if it broke through the front-line trench. The only defence was to retake the trench immediately meaning the role of support troops was purely offensive.

There were no communication trenches either, other than the one on the extreme right of the Brigade front which was only about fifty yards long. Therefore, reliefs had to be carried out at night in the open, a particularly dangerous task if it was a bright moonlit night and the enemy became aware of what was going on. There were two methods of relieving the trench. Either the new men simply jumped in and hoisted out the incumbent troops or they filed in one end and gradually

Cpl Gordon Bartlett. By kind permission of Richard "perce" Percival.

Unknown Liverpool Scottish. By kind permission of First World War Tommies Not Forgotten Post Cards from the period.

pushed the troops out the other end. Neither method gave the incoming troops time to find out where the danger spots were or any other details that might be of use to them during their tour.

The trenches had no dugouts, no duckboards, no pumps and any repairs had to utilize material from planks and lumber taken from ruined houses. There were also few sandbags. After heavy rain or a heavy thaw men would sometimes have to be dug out of the mud as they were incapable of moving unaided. Shoes and spats were useless as the mud sucked them off, something the men often failed to notice until the circulation began to return to their feet. These were soon withdrawn and replaced with boots and puttees. There was virtually no sanitation other than the ground behind the trenches which resembled an open sewer. From the twenty-six officers and 829 other ranks who entered the trenches on 27 November only 370 remained by the first week in January.

There was also a lack of hot food. Although tea was sent up in Dixies from HQ a mile and a half away, much of it was spilt on the way and what survived the journey was invariably cold by the time it arrived. Transport did not include field cookers so hot stews were impossible. It was also impossible to get uniforms dry when back in their billets after their tours in the trenches. The officers had a set of dry clothes in their cases they could wear while their clothes were drying, but the men remained in wet clothes. It was impossible to shave in the trenches as there

Men of 'Z' Company, relaxing behind the lines. By kind permission of Liverpool Scottish Museum Trust.

was not enough water to spare so the men were allowed to grow beards. However, after a few weeks the Battalion looked so bad that only those whose beards looked reasonable were allowed to continue, the rest had to shave them off.

The other inconvenience was having to use the old Lee Enfield rifle, unlike the regulars who were issued with the new SMLE. This caused problems because it was not designed to withstand the heavier charge of cordite in the new Mark VII ammunition. This meant special stocks of Mark VI, in addition to the 150 rounds each per man, had to be taken into the trenches. The old rifle was also not as easily protected

Unknown Liverpool Scottish. By kind permission of First World War Tommies Not Forgotten Post Cards from the period.

from the mud and its protruding barrel was particularly prone to filling up with dirt. It was also better suited to target shooting than the rapid fire which was necessary in close range warfare.[12]

On arrival in the trench for the first time the men were surprised to find that although the right section was reasonable and the parapet was sound, it had no traverses. The left section was not a trench at all but a series of unconnected pits that only held three or four men. These were so shallow they could not sit upright without exposing themselves to enemy fire. The men immediately set to work with their trenching tools to deepen the pits and join them up. By the end of their tour they could go from one end to the other without leaving the trench.

The distance from the enemy varied from 200 yards on the left to about thirty-five yards on the right. Here the Germans had dug out a sap so the British trench ran sharply back. This trench was manned by the Royal Fusiliers.

The first tour was quiet with only two casualties but by the third day it was raining heavily and the trench began to turn into sticky mud. The men were also thirsty as they only had one water bottle per man plus their nightly cup of tea and had run out of water by the end of the second day.

Kemmel village itself had so far suffered little damage with many inhabitants carrying on as usual. Away from the front line the houses provided excellent billets and the men were able to vary the monotony of army food by eating at numerous places where they had excellent omelettes. The men had little difficulty buying omelettes, but the officers could not buy any eggs. Eventually the president of one of the company officers' messes sent out two batmen with the express orders they were not to return without eggs. They returned late at night with ninety-one eggs, but as the Battalion was moving the next day most were given to the men instead.

The church at Kemmel was intact and one of the men from the Honourable Artillery Company played the organ regularly. However it was noticed that although the clock did not work the hands regularly changed position. A watch was kept on it until a man was caught red handed. He was subsequently arrested for signalling to the enemy.

On 8 December a Company of Lincolns who had already spent two days in the front line, were ordered to attack an enemy trench and the Battalion were detailed to find supports and reserves in case of a counter-attack. The trenches the Lincolns had been in were among the worst on the line. After forty-eight hours in waist high mud and water many were incapable of dragging themselves out when the signal was given. Those who succeeded managed to reach the German trench despite heavy rifle and machine-gun fire, but were too few to hold what they had

---

12. These were replaced in early 1915 although some of the men who returned from the hospitals still had the Lee Enfield as did new drafts of replacements. It was not until immediately before the Battle of the Somme in 1916 that the Battalion was completely armed with the SMLE.

Pte Michael John O'Connor. By kind permission of Joe Dwyer.

Unknown Liverpool Scottish. By kind permission of First World War Tommies Not Forgotten Post Cards from the period.

won. Eventually they were forced to return back to their trench after taking heavy casualties.

Seeing the dreadful condition of the survivors, Captain D. McLeod, OC of Y Company, suggested his company take over the trench for the remaining twenty-four hours of the tour and Lieutenant Colonel Smith gladly accepted. On their way back the following night they were met on the Kemmel road by the company of Lincolnshires they had relieved and given tots of rum, hot tea, a change of socks and a chance to warm themselves at a brazier. From that day on the Lincolnshires always called the Liverpool Scottish the 'Lincolnshire Scottish'.

Christmas day dawned after a hard frost and the ground was dry for once. The Battalion were out of the line so at 12.30 pm they paraded in the field close to their billets. Here they received their presents from the officers' wives and their relations and then they were addressed by Lieutenant Colonel Davidson. This was followed by the Pipe Band and Christmas hymns by the Battalion. The Quartermaster made a dramatic entrance at full gallop on a GS Wagon with Princess Mary's gifts of a pipe and tobacco in a gilt box for every man followed by plum pudding for the men, a cigar for the NCOs and a full Christmas dinner for the officers provided by Lord Derby. In addition there were nearly 250 sacks of Christmas mail, most of which contained food.

The weather in January was atrocious but in an effort to ameliorate this the men were given braziers in the trenches to make tea and goatskin coats were issued. When they were out of the line boxing matches and concerts were held in the school in Locre and football matches took place against other battalions in the brigade.

The Battalion was considerably under strength so when they went into the line it was necessary to send the whole battalion. Inter-company reliefs were carried out regularly to prevent too much strain on the men, but they were very relieved when 4 officers and 302 other ranks arrived at the end of the month. These were distributed amongst the companies.

On 15 February the 9th Brigade was ordered up to Ypres to take the place of the 85th Brigade in 28th Division. Although the battalion was initially ordered to follow the Brigade these orders were subsequently cancelled and instead they remained in the Kemmel sector and were attached to 85th Division when it arrived back from Ypres. The Battalion did one more tour in the trenches before being relieved by the 1/4th South Lancashires, another Lancashire territorial battalion.

On 28 February they were reunited with 9th Brigade in Ypres and they moved north to Ouderdom. 9th Brigade was now part of 28th Division so no longer part of 3rd Division and when the Battalion re-joined 9th Brigade it too ceased to be with them.

The Battalion was billeted in farms in the Busseboom area until 10 March, their time spent training and route marching. When they weren't training they could enjoy the entertainments. These included a prize for the best mouth organ band which was won by twelve performers from No 10 Platoon. HQ officers and Company Commanders went off to see the trenches on the 9th and on the 10th the Battalion headed to Ypres and their first experience of the salient.

At this time the damage in Ypres was largely confined to the Grande Place and the houses near the two easterly exits from the town, the Menin and Lille Gates. Several shops were still open carrying a good trade of tobacco, picture postcards, lace and other knick-knacks and there was even a photographer.

The Liverpool Scottish marched through on their way to the trenches at Hill 60, east of Zillebeke. As X and Y Companies went into the front line and supports V and Z Companies remained in reserve in the Infantry Barracks in Ypres. HQ was in a cellar just behind Zillebeke.

These trenches were a complete contrast to those at Kemmel, dry and deep. They even had a shelter where men could sleep when off duty and a communication trench where supports could reinforce the firing-line. However, although the trenches were better, the disadvantage was that this part of the line was considerably more active. Although no heavy shelling took place the Battalion suffered many casualties from the numerous 'whiz bangs'. Even worse, the enemy were digging tunnels.

On 12 March the ground shook violently as a giant explosion erupted immediately to the left of their position. The ruins of a house were immediately

Pte Brisco Francis MacSwiney. By kind permission of Old Birkonians (Memorials)

Unknown Liverpool Scottish. By kind permission of First World War Tommies Not Forgotten Post Cards from the period.

over the mine and a vast quantity of bricks, earth and debris were flung high in the air burying the platoon of Royal Scots Fusiliers to their left under the rubble. No 9 Platoon took thirteen casualties, some of which were serious.

The destruction of the Scots Fusiliers' position left a dangerous gap in the line. Captain B. McKinnell, the machine gun officer, immediately posted a machine gun to cover the gap and under heavy fire he and the remaining Scots Fusiliers managed to dig out some survivors from the mine explosion.

The Battalion remained in the Hill 60 sector for twelve days during which time fourteen men were killed and forty-two wounded. They were relieved on 21 March by the Liverpool Rifles.

The next sector to be occupied by the 9th Brigade was the Bluff which lay south of Hill 60 between it and the Ypres-Comines Canal. On the eastern end of the ridge formed by the spoil bank of the Canal was Slaughter Hill.

'International trench' was occupied by both the British and the Germans. Each held one end with about twenty yards of no man's land in the middle protected at either end by a strong sandbag barricade. This sector was better suited to a four battalion brigade so the Liverpool Scottish were split up and attached by companies to the other Battalions; V Company to the Northumberland Fusiliers, X Company to the Lincolns, Z Company and half of Y to the Royal Scots Fusiliers and the remainder of Y into reserve dugouts on the Canal bank.

On 1 April Slaughter Hill was heavily shelled and X Company and a team from the machine gun section suffered heavy casualties. Whilst being relieved that night they were again shelled and suffered eight more deaths and several wounded.

The 9th Brigade was relieved on the night of 3/4 April by 85th Brigade and the Liverpool Scottish were delighted to hear that they were to rejoin 3rd Division which was occupying the St Eloi sector. This proved to be a relatively quiet sector, the main enemy activities were night sniping and shelling.

On 14 April they were again involved in an enemy mine explosion. The left end of Q2 trench was masked by a small advanced trench, Q1, which lay about eighty yards in front. It was manned by the Northumberland Fusiliers and under the left portion the enemy had dug a mine. At 11.00 pm the Germans opened up with rapid fire and then the mine exploded. The left end of Q1 was destroyed burying thirty-five men under it. Many were dug out and the men set to repairing the trench. By the morning it was repaired and fit for defence.

Pte John Godwin Raschen. By kind permission of Old Birkonians (Memorials).

Unknown Liverpool Scottish. By kind permission of First World War Tommies Not Forgotten Post Cards from the period.

Pte Wilfred Coop. By kind permission of Old Birkonians (Memorials).

The 10th Battalion were in Ypres from 24 March to 8 April. At night men in kilts could be seen lying in the square in front of the famous Cloth Hall drinking hot tea from the field cookers round the light of a candle. During the day the weather was fine and sunny and Captain Bryden McKinnon even found time to climb the tower of what remained of the Cloth Hall. Once above the clock he squeezed into one of the small turrets and disturbed some nesting jackdaws. The turret afforded him a magnificent view of the surrounding countryside and he also found time to explore the cathedral.

When they were off duty the men could buy drinks at a place they named 'Marie's' after the barmaid. Lunch and dinner were often bought at 'Julia's'. Tea was held at the 'Patisserie' which the men were told meant 'among the ruins'!

Their Headquarters was billeted in 64 Rue de Chien, a rather comfortable private house which belonged to a local brewer. The brewery itself had been destroyed by a shell and only the house remained. Inside there was a piano, a gramophone and even some crockery.

Three weeks later Captain Bryden McKinnon found himself in the trenches near St Eloi where the Liverpool Scottish were holding the line. On the left the battle raged. The noise of the fighting was deafening. But the roaring of the 17-inch guns, hurtling past from thirteen thousand yards away towards their target over three miles away, shook their dugouts so much that it appeared the shell was whistling past the front of their trench. Clouds of red brick dust and flames lit the sky in the distance as Ypres was pounded into a ruin before their eyes.

On 26 May the Battalion was relieved by the Queen Victoria's Rifles from 13th Brigade and they moved back to the huts at Dickebusch. Although 9th Brigade again took over the trenches two days later the Liverpool Scottish remained in reserve in a camp near Vlamertinghe and supplied working parties at night to dig support trenches and strong points behind the line. To do this they had to pass through Ypres which was now almost unrecognizable. The 17-inch guns had caused considerable damage and the shelling continued with smaller guns. Everywhere they looked buildings were burning out of control and the streets were filled with rubble and masonry, making it difficult to pass through. Ypres had almost become a deserted ruin.

In the evening of 1 June 1915 officers from each battalion of 9th Brigade inspected the trenches north of Zillebeke and on 2 June, 9th Brigade moved up to the trenches to relieve the 83rd Brigade.

The King's (Liverpool) Regiment left E Camp on the Vlamertinghe-Ouderdom Road at 6pm that night. They halted at Kruisstraat to have tea before continuing on to the trenches on the east edge of Armagh wood. They finally reached the trenches at around midnight and took over from the East Yorks. To their relief these trenches were well dug, being very deep and dry. They had 470 rifles and 48 machine guns in the fire trench and 38 rifles in a small support trench on the right. There was also a small garrison of one NCO and nineteen men in a redoubt in Sanctuary Wood. A small company of Royal Scots Fusiliers, who also came under the command of the King's (Liverpool) Regiment's CO, were in reserve. HQ was established about thirty yards behind the firing line and the men settled down to wait.

The next couple of days were reasonably quiet and the men in the support trench took the opportunity to snipe at any enemy targets that unwisely presented themselves. Unfortunately, because the trench was open to enfilade fire from German machine gun fire, there were several casualties until the traverses could be improved.

Unknown Liverpool Scottish. By kind permission of First World War Tommies Not Forgotten Post Cards from the period.

Unknown Liverpool Scottish. By kind permission of First World War Tommies Not Forgotten Post Cards from the period.

On 5 June the Royal Engineer in charge of mining operations blew up a small charge to prevent the enemy making similar repairs to their trench, but it had little effect. With little else to do the men continued making various other repairs and improvements including making loop holes. The Brigade was relieved on 6 June by 150th Brigade and the 5th Durham Light Infantry took over the section from the King's (Liverpool) Regiment. The battalion found itself marching back to Vlamertinghe arriving at about 4.00 am on the morning of 7 June. Billeted in A Camp were A and C Companies with B and D Companies in B Camp and HQ in a house near to the station.

On 9 June orders were received that 3rd Division were to go back for ten days' rest and that some men would be granted leave. The Battalion packed up and marched cheerfully back to a point near Busseboom. Here they camped in the same field where their transport had been billeted for some time and waited for their much deserved time off. But within hours their orders had been rescinded.

The next five days were spent training for an operation planned for 16 June. The training concentrated on advancing wave by wave in open order and attacking imaginary trenches which were marked by sticks in the ground. Consolidation would follow while the next wave passed through and continued attacking the enemy with bombs and bayonets. Particular attention was paid to bombing. It was hard work and very tiring but the weather was good and it made a change from the monotony of life in the trenches. Captain McKinnon even found time to ride at the end of the day and the QM, CQMS, R.A.S. McFie, invariably made sure tea was ready when they arrived back ravenous and tired from their training. This would tide them over until they had their evening stew. He had also arranged for tents and blanket bivouacs which was fortuitous as it rained all night on 12 June.

Whilst they were training a ceremonial parade took place that same day. A composite Company under Captain R. F. B. Dickinson attended and GOC 3rd Division, General Haldane presented DCMs to NCOs and men of the Brigade. One of these was Private Howarth of B Company.

The next morning they were told their leave was indefinitely postponed and in the evening the Colonel called the Officers together for a conference.

Chapter 7

1st Battalion
Lincolnshire Regiment

There were five Battalions in the Lincolnshire Regiment at the start of the war: the 1st and 2nd Regular, 3rd Special Reserve (formerly Militia) and the 4th and 5th Territorials. The 1st Battalion was commanded by Lieutenant Colonel W. E. B. Smith and based in Portsmouth. They were part of the 9th Infantry Brigade, 3rd Division and brigaded with the 1st Northumberland Fusiliers, 4th Royal Fusiliers and 1st Scots Fusiliers.

On 4 August at 6.00 pm the 1st Battalion received their mobilization orders. Out of the 673 other ranks most were young soldiers whose service ranged from a few weeks to two years. There were twenty-four officers and very few old soldiers. They were joined by 543 mobilized reservists from the depot in Lincoln on 8 August. They had already been kitted out with their clothing and equipment and the next few days were spent in strenuous training in preparation for going overseas. Mobilization was finally complete by 12 August and all those who were considered to be insufficiently trained were despatched to the 3rd Reserve Battalion together with those earmarked as reinforcements or cadres for new Battalions. One officer and 100 men were designated to be the first reinforcements, ready to leave at a moment's notice. They remained in Portsmouth.

Lt Allan Dixon-Walker. The Stone Frigate, 1914.

At 6.15 am on 13 August the right half of the Battalion marched out of Victoria Barracks to the train station and entrained to Southampton. The left half followed an hour later. Once in Southampton the men boarded the *SS Norman* while their transport was loaded onto the *SS Italian Prince*. By the time the ships put to sea it was dark and as they watched the lights of Southampton fade into the distance men and officers wondered where they were going.

They landed in Le Havre in France at about 2.30 am on 14 August and began disembarking immediately. They formed up in companies in a large shed at one end of which there was a French civilian serving hot coffee from a large, steaming portable boiler. The men settled down to wait, the lucky ones able to snatch a few hours' sleep, while others thought of loved ones or wondered what lay in front of them.

At 10.00 am the mist cleared and the sun began to beat down. For the men laden with packs and equipment it was just the beginning of a gruelling six-mile march on rough roads through the town and up the hill past Harfleur[13] with its historic connotations. Finally they reached the designated concentration area on the plateau where, to their relief, there was an orchard to shelter them from the heat of the afternoon sun. Fortunately the tents arrived later that evening as a violent thunderstorm struck the area that night. The following day it rained incessantly as the men marched to Havre station and entrained to Landrecies where the BEF were concentrating before moving to their allotted position on the left flank of the French Fifth Army. The 3rd Division was concentrated between Le Cateau and Maubeuge, east of Foret de Mormal.

By 10.00 am 22 August the 1st Battalion had arrived in Frameries. They were greeted by streets decorated with assorted flags of the allied nations, shouts of welcome from the local population and numerous gifts of food, fruit, cigarettes, matches, handkerchiefs and towels. Although they were originally planning to halt in the town orders had now changed and they carried on through until they were in position to take up the line along the Mons-Conde Canal from Nimy to Mariette.

However, before they could do so they were relieved by the 4th Royal Fusiliers, 1st Scots Fusiliers and 1st Northumberland Fusiliers. 9th Brigade HQ and two Companies of Northumberland Fusiliers, the 1st Lincolnshire, Transport B, 23rd Brigade RFA and the ammunition column retired to Cuesmes to wait in reserve. As they waited in the village Captain Ellison fired the Lincolnshire's first shot of the war at a German aeroplane that flew over them.

The following morning, as the German infantry advanced towards them, they marched rapidly along the cobbled streets to Mons. Here they began building barricades along the straight avenue that ran northwards to the centre of town. With the aid of civilians, including a young girl, they built four barricades using paving stones, sawn down trees, piles of logs and iron piping. The barricades were held by D Company and the machine gunners while C Company on their right formed an enclosed area and held the side roads. On the open ground to the left A Company began digging trenches. This only provided a field of fire of about 200 yards though as a row of houses to the north of their position obscured any further view.

By 2.00 pm the Royal Fusiliers at Nimy had withdrawn, passing through the Battalion on their way to Ciply. The Lincolnshires braced themselves, ready to meet the enemy. They did not have long to wait as soon the streets were swarming

---

13. The siege of Harfleur, Normandy began on 18 August 1415 and ended on 22 September when Harfleur surrendered to Henry V and the English. It was part of the 100 Years' War and just before he won the Battle of Agincourt which took place on 25 October 1415.

with German infantry. They opened fire immediately causing the Germans to fall back into the surrounding houses where they returned fire. After a brief fire fight the Germans turned westwards leaving the Battalion to tend to their first casualties. Within hours the Battle of Mons was over and the Retreat had begun. In two days the Lincolnshires had lost 4 officers and 130 other ranks, but worse was to come. The Retreat from Mons would claim more lives than the Battle itself and by 5 September they had marched 237 miles and fought two big battles.

The Germans were now within thirty miles of Paris and the French prepared for a siege. Both the French 5th and 6th Armies and the BEF were exhausted following the retreat. The German 1st Army under Alexander von Kluck was ordered to encircle Paris and the French Government left for Bordeaux. In response Joseph Joffre decided to launch a counter offensive. On 6 September, 150,000 men of the 6th Army under General Maunoury attacked the German 1st Army. As they turned to meet the attack a thirty-mile gap opened up in the German lines between the 1st and 2nd Armies. As the right wing of the French 5th Army attacked the German 2nd Army under Karl von Bulow, the BEF joined the rest of the French 5th Army in pouring through the gap.

Despite this the Germans almost succeeded in breaking through and were only defeated on 7 September by the arrival of 6,000 French reserve infantry troops ferried in by 600 taxis.

The following night the 5th Army led by General Franchet d'Esperey launched a surprise attack on the German 2nd Army and widened the gap even more. It was enough. On 9 September the Germans began to retreat pursued by the BEF and the French. But the advance was too slow and after forty miles the Germans stopped north of the River Aisne and began digging the trenches that would remain for several years. Casualties were heavy with an estimated 250,000 French losses and 12,733 from the BEF.

The 1st Battalion began their advance on 6 September at 6am. The men fell in and marched down long dusty roads in the hot sunshine, finally arriving at Chateau de Lumigny in the late afternoon. The next day the advance continued in a north easterly direction to Chauffry where they were joined by a second draft of reinforcements and billeted in La Bretonniere. Although the 9th Brigade was to remain in reserve on the following day the Lincolnshires left La Bretonniere at 6.00 am arriving five hours later at a small village north of Rebais called Gibraltar. Here they took up positions overlooking the valley of the Petit Moran. They waited while the 7th and 8th Brigades cleared the woods and hills and then crossed the Petit Moran at Orly. They were now designated as the advance guard for 9th Brigade and the 1st Battalion were detailed to form outposts west of Villare.

The 3rd Division crossed the Marne at Nanteuil and by 10.30 am Brigadier General Shaw had established 9th Brigade HQ at Bezu. The 1st Lincolnshires were halted in a field nearby when Lieutenant Colonel Smith and two companies, C and D, were sent to capture a German battery that was inflicting high casualties on the Brigade. They succeeded in shooting down the German gunners, but on the way back were fired on by the 65th (howitzer) Battery who mistakenly thought they were Germans. Thirty-four officers and men were either killed or wounded.

As the BEF continued its slow, steady advance the 9th Brigade spent more time as the advanced guard. On 12 September the 1st Battalion marched to a plateau overlooking the valley of the Vesle. At 10.00 am Brigade HQ received a message from General Allenby stating his Cavalry Brigade had captured the bridge at Braisne and that it was intact. However the outskirts of the town were still in enemy hands.

While the Northumberland Fusiliers crossed the bridge and moved to the west of the town, the Lincolnshires were ordered to move to the right of the town and take the railway bridge half a mile to the east, then sweep north. They took the chateau with little difficulty and then began searching the town. Here they found a few wounded Germans, a machine gun and ammunition limber with a horse. They moved out towards a large wood south west of the town and took some more prisoners before retiring to their billets in Brenelle. But there was little rest. It was raining hard and the men were wet through, supplies had not reached them so they had to eat their iron rations instead and still not one bridge over the River Aisne was in British hands.

The next couple of days saw the 1st Battalion in the thick of the fighting, the heaviest of which was on 14 September, a day on which they lost 8 officers and 180 other ranks either killed or wounded.

For the next few weeks the Battalion continued to fight on the front line, through the Battles of La Basse, Armientieres and Messines. By 1 November the Battalion had taken very heavy losses – eight Officers and 293 other ranks either killed or wounded. Despite their exhausted and depleted state the 1st Battalion continued to be in the front line between 8 November and 11 November, suffering incessant attacks between the Lys and Menin Road. This continued until they were relieved by French troops on 20 November. Having spent two weeks in the flooded trenches their feet were in a dreadful state but they still marched twelve miles through snow and a heavy frost that made it almost impassable for the horse drawn transport, only to arrive at Westoutre to find no billets had been provided.

The rest period was short lived and they were soon back on the front line in sodden trenches, up to their knees in thick glutinous mud, before attacking the German trenches on 8 December. They reached the first trench, but although it was full of water it was empty of men. Then they came under heavy machine gun and rifle fire forcing them to withdraw back to their own trenches.

At this time the elements of the 3rd Division spent three days in the frontline trenches, three days in immediate reserve trenches and three days back in Westoutre. The 560 yards of frontline trench would be manned by 395 men, the 130-yard support trench by 50 men and the reserve dugouts occupied by 1,980 men. This changed later in the war with the front trenches only lightly manned and the bulk of the Garrison much further back. But at this time the wire entanglements only presented a slight obstacle and machine guns were few and far between. The two main forces' infantry were face to face in assault positions and any attack could be halted by intense rifle fire, thus they needed a strong presence on the front line. They were also too close to the enemy to bring artillery fire on the opposing trenches and they didn't have enough accurate short range high angle mortars until later in the war. It was the increase in trench mortars that led to the thinning of frontline trenches.

Christmas was spent in Locre and New Year back in the trenches. By the end of 1914 most of the Battalions of the BEF had lost virtually all their original men. Survival rate, on average, was around one officer and thirty other ranks.

During January, and until 17 February, they were in a reasonably quiet part of the line, east of Kemmel. Then they were ordered to Ypres to relieve the troops in that area. They moved into their new trenches on 2 February and found they were only fifteen yards from the Germans who were actually in the same muddy, water-logged ditch as they were, with traverses in between. In other places the Germans were also behind them meaning sentries had to be posted to the rear as well as the front.

On 22 April they relieved the 1st Duke of Cornwall's Light Infantry (5th Division) in the frontline trenches on the Comines-Ypres Canal and were there for five weeks. As the Battle of Ypres continued into May they watched the damage inflicted on Ypres and by 26 May, despite the relative inactivity in their area, had suffered more casualties – 8 officers and 125 other ranks.

Between 1 June and 5 June they spent more time in the trenches in the neighbourhood of Hooge and Zouave Wood taking more casualties – two officers and 101 other ranks killed or wounded. On 5 June they were moved to Brandhoek, four miles west of Ypres. Here they stayed until being bought up for the attack on Bellewaarde.

Chapter 8

1st Battalion West Yorkshire Regiment

At the outbreak of war the 1st Battalion West Yorkshire Regiment, part of 18th Infantry Brigade, 6th Division, was based in Lichfield. By the time they left Lichfield for Dunfurmaline on 7 August mobilization was almost complete. On 13 August the whole of the 18th Infantry Brigade left for Cambridge where 6th Division were ordered to concentrate. This was soon complete and on 7 September they marched to Newmarket and boarded a train for Southampton. Here the West Yorks embarked on the *Cawdor Castle* and sailed at 6.15 pm for France. The total strength of the battalion was 27 officers, 959 other ranks, 57 horses, 17 vehicles and 19 bicycles.

They reached St Nazaire on 9 September and three days later were billeted in the Coulommierrs–Montcerf–Marles–Chaume area. In command of 6th Division was Major General T. L. Kier and 18th Infantry Brigade was commanded by Brigadier-General W. M. Congreve VC. The West Yorks, under the command of Lieutenant Colonel F. W. Towsey, were billeted in Croupet.

1st Battalion The Prince of Wales Own (West Yorkshire Regiment) Cambridge 1914 kind permission of The Prince of Wales Own Regiment of Yorkshire Museum http://www.pwoyorkshire.co.uk/

At this time the BEF, consisting of five infantry divisions and one infantry brigade (1st, 2nd, 3rd, 4th, 5th Divisions and 19th Infantry Brigade), one Cavalry Division and one Cavalry Brigade, were positioned south of the River Aisne. Meanwhile, I Corps (1st and 2nd Divisions) were in Beugneux, three miles southwest of Arcy and Bruyeres, southwest of Rocourt, Oulchy le Chateau, II Corps (3rd and 5th Divisions) were at Hartennes, west of Beugneux and III Corps (4th Division and 19th Infantry Brigade) were at La Loge Farm to Chuoy. The Cavalry Division at Loupeigne and the 3rd and 5th Cavalry Brigades were at Parcy Tigny, six and half miles west of Arcy, and British HQ was at Coulommiers.

The French 5th Army was on their right and on their left was the French 6th Army. While the battles raged on the River Aisne the 6th Division gradually moved forward arriving at Villemontoire on 16 September.

At 4.00 am on the morning of 19 September and in heavy rain, 18th Infantry Brigade set out for Bourg. Here they took over the positions held by the 2nd Infantry Brigade (1st Division) and the 1st Infantry Brigade. The 1st West Yorks now held the extreme right of the British Line linking with the left flank of the French 5th Army, a regiment of Tireulleurs d'Afrique. Both A and B Companies, under Major A. W. Ingles, were in the line of fire just south of Chemin des Dames while C and D Companies were in the support trenches in the rear and to the right of the two forward companies.

Although the enemy began sniping at them before they were properly settled in the trenches, there was no infantry attack. The trenches here were totally inadequate. They were little more than a series of excavations in the ground, there was no communications trench and the only connection to the support trenches was by field telephone. The men had little option but to spend the night trying to improve the trench and constructing overhead cover.

Heavy shelling began on the French troops on the right flank just after 3.00 am followed by an infantry assault on the Tireulleurs d'Afrique who, having suffered heavy casualties and having lost all their officers, withdrew. This left the right flank of the West Yorks open. Twice the West Yorks tried to rectify this but each time they sent out a forward patrol they were fired on. They eventually decided that the French must have re-occupied the trench and were firing at the British, mistaking them for the enemy. The Battalion took several casualties; one killed and twenty-seven wounded.

At 8.00 am they came under heavy rifle fire again. The heavy firing continued all morning and again the French on their right left the trenches. At the same time A Company of the Royal Sussex and a Squadron from the 18th Hussars were bought up to strengthen the right flank but telephone communications with the support troops had now broken down, meaning the only communication was by runner.

At 1.30 pm they received a report that the Germans were advancing on the right flank which the French had left. They immediately began enfilading the West Yorks with rifle and machine gun fire. Within a short while the front trenches had been overrun and the frontline companies captured. Information received

Cpt Barber & Lt Hutchison. Kind permission of Nick Balmer.

afterwards suggested that the Germans had advanced under a white flag on the right flank and when the West Yorks went out to meet them they were surrounded and the Germans opened fire. Many were killed and 8 officers and 436 other ranks captured.

The CO, Lieutenant Colonel Towsey was wounded so at 3.00 pm Major Lang signalled the advance and Battalion HQ with C Company went forward to occupy the trenches previously held by A and B Companies. They were relieved at 8pm by the Sherwood Foresters.

The official casualty list for 20 September was 7 officers killed, two officers wounded, 8 officers missing, 21 other ranks killed, 110 wounded and 436 missing. The Durham Light Infantry and the East Yorks also took heavy casualties, but the line held.

On 21 September Major Lang assumed command of the Battalion which was reformed into HQ, C Company and one platoon. They returned to the line on 24 September suffering more casualties with nine killed and two wounded. The next day the first reinforcements of one officer and ninety-six men arrived and the battalion marched back to Pargnan and into Divisional Reserve. Further reinforcements of one officer and ninety-two other ranks arrived on 2 October followed by a further two officers and 326 other ranks three days later. This enabled them to reform B Company. A few days later four more officers arrived increasing the strength of the Battalion to 13 officers and 848 other ranks, but they were still short of 13 officers and 130 other ranks. Despite this they set out with 6th Division to St Omer.

After reaching St Omer on 11 October, III Corps (4th and 6th Divisions) headed east towards Hazebrouck. On 13 October they advanced against the Armentieres – Wytschaete line. The first objective of the 6th Division was the Vieux – Berquin – Merris line and they moved forward in two columns. The right column under Brigadier-General Congreve VC, which consisted of the 18th Infantry Brigade, 38th Brigade Royal Field Artillery, 18th Field Ambulance, Cyclists and Engineers, started at 7.30am and reached Vieux Berquin about midday. They relieved the 2nd Dragoon Guards and prepared to attack the enemy in Bleu.

The assault began at 1.30 pm with the East Yorks on the right, the West Yorks in the centre and the Durham Light Infantry on the left. The village was captured at 4.30pm with the West Yorks suffering more casualties. One officer was killed, two were wounded, nine other ranks killed and thirty-two wounded. The Battalions dug in for the night.

The line now held by the 18th Infantry Brigade extended from Bleu-Haute Maison to the railway south of Merris.

On 14 October they carried on eastwards with the 6th Division marching in three columns. Their destination was La Verrier, but the German rear guard, which consisted of cavalry with machine guns, prevented them from progressing any further than a line a third of a mile north of La Verrier. Here they set up an outpost.

Lieut Donald H Hutchison. Kind permission of Nick Blair of Merchiston College.

Over the next few days the Germans began concentrating fresh forces along the line from the Belgian coast to right of II Corps and on 20 October they attacked. The 6th Division's part of the line was five miles long and thinly held. Despite orders to hold the line at any costs they found it impossible to do so against the ferocity of the enemy assault. At 8.40 am the enemy began massing south and west of Escobecues. With Radinghem having fallen, the brunt of the attack fell on the 18th Infantry Brigade at Ennetiers.

The West Yorks, whose line was 700 yards long, were attacked in force at 11.30 am. As the regiments around them retired, the enemy was able to attack on several flanks leaving the West Yorks in a precarious position. But somehow they managed to hold on despite losing four officers and thirty-four other ranks, either killed or wounded.

November was a quiet month and the 1st Battalion spent much of their time wallowing in the mud of the trenches. A further 101 reinforcements arrived;

two officers and ninety-nine other ranks, but the Battalion suffered eighty one casualties of all ranks in November and December mainly from sniper fire and shell fire.

By the middle of March the weather had improved. Work on the trenches continued day and night and more reinforcements arrived having been despatched from the Reserve Battalions (3rd and 4th West Yorkshires) in England.

By the end of April the Battalion had been in every trench from Neuve Chapelle to Le Touquet and although there had been little fighting they had still suffered numerous casualties from sniping and sickness.

On the 30/31 May they marched north to Ypres and were billeted northwest of the town. Although they were pleased to have left Le Touquet their first sight of Ypres was not very reassuring as the town was in flames. Although they were not involved in any fighting the guns were never silent and the constant heavy shelling was responsible for all the casualties at this time. They soon found life in the trenches here was no better than anywhere else. Rain had fallen heavily in the middle of the month causing the communication trench to fill with water and the parapets and frontline trenches to collapse.

Chapter 9

1st Battalion Royal Scots Fusiliers

The 1st Battalion Royal Scots Fusiliers returned home from South Africa in March 1913 and were based at Gosport. On 13 August 1914 they left for France via Southampton under the command of Lieutenant Colonel Douglas Smith. Over half their number were Reservists and the men were in good spirits. From Havre they moved swiftly to Landrecies and on 22 August to Ghlin, some two miles north of Jemappes. Here they withdrew south of the Conde Canal which was held by II Corps. The 9th Brigade held the six miles of the canal bank from Nimy Bridge to Mariette Bridge. The 4th Royal Fusiliers were on the right, the 1st Battalion were in the centre, holding the Jemappes section and the 1st Northumberland Fusiliers were on the left. They had no idea that eight German Divisions were marching against the two British Divisions who were stretched out thinly in a chain of groups over a thirteen-mile front.

Sgt William Nash.

At 2.30 pm the following day they were ordered to withdraw back three miles to Frameries and most of the bridges behind them were blown up by the Royal Engineers. A vigorous rearguard action in numerous houses with rifles and machine guns managed to delay the German advance and most of the Battalion escaped with few casualties, except on the right where the Jemappes bridge was not destroyed in time. As the men retreated among the slag heaps and cottages there was fierce hand to hand fighting. The ground was difficult and the German machine guns wreaked havoc on the retreating men. They were heavily outnumbered and B Company was in serious danger until the arrival of the Northumberland Fusiliers who provided cover for them to withdraw. Two officers were killed and 100 other ranks were also killed or wounded.

By 13 September the open warfare of the first few weeks had ended, the line had stabilized and the Germans were heavily entrenched on the north bank of the Aisne. The BEF had regrouped and it was time to attack.

As II Corps attempted to cross the River Aisne in the section between Vailly and Missy 3rd Division used the Vailly Bridge. It was late in the afternoon by the time

8th Brigade had crossed and set up outposts up to Vauxelles. 9th Brigade crossed in darkness, but by the morning of 14 September 7th Brigade was still on the south bank and the only communication between them was a single plank footway.

The general advance began on 14 September when 9th Brigade moved out of Vailly to the spurs north east of the village which were secured by the 1st Battalion Lincolnshire Regiment and 4th Battalion Royal Fusiliers. At 7.30 am the Germans, whose trenches were only 600 yards away, began firing, the attack backed up by machine guns and artillery. The Northumberland Fusiliers were sent up on the left of the Royal Fusiliers and the three battalions continued to advance. It was crucial for them to take the high ground on the spurs otherwise the Germans could accurately shell the pontoon bridge. At 9.00 am the Germans counter attacked against the 8th Brigade at Jouy and managed to drive them back.

Meanwhile 9th Brigade had fought its way out of the wet trees in thick fog and found themselves in open beet fields. Here they immediately came under devastating machine gun and artillery fire. They tried to dig in, but the Lincolns on their right had to fall back and this led the whole Brigade to withdraw. The situation was becoming desperate so the 1st Battalion, which was in reserve, were ordered up in support and A and D Companies came up to support the Lincolns. They too came under the same withering machine-gun fire and after struggling knee deep in muddy roots were forced back after taking heavy losses.

The situation was now critical as 9th Brigade was on the extreme right of II Corps with a gap of nearly two miles to I Corps. If the enemy advanced the BEF was in danger of being cut in two. However reinforcements in the form of 1st Wiltshire and Irish Rifles from 7th Brigade were on their way and this enabled the Brigade to secure the spur. The Battalion took heavy casualties during this action with eight killed, sixty-seven wounded and a further ninety missing.

Up until 18 October II Corps had been mainly opposed by German Cavalry and this had allowed them to make progress. Now they found themselves facing the centre of the German VI Army. The German VI Army was under the command of Crown Prince Rupprect and consisted of, amongst others, the 16th Bavarian Reserve Infantry Regiment, known unofficially as the 'List' Regiment after its original Commander Colonel von List. The List Regiment had entrained for France on 21 October 1914 and was immediately attached to the 6th Bavarian Division in the VI Army which was embroiled in the First Battle of Ypres. In the 1st Company of this Regiment was a young man called Adolph Hitler and also in the List Regiment was another volunteer, Rudolph Hess.

The 9th Brigade was detailed to take Herlies and the objective of the Scots Fusiliers was the chateau in the wood south of Herlies. The terrain they had to cover was in a dip and was a maze of ditches. North of the wood the land sloped up to La Basse road and the Germans were entrenched with machine guns to the south, east and west of the wood. The Scots Fusiliers advanced towards the centre, the 7th Brigade on their left, the Northumberland Fusiliers on the right. They immediately came under heavy artillery and rifle fire. When they were within 500 yards of the wood they realized that their left flank was exposed. They had no option but to halt and so remained there all day under intense artillery bombardment. They continued the advance at 5.30 pm after C Company, Honourable Artillery Company (HAC) came up to support them. But although they were only sixty yards from the wood the advance stalled and eventually they were withdrawn. Again casualties were heavy with 127 all ranks killed or wounded.

From 19 October onwards, the battalion, along with the rest of 3rd Division, were on the back foot, struggling to hold the defensive line which ran from Givenchy east in a salient north of the La Basse-Lille Road and westwards towards Aubers. Between 2 and 7 November the weary, depleted Battalion fought to hold their trenches under pressure from an enemy with superior numbers and more guns. The line had been forced back to Givenchy, Festubert and Estaires.

On 7 November they moved to the Ypres Salient and became part of 7th Division Reserve. At just after 8.00 am on 11 November the 1st and 4th Brigades of the Prussian Guard attacked on both sides of the Menin Road. To the Scots' astonishment they marched forward in parade form making easy targets for the British troops facing them. But such was their discipline they managed to break through the British lines and took some woods to the west. The 1st Battalion were in reserve in Inverness Copse (named after their success) and played a large part in driving back the German attack, taking up a new position half a mile east of Herenthage Chateau. The following day A Company, which was a composite company of 4th Battalion Fusiliers and Northumberland Fusiliers, attacked a German trench, but unfortunately were too exhausted to take it. The Germans crept forward and managed to take up positions in the stables near the chateau and were only evicted after repeated bayonet charges.

Although 8th Brigade had arrived at the Ypres salient with 2,200 men it left with only 850. The 1st Battalion had 284 casualties, officers and men, dead and wounded.

By the middle of the month the fighting began to die down. French reinforcements arrived and relieved the exhausted British troops who had held the trenches for four weeks. As the weather changed for the worse the First Battle of Ypres finished in snow blizzards and gale force winds.

The next few months were spent in the trenches between Ypres and La Basse. The Battalion was now largely made up of the new drafts which still needed to be trained in between trench duty. Because digging trenches in the Ypres Salient was impossible due to the waterlogged ground, defences consisted of breast works, 7ft high in places with fire steps and the trenches were often over fifty yards apart.

William Nash as a child.

The 1st Battalion remained in 9th Brigade, 3rd Division, II Corps, but II Corps had a new Commanding Officer, Sir Charles Fergusson as did 3rd Division, Major-General Aylmer Haldane.

In the middle of February the 9th Brigade was moved to 28th Division which, together with the 27th Division made up Sir Herbert Plumer's new V Corps. They were sent to the muddy trenches south of Ypres where they took several casualties from mines and shells. Despite not being in the heaviest fighting during the Second Battle of Ypres they still suffered casualties.

On 20 April they held the front from northeast of Zonnebeke to the Polygon Wood. The Canadians were on their left and the 27th Division were on their right. That night the Germans began bombarding Ypres with heavy shells. Two days later the Germans launched the first gas attack which forced the French back behind the canal and forced a large gap in the Allied lines. The Canadians held the line despite the gas and the next three weeks saw the Second Battle of Ypres. The 1st Battalion were not involved in any of the heavy fighting but in April forty men were killed including two officers and another thirty were wounded. On 5 May they came under a gas attack and on 26 May they took over from the 85th Brigade. Their casualties in May were one officer and ten men killed and two officers and sixty-seven men wounded.

They moved up to the trenches near Bellewaarde ready for the assault on the 16 June.

Chapter 10

3rd Battalion Worcestershire Regiment

On the evening of 4 August the Battalion received the order for mobilization. They were already based at Tidworth as part of 3rd Division and during the following week hurriedly completed their preparations including making their weapons ready, receiving ammunition, equipment and other stores. Officers and men needed to have their medical inspections to be passed fit for service and additional horses had to be requisitioned and regimental property had to be stored away, especially the Regimental Colours which were taken under escort to Worcester Cathedral and handed to the Dean and Chapter for safe keeping. Like many of the other Battalions it was under strength so it needed to be made up to war strength by reservists. The depot at Norton Barracks was so crowded with reservists and volunteers they were sleeping out on the cricket ground and adjoining fields.

Colonel B. F. B. Stuart. Source unknown.

By the second week the mobilization was complete, although there was the usual general discomfort and organized chaos that preceded a move. Tense and excited the men settled down impatiently to wait for orders.

The movement of the BEF on 9 August was conducted in such secrecy that for several days the enemy were unaware they had mobilized. The 3rd Battalion finally received their orders on 12 August and at 5.00 am left for Southampton, arriving two hours later. They sailed the following day on the *SS Bosnian* and arrived before dawn on 15 August at Le Havre. Because of the tides and numerous other transports the area was overcrowded so they did not sail onto their destination at Rouen until the next day. Finally, at 1.30 am on 16 August, the *SS Bosnian* sailed up the River Seine. The banks were filled with people cheering the troops as they passed and this increased the excitement on board. They disembarked at 9pm and spent the night in a long shed next to the ship. The following day they marched through the streets to the station and caught a train to the front.

It was extremely hot, the trains moved slowly, there were few places to sleep and they spent several periods of marching and then retracing their original steps. By the end of five days the men were worn out, bad tempered and their boots were starting to show the strain.

They finally arrived at their billets in Ciply in the early hours of the morning of 23 August. The men rested while their dinners cooked, but, just when they were ready to be eaten, orders came to advance. The first shell they had seen since arriving in France burst behind them as they marched off towards Mons. Although they were rested their feet still hurt and now they were hungry as well.

The rapidly advancing Germans were moving towards the Belgium/French border. The original intention was for the British and French armies to support the Belgians but the speed of the German advance had caught them out so the BEF had taken up defensive positions along the Canal. Because they had little information about the strength of the enemy the British had organized themselves with strong supporting positions on which the front line could fall back if necessary. By the time the Worcestershire Battalion arrived there was already heavy fighting.

Pte John Henry Pitt. By kind permission of David Pitt.

While the 5th Brigade had been digging trenches near Bougnies, 7th Brigade had taken up position near Ciply, some two miles nearer Mons. This was the second line of defences held by the 3rd Division. By the afternoon the 3rd Battalion were entrenched in the rough ground south west of Ciply Station. On their right were the 2nd Royal Irish Rifles with the 2nd Lancashire on their left, holding the forward slope of the low ridge between Ciply and Frameries. The 1st Wiltshire were back in reserve.

The front line along the canal was thinly held and the men had orders to fall back on the second line if they were unable to hold it. It was nearly dusk by the time the 3rd Battalion were securely entrenched. The British artillery was behind them as well as to their left and right. In front of them a field battery was firing at them from the rearward slopes of Mount Erebus so they had dug in amid gun fire from all sides.

Although German shells had yet to reach them they could see the shell bursts over the houses and slag heaps of Cuesmes. There were fires burning in every direction and the roads and tracks were filled with terrified inhabitants fleeing the shelling. Among the civilians were wounded soldiers and soon word came that the BEF was falling back. Although they received word that German soldiers were in Mons and Hyon, Mount Erebus hid them from view and the 3rd Battalion could not find any good targets for their rifles to fire upon.

As darkness fell the British fell back and the field guns moved back to a new position in the rear of the 3rd Battalion. The 8th Brigade had withdrawn back to Nouvelles and the 9th Brigade had withdrawn back in line with the South Lancashire. By 9.00 pm there were no troops in front of the 3rd Battalion and they remained on alert, expecting an attack at any moment. They did not have long to wait. At 6.00 am German infantry swarmed over the crest of Mount Erebus and the right flank of the 3rd Battalion opened fire. They were so effective that the attack was halted about 500 yards from the British lines. Taking cover the Germans began bombarding the British with rifle and machine gun fire.

The fighting grew more intense and orders reached Colonel Stuart that 7th Brigade was to withdraw. Platoon by platoon the 3rd Battalion retired back through the reserve position held by the 1st Wiltshire, all except 'D' Company who were ordered to cover the withdrawal. The shell fire became so intense that they were eventually forced to retire in single sections to avoid the shell bursts while the South Lancashire acted as rear guard to the brigade, taking heavy casualties in the process. The whole of 3rd Battalion escaped with only fifty casualties and reassembled south of Ciply.

At Genly where 7th Brigade were reassembling new orders arrived. The 3rd Division withdrew to the new defensive line which ran east and west through Bavai and on arrival received a meal and were able to rest. But not for long. That afternoon more orders arrived with the news that the enemy were threatening to cut off the outer flank of the retreat. 3rd Division immediately set off to support the beleaguered troops from 5th Division who were engaged in fierce fighting near Elouges.

The 3rd Battalion settled down along the road from St Waast to Wargnies with some outposts further forward on the railway line. There was no sign of the enemy and the night was quiet apart from the sound of gunfire off to the west.

The next morning dawned in thick mist and the sentries strained their eyes for any sign of the enemy. Suddenly, out of the mist, the sentries spotted a patrol of Uhlans riding towards them. They immediately opened fire, killing two German Lancers before they could escape. The mist lifted and there was no further sign of the enemy so the men lit small fires, brewed some tea and settled down to wait.

As the rearguard for 3rd Division's retreat they prepared to hold their ground, but at 8.00 am they were ordered to pull back, leaving D Company to act as rear party. The Germans were now in sight, but did not attack.

Eventually, D Company too, pulled back and joined the steadily retreating BEF. The next few hours were a mixture of marching, briefly holding positions and yet more marching as they fell back even further. The skies were cloudless and the relentless sun beat down on the weary men. At 5.00 pm, they finally arrived in Solesmes. But to add to their misery the heavens then opened and a thunderstorm broke above them. The rain was now falling in torrents and the men were drenched, but they couldn't move. All around them were civilian carts and the guns and transports of retreating British and French soldiers. The narrow streets were completely blocked.

To gain time for the streets to clear the 7th Brigade was ordered to take up positions outside the town. The Battalion was sent to occupy a position on the high ground to the south and the tired, hungry, men settled down in the pouring rain to wait. To the north they could hear gunfire and as the light faded shells could be seen bursting over the town.

The traffic jams remained and in the dark many retreating troops lost their way. Eventually the Royal Irish Rifles, some of the Wiltshires and the brigade transport moved towards Le Cateau. The rest remained in position until 10.00 pm then began to withdraw. By now the 3rd Battalion were soaked through, but they too moved off towards Caudry, arriving at midnight. To their astonishment the shops were still lit up with people sitting at café tables. Outposts were established on the main road north of the town and the men rested. After barely two hours' sleep they were woken. Although defensive positions had already been prepared by the town they had not been able to inspect them in the dark. When they arrived at the trenches in the north and northwest of the town they found they were not deep enough so the weary platoons filed in and began working to improve them. As the mist cleared and the dawn broke it was the sound of shells bursting over the town which woke the exhausted dozing men.

The German Cavalry and guns were in the wooded valley north of Beauvois but before the machine guns could engage them two guns of I Section Royal Horse Artillery fired and the Germans withdrew to a safer distance.

Several small fire fights broke out and although the units were now intermingled they soon dealt with the small parties of the enemy they saw. Soon the enemy fire died down and there was a lull in the fighting.

The men breakfasted on food procured locally by the QM as the divisional train had not yet provided any supplies. But soon the bombardment opened up again, this time the shelling so severe that C Company were ordered back to positions near B Company on the edge of town.

Three batteries of British Field Artillery (XXXth Howitzer Brigade) were behind the ridge southeast of Caudry but their position was becoming increasingly precarious. A Company was selected to escort the guns back through streets that were increasingly full of terror stricken residents streaming southwards to escape the shelling. The battle raged for the next few hours until eventually they too were ordered back to a new position.

Battalion HQ had moved from the north of the town to a building near the railway embankment. The building took a direct hit from a large shell killing and wounding several men including the Second in Command Major W. R. Chichester. Between 3.00 pm and 4.00 pm 7th Brigade fell back from Caudry and marched down the road to Montigny. The Battalion had lost 100 men including three officers.

Pte John Henry Pitt. By kind permission of David Pitt.

The retreat continued until 5 September when the joyous news went round the ranks that it was over. The German army was moving in a south-easterly direction leaving their right flank open to assault by the French VI Army and the BEF. Tomorrow they would attack. The German columns were now in full retreat pursued by the BEF.

They left their outpost line at Les Chappelles Bourbon at 5.00 am on 6 September joining the 7th Infantry Brigade in their advance to the Forest of Crecy. While two battalions from 7th Brigade advanced to Hauteville to the line of Grand Morin the remainder were billeted for the night in Faremoutiers. 7th Brigade remained in reserve while the rest of 3rd Division advanced to Vailly.

Early on the morning of 20 September they came under heavy shelling followed by infantry attacks. These succeeded in penetrating the 1st Wiltshire's line on their left. Desperate fighting followed and Battalion HQ was attacked. Further to the left the Royal Irish Rifles were also in trouble and the line was broken. Two platoons were sent to reinforce the stricken left flank taking heavy casualties with both platoon leaders and a number of men killed.

On the right of the Battalion there was also heavy fighting. To stem the enemy advance a platoon from D Company was sent into the woods. The undergrowth was dense and at first they couldn't see anything. As they peered into the gloom they suddenly spotted a large bearded man wearing a spiked helmet and immediately opened fire.

Within moments the Germans began a mass assault. There was a short fierce fire fight forcing the Worcestershires back to the western edge of the wood. Here they held on for some time until they were reinforced by two more platoons from D Company. Under intense pressure they fell back across the open and took up new positions on the edge of a little hollow facing the wood, about 100 yards from the western edge. The three platoons now formed the defensive flank on the right of the battalion.

The enemy lined the edge of the woods and a fierce battle started. They held firm despite taking heavy casualties. Eventually the firing tailed off and they cautiously sent a patrol into the woods to check. The Germans had gone leaving behind more than forty dead, their bodies lying in the undergrowth; D Company had suffered over eighty casualties, killed and wounded.

On the night of the 21/22 September several changes were made to the British army on the River Aisne. On the right flank of the British line 2nd Division were relieved by 1st Division and further to the left of the 3rd Division line 7th Brigade were relieved by 16th Brigade. The 3rd Worcesters were relieved and withdrawn back across the river.

On 1 October the 3rd Worcesters began their move to Flanders. They rested by day and marched or entrained by night in an attempt to keep their movements from the enemy. On 20 October they relieved the Royal West Kents (RWK) in trenches near Le Hue. Whilst they were settling in the German guns opened up and their infantry attacked en masse. The RWK were bought back up to support the right of the line where the Lancashire's position was under threat. That night a thick fog formed and it was ominously quiet. As dawn broke, through the dense mist, they heard the enemy guns firing in the distance. This was almost immediately followed by a stampede as the line broke and the enemy swarmed through. The rapidly retreating Lancashires fled past the right flank of the Battalion as it wheeled back in the thick mist trying to form a defensive back. Mixed up with them were numerous advancing Germans.

Drawn by the sound of the fighting other Germans pushed on and found their way to the farm where Battalion HQ was sited. They only just escaped in time. Simultaneously the Germans launched an attack on the left flank of the Battalion and it too began to retire. But the mist that had allowed the Germans to get so close eventually proved to be their downfall. As it swirled around it caused them to lose direction and the British were soon able to pick them off. By the time the mist had cleared the Germans were surrounded on three sides and they called off the attack. Battalion HQ was re-established and by nightfall the trenches had been retaken. But the attack had cost them over 100 men including 7 officers.

The line had been restored at considerable cost, but it now stretched from Aubers to Givenchy and was too shallow to be sustained. Fresh enemy reinforcements were pouring in and the men were weary after ten days of continuous fighting. Reluctantly orders were given to withdraw. As they did so 5th Division, on the right of 3rd Division, began to lag behind. At dawn the enemy attacked all along where the line had been.

On the 3rd Division front they only found empty trenches, but on the 5th Division front the Cheshires were still there and took the brunt of the fighting. The line gave way and 5th Division requested urgent help. The Battalion moved forward to the crossroads at La Tourelle while 5th Division began a counter-attack against Rue du Marais. The men of Z Company went forward to assist Duke of Cornwall's Light Infantry who were fighting in the ditches and hedgerows north of the village, but the Manchesters could not get forward.

There was no communication with Brigade or Division so it was impossible to summon artillery support. Although 3rd Battalion held on to the northern edge of Rue du Marais it was soon apparent the counter-attack would have to be abandoned. The troops fell back to the new line which had been adjusted to run with that of 3rd Division on its left. They were now attached to 5th Division where they remained until the end of October when they rejoined 7th Brigade on the northern side of the Lys valley. They had lost over 300 men including 8 officers.

On 1 November they were attached to 4th Division who were having difficulty holding Armentieres and the area around Ploegsteert Wood. The trenches on the edge of the wood were shallow, waterlogged and overlooked by the Messines Ridge on the left. Firing was constant and communications difficult. On 17 November they were attached to 8th Brigade and spent the winter in the trenches on the high ground that divided the River Lys from the lowlands around Ypres. In the middle of December 3rd Division began a number of attacks with the aim of harassing the enemy and preventing the transfer of reserves to the Russian Front. On 14 November they had unsuccessfully attacked the Messines Ridge and taken heavy casualties. The operation was halted and 7th Brigade took over the line which, despite the fighting, was virtually unchanged. The only difference being that the trenches were now full of the dead.

On 25 December 1914 the famous Christmas Truce between British and German troops took place near Ploegsteert Wood where they played football and exchanged gifts. However, this did not happen on the whole length of the front. Five miles away, near Spanbroekmolen, the 3rd Worcesters were holding the line. Here casual sniping continued as usual throughout the day killing Joseph Stanley whose name can be found on Panel 34 of The Menin Gate Memorial.

The 3rd Battalion had spent the winter in the defences facing the Messines Ridge or in billets behind the line at Locre or Dranoutre. The heavy clay soil restricted the drainage of the trenches and they had a tendency to dissolve in a welter of sticky slime after heavy rainfall. At one point the muddy slush was so deep that the sentries had to be stationed in barrels which almost floated away on the sea of liquid mud. The battalion was relieved regularly – in January every four days which was extended to every seven days in February. Sniping and shelling continued to take its toll with nearly 100 wounded or killed between the New Year and March 1915. Finally, in February, the weather improved and the soil gradually began to dry out making it possible to carry out active operations.

After spending 4 March to 11 March in billets in Locre 7th Brigade was ordered to take and consolidate Spanbroek Mill as a preliminary to a further advance. The assault was timed for 8.40 am on 12 March and the battalions detailed to take part were the 3rd Worcesters, 1st Wilts with the 2nd South Lancs in support. But as morning came they were surrounded by thick fog and, although the British artillery had been pounding the enemy since 7.00 am, they were unable to see the result. The Assembly Trenches were only half dug and were full of water and afforded little cover against the increasingly accurate German shells causing many casualties. While the staff tried to work out whether the attack was likely to be successful, they received a message stating that the 1st Army was making excellent progress and that the Germans were withdrawing men from this area to provide support further south. Therefore the assault should happen without delay.

The artillery opened fire at 2.30 pm and two hours later the men pulled themselves out of the waterlogged ditches, crossed the frontline trenches by means of plank bridges under a hail of rifle and machine gun fire and staggered through knee deep mud. The German fire was deadly accurate cutting

Pte John Henry Pitt 3. By kind permission of David Pitt.

down swathes of men. But the survivors struggled on through the mud, reached the wire entanglements and broke through the gaps they could find. The leading party finally broke through and took the trench. To their right another group broke through the German lines and seized a number of ruined houses. The rest of the two attacking companies of the 1st Worcesters were dead or dying in the mud, the remaining two companies had been ordered not to move from the Assembly Trenches.

The Germans counter-attacked, but the Worcesters who had broken through held on for three hours before being killed by the British artillery who assumed they were Germans and began pounding their positions. The losses were severe with virtually all the men of the two attacking Companies killed, 180 dead including two officers.

While the British 1st Army was fighting at Aubers Ridge and the 2nd Army was fighting in the Ypres salient the 3rd Division was in between the two fronts. There was little fighting, but sniping and bombing continued.

On 25 May the 2nd Battle of Ypres ended with the German defenders forcing the British back from the high ground around Bellewaarde and Hooge. The 3rd Division was bought up to relieve the exhausted divisions who had borne the brunt of the attack.

The 8th and 9th Brigade left first, followed by 7th Brigade. On the evening of 5 June the Brigade moved forward through Ypres, up the Menin Road to Hooge.

Just short of the ruins of Hooge the guides led the 3rd Battalion into half dug trenches on the south of the road relieving a mixed force of Royal Horse Guards, Royal Dragoons and Royal Fusiliers. The front taken over by the 3rd Battalion ran from the Menin Road on the left to Sanctuary Wood on the right and on that line the Battalion fought for the next four days.

Late on the evening of 9 June they were relieved by the 2nd Royal Irish Rifles and moved back in pouring rain down the Menin Road through Ypres to Busseboom just east of Poperinghe where they bivouacked. They were joined by the rest of 7th Brigade on 11 June.

Chapter 11

2nd Battalion South Lancashire Regiment

The 2nd Battalion South Lancashire Regiment landed in France on 14 August having mobilized at Tidworth. Their strength was 980 other ranks and twenty-seven officers. Upon arrival at Havre they travelled by train and route march to Maubeuge, the concentration area that had been selected for the BEF during the pre-war talks between the British and French General Staffs. Although the BEF was not under the command of the French, Sir John French was ordered to co-operate fully with them, but not to endanger the safety of the British Forces. The plan was for the BEF to serve on the left of the French 5th Army.

On 21 August at 8.00 am the BEF marched towards the Belgian border arriving at Frameries at teatime the following day. They were informed that the Germans had occupied Brussels and that the following morning the British would move forward to attack them.

Air Chief Marshal Trafford Leigh-Mallory KCB, DSO (1944).

After breakfast on 23 August they left Frameries by the Ciply road expecting another long march. Instead they arrived at Ciply and were told to collect all the picks and shovels they could find. Once they had done this the march continued and before long they could see the shells bursting over Mons, two miles away. By 5.30 pm the Battalion were entrenched, holding the left sector of 7th Brigade with the 3rd Battalion Worcester on their right.

Shortly after 4.00 am the German infantry attacked en masse straight at their positions. They were met with a hail of rapid, accurate rifle and machine-gun fire. A little while later the enemy artillery opened up on Frameries and within moments the whole place had caught alight. Despite being outnumbered by five to one, the British artillery held its ground. The German battery then took up a position on a hill 1200 yards to the left of the line and began to enfilade the trenches. Almost immediately the British artillery dropped two shells in the middle of them completely obliterating them.

Once the town was on fire the six battalions holding it began to withdraw and the German batteries advanced into it. This placed them behind the 2nd Battalion's left flank and they began enfilading the rear of their position. At the same time the German infantry lined the railway embankment on their left and swarmed under the railway bridge, forming up behind some houses on the South Lancs' side of it.

To start with, D Company and their two machine guns held their ground, mowing down the enemy with comparative ease, but the Germans came on relentlessly. Eventually they had eight guns and two battalions within 400 yards of them, enfilading the whole of the line with the exception of D Company and the machine guns. Lieutenant Colonel C. Wanliss, the CO of 2nd Battalion sent several messages to the Brigadier requesting support from the 7th Fusiliers. After about twenty minutes they received orders telling them to withdraw and although I Company, 7th Fusiliers, had arrived, they were unable to save the situation. The machine guns and D Company had accounted for about 1,000 Germans. They reluctantly retired, their withdrawal covered by A and B Companies. The Retreat from Mons had begun.

Between 25 August and 26 August they marched southwards, enduring sweltering heat and roads crammed with fleeing refugees and transport. They were detailed to cover the withdrawal of 7th Brigade which itself was rearguard to 3rd Division and at Solsmes on the evening of 25 August they and the 1st Battalion Wilts successfully held up the German pursuit.

Because of the fighting at Mons and Solsmes the men had become scattered. Their transport had become separated and was nearly captured by the German cavalry. It was rescued by Quartermaster Lieutenant Sidney Boast who managed to save all the personnel and vehicles under heavy fire without any casualties. The rest of the battalion were waiting at Caudry, but it was nearly daybreak before all the Companies were safely in. The long retreat continued and by 31 August they had reached Coyolles, south of the River Aisne. The retreat plus the heavy fighting had reduced the Battalion to only 14 officers and 400 men, half its original strength. It was not re-equipped with the machine guns it had lost at Mons until 22 September.

By 5 September the whole of the BEF was south of the River Marne. With little food and even less sleep they had marched and fought over a distance of more than 200 miles in thirteen days. During the retreat they had taken part in two general battles plus numerous smaller skirmishes and lost 5 officers and 149 men. A further 7 officers and 301 other ranks were wounded or missing.

On the following day, together with the rest of the BEF, the Battalion began forcing the Germans back, eventually driving them back to the River Aisne. By 13 September the 8th and 9th Brigades of 3rd Division had succeeded in reaching the Chemin Des Dames, a prominent ridge on a plateau north of the River but 7th Brigade were still on the south side. The Wiltshire and Royal Irish Rifles crossed the river the next day by means of a single plank which was laid across the remaining girders of the railway bridge at Vailly. The South Lancs crossed the same way later that day under continuous heavy shell fire from the enemy who were concealed in the wooded valleys beyond the river. By midnight they were all safely over and on 15 September they occupied some shallow trenches north of Vailly. It was their first experience of trench life.

There were now problems with supply. The roads south of Aisne were under continuous shell fire which restricted movement by day and they were unable to cross the pontoon bridge built by the Sappers near the demolished road bridge. To overcome the problem, under cover of darkness, the QM dumped rations and ammunition at a spot on the south bank north of Chassemy and the Companies sent parties to pick this up and distribute them to the front line. The Battalion remained there until 21 September when they were withdrawn back to Augy, south of the Aisne. Back in the comparative peace on the south bank they received a replacement draft of officers and men raising Battalion strength back to over 800 men of all ranks.

At the beginning of October it was decided to withdraw the BEF from the trenches on the Aisne as stalemate had set in. To try and outflank the German armies further north they moved to the muddy plains of Artois and Flanders. On 12 October they moved to Lacouture. Here they encountered stubborn resistance from the German cavalry supported by Jaeger and Cyclist battalions who fought over every barn, building and hedge. By the evening they had finally taken Givenchy and they spent the night sleeping in the open, grateful for their new greatcoats issued before leaving the Aisne. On the following days they pushed on until 20 October when the arrival of fresh German Divisions halted their advance.

In the waterlogged trenches near Le Transloy the battalion repulsed a German assault on 20 October but the following day they were eventually pushed back together with the 3rd Worcesters on their right. They had lost seven officers and over 200 other ranks in one day. They remained out of the line until 26 October when they headed back to Neuve Chapelle after the enemy had made several serious assaults of the 3rd Division front and captured the trenches in and about the village.

By dawn on 27 October the Germans had forced a salient in the British lines allowing them to exploit their previous successes. A composite force of the 2nd Battalion, Royal Fusiliers, Northumberland Fusiliers and a detachment of French Cyclists made a brave effort to retake Neuve Chapelle. Although it was supported by four British and seven French Batteries they made little progress against the German machine guns and snipers.

Lt Edmund Lionel Frost.

Meanwhile the Germans had broken through east of Neuve Chapelle. But they were met 500 yards from the village by two companies from the Battalion and the Wiltshire's Reserve Company, 250 men in total, who drove them back with several casualties.

In the evening the exhausted survivors returned to billets only to be sent back again the following day where they stayed until 29 October. There was no peace in their billets in Richebourg either as they were shelled at 4.00 pm and Battalion HQ took a direct hit causing severe concussion to both Major Ashworth and Captain Melvill leaving both unfit for duty.

They moved back to Lacouture where Captain L. W. Herbert from 3rd Battalion assumed command. Although sorely needing a rest the situation created by the First Battle of Ypres meant they were soon back in action and 6 November saw them occupying the cold, wet trenches in Zwarteleen, near Hooge. The battle raged for over two weeks with furious artillery bombardments and violent infantry assaults. The Menin Road beyond Hooge was so heavily shelled that the only way through was to use a narrow path leading up to their positions. The mud here was so deep that horses were belly deep in it and only half limbers could be used. The rear portions were left in Hooge and collected on the return journey. Once near the front line carrying parties had to transport the rest of the supplies to the scattered posts, a difficult job for men already weary enough to drop from exhaustion. Rifle oil was also scarce and the men had to use their ration of brown fat to grease the working parts on their rifles which were frequently clogged by the thick sticky mud that pervaded everything. Despite this, the men from the 2nd Battalion, languishing in their shallow waterlogged trenches and scattered shell holes, held on grimly, defying the overwhelming numbers and defeating the enemy's attempts to break through the line. By 23 November the attacks began to diminish and the First Battle of Ypres was over.

The next few months were spent in arduous trench warfare east of Kemmel, battling against the cold wet weather, lack of stores and a shortage of reinforcements. Up until December only two new officers and 150 extra men could be mustered. It was here that hand grenades and improvised trench mortars began to be used, many almost as dangerous for the users as they were for the enemy.

In January 1915 Lieutenant Colonel F. A. Dudgeon, previous commander of the 1st Battalion in India, gave up a staff job with the Indian Corps to take up command of the 2nd Battalion.

The Battalion spent the first few months of the year on the lower slopes of the Messines Ridge near Lindenhoek, Kemmel, Spanbrockmolen, Wytschaete and St Eloi. As both sides had fought to a standstill in the First Battle of Ypres the British had dug in wherever they could. The front line consisted of disconnected lengths of muddy field works, partly trenches and partly breastworks. There were few traverses and little protection from enemy shelling. Duckboards, communication trenches and deep dugouts were non-existent meaning there was an urgent need for improvement.

At this time the normal tour of the front line was twenty-four hours with no hot food or ability to dry out clothes. Even worse, dead bodies had been built into the parapets so it wasn't unusual to find limbs protruding from them. A platoon officer's command post was often a few sandbags supported by a dead body covered with a few inches of earth. There were no active operations in January and February, but sniping and patrolling were constant as was artillery bombardment and few days passed without someone being wounded or killed.

As the Second Battle of Ypres commenced the Battalion arrived at Dickebusch for a much needed rest. They had just spent seventeen days in the trenches at St Eloi and taken part in an assault to retake Hill 60 on 17 April. It would be the first time in over a fortnight the officers and men would be able to sleep without their boots and puttees on. But their rest was short-lived as the new German offensive began and the Battalion headed to the woods north of Voormezeele. Here they cut up bodybelts, impregnated them with urine and used them as improvised gas masks. The rest of the night was spent digging a switch line under intermittent shell fire in case of an enemy break through.

On 6 May they moved to the Hill 60 area to relieve troops of the beleaguered 5th Division. They spent five days on Hill 60 improving the defences, clearing the dead and keeping the enemy at bay. The majority of the dead were Germans belonging to the 53rd Cavalry Regiment and the 105th, 117th and 139th Infantry Regiments. Many had black faces and the metal parts of their uniforms, arms and equipment were covered in a thick green substance, the result of breathing their own gas. Others had been shot through the head whilst withdrawing back to their own lines.

They were relieved on 12 May by the 1st Battalion Gordon Highlanders and returned to their old billets in Dickebusch. The rest of the month was spent digging a trench in the exposed site between St Eloi and the Ypres-Comines Canal. The work could only be carried out at night, usually in the pouring rain and under incessant machine-gun and rifle fire.

At the end of the month they moved back to the salient carrying out pioneering work in the dangerous areas around Hooge and Sanctuary Wood.

They took many casualties here including another officer, Captain Salter. The Battalion now only had one of their original officers left, Captain Sydney Boast.

On 9 June three men were awarded the Distinguished Conduct Medal for the fighting round Ypres in November, CQMS J. Fearnehough and Lance Corporals A. Cleveland and S. Yorke. It was also at this time proper gas masks were issued. These were smoke helmets which afforded complete protection against chlorine. The men now prepared for the attack on Bellewaarde on 16 June.

Chapter 12

1/4th Battalion
South Lancashire Regiment

The Territorial Force (TF) was formed in 1908 by Lord Haldane who was then Secretary of State for War. The existing volunteer units were reorganized into fourteen Divisional Infantry complete with artillery, engineers and ancillary services based on large towns or counties. They were intended primarily for home defence and the volunteers had no obligation to serve overseas unless they specifically signified their assent to overseas service in a national emergency.

When the TF came into existence, the 1st Volunteers (Warrington and Newtown) became the 4th Battalion. They received their orders to mobilize on 4 August and notices calling all ranks to the Colours were posted in Warrington and neighbouring parishes by the evening.

By 9 August over ninety per cent of the Battalion had volunteered and they had 15 officers and 853 men. By 12 August they had a further sixteen officers and 489 other ranks. On 13 August they were sent to camp in Dunfermline for training whilst recruiting continued. In October they moved to Tunbridge Wells and spent the rest of 1914 training.

Their orders for overseas came on 22 January and on 12 February they left Southampton for Havre. The Battalion was up to full strength with 31 officers and 1,038 other ranks. Two days later they were in billets at Grapperies and on 21 February they marched to La Clytte to join 7th Brigade. Here they were attached to 2nd Battalion for training in trench warfare. At this time the 3rd Division were holding the lower slopes of Messines Ridge, south of the Ypres Salient. Their trenches were more like waterlogged ditches; they weren't continuous and were often only fifty or sixty yards away from the enemy. The roofs on the dugouts were corrugated iron which provided no protection from shelling, although it did provide protection from the constant rain. There were virtually no communication trenches, very few supplies of food and ammunition and the weather was atrocious, heavy rain, blinding snow blizzards and hard frosts.

On 26 February, together with 2nd Battalion, A and B Companies occupied parts of F and G trenches in front of Kemmel and it was here they took their first casualties with twenty other ranks killed and three wounded. The other Companies also took their turn in the trenches and when not in line of fire they carried out work parties digging support and communication trenches. On 25

March they moved to Dickebusch and into trenches opposite St Eloi. Here the field drains were so near the surface that it was impossible to dig trenches so breast works were used instead. They remained here until 1 April when they went back to billets on the Dickebusch – La Clytte Road. They spent the rest of the month in normal trench routine with the 2nd and 4th Battalions relieving each other at regular intervals, with work parties when out of the line.

On 1 May they took over from the 2nd Battalion in the line near Elzenwalle Chateau and the following day suffered some ill effects from the clouds of gas drifting over from Hill 60.

Corporal Sidney Thomas Ince

24th Monday (Whitsun)
Hard lines. Another holiday gone west. Heavy bombardment commences at 3:00am. We receive our first taste of gas in early morning and again in the evening.[14]

They remained here until the end of May and although they had no serious engagements they still suffered casualties from the constant sniping and shell fire.

At the beginning of June they moved into the Salient relieving the 2nd Life Guards and 8th Hussars at the south edge of Sanctuary Wood near Hooge on 5 June. Corporal Ince wrote:

7th Monday
This position runs through a wood, the enemy's lines varying in distance from 50–500 yds. Don't like this place at all. Vastly different from Dickesbusche. Five hit today.[15]

---

14. Contributed by Perce from the diary of Sidney Thomas Ince.
15. Contributed by Perce from the diary of Sidney Thomas Ince.

Chapter 13

1st Battalion Wiltshire Regiment

During the First World War, The Duke of Edinburgh's (Wiltshire Regiment) raised a total of ten battalions from its pre-war establishment of two regular, one reserve and two territorial battalions. The 1st Battalion, The Wiltshire Regiment were based at Tidworth with 7th Brigade, 3rd Division when war broke out in August 1914 and on 4 August at 5.45 pm orders were received to mobilize.

The next few days were spent on musketry drill, practising on the ranges, route marching, being inspected and having the dreaded inoculations for enteric. On 13 August they left in two separate trains for Southampton. The first train, commanded by Lieutenant Colonel A. W. Hasted, embarked with 505 men of all ranks. The second train, commanded by Major A. S. Barnes, held the remaining 509 men of all ranks. The first train arrived at Southampton at 9.12 am and the men detrained at Shed 23.

At 11am they began boarding the *SS South Western* only to face considerable delay as the vehicle hatch was too small so all the shafts and wheels from the GS Wagons had to be removed. All horses and vehicles were finally on board by 2.15 pm, the troops quickly boarded and the ship sailed at 2.30 pm. They sailed as far as Sandown Bay and then anchored there. Meanwhile the second train arrived safely in Southampton and the men immediately embarked on the *SS Princess Ena*, also sailing at 2.30 pm.

At 5am on 14 August both ships sailed for France, the *SS South Western* arriving at 8.45 am and the *SS Princess Ena* at 7.30 am. On arrival they marched to the camp at Mont St Aignon and spent the next few days marching towards Ciply, which they reached on 22 August. The following day three Companies were dug in north of Ciply facing Mons.[16] Despite the fact the Germans were already shelling the area the men continued to dig themselves in. The shelling went on until nightfall and after dark the digging continued.

After little sleep they were woken abruptly at dawn by heavy shelling of their trenches. This continued until lunchtime. 7th Brigade was now ordered to retire to St Wass. During the withdrawal Captain Dawes and three men were killed, a further twenty-two were wounded, and the CO had his horse shot from under

---

16. C Company had been sent first to set up an outpost at Harmignies, then to Nouvelles to protect the artillery and then back to Harmignies.

him. Three days later they were again in the thick of the fighting as they doggedly held onto the northeast edge of Coudry for the whole morning despite heavy shelling and several infantry attacks. They took nearly 100 casualties. The retreat continued, back to Hagicourt, Vermand and Ham where they formed the advanced guard during the night march.

On 30 August they were the last Battalion to cross the bridges across the River Oise near Varenne before the bridges were blown up. From here the retreat continued back to Vic Sur Aisne. The following day B Company came under attack from an Uhlan patrol and, after a long, hot and very tiring march, the men fell back to Coyelles.

The retreat continued until the beginning of September when the BEF halted, regrouped and prepared to attack.

By 14 September the BEF were back on the front foot and at 5.00 am the 1st Wiltshire Regiment formed the advanced guard to the Brigade through Brenelle to the high ground of Chassemy. From here they pushed on to cross the River Aisne using the bridge the engineers had made overnight, despite being under constant fire from the enemy. 8th and 9th Brigade had already crossed under cover of darkness and were under attack on the north bank. The GOC of 8th Brigade asked for the 1st Battalion to be sent to his assistance and 1 Wilts set off via the woods to cross by the railway bridge between Vailly and Presles. The bridge had been demolished but a plank had been put across the breach to enable them to cross.

However, on approaching the bridge they could see that the Battalion on the right of 9th Brigade was falling back and had already reached the broken bridge. The 1st Wiltshire took up positions and began covering their retreat.

Lieutenant Colonel Bird of the Royal Irish Rifles arrived to take control and ordered them to advance and take the hill to the north, part of which was still held by 9th Brigade.

Despite A Company taking several casualties the Battalion managed to cross the bridge and made their way onto the hill north east of St Precord, north of Vailly. The Royal Irish Rifles crossed behind them and extended the line to the left leaving the Battalion to set up outposts and entrench as night fell. The enemy attacked in strength at 11pm but were eventually beaten back. For the next five days they remained dug in despite torrential rain, intermittent shelling and several exchanges with small assault parties.

They received some much needed reinforcements on the 20 September, a draft consisting of ninety other ranks under Lieutenant Gaskill. On the front line the trenches again came under attack for an hour from 8.00 am and at 11.00 am heavy shelling began and lasted another hour. Then 200 Germans with machine guns broke through the dense woods in the line and crashed through the trenches held by the Worcestershires. This threatened the right of their position, but the enemy were eventually halted within fifty to 100 yards of their trenches. There was lots of hand-to- hand fighting but finally the British artillery began shelling the Germans and they began to fall back. However, they were entrenched on the two bare knolls that they had gained and this gave them a commanding view of the area. The British artillery continued to shell them and eventually forced them back.

At 5.00 pm the troops on the right (200 men from Wilts, Worcs and South Lancs) were ordered to advance and three quarters of an hour later they had regained the line and reconnected with the Companies on the left. During the action Lieutenant Colonel Hasted had been wounded and Captain Reynolds killed. Lieutenant Cruickshank was missing so Major T. Roche took command of both the Battalion and the right section of the area held by 7th Infantry Brigade (one Coy Worcesters and one Coy South Lancs). They were reinforced by four machine guns from the 12th Lancers and two from the 19th Hussars. On 23 September they were finally relieved by the Norfolk Regiment.

General Sir Horace Smith-Dorien (Commander 2 Corps) and General H. Hamilton (Commander 3rd Division) visited on 29 September. Since their arrival in France the Battalion had lost 12 officers and 362 other ranks and their strength was down to 23 officers and 925 men. They had received four reinforcement drafts of ninety men each.

On 23 October they marched to a position west of Neuve Chappelle. The trenches here had been partially dug by the Royal Engineers so they immediately began digging and making the trenches bomb proof until the sniping became too bad. They stopped until dusk and then continued entrenching and strengthening the supporting works. During this two more men were killed and three wounded.

At 12.30pm on 24 October the Germans attacked. The heavy fighting went on for two hours but eventually they forced the Germans back. Afterwards they set about repairing the trench as best they could under continued enemy sniping and managed to get all troops except HQ troops out of the buildings by daylight. At 9.45 am heavy shelling of the village and trenches began, stopped for a while and then continued for three hours in the afternoon. The trenches were blown apart by the ferocity of the shelling which killed eight, wounded thirty-six and left twenty-three missing, presumed buried in the collapsed trench. The village also suffered considerable damage.

On 25 October Battalion HQ moved further back west of the village. The shelling continued all day reducing the village to ruins and the damage to the roads by the shelling made it difficult to get supplies up. The Battalion had lost another thirty-seven men killed with forty-two wounded and by the next day Battalion HQ had moved back to the farm. While B and C Companies and two platoons of A Company remained in the trenches, two platoons of A Company in support of C Company, about eighty men, were held in reserve.

At 1.00 pm heavy shelling began and the regiment on their left were virtually cleared out of their trenches. At 4.30pm they heard the enemy coming up on the left so they sent in two platoons in support and moved C Company. They were just in time to meet the Germans arriving on the west side of the village. They came within 200 yards of the road before they stopped and dug themselves in as it was getting dark. Three platoons from C Company were deployed with bayonets and drove them out of the burning village. There was now a great delay in moving the line forward as there were five different units with no senior officers to take command.

After waiting an hour for a Regiment on their left to come up, the five Companies from 7th Brigade (Wilts, S Lancs and Royal Irish Rifles) decided not to wait any longer but to push on to relieve their colleagues in the forward trenches. They advanced through the village with little opposition other than from snipers. On arrival at the Royal Irish Rifles' trenches C Company Wilts discovered they were now occupied by Germans. A fierce hand-to-hand battle ensued as they attacked with bayonets, finally making the Germans withdraw. They reoccupied the trenches and held them until the rest of the Royal Irish Rifles came up.

It was decided the north end of the village could not be cleared of enemy troops without artillery support and they would have to wait until daylight for this. The village was now burning out of control and all units had withdrawn about half a mile west, roughly the line the Royal Fusiliers had been halted on several hours earlier.

They continued to fight in the area for the next two weeks. Often outnumbered and sometimes partially surrounded they still managed to restore the line on at least two occasions.

Having been reinforced again they marched northwest on 30 October for three days until they reached Locre, south of Ypres. Their War Diary of 30 October 1914 records that in the first ten weeks of fighting they had lost 28 officers and over 1,000 men.

After spending some time in the trenches at Hooge in November they moved to the Kemmel Sector, southeast of Ypres on the Messines Ridge where they spent the next few months in waterlogged trenches engaged in trench warfare until March 1915.

On 12 March they left their billets at Locre at 2.45 am and marched towards the trenches known as 'F' in front of Spanbroekmolen. They arrived in position at dawn, about 5.30 am, and occupied four lines of trenches on the reverse side of the hill. The Worcestershire Regiment were in similar trenches on the right. The Battalion HQ was in the trench known as 'F2' about fifty yards in front of the trench in which the Battalion was situated. The trenches were about twenty-five yards apart.

The morning was dull and misty and other than some desultory gun fire and odd sniper fire everything was quiet. At 1pm the mist began to clear and by 2.30 pm had gone completely. The artillery bombardment began and continued until about 4.10 pm with only a slight break. The field guns fired shrapnel to cut through the enemy barbed wire and large quantities of heavy HE beat down the German parapets and blew in the trenches. However, although it appeared to have been successful, it was later discovered that the frontline trenches were almost completely intact.

As the artillery fell silent the infantry assault was launched by two Companies of the Worcestershire Regiment with a small party of Royal Engineers. Now A Company rushed forward crossing over the F2 trench by means of flying bridges which had been placed there in the early hours of the morning, passing through gaps in their own barbed wire that had been made opposite the bridges.

No sooner were A Company across the bridge, than the enemy opened fire with rifles and machine guns. Only a few isolated parties made it to the enemy wire, a distance of about 200 yards. Also coming under fire were B Company, unable to get more than fifty yards from F2. The Worcestershire Regiment, on their right, were also struggling. They tried crawling forward on their stomachs but still didn't get very far and about midday they reluctantly turned back. Unlike the survivors of A Company who had retreated under cover of darkness, B Company took heavy casualties. At 7.00 pm the Battalion withdrew and returned to their billets at Locre. Casualties were heavy with thirty-two men killed, forty-eight wounded and twelve missing. The survivors spent April and May in the trenches at the Dickebusch area southwest of Ypres. On 4 June they moved to Hooge where they relieved the Lincolnshires. The trenches here were in a terrible state and they spent 5 June, a fine, hot day, working to improve them while C and D Companies went into reserve in Zouave Wood. The following day was also hot but not quiet. The Germans opened fire on the west of Hooge with several very heavy, and one medium, minenwerfer. In all twenty-one shots were fired until they were finally silenced at about 11.30 am by the British Artillery firing their 9.2 howitzers. The Battalion had taken more casualties with two dead and twenty wounded.

The next day, 7 June, was still hot and despite enemy fire and the loss of two more dead and six wounded they managed to put a large quantity of barbed wire in front of the trenches.

On 8 June they were relieved by the Honourable Artillery Company and the next day returned to Ypres and into billets in the ramparts. On 10 June they marched a mile west of Ypres and spent the next four days resting and training. During training with a lyddite grenade on 12 June there was a terrible accident which left two men dead, one of whom was Second Lieutenant Stansfield Smith, and a further twenty-three men wounded.

On 15 June they marched to the Assembly Trenches on the Menin Road, west of Hooge, arriving at 11.45 pm.

Chapter 14

1/4th Battalion Gordon Highlanders – 8th Brigade

On 30 July 1914, as news reached them of the general mobilization, U Company 1/4th Battalion Gordon Highlanders were finishing their two-week camp at Tain on the shores of the Dornoch Firth. From sitting round the large campfire singing songs with the help of several bottles of beer, the 132 soldiers of U Company now found themselves preparing for war. As they made ready to leave the heavens opened and the special train that was supposed to take them home was cancelled. By the autumn of 1914 the Regiment's four Territorial Battalions had all volunteered for overseas service. Coming so close after the annual summer camp many found the transition to serving with an operational battalion bewildering.

Murdo Murray.

With U Company were the territorials of the 4th Battalion Gordon Highlanders. The 'U' stood for University and they were all undergraduates of Aberdeen University. They had been formed in 1908 as one of the eight rifle companies of the local territorial battalion, 1/4th Gordon Highlanders. Although the majority were from Aberdeen and the northeast, there were also students from Caithness and the Lothians as well as Gaelic speakers from the Hebrides and the Western Isles.

Sergeant Alexander Rule remembers that they were happy enough to be mobilized provided they could retain the original title of the University Unit. However, before they left for France, the Battalion's original eight companies were reduced to four to meet army requirements and U Company became D Company. But within the Battalion the men kept their own title and took great pride in that it consisted of student soldiers.

Their officers were also ex-students so they understood the men under their command. Commanding Officer of the 1/4th Battalion Gordon Highlanders was Colonel Ogilvie. Company Commander was Captain Lachlan McKinnon who'd been a law student and who had graduated four years earlier. His second in command was Lieutenant J. D. Pratt. Most of the sergeants had degrees including two who had honours degrees. Even some of the men in the ranks had degrees, but Colonel Ogilvie had not allowed them to apply for Commissions because to do so could have deprived the Battalion of its best men and this could have prejudiced their opportunity to go to France. At the time of mobilization it was still considered that the war would be over by Christmas or early 1915 and the Colonel was determined nothing would prevent the Battalion deploying.

The Battalion left Bedford on 19 February on three trains at 5.45 am and 7.10 am, and arrived at Southampton at 9.45 am. They boarded the *Archimedes* (requisitioned as a British Expeditionary Force supply ship from 1914 to 1919) and sailed for France at 7.00 pm.

After arriving at Havre they marched to No 2 Rest camp where they were issued with clothing and other necessities. Two days later they left the rest camp for Bailleul arriving half an hour later. Here they were billeted in the Grapperies until 27 February when they marched to La Clyette to join the 8th Infantry Brigade.

Over the next few days each Company accompanied a regular Battalion into the trenches for a few days of instruction. A Company went with the 4th Middlesex Regiment, B Company with 1st Gordon Highlanders, C Company with 2nd Royal Scots, 1 Machine Gun Section with the 1st Gordon Highlanders and D Company with 2nd Suffolk Regiment.

The next few months were spent enduring the cold, biting wind and torrential downpours in the dank, waterlogged trenches. Time was spent on fatigues which the men found boring, on working parties and on supplying the front lines with sacks of coke, rolls of wire, timber, stakes, ammunition and other items. They made several trenches, latrines and dugouts and, on numerous occasions, went out into no man's land among the rotting corpses with wiring parties.

Sgt James Fraser. Kind permission of John Blomfield.

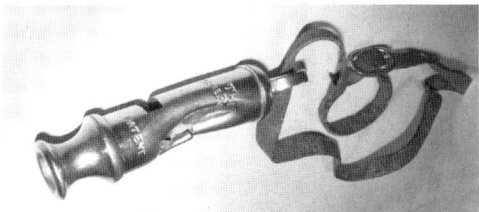

Acme whistle belonging to Sgt James Fraser. Kind permission of John Blomfield.

On 14 March they were ordered to take over trenches G3 and 4 and H1. Two Companies remained in billets in Locre while C and D Companies prepared to take over the trenches. The whole move was cancelled after the German attack on St Elroi but two days later they again prepared to move. This time they took over the trenches as planned and also trenches H2, 3 and 4. Throughout March and April they took eighty-four casualties who were either killed or wounded.

Although they had been soldiers for almost a year they still considered themselves students. Their intention was to enjoy themselves where possible and rough it out when necessary. One of their favourite past times was singing, either the traditional Scottish Airs which were not entirely understood by the Suffolk and Middlesex men of 8th Brigade, or songs from the student song book.

The Muckin' o' Geordie's Byre was popular with the English because although they couldn't understand the words they could stamp their feet along to the ever-increasing tempo. A different song became popular for another reason after a Suffolk man requested *Where's me fourpence Charlie?* This caused much confusion until it was finally understood to be the Jackobite song *Wae's Me For Prince Charlie.* As the story quickly spread U Company began singing the revised version instead.

At the beginning of May D Company moved to Siege Farm in the dark to relieve a Company of the 1st Gordon Highlanders so they could act as Brigade Reserve in the trench area. The next few days all companies spent time in trenches *K2, K2A,*

Sgt James Fraser 1938 (2). Kind permission of John Blomfield.

Sgt James Fraser 1938. Kind permission of John Blomfield.

K2B, L1 and L3.[17] While there they practised putting on the special respiratory pads provided to protect them against the gas attacks.

On 9 May they received orders to be ready to move at the shortest possible notice and that they were to hand over the trenches that night to the Nottingham and Derbyshire Regiment. After this they were to proceed to Rozenhill Huts where the whole Battalion was assembled by 4.30 am the following day. Other than a practice attack in the afternoon and an emergency turn out in the evening most of the day was spent resting. They remained at Rozenhill Huts until 2.30 pm on 12 May when they moved with the rest of the Brigade to the Chateau, one and a half miles south west of Ypres. At 8.30 pm that night they moved to dugouts three quarters of a mile west south west of Zillebeke.

The next day they dug a new switch line during which twelve men were wounded. The following day another man was wounded whilst carrying out fatigues and guiding parties. This pattern continued over the next five days when another ten men were wounded.

By the middle of May, after moving from the quiet sector in front of Kemmel to Hill 60, U Company had lost twelve men. They were buried in their own small cemetery; others who were wounded had returned home, leaving noticeable gaps in the small Company.

Finally, on 20 May, they moved with the rest of the Brigade back to La Clytte and into huts in Rozenhill. Although they received orders to go back into the trenches on 24 May the orders were rescinded and they found themselves marching with the rest of the Brigade to a point half a mile east of Vlameringhe where they were held as 5th Corps Reserve.

On 26 May they took over the line trenches from 1st Battalion Rifle Brigade and 2nd Battalion Shropshire Light Infantry and part of 3rd King's Royal Rifle Corps (KRRC). They also took over KRRC HQ. Over the next few days a further ten men were killed and thirty-five were wounded. On 2 June they again found themselves under heavy bombardment, although this time casualties were relatively light. The German infantry made a further two attacks at night on the trenches near Hooge, but were beaten back by the Cavalry.

Sergeant James Fraser enlisted in to the Aberdeen University T.A. in 1911 and graduated in 1914. He had embarked on a medical course when the war started.

Sergeant James Fraser

5th: *Digging till 3am, back to our trench, stood to, not much doing, very hot day. In the evening back to digging till well into morning.*

6th: *Similar day to yesterday, very hot. Were allowed to take off our boots in relays as we had not had clothes off for over ten days, we were very lousy.*

7th: *Digging ad nauseam, hot. Got back to our own line about dawn.*

---

17. G3 & 4, H1,2,3 and 4 had changed their names to K2,A,B & C on 17 March.

Sgt James Fraser, front row, right, at Blendeques. Kind permission of John Blomfield.

8th: Back to familiar country, thunder and heavy rain. Used the cart for several journeys to front line, mud awful.

9th: Still raining, carried up knife rests of barbed wire and set them out in front of the trenches, rather trying as there was nothing between you and the Germans.

10th: Rain in morning. J.K. Forbes and I lost our breakfast. Just behind our trench there was a big heap of 'slack', had been used for steam engines, I was frying our bacon in my mess tin lid when a shell fell right in the slack and exploded. We disappeared in a cloud of black dust but there eventually emerged two dirty black figures. I still held on to my mess tin lid but as well as bacon it was full of coal dust.[18]

11th: Recalled to see Brigadier, saw Col. Ogilvie at 9am. Brigadier at 10am. got all papers signed, so set for cadet school in about a month.

12th: Back to ordinary duties, digging etc. shelled a bit.

13th: New horror. Minenwerfer. This lady threw large bombs (about fifty pounds). One could see them coming and had sentries calling, bomb right, bomb left as the case may be, thank goodness they were very accurate but they made a mess of a

---

18. This incident is recorded in Peter Diack's book *J.K. Student and Sniper Sergeant*. The Forbes students' residence is named in memory of J.K. Forbes.

Sgt James Fraser at Blendeques, second row, second from left. Kind permission of John Blomfield.

> strong point we had made of a farmhouse just ahead of our front line, several men were killed there from 13 platoon.
>
> 14th: Rumours of an attack, did some hard work on the support trench, as it was to be our starting point. Germans broke the rule tonight, after 10 minutes hate at nine o'clock, they proceeded to shell up and down the Menin road from our front line to the Menin gate. Caught two battalion transports and we had frightened mules and horses all over the back area. Two mules tore up the Menin road, cleared our barricade and possibly became POWs we never saw them again.
>
> 15th: Orders for attack tomorrow were issued; we were to start with the second wave from the support trenches. We went up to support trench and made it more habitable. Germans shelled the Menin road again, but this time it was deserted.[19]

From 2 June to 14 June the Companies alternated between the fire trenches and reserve taking twenty-three casualties. During this time Lieutenant J. D. Pratt had sent a platoon from U Company, a sergeant and seven men, into Ypres. When they were due to be relieved twenty-four hours later they requested that they be allowed to stay longer. When asked why they explained that Ypres was full of

---

19. Kind permission of John Blomfield.

people from all different regiments merrily helping themselves to the possessions left behind by the fleeing civilians, especially the alcohol.

On 14 June A and B Companies were in the fire trenches and C and D Companies were in reserve. During the day and night the wire entanglements of the enemies, front row trenches were carefully inspected and at night the wire in front of the Battalion trenches was cut ready for an assault on 18 June. But this order was subsequently cancelled. Meanwhile the Germans were busy shelling the road although there were no further casualties. On 15 June they made their way to Ypres which was now a city in total ruin. The streets were covered in brick dust which muffled the sound of their boots as they

Sgt James Fraser graduation 1914. Kind permission of John Blomfield.

Sgt James Fraser U Company Aberdeen 1911. Kind permission of John Blomfield.

The Gordon Family, Christkirk. c1911. Jenella, George, Robert, James, Constance, James A. Gordon, Christina, John, Mrs Jeannie Gordon.

picked their way carefully through the shell-shattered buildings. Everywhere they looked was utter devastation. The fronts of buildings had been ripped off leaving jagged edges and floors clinging precariously to the remaining supports. There were possessions strewn all over the streets and the air was filled with the foul stench of the damaged sewers and the smell of smoke from the untended fires. The interior of the Cloth Hall was completely destroyed, its clock laying at the base of its square tower, the works twisted and mangled.

Only one altar remained undamaged from the ruined Church of St Martin's near the Grand Place. Outside there was an empty pedestal and at its base a statue of a corpulent civic dignitary, complete with robes and chains of office lay as if taking cover from the shelling. This caused

Pte Robert Patrick Gordon. By kind permission of James M Grant (www.kinnethmont.co.uk.)

a certain amount of ribald laughter from the men as they marched through Ypres on their way to the salient. They were in no doubt as to what lay ahead of them and singing in the deserted town seemed inappropriate. So they marched in silence, the gloom only lightened when they came across the ruins of a building with a sign above it stating it was the English Ladies' Seminary. As they marched past one man began whistling a few bars of *Gaudearmus Igitur*. This was a song that as students they would whistle outside the women students' hostel in Aberdeen after lights out. It would always bring at least one woman to the window and they would then share friendly banter. The few bars were just enough to remind the men of happier days, briefly giving them something to smile about as they continued through Ypres.

They continued to march towards the Menin Gate only to find their route blocked at intervals by the swollen rotting corpses of dead horses. The flies and stench of decay was enough to make them hold their breath and they only relaxed as they left the city wall and crossed the moat. From here their route took them past a water tower and a heavily shelled cemetery until eventually they reached the trenches at the tip of the salient, south of the village of Hooge.

They continued on past Hell Fire Corner until they reached Birr Crossroads on the right of the Menin Road. Although 8th Brigade was not intended to be in the forefront of the attack, 7th and 9th Brigades were.

Chapter 15

2nd Battalion Royal Irish Rifles

Sgt Jackson Clarke. By kind permission of Stephen Kerr.

In the spring of 1914, the Royal Irish Rifles were based in Bhurtpore Barracks in Tidworth. Their commanding officer, Lieutenant Colonel W. D. Bird from the Royal West Surrey Regiment, had taken command in September 1913 and immediately run into trouble with other senior officers after trying to turn the billiard room into a lecture room.

The country was in the middle of a political crisis after the government had attempted to bring in Home Rule in Ireland. Ulster Unionists had formed the Ulster Defence Force (UDF) after vowing to fight Home Rule at all costs. In March 1914 many officers based in the Curragh in Co Kildare had resigned rather than be forced to move against the UDF and there was fear that the UDF would raid the police and army barracks there to procure arms and equipment. Lieutenant Colonel Bird was believed to have offered the Regiment for active operations in Ulster which caused considerable animosity amongst the other officers and men. Although the order was subsequently withdrawn it had a long lasting effect on the relationship between Lieutenant Colonel Bird and his senior officers, particularly Captain Bowen-Colthurst.

The Battalion was ordered to mobilize on 4 August at 6.00 pm and formed part of the 7th Infantry Battalion under Brigadier General F. W. N. McCracken in 3rd Division. The mobilization was complete by 9 August although the men suffered considerably from their enteric inoculation which made them feel very ill. Their ranks were swollen by the reservists who were soon in uniform and ready to go.

At 2.30 pm on 13 August the first half of the Battalion went by train to Southampton and embarked on the *SS Ennisfallen*, a Cork cattle steamer. They sailed at 8.00 pm arriving at Le Havre at 5.00 am the next morning. They carried on up the River Seine and disembarked at Rouen at 7.30 pm and then marched to the rest camp at Mont St Aignan. The second half left Southampton on the *SS Sarnia* and did not stop at Le Havre, instead making their way straight to Rouen and St Aignan arriving before the first half. That night the heavens opened turning the camp into a quagmire, but they stayed there until 15 August meeting up with the other regiments of the brigade, the South Lancs, 3rd Worcester and 1st Wiltshire Regiments. The following day they boarded the train for Aulnoye via Amiens. Here they were billeted in a large foundry at L'Usine Monbart, one and a half miles from the station.

The next few days were hot and sultry. The men spent their time marching, training and gradually making their way to Ciply, a small industrial town of about 1,000 people, two miles south of Mons. On 23 August they were warned that contact with the enemy was imminent. Having marched a short distance past Nouvelles, they were abruptly halted and then began to retrace their steps halfway back to Ciply.

Their first sight of the war came at 11.00 am when they were confronted with the sight of several riderless horses, all that remained of the 9th Cavalry. At Harmignies they heard that the 15th Hussars, the 3rd Division Cavalry, had been driven back. Virtually all the returning men and horses were wounded.

The Battalion was quickly sent to reinforce the Royal Scots on the high ground north of the station and began entrenching on the right flank of the British defences. At 3.45 pm the enemy artillery opened up aiming straight at C and D Companies (A and B Companies had remained in reserve on the Givry-Mons Road). They now found themselves separated from the rest of the Brigade as the Germans had already crossed the Monde Canal and 3rd Division had withdrawn to a new defensive line south of Mons.

The German infantry began to advance and the Battalion opened fire. Advancing in close formation the Germans were an easy target for their rapid rifle fire and within moments they had been mown down, the attack an utter failure. But their elation was short-lived as orders were soon received that the BEF was withdrawing. This was the beginning of the Retreat from Mons and the Germans were in close pursuit. On 25 August, after a full day in action the Battalion was tasked to form the rearguard to the Brigade. After marching forty-five miles in forty-eight hours they finally reached the billets in Maurois.

The retreat continued and on 26 August they reached Caudry village at Le Cateau. 3rd Division now occupied the Troisville-Audencourt-Caudry line with 7th Brigade occupying the line north of Caudry. The Germans were drawing ever closer and in danger of overrunning them. The Commander of II Corps decided that they needed to make a stand. This would slow up the enemy advance and allow them to continue to make a safe retreat. Despite having been in continuous action since the retreat began, the Battalion were ordered to take up positions on the second line of defence. This was some high ground on the Audencourt-Caudry line, about halfway between Caudry and Montigny. Supporting them were the 41st battery of Royal Field Artillery.

A fierce battle ensued with repeated enemy frontal assaults on the beleaguered units of 7th Brigade. The perpetual fighting had weakened them considerably and an imminent breakthrough was feared. Now B Company and part of A Company were ordered up to positions on the right of the Worcesters in Caudry. Here, after savage close quarter fighting, they helped force the enemy into a temporary retreat from the village.

As fighting flared again later 7th Brigade finally withdrew back from Caudry leaving the Royal Irish Rifles to cover their retreat. This proved doubly difficult as they had to also cover the retreat of the Royal Field Artillery units attached to the brigade which had been previously shelling the enemy. Their first orders were to proceed to Market Square, but the area was being heavily bombarded and several men were killed and wounded. To minimize casualties they made their way to the north edge of the town where they met up with the remnants of the Worcester Regiment on their left and other mixed regiments on the right.

Their orders then required them to double to the road which commanded the approaches to the village. As they lay there on their stomachs, they realized to their horror that they were within 100 yards of a gasometer. However, despite the best efforts of German heavy artillery it remained intact throughout the fight, although the village and its inhabitants suffered considerably. They eventually retired between 5pm and 6pm but not before one more last stand at the stud farm in Montigny. Here their transport was surrounded so Major Charley, Captain and Quartermaster Clerk, handed out all the ammunition, some 750 rounds, to the thirteen men. With this they held out for several hours, killing many of the enemy before they were finally overrun. Practically every man was killed or wounded.

The weather from the 13 September to 21 September was cold and wet. By now the Royal Irish Rifles were in the trenches due south of Rouge Maison and life was miserable. The men were unable to take off their boots because of the waterlogged trenches.

There were no cooking facilities so they did not have any hot food and they were under constant shell fire. On 15 September a patrol from D Company under Lieutenant Dawes was ordered forward to see where the enemy were. They immediately came under heavy fire killing one man and wounding Lieutenant Dawes and another man. To receive medical help they were sent back to a cave that was already filled with injured men, many who were from their own regiment. As they stood outside waiting for treatment they heard a strange noise that resembled that of a fast train approaching. It wasn't. Instead it was a heavy shell and as it came nearer they crouched down trying to

Rifleman Frederick Watling. By kind permission of Sue Holmes.

protect themselves from the inevitable. The wounded squirmed lower and lower into the ground, but to no avail. The burst when it came sounded like it was right on top of them and when Lieutenant Dawes eventually felt it was safe to raise his head he was horrified to see that the shell had killed all the wounded.

The following morning A Company were ordered forward across several hundred yards of hard bare ground to attack a German trench. There was no cover and as they reached within a few hundred yards of the German lines the enemy opened fire. Within moments they were showered in a storm of flying metal from rifle fire, shrapnel and machine guns. Although part of the Company was able to reach the trenches, there were too many Germans and they were too well dug in. Eventually they had no option but to retire. Two officers and half the men were killed.

During the assault on the River Aisne the trouble between Lieutenant Colonel Bird and his subordinate worsened with Lieutenant Colonel Bird accusing Captain Bowen-Colthurst of a lack of judgement, although not of personal courage. The dispute arose in relation to an event on 12 September. At the time the Lieutenant Colonel had taken charge of the Wiltshire Regiment as well as his own and on that day the advanced guard had crossed the river and occupied the heights of the right bank near Vailly. On reaching the heights he found that Major Spedding had sent Captain Bowen-Colthurst's company to occupy the northern edge of the copse some 400–500 yards ahead of the line. The idea was to outflank a German trench they could see about 750 yards away. The Major assured the Lieutenant Colonel that the Captain had been ordered not to go any further. However, the Captain had reached the edge of the wood and seeing the German trench had gone forward and captured it. Unfortunately the enemy had immediately retaliated with heavy artillery and as they were driven back they took heavy casualties. Four officers and seventy-five NCOs and men were killed or wounded. This account was robustly disputed by the Captain who produced seven sworn witness statements to the effect that Major Spedding had known about the attack and had actually supported it. The truth appears to be that while Captain Bowen-Colthurst made the attack with one company, Major Spedding and Lieutenant Colonel Bird thought the whole company was attacking so the Major committed further troops to an attack that was already defeated.

The Battle of La Bassee was overshadowed by the fighting further north, but it was also a critical moment in the Race to the Sea. If the Germans had succeeded in consolidating the Aubers Ridge it could have influenced future campaigns. The Germans were holding Croix Barbee and the woods to the south. Their artillery was behind and they had trenches running in front of the village. As the British artillery were going to shell Croix Barbee the Royal Irish Rifles were ordered to withdraw from close proximity to the village to a group of houses midway between Croix Barbee and La Couture. Three Companies went into the front line with the Middlesex Regiment on their left and the South Lancs to their right. The other company went into reserve. The artillery began pounding enemy positions just before dark and succeeded in driving back the few Germans seen advancing down the road.

On 13 October the Rifles advanced under heavy machine-gun fire and reoccupied the old position just short of Croix Barbee. There was heavy firing by both sides over night, but there was a pause the following day due to counter-attacks and the death of 3rd Division's Commander. His replacement was Major General C. MacKenzie.

The advance continued on 17 October to the high ground of Haut Pommereau on the slopes of Aubers Ridge where the men stopped and watched as German reinforcements moved towards La Basee. The following day they were relieved by the King's Own Yorkshire Light Infantry (KOYLI) and moved back to Pont Logy. Later that day they moved forward to the outpost line in front of the Bois de Biez and remained there until they withdrew back to billets on 19 October.

The next day the Rifles marched back to their former position and after relieving the KOYLI they endured a day of heavy shelling, but fortunately took no casualties. On arrival at Neuve Chapelle on 22 October they placed three Companies in the trenches and one in reserve. Despite continuing rifle fire from an advanced German outpost, most of the day was spent digging reserve and communication trenches.

The Battalion was now down to 700 men but still in good spirits. However they were at a considerable disadvantage. The 8th Brigade were positioned some way back, a road on their left flank led to the enemy and on it were several houses that had not been destroyed. The area was full of wire entanglements and entrenched machine guns so they could command a good view of the road. During the night they were hit by friendly fire from 8th Brigade and returning patrols were fired at by other units killing several men.

The Germans attacked in force the next night, but because they attacked in close formation were easily beaten back. Hundreds were mown down by rapid rifle fire at close quarters. German shellfire increased on 24 October and casualties increased. The situation was made worse when the recoil spring in the field gun in the centre of the frontline trench broke leaving only one gun in action. The enemy commenced heavy shelling of Neuve Chapelle from La Bassee and soon after dark another assault was attempted. Again they were beaten back, this time with bayonets as the men fought hand-to-hand in the muddy, slippery trenches. The Germans took heavy casualties, many of the wounded and dead lying close to or in the Royal Irish Rifles' trenches.

By 25 October the Germans had established themselves in the houses near the left flank of the trenches and in the morning they rushed the end trench. Although they managed to capture the field gun, it had already been sabotaged by the British gunners and overturned after only one round had been fired.

The enemy was eventually driven out, but the trench could not be reoccupied as it was now being shelled by British artillery. The fighting continued unabated for the next few days and by 5 November the Battalion was down to only 250 men.

From here they marched through Ypres to Hooge to relieve the 7th Division incurring more casualties on the way. Although they were only on the periphery of the fighting over the next two weeks casualties continued to mount and by 19 November their strength was reduced to only forty men. They were finally relieved by the 5th Fusiliers that day and the following day marched the fourteen miles to Westoutre. Here much needed reinforcements of four new officers and 507 men arrived. But they bought their own problems and ignorance of military code increased the number of court martials to thirty-two in one month for a variety of offences including neglect of duty, drunkenness, insubordination, assault of NCOs and desertion. This cycle of alternating between the trenches, Weststoutre and Locre continued to 12 March. From January until March the Rifles suffered a further eighteen killed and seventy-eight wounded.

Frederick Watling and Family. By kind permission of Sue Holmes.

On 6 May the Royal Irish Rifles and the South Lancs were lent to 5th Division. They left the camp at 3.00 pm and arrived at the crossroads to wait for the guides who were to take them to the trenches. As evening arrived they brewed tea and sang songs about dying heroes, but there was still no sign of the guides. Finally, at 9.00 pm, a cycle orderly arrived with a note and at last they set off. Arriving at a neighbouring crossroads they were warned not to hang about too long because the enemy regularly shelled the area. The man had only just spoken when a shell whizzed over about 2ft above their heads. Fortunately the shell was a dud and fell harmlessly into the soft mud behind them.

The Royal Irish Rifles reached Shrapnell Corner safely, but as they made their way in single file along the side of Zillebeeke Lake the Germans shelled them constantly. Their way was further blocked as the sides of the path were covered with stretchers carrying the wounded and those who had been gassed, coughing up white froth as the chlorine gas ate away their lungs.

The Brigade HQ was only 100 yards away from the path and chaos reigned. As well as Regiments relieving each other, the Brigades were also changing over so no one seemed to know what was going on. Their guide continued, taking them to the trenches along the top of the embankment, rather than via the sheltered path. The path was fully exposed to shell fire and the first sight that greeted them was a dead soldier with his face covered.

Within moments they came under fire from Hill 60 positions, but finally reached Dormey House where Battalion HQ was situated. The frontline trenches were further on and the confusion continued as HQ orderlies delivered their food supply straight to the Germans. The Bedfords, who they were meant to relieve, had already sent their own food supply away. But they shared half a bottle of whiskey and some army biscuits with them.

It was now 1.00 am and the assault on the German trenches was timed for 2.30 am. The orders, written on the back of an old envelope, stated that the Germans were supposed to be positioned in a portion of the frontline trench which was held by the British on either side.

The idea was for the South Lancs and Royal Irish Rifles to bomb either flank simultaneously whilst the KOYLI rushed the trench. Owing to delays reaching the trench they only reached their positions five minutes before the attack and then found the position was not as described. Before reaching the Germans they had first to pass through a long communication trench. This trench had been under German machine-gun fire and was in a bad state. When they did reach their objective they found the bombs were deficient. Several men were killed and wounded and those making the frontal assault disappeared. The attack failed miserably and they remained in the trenches for another week until relieved by the 3rd Worcestershire on 16 May. They returned to Dickebusch on 20 May.

On 1 June Major E. M. Morris of the Devonshire Regiment took command and over the next few days they began taking barbed wire entanglements to the Ypres Salient. On 8 June the Battalion moved to a camp 300 yards west of the camp south of Vlamertighe-Poperinghe Road. Meanwhile the CO, Adjutant, Machine Gun Officer and two officers per company visited the new line of trenches west of Hooge.

On 15 June 2nd Royal Irish Rifles marched to the Assembly Trenches between Witteport Farm and the Ypres-Roulers railway ready to support 9th Brigade in the attack on Bellewaarde.

Chapter 16

Army Service Corps

Lieutenant G.H. Fearnley-Whittingstall joined the Army Service Corps as Second Lieutenant in September 1914 and served with them at Boulogne before transferring in May 1915 as (temporary) Lieutenant to the 1st Battalion Northumberland Fusiliers.

Other than during the opening and closing phase of the war on the Western Front there was little movement of the troops and this reduced the need to move large quantities of supplies over long distances. France had several large towns with ports that were equipped, to some greater or lesser degree, for dealing with stores and supplies in bulk. Although planning was needed, it was not on the same scale as that needed in the other theatres of the war. The Western Front was also close to Great Britain and the supply was not particularly threatened by enemy submarines. However, it was still an enormous task to supply such a large force, especially as it was done with little increase in the number of officers. Instead the majority in charge of the supply chain were employed in ranks one or two above their own. These men provided practically all the personnel for the transport of the men and animals. There were also many different races in the BEF who also needed to be catered for.

An advanced supply depot was arranged at Amiens, but the condition of the railways and the rapid advance of the enemy meant they couldn't use it. Two weeks after the evacuation of Amiens the supplies had to be evacuated to Le Mans, 100 miles southwest of Paris. These fed the whole of the BEF for several weeks.

The final link in the chain of supply depots from the bases to the front were the Field Supply Depots in each Army area. Their function was to hold a number of reserves of rations for the men and animals in case there were any shortages at railheads. They could also hold any surpluses from the railheads. Normally each of the five Armies was allocated two of these but they could have up to thirty if needed.

Bakeries were established at all Base Supply Depots except St Valery, Cherbourg and Etaples. They were initially equipped with Aldershot ovens but early in 1915 these were replaced with Perkins ovens producing millions of pounds of bread per month.

Demand for petrol also grew as the numbers of aircraft and mechanical transport grew. The largest depots were at Calais and Rouen. Attached to these were the refuelling and repair plants as well as can and case making. In the early days of the war coal came from England and any shortfalls were supplemented by local purchases in France.

France was a rich agricultural country so the BEF were able to make extensive use of local produce. Hospitals obtained large quantities of fish, eggs, milk and fresh butter. Forage was also bought locally on a large scale.

The Army Service Corps had its own Investigation Department in the Directorate of Supplies. This was manned by accountants, actuaries and businessmen who kept track of the £80,000,000 worth of supplies per year.

The original BEF had 950 lorries and 250 cars. By 1918 there were in the region of 33,000 lorries, 1,400 tractors and 13,800 cars plus thousands of motorbikes. In 1914 all heavy repairs to mechanical vehicles were done in the Army Ordnance Departments at the bases while light repairs were completed in the mobile workshops of the Army Service Corps. By October this system was so overloaded that the ASC took over all the heavy repairs. Base Mechanical Transport Depots had already been tested in pre-war army manoeuvres. In the field the Personnel or Reinforcements Branch increased from its original 80 to a floating population of about 1,500 men and evolved into an organization that could train, equip and despatch about 2,000 men to the front per month. By spring 1915 an additional Depot was established in Calais. There were also schools set up to train drivers in Rouen and Calais.

There were two main depots for horse transport. The base depot was in Le Havre. The Advanced Horse Transport Depot was at Abbeville and its main duty was to supply men, vehicles and animals to units and to train teams of animals with harnesses for special purposes.

In 1914 the ASC was also responsible for Labour Companies for work on lines on communications, but by 1915 the demand for labour was so great that the Royal Engineer and Infantry Labour Units appeared.

The ASC was organized into Companies, each fulfilling a specific role. Some were under the orders of, or attached to, the Divisions of the army, the rest were under direct orders of the higher formations of Corps, Army or the GHQ of the army in each theatre of war. The 3rd Divisional Train consisted of four Companies ASC: the 15th, 21st, 22nd and 29th. There was also HQ which comprised five officers, two Staff Sergeants and Sergeants and nine other ranks. HQ Company consisted of six officers, one Warrant Officer, 10 Staff Sergeants and Sergeants, 25 Artificers, one Trumpeter and 220 other ranks. Making up each of 1, 2 and 3 Companies were five officers, one Warrant officer, 10 Staff Sergeants and Sergeants, 14 Artificers, one Trumpeter and 159 other ranks. This was around 657 personnel plus 660 horses.

The lines of communication or logistics they were responsible for were the supply lines from the port to the front line plus the camps, stores, dumps and workshops of the rear areas. In 1914 there were 120,000 men and 53,000 horses in France (by 1918 there were up to three million men and 500,000 horses). This meant a monthly supply of 3,600,000 pounds of meat, 4,500,000 pounds of bread, 5,900,000 pounds of forage and 842,000 gallons of petrol.

Chapter 17

1st Battalion Honourable Artillery Company

Pte George Neal.

On the same day that General Haldane assumed command of the 3rd Division the war situation was considered so serious that 1st Battalion Honourable Artillery Company (HAC), a Territorial Battalion from the City of London, joined the Division and was rushed into the front line. The 1st Battalion HAC was manned by men with potential officer material and they had initially been used to reinforce regular battalions with individual companies.

On 4 August 1914 the HAC had consisted of just two four-gun batteries of Horse Artillery and half a Battalion of Infantry, known as 'army troops'. Although former members who were still fit for service immediately rejoined and recruits flocked in, the HAC could not take them on as orders were for all new recruits to join the New Army. This left the Territorials short of men. However, once the Earl of Denbeigh had spoken to Lord Kitchener, the Battalion was quickly bought up to full strength, extra officers were promoted from the non-commissioned ranks and very soon the HAC was ready to mobilize.

The 1st Battalion, now a thousand strong and under the command of Colonel E. Treffy, remained at HQ until 12 September when they were inspected by His Majesty the King. After this they marched to St. Pancras and went by train to Purfleet Rifle Range Station and from there to Belhus Park in Essex. They expected to stay there for up to three months training, but events in Europe were to accelerate their departure. Having spent the first two days on field exercises, route marching and musketry, the Commanding Officer was surprised to receive a message from the War Office warning they would be leaving for France much earlier than anticipated.

On 16 September orders arrived for 800 men and 29 officers to leave in two trains on 18 September at 6.25 am and 8.30 am. They had no equipment, no rifles, no ammunition and only a motley assortment of vehicles including Pickford vans, a Frederick Gorringe Delivery cart, a four-wheeled milk cart and a large wheeled tank used by a London Borough Council to water the streets. This was to become their water cart.

Their equipment finally arrived at 5.00 pm followed at 10.00 pm by the rifles. It took until 1am on 16 September before everything had been issued. Colonel Treffy left with the right half of the battalion at 3.15 am followed by Major Hanson with the left half an hour later. Despite the difficulties in loading up in the dark the Battalion left on time to catch their respective trains. At 4pm the 1st HAC left Southampton aboard the *SS Westmeath*, arriving off St Nazaire at 10.00 am on Sunday 20 September where a splendid civic reception was given in their honour.

On the Tuesday, Captain Ward and 3 Company left for Nantes. 4 Company remained at St Nazaire while the Battalion HQ and Number 1 and 2 Companies went by rail to Le Mans.

Pte Roger Ballard. Kind permission of Paul Ballard.

Just over a month later, at 7.45 pm on 31 October, the Battalion left Le Mans and arrived at St Omer. While waiting to detrain they heard that the London Scottish had been in action. They realized that it was only the failure of HQ to arrive with their transport, machine guns and reserve ammunition in time that had prevented them from also being involved. At St Omer, under Brigadier General Chichester, they spent their time digging reserve trenches as part of a reserve line in case the Germans broke through at Ypres.

On 3 November Colonel Treffy met the Military Secretary to the Commander in Chief, General Lambton, and suggested the HAC should spend time in reserve first to give them time to acclimatize themselves to shell and rifle fire, especially as many had not yet fired their rifles. They spent the next day using the 200-yard range under the town walls. But time for practice was short as the following day they were sent in buses owned by the London General Omnibus Company to Bailleul.

Four days later, the CO took the 1st and 4th Companies across the Belgian border to Estaires, the HQ of the Lahore Division of the Indian Corps. By the time they arrived the battle had eased, but they could still see and hear the shells busting around Mount Kemmel. From here they marched to Les Lobes, the HQ of the 8th Infantry Brigade, arriving at 1.00 pm. Before reaching their billets they marched past General Sir John French. After commenting on the height of the men of the 1st Battalion – an average of 6ft – he asked if there was anything he could do. The Colonel immediately asked if he could lend him some machine guns as he had lent his to 1st Division during the First Battle of Ypres and had not yet had them back.

General Sir John French instructed General Lambton to recover the guns. Three days later the two machine guns turned up, plus two new ones. Captain Holliday and his gunners were delighted. Captain Holliday was especially pleased as they had been rather peeved that 1st Division had only taken guns and ammunition despite being offered men as well.

On 10 November General Sir James Wilcocks, Commander of the Indian Corps, inspected the Battalion. He informed Colonel Treffy that Companies of the HAC would initially be attached to regular battalions as a way of gradually acclimatizing them. Once used to the trench warfare they would be able to operate as a separate unit. So while attached to 8th Brigade, under the command of Brigadier General Bowes, they spent most of their time digging near Rouge Croix and Croix Barbe, close behind the firing line.

Six days later they marched in heavy rain to Bailleul, arriving at 2.00 pm and going straight to their billets. General Smith-Dorien inspected the battalion on 21 November after which Major Cooper and A Company went into the front line attached to the 4th Middlesex. For the next six days they remained at Neuve Eglise, opposite Messines and each Company took two turns in the frontline trenches. The two sides were separated by the River Douve and were only 500 yards apart. The HAC took a few casualties whilst here but there was little time to mourn as on 27 November they were moved to Westoutre and then Sherpenberg.

On 3 December King George V arrived, accompanied by the Prince of Wales, General Smith-Dorien (the Corps Commander), General Haldane (the Divisional Commander) and Brigadier General Bowes. The King remembered his previous meeting with Colonel Treffy and after speaking to him he, and the Prince of Wales, entered the Sergeant's hut where he first chatted to some of the sergeants before entering another hut and speaking to the men there.

The 2nd Royal Scots were joined by A and D Companies in the front line north of Kemmel while B and C Companies with Battalion HQ provided a support role at Shrapnel Farm alongside Kemmel Chateau. On 6 December the Brigade was relieved and returned to Westoutre. After a brief rest they returned to the line three days later to relieve the Royal Scots Fusiliers in front of Spanbrock Moelen. It was the first time they were in the front line as a Battalion, rather than as separate companies attached to other Battalions and it was a baptism of fire. For the next three days they endured atrocious weather conditions with either continuous rain or intermittent snow. At the end of the three days they finally understood why the Yorks swore so much.

Pte Harry Dunkinfield-Jones. Kind permission of John Hamblin.

The HAC had been tasked to take over the F trenches of Kemmel which lay to the right of the line held by 3rd Division. The trenches were in the centre of the Wytschaete-Messines Ridge and virtually opposite the Spur of Spanbrock Moelen. The Spur was one of the most heavily defended areas of the German Line on the ridge and unfortunately for the men of 1st Battalion HAC it completely dominated F trenches. On their right were the 5th Division and on the left of the 3rd Division were the French, the right of their line positioned opposite the Hollendischur Spur. As the British Army increased in size it gradually took over from the French heading northwards towards Ypres.

The trenches the HAC moved into had been built by the French and were little more than ditches filled with liquid mud. There was no wire or any other type of protection in front of them and there were no communication trenches. This meant that the only way into the front line was by crossing a sea of mud in the open leaving the men totally exposed to German fire. The parapets offered little protection against the bullets which passed easily through them. In some parts of the trench the parapet was only chest high and the men had to spend the day sitting on the floor of the wet muddy trench, sometimes on the rotting bodies of dead Frenchmen whose corpses had been there several weeks. The German line was only 100 yards away and completely dominated the area.

They were finally relieved by the Royal Scots Fusiliers on 12 December. The Adjutant, Captain Whyte and Captain Gibson, Lieutenant Byron and the doctor, were all very sick and the remaining men exhausted and suffering from exposure and frostbite. The three days in the trenches had cost the Battalion 12 officers and 250 men.

The Battalion continued to fight on the front line throughout the next few months during the 2nd Battle of Ypres. When the Germans broke through on the north of the Ypres salient, opening up a gap of about eight miles, it was considered highly likely they would try to break through to St Eloi, probably with the use of gas.

Now 7th Brigade made preparations to withdraw, leaving instructions that the HAC were to hold trenches P1 and P2 to the last man in the event of an attack. On the night of the anticipated attack a mine went off under RB trench which was then occupied by the Northumberland Fusiliers of 9th Brigade with the Liverpool Scottish in support. The Liverpool Scottish immediately retaliated with machine and rifle fire onto the enemy parapets and nothing further happened. However, during one of their rest periods, the HAC in billets in Dickebusch were heavily shelled and A Company lost three more men with another nineteen injured. Nearly all those from the HAC who died during this time were buried in the garden behind Elzenwalle Chateau.

On 3 June, 3rd Division was relieved by 85th Brigade and they moved out of the lines to Ouderdom. Two days later 7th Brigade was sent to the ramparts of Ypres to relieve the 7th Cavalry Brigade. As the HAC were the lead Battalion they were expected to move into Ypres during daylight. The area was under continual enemy observation so the CO tried to have the timings changed. Unfortunately he was unsuccessful and the HAC came under heavy sustained shelling as they approached the Lille Gate. The Battalion was meant to relieve the 3rd Dragoon Guard, but as the shelling and firing intensified and the ramparts were bombarded with salvos of 5.9s (150mm) from German field howitzers they were understandably reluctant to leave the relative safety of their positions. This meant it was impossible to get everyone under cover and the HAC lost several more men, either killed or wounded. As they finally entered the town they were met with total devastation. Everywhere they looked fires were burning out of control, the acrid black smoke mingling with the smell from rotting corpses and fractured sewage pipes.

Pte John Thompson.

Three days later they were sent back to the front line, relieving the 1st Wiltshires in the Hooge pocket at the point of the salient. The Battalion left Ypres in Companies at intervals of ten minutes via the Salle Port, a narrow culvert under the ramparts near the Menin Gate that was just big enough for a man to lead his horse through. Somewhat surprisingly they reached the leafy glade of Zouave Wood with no casualties. At this time the woods were still full of trees and shrubs and the air was filled with the sound of birds singing. Within two months there would be nothing left but tree stumps.

They were relieved by the 5th Border Regiment three days later and returned to the Lille Gate, this time under cover of a mist which hid their movements. They counted themselves lucky in that casualties had been light with only one man killed and eleven wounded.

On arrival they found that the whole of 3rd Division was now resting, but this would not last long.

Chapter 18

Queen's Westminster Rifles

On 1 March 1914 the Queen's Westminster Rifles held a practice mobilization at Battalion HQ in Buckingham Gate as part of the normal training of all Territorial Forces. They had no idea how soon it would be before the practice became real.

The Territorial Force began every year on 1 November with a progressive training scheme in preparation for the annual fourteen-day training that took place in August under either Division or Brigade. During winter the training was mainly confined to marching through the London streets with some occasional miniature range work and lectures at Battalion HQ. But once spring arrived exercises were carried out in Richmond Park and other open spaces around London. In addition there was frequent Sunday and weekend tactical training for officers with more elementary tactical training for NCOs. An important part of this training was in musketry and in the years before the war the Queen Westminster Rifles were consistently highly placed in the musketry returns from the district.

In Easter 1914, as in most other years, the Battalion was attached to a Battalion of the King's Royal Rifle Corps (KRRC) in the barracks at Aldershot for musketry and field training. The annual training camp was designed to cover a wide range of military requirements. For the Battalion two other camps that provided useful experience were the one in Minster in the Isle of Sheppey in 1911 where they took place in large scale manoeuvres and the one in Abergavenny in 1913. Here they were marched to a deserted place in the Welsh mountains called Tal-y-Maes where they bivouacked for several nights and carried out strenuous training in attacks, outposts and defence. The approaches to the camp were so steep that none of the transport could get there except the Battalion wagons. All baggage and supplies had to be manhandled several miles over rough terrain, perfect training for what was to come.

On the morning of 2 August the men boarded a train at Paddington for Perham Down, Salisbury Plain, for the annual camp. By now rumours were rife that war had been declared and mobilization was imminent. An air of excitement and anticipation was everywhere so when news reached them later that evening that French patrols had crossed the German border cheers were heard throughout the camp.

At 9.30 pm the Battalion was ordered back to London, arriving at Paddington in the early hours of the following morning. On arrival at HQ the men were sent on leave with orders to be ready for immediate mobilization. The next day war was declared and the Battalion mobilized with strength of 511 under the command of Lieutenant Colonel R. Shoolbred. However, now war was declared, the old members of the Battalion immediately flocked to HQ and in less than forty-eight hours the Battalion was up to full strength. The men reported to their Companies in the playground of the Endowments School in Palace Street, Westminster. After their kit was examined and notes made of any deficiencies they proceeded to HQ where they had a medical examination and particulars of their next of kin were taken.

The scene in the drill hall was one of mass activity as recruits poured in and mobile stores of every description were collected and issued under the direction of QM, Major A. S. Pridmore. Machine-gun belts were fitted and ball ammunition doled out to the men. Even the issue of identity disks and orders for immediate move did not dampen the spirits of the men who couldn't wait to get into the action. The Battalion transport for annual camp was provided by department store James Shoolbred and Company and they were also to provide the war transport. With everything ready to go the men were then billeted out at the Endowed Schools. Concerns about the serious probability of a German landing on the east coast now the BEF was in France prompted new orders on 5 August. They were to be ready for an immediate move which meant sleeping in their boots and puttees and two days later they marched to the Tower of London to draw their rifles from the armoury.

At the outbreak of war they were part of the 4th Infantry Brigade of the 2nd London Division. The Brigade consisted of The Kensingtons (13th London), The London Scottish (14th London), The Prince of Wales' Own Civil Service Rifles (15th London) and the Queen's Westminster Rifles (16th London). Commanded by Colonel F. J. Heyworth they were known as 'The Grey Brigade' because of the colour of the uniforms of the constituent units.

By 16 August Battalion HQ was established in a village school in Leverstock Green near Hemel Hempstead and the companies were billeted on various farms in the area where they carried out a minimum of seven hours training a day except Sunday which was a rest day and Saturday which was half day. All training was carried out with a full regulation pack and some 250 rounds of ammunition. Soon the men were at the peak of their physical fitness but unfortunately the exercise and good food meant many could no longer fit into their uniforms.

Finally, on 27 October, they received the order they were waiting for. They would embark for the continent on 30 October. As they readied themselves to go, the Battalion was now completely re-equipped with new rifles known as Long Charger-Loading Magazine Lee Enfields. However, these were not adapted to fire the new Mark VII cartridges which had a pointed bullet and every short rifle was earmarked for the Regular army. There was no time for the men to practise on their new rifles or even to fire sighting tests so Sergeant A. G. Fulton, his father, Armourer Sergeant G. E. Fulton and other expert shots tried to sight in as many as possible before they left.

The khaki uniforms available for mobilization were of very poor quality and incapable of withstanding even moderate wear so the Battalion had arranged for a supply of better material and received permission to use it. But they were still not ready so the men went in their pre-war kit which, despite being old and patched, was still considered of better quality than the mobilization uniforms. Their transport wagons were also replaced with government-issue wagons and limbers and they picked up new water carts and a travelling field kitchen at Dartford.

They left Leverstock Green in two detachments at 9.00 am and 10.00 am on 1 November to the strains of *Auld Lang Syne* played by the Regimental band. The Battalion now numbered 892 officers and other ranks and at 2.00 pm they caught the train at Watford for Southampton Docks. They met up with the Liverpool Scottish and embarked together on *The Maiden* to Le Havre where they spent one night in the rest camp about the town.

The next morning their Sam Browne belts were replaced with webbing, their swords replaced with walking sticks and maps of Northern France and Flanders were issued to each company.

Their first destination was given as Rouen but that was quickly changed to St Omer. Their route was circuitous and on a brief stop at Calais that night some thirty men stepped off the train to boil hot Oxo for the men in Dixies on the platform. Without warning the French train pulled out leaving them stranded and the men on the train without their hot drink. The driver refused to halt the train or go back so the men went without and those left behind had to be bought up by goods train some time later.

They spent four days training at St Omer and then marched fifteen miles to Hazebrouck and then onto Bailleul. Their progress was hampered by the crowded roads crammed with refugees, old people riding in carts, younger ones walking and pushing prams piled high with various motely assortments of household goods.

The Battalion now had to reorganize from an eight-Company system to the four-Company system used by the regular army. All Territorial Forces had to do this once deployed as they were not allowed to do so at home. This caused considerable confusion while the commanders and the men adjusted. At Bailleul they were billeted in a large convent that had previously been used as a hospital for the Indian Troops. From here they could hear the unceasing artillery and watch the flashes from the guns lighting up the sky over Ypres.

On 12 November they marched to Erquingham, a small village about a mile and a half southwest of Armentieres. The roads were even more packed with refugees fleeing the heavy shelling in Chapelle d'Armentieres, a suburb of Armentieres. This part of the town had been particularly badly hit with parts of it on fire and dense smoke rising from the burning houses. The occupants of the village were delighted to see them and many told tales of the cruel German occupation where their food, forage and horses had been seized without payment. They treated the British as their saviours and made the men as comfortable as they could.

In the afternoon they were lined up in single rank along the narrow street with the Durham Light Infantry in the village for an inspection by Field Marshal Earl Roberts. He was an elderly man but seemed in good health as he stopped and spoke to several of the men. Two days later he was dead.

The Battalion was now in 6th Division under Major General J. L. Kier, having been posted to 18th Infantry Brigade commanded by Brigadier General W. N. Congreve VC. The Brigade consisted of 1st Battalion the Princess of Wales' Own (West Yorkshire Regt), 1st Battalion the East Yorkshire Regiment, 2nd Battalion the Sherwood Foresters (Nottinghamshire and Derbyshire Regiment), 2nd Battalion Durham Light Infantry. On 13 November Division and Brigade officers attended a conference at Brigade HQ when they were informed by General Kier that all trenches were to be held at all costs and there would be no retirement without express orders.

During the next few days the men had some musketry practice in a hastily constructed range just outside the village and spent much of their time constructing a new defensive line to the east of Erquingham. An occasional plane flew over and was fired at with the pom-pom gun (QF one-pounder gun). It was quite useless as the plane was out of range, but it was a novelty at that time and it broke the monotony.

On 16 November the Battalion came under fire for the first time while carrying out work for Brigade HQ which was based at Calvart Farm only a few hundred yards behind the firing line. This work consisted of carrying fascines and taking material from HQ up to the waterlogged trenches and although there were frequent bursts of rifle and machine gun fire there were no casualties. The next day they moved up to billets at Gris-Pot and La Vesee. The civilian inhabitants had left their homes hurriedly and only take portable possessions. In some places the chickens and rabbits were still in the tiny backyards of the cottages. That night No 2 Company was due to support 16th Infantry Brigade so they reported to Calvart Farm soon after dark. One platoon was employed as a carrying party to the front line; the remainder dug a communication trench forward from the farm at La Flamanderie. The enemy began shelling the farm and within minutes they had come under heavy rifle fire too. This went on for about twenty minutes. The carrying party got under cover and the digging party lay down in the trench even though it was only eighteen inches deep. Miraculously no one was hit. The night had turned bitterly cold and in the morning the ground was white.

That night 18th Infantry Brigade had extended their front by 700 yards and the following night No 1 Company the Queen Westminster Rifles relieved a company of 1st Battalion East Yorkshires in the trenches facing La Houssoie to the south of Rue de Bois. This was about 300 yards from the enemy front line. They received a warm welcome from the East Yorks who were exhausted after several months of heavy fighting. They also gave them a lot of help. This ranged from explaining the duties of sentries in the trenches to the art of keeping the charcoal fire alight in a bully beef tin and cooking a dinner over it in a mess tin. The only fuel available in the trenches was a small piece of charcoal each man took in with him for cooking and warmth.

The night started warm and damp but it soon turned to heavy snow and in the morning the ground all around was a white wasteland. The stout wooden poles of the wire entanglements stood in stark relief to the frozen root field giving a false sense of security and glistening in the icy air. They were relieved by No 2 Company on 20 November for forty-eight hours and then by No 3 Company. The weather was now bitterly cold and the bolts of the rifles began to stick. One of the reasons for this was the lack of rifle oil so the men resorted to using bacon fat as a substitute. To prevent the bolts sticking sentries were told to work the bolts of their own rifles and those of the reliefs every fifteen minutes as a precaution.

On 24 November the Queen Westminster Rifles went into the trenches as a unit for the first time, relieving the East Yorks. These trenches, a 600-yard front, were in Number 1 section on the right of 18th Brigade line which ran from a point due west of La Houssoie to the Boulogne-Lille Road, northwest of Macquart. The defence was a single line of very narrow fire trenches about four to six feet deep with lengths of a lateral communication trench dug in places a few yards behind. There were only two communication trenches at this time, a deep one of about eighty yards long linking Battalion HQ to the front line, and another on the extreme of the Battalion front. The approach to all other parts of the line was across open ground. The Support Company were accommodated in a series of shelters at the side of the road near Battalion HQ. The shelters for the troops in the frontline trenches consisted of a number of hollows scooped out under the parapet. The roofs were supported by wooden struts. The entrance was about 2ft 6in high and the shelter held between one and three men. They were universally known as 'funk holes', 'cubby holes' or 'bug hatches'. The trenches were not re-vetted as there was no material for doing so and sandbags were non-existent. The wire was a single curtain fence with a narrow belt of trip wire a few yards in front. Fortunately for the Queen's Westminster Rifles the Germans had been beaten to a standstill so even though the line was weak it was enough to prevent them from moving forward.

Trench routine was simple. Sentries were one man per section per day, and one man in every three by night. They would remain on duty for two hours. At night the men could expect to get four hours of sleep out of six, but the nights were rarely that peaceful. Most nights there were alarms with the Battalion having to 'stand to'. Each man stood at his post in the trench ready for any emergency. Initially the rifles, with bayonets fixed and five rounds of ammunition in the magazine and none in the chamber, were left resting on the parapet at night. But as the weather became increasingly cold the men were ordered to sleep with their rifles to prevent the oil from freezing. The whole Battalion would 'stand to' just as it was getting dark and again at dawn after which they would be dismissed. There were rifle inspections in the morning, the officers were always on duty and NCOs patrolled the trenches frequently to ensure sentries were at their posts and alert and everything else was in order. Days were spent working in the trenches and at night working parties were sent out to repair the wire and do any other work above ground that needed doing.

On 25 November a thaw set in followed by heavy rain. The trenches began to crumble and one collapsed killing Rifleman Brooks of 4 Company. His brother who was sleeping next to him had his leg badly crushed. At this time most of the shelling came from the enemy. Due to a severe shortage the British guns were strictly rationed as to the number of shells they could fire and they were restricted to special targets. However rifle fire was continuous. Both the enemy parapets and the British were provided with loopholes. These formed a favourite target. A large number of wooden loopholes for fitting into the parapet arrived and these proved to be very dangerous. Not only did they provide a useful target but bullets which struck the loophole were deflected into the trenches. After there had been several casualties orders were given not to use the loopholes but for sentries to look over the top instead. This led to an increase in men being hit in the head. It wasn't until steel loopholes and periscopes were introduced that casualty rates of sentries began to fall.

The Battalion's first tour in the trenches had lasted eleven days with three men killed and ten wounded. They returned to the trenches again on 9 December for another nine days, relieving the Durham Light Infantry in No 3 Section opposite Wez Macquart. The conditions were even worse than before. Drainage in the low-lying ground was impossible and bailing the water out was exhausting and ineffective. After nine days they had four days' rest before again returning to the same trenches on 23 December, this time relieving the 1st Battalion Royal Fusiliers. The water was waist deep and only those lucky enough to find a dry plank could get any sleep. The next day enemy snipers were very active killing one man and wounding four others. As night fell lights could be seen on the enemy trenches which they fired at. The lights went out but there was no answering fire. As the evening wore on lights again began to appear all along the length of the German line and then they could hear singing as the Germans launched into carols, songs and finally finished with the German and Austrian National anthems. The singing echoed across the land and when it finished the Germans began calling and cheering. The rest of the night passed without a shot being fired. Christmas Day began with a thick mist hovering over the frozen white ground. The Germans began to sing at daybreak and the Battalion soon joined in.

'Good morning Englishmen, Merry Christmas, you no shoot, we no shoot' – the shouts echoed down the line. At one point it was arranged for a representative of either side to meet halfway and gifts of wine, cake, chocolate and cigarettes were exchanged. One German saluted and explained that he was an officer and he came from Catford! The same sort of thing was happening on the front of the units on either flank and on the right a formal truce was agreed to allow each side to bury its dead. Slowly the mist cleared and to their astonishment they could see Germans standing on their parapet. Once they had heard that a truce had been agreed the British did the same. Permission was given for the men to go out although they were not allowed to go more than halfway. They were also to make sure none of the enemy approached the British lines. The men returned to their trenches for Christmas dinner but in the afternoon groups of men from both sides could be seen chatting and laughing and exchanging gifts. The Germans were healthy and well-fed and from Saxon Regiment 107th. They had no idea where they were or what was happening in the war. Some believed they were near Paris others thought that the Germans had reached London. Others spoke of their hatred for the Prussians and warned the men not to trust them. The men withdrew back to their lines before dark and a note came across from the Germans to say that at midnight the officer would fire his automatic pistol and the war would start again.

On 1 January they relieved the Durhams on the left of the 18th Infantry Brigade. The trenches covered about half a mile with the left edge resting on the River Lys opposite the village of Frelinghien. But by the end of the first week heavy rain was beginning to make the trench untenable. The river continued to rise over the next few days and the men fought a losing battle against the collapsing parapet and collapsing barricades. On 8 January the enemy made an attempt to flood the British lines, but was defeated when a party under Lieutenant W. M. Henderson-Scott, a mining engineer by profession, spent all night piling up sandbags. Sleep was out of the question, everyone was permanently wet through and many of the men became ill. Because of a shortage of doctors they were not allowed to come into the trenches so the sick had to struggle back to Houplines at night. The Battalion was very low on numbers so only the sickest men were taken out of the line, the rest spending a night at the dressing station and having to return to the trenches at dawn. By the end of January one officer and six other ranks had died and a further twenty other ranks were wounded.

On 1 February the new draft of three officers and 244 other ranks from the 2nd Battalion arrived. On 18 February they were joined by a half-Company of the 3rd Battalion (Toronto) Canadian Regiment who were in the line for the first time to be instructed in trench warfare. They were followed the next day by the other half. The rest of the month was spent alternating between trenches and reserve but at least their equipment had improved. Each man now had a warm, soft service cap and fur waistcoat and there was a good supply of waterproof capes and gum boots. There was also a small number of Very lights and pistols available in the trenches. But casualties continued to mount and by the end of February they had lost a further five other ranks killed and eighteen other ranks wounded.

In March artillery fire from both sides increased and bombardments of the Battalion front with rifle and heavier grenades was an almost daily occurrence causing several casualties. By the end of the month they had lost another officer and eleven other ranks were killed with twenty other ranks wounded. April, by contrast was relatively peaceful. Work was done to improve the defences and the mining operations begun by a platoon of miners from the Sherwood Foresters in March was continued. April casualties were three other ranks killed and seventeen other ranks wounded.

The Battalion was relieved on 1 May by the Sherwood Foresters and went into billets at Houplines and Le Bizet. The following day the whole Battalion was billeted at Houplines with one company occupying the reserve trenches at night. This was the first time the whole Battalion had been at rest for four months. But they would not enjoy their peace for long as on 3 May the village was heavily shelled in retaliation for the explosion of a mine at Frelinghien. The church was destroyed and some of the debris destroyed the Battalion machine guns. There were many casualties among both the troops and the civilians. The Battalion suffered three dead and eight wounded.

The men were treated very well by the villagers who had refused to leave their homes. On returning from the trenches they found hot coffee and some other luxury waiting for them, their washing was often done and some even had beds with clean sheets on, a real luxury after being in the trenches. They relieved the Sherwood Foresters in the trenches north and south of the river on 7 May and then remained there until relieved by the West Yorks on 14 May.

They paid one last visit to the trenches on the Armentieres front on 26 May before the 18th Infantry Brigade was replaced by the 27th Division. The Queen Westminsters handed their portion of the line over to a battalion of Canadian Territorials and joined the rest of the Brigade in marching to Bailleul, arriving at 3am on 29 May. A further four men were killed and 114 wounded in May. Out of the line for the first time in many months, 18th Infantry Brigade was now billeted in the town. Later that day the Brigade was inspected by the Commander in Chief, Field Marshal Sir John French. The following day at 5.00 am the 18th Infantry Brigade left for the Ypres salient. They marched via St Jans Cappel, Berthen and Boeschepe to the area between Wippenhoek and Poperinghe where they stopped for the night. The next day they went by bus to Vlamertinghe and then marched through Ypres, which was still smouldering from the German bombardment a week earlier. Here they relieved the 9th Infantry Brigade which was holding the line between the Ypres-Roulers railway and the Ypres- Verlorenhoek road.

The Westminsters first went into the support trenches over the Ypres-Verlorenhoek road east of Potijze but on 2 June moved further south relieving the East Yorks and a battalion of Royal Scots in support trenches north of the Ypres-Roulers railway. For the next two weeks they suffered the monotony of trench routine. Despite the enemy heavy bombardments they did not have the means to retaliate effectively so remained largely inactive. On 4 June several HE shells almost demolished the support trench leaving nine men dead and twelve wounded. Later that night B and D Companies moved forward to the fire trenches east of Potijze leaving the other two companies in support.

They were relieved on 8 June by the East Yorks and after two days in hutments west of Ypres they moved to dugouts on the east bank of the Yser Canal. Because the trenches were in a dreadful state, the communication trench full of water and the parapets and traverses collapsing, the men spent their rest period rebuilding the defences. By the time they had done this it was 16 June.

Chapter 19

42nd Brigade 14th (Light Division)[20]

5th Battalion King's Shropshire Light Infantry

On 6 August, two days after war had been declared, Captain G. A. Deme-Murray, Captain R. Fort, Second Lieutenant R. H. Shears and thirty other ranks of the 1st Battalion, left Tipperary to form the nucleus of the 1st Service Battalion. Major M. H. Smith was appointed to command and men were accommodated in hutments at Blackdown Camp in Aldershot. The Battalion left the depot by Companies, the last company leaving on 27 August 1914.

There was no real recruiting in the ordinary sense of the word, just a printed notice signed Kitchener, Field Marshal, informing those who read it that 'Our King and Our Country needed its able-bodied men in this great emergency'. Thousands of men from Shropshire, Herefordshire and the bordering Welsh counties flocked to the Regimental depot at Shrewsbury. The 1st Service Battalion was designated the 5th King's Shropshire Light Infantry and allotted to 42 Brigade of 14th Light Division. The Brigade Commander was Brigadier General C. J. Markham and other Battalions in the Brigade were the 5th Ox and Bucks, the 9th KRR and 9th RB. The Divisional Commander was Major General V. Couper.

Drafts arrived at Blackdown at intervals of a few days and Companies were quickly formed; A Company first, followed by the other three. At first they were without equipment and uniforms so there was great excitement when C Company arrived at the depot in khaki with rifles and equipment. But it was short-lived. The Retreat from Mons had taken its toll and their uniforms and equipment were taken away to be sent to France.

The weather was hot and training began at once. At first, because everyone was so keen, they trained hard every day including Sundays. But after two weeks Sunday became a day of rest and the training during the week was modified to suit the men's capabilities. Some officers came from the OTC (Officer Training Corps) at Shrewsbury School, but most of the men were ignorant of military matters. The Marines lent some Sergeants to help with training but most of the officers and NCOs learnt whilst teaching.

---

20. I have not included these Battalions in the previous order of precedence because they are from a different Division and did not take part in the battle. However, they did suffer casualties on their way up to the lines so I thought it was important to include them as well.

From Blackdown the Brigade moved to North Camp, Aldershot, sharing Malplaquet Barracks with the 5th Battalion Oxfordshire and Buckinghamshire. On 27 November they marched sixteen miles to Chiddingfold in Surrey. Training was now more advanced and clothing and equipment was gradually completed. On 23 January, together with thousands of other troops, they were inspected by Lord Kitchener and a representative of the French Government at Witley. To show the French how well equipped they were the men were not allowed to wear their greatcoats, so they stood in a blizzard without their coats throughout the whole inspection.

On 19 May Major J. G .Forbes, Lieutenant S. G. Beaumont, Lieutenant J. C. B. Firth, 109 other ranks, seventy-nine horses and mules and all Battalion transport sailed for France. They were followed on the next day by twenty-eight officers, 797 other ranks and Colonel H. M. Smith. They left Aldershot on two trains at 5.20 am and 5.45 am to Folkestone, went on to Boulogne and from there to Osterhove rest camp on the outskirts of the town.

On 21 May they were on their way to Cassel. They had a long and tiring march to Erkelsbrugge where they were billeted in Companies on local farms. They stayed there for six days before moving to Eecke, sixteen miles away. On 30 May, A and B Companies and the transport went ahead to Dickesbusche followed by the rest of the Battalion. The Battalion was now addressed by General Sir Charles Ferguson to whose division it was attached for instruction. On the same day two Companies moved to some dugouts near Ypres and in the evening the Battalion came under fire for the first time. There were some new trenches being constructed at Zillebeke, not far from Hill 60. Colonel H. Smith and 550 other ranks went up to help with the digging which was being done at night. However the Germans were constantly throwing up Very lights and although the diggers were not visible to them they kept up a continuous unaimed rifle fire resulting in the death of Sergeant A. R. Diss and the wounding of three others. There was more shelling on 1 June and 2 June but fortunately no casualties.

On 3 June the Battalion moved back to Canada Huts near Dickebusch where they remained for three days. However, every night a proportion of the men were involved in digging and this left another two dead and ten wounded. On 6 June they marched to Locre to experience life in the trenches. The line here, in front of Locre, was manned by a Brigade of the Sherwood Foresters (TF) whose HQ was at Locre. The Brigade band played every evening and after their experiences in Ypres it seemed like a peaceful place. Dickebusch was still undamaged at that time although German shells did fall quite close to the town several times a day.

At this time C and D Companies went up past Kemmel to the trenches, D Company attached to the 6th Royal Scots Fusiliers and C Company attached to the 8th Royal Scots Fusiliers. They spent two days in the trenches before being relieved by A and B Companies.

On 11 June A and B Companies returned to Locre and the next day marched back to Canada Huts. Two days later they marched to huts just south of Vlamertinghe.

The 1st Battalion passed through Vlamertinghe on route to the trenches and the 5th lined the streets to cheer them on. The first draft of ninety-nine men arrived that evening.

9th Battalion King's Royal Rifle Corps

The Battalion was formed during the early days of August 1914 and was initially stationed at Blackdown Camp before subsequently moving to Blenheim Barracks Aldershot, which they shared with the 9th Battalion Rifle Brigade. In November both Battalions were moved to Petworth.

On 22 January the Battalion marched to Witley, a camp that was under construction and only half completed. The night was spent in huts with no windows or doors and snow falling steadily outside. The following day they joined the rest of 14th Division at Hawkley and after standing to attention for five hours in a snow blizzard the men began the five-mile march back to Witley. But the accommodation was so bad they decided to make their way back to Petworth. By now the weather had deteriorated even more and the snow was two feet thick in places. It was pitch black and men and horses were slipping and sliding on the frozen ground with several falling over.

On 25 March the Battalion moved to Talavera Barracks in Aldershot and more training in musketry and firing on the range. Once this training was complete they reverted back to marching and digging and on 11 May they received their orders to mobilize. On 19 May the Transport with the Transport Officer and Machine Gun Officer left Aldershot for Havre. They were followed the next day by the rest of the Battalion who arrived in Boulogne at 2.00 am on 21 May. They arrived at Cassel the next day and were joined by their transport. By the time they reached Zeggars Cappel their strength was 29 officers and 842 other ranks.

On 30 May they marched to Dickebusch, four miles southwest of Ypres and the next day they were addressed by Sir Charles Ferguson, the Commanding Officer of 2nd Corps. At 7.00 pm that night they marched three miles to a point on the Yser Canal, one and a half miles southwest of Ypres. Platoons marched at 100 paces apart and progress was slow. It was still light and they didn't want the enemy aircraft to see where they were going. The skies above them were full of their own planes dodging German anti-aircraft shells and it wasn't until the light fell and the planes returned to the ground that they moved on. There was no smoking or talking as they walked the next couple of miles and then halted.

Their first task was to dig a trench. Compared to digging in the Petworth clay this was comparatively easy. Behind them the sky was lit up by the flames from the burning buildings in Ypres. All around them was the sound of shelling, and their ears were deafened by the shriek of the shells as they passed and the ground was pitted with shell holes. They dug until 1am and then returned to their billets, the next two nights were spent the same way but they were lucky and took no casualties. On their right the King's Shropshire Light Infantry were also digging but they were not so lucky suffering several casualties.

On 3 June, B and C Companies moved into some dugouts in Ridge Wood while A and B Companies were in nearby farms. The following night they again escaped casualties when Lieutenant Stow, fifty NCOs and men from D Company took some stores up to the frontline trenches. Two days later, as reports reached them that the Germans were massing near Ypres, the 7th Battalion took over their dugouts and they returned to Canada Huts.

It was now time for them to experience life in the trenches so C Company was attached to the KOYLI while D Company was attached to the West Kents. The trenches here were awful, in many places only breastworks. They had been dug in a hurry by the French on their running fight to the sea, there were many dead Frenchmen buried in the parapets and the stench was dreadful.

On 11 June they marched to Vlamertinghe to join back up with 42nd Brigade. That night Vlamertinghe was shelled and the next day was spent hastily digging dugouts. This was just as well as that night they were shelled again, this time with high explosive. Fortunately for the Battalion they were not the target this time as the shells were aimed at the railway line a quarter of a mile to their left.

On 15 June they marched out on to the Ypres Road round the outskirts of Ypres to the railway embankment just north of the Lille Gate. They spent the night digging themselves in to the embankment and at dawn the next day lay down to try and grab a little rest.

9th (Service) Battalion Rifle Brigade

The 9th (Service) Battalion Rifle Brigade was formed on 21 August 1914 at Winchester and billeted in Blenheim Barracks in Aldershot. In November, after learning the basics of drill and discipline, they moved to Petworth. They now had their uniforms, and rifles and their days and nights were spent training.

In January they marched to Hawkley where the whole of the 14th Division was drawn up for a mass inspection by Lord Kitchener and the French War Minister, M. Millerand. The weather was dreadful, the roads thick with snow which delayed the arrival of Lord Kitchener and his guest. The whole Division was kept waiting for five hours in a snow blizzard so they were glad when the inspection was over and they were able to march the five miles back to Witley.

At 10.00 am on 19 May three officers and 106 other ranks, plus all the 1st Line Transport, left Aldershot and embarked at Southampton for Havre, arriving the following day. That evening the remainder of the Battalion left Aldershot, crossing from Folkestone to Boulogne in the early hours of 21 May. They went into the rest camp at Ostrohove at 5.30 am and at 4.20 pm marched to Pont de Briques Station where they caught the

Unknown Rifleman

train from Havre which was carrying the rest of the Battalion. They arrived at Cassel at midnight and with great difficulty, due to the shortness of the platform, the Battalion detrained. From there they marched to billets at Zeggers Cappel arriving the next morning. On 30 May they went into huts south of Zevecoten and the following day, together with the 5th Battalion Ox and Bucks were addressed by General Sir E. Fergussen. That evening they began work on entrenchments.

The following few days were spent marching eleven and a half miles to the trenches to work and then back. On 3 June they came under fire for the first time in the camp at Zevecoten. Two days later they were informed that from the following day the Battalion would be attached to the 137th Infantry Brigade for instruction. That night half the machine-gun section reported to the HQ of the 1/5 Battalion South Staffordshire Regiment and went into their trenches. The following day the Battalion marched to Bailleul and went into billets; A Company was attached to the 1/5th Battalion South Staffordshire and B Company was attached to 1/5th Battalion North Staffordshire Regiment. They spent the next two days in the trenches and were then relieved by C and D Companies on 9 June.

On 11 June the whole Battalion was back in billets at Bailleul, from here they marched to M17.6 where they camped. The following day they were on the move again to H14 and from there to the trenches between two railway embankments on 15 June.

5th (Service Battalion) Oxford and Buckinghamshire Light Infantry

The 5th Battalion was raised in August 1914 at Camberley and was up to strength by 8 September. It was commanded and partially staffed by Regular officers and non-commissioned officers and ex-non-commissioned officers of the Regiment. After a short time it moved to Aldershot, and then to Cranleigh. As part of the 42nd Infantry Brigade, 14th (Light) Division, it was inspected by the King on 26 September. In February 1915 they moved to Salamanca Barracks in Aldershot and proceeded to France on 20 May 1915, landing in Boulogne the following day.

They carried out some training in trench warfare in the area south of Ypres and commemorated the King's birthday on 3 June with a rapid burst of fire on the German lines. This was carried out by each trench garrison at 'morning stand to' but there was no reply from the Germans. On 6 June British miners detected a German tunnel being dug towards them. A counter mine was successfully prepared and the German mine blown up destroying their tunnel. The British tunnel was then maintained as a defensive measure.

From 10 June to 14 June the Battalion was attached to 14th Division and provided work parties with the 7th (Service) Battalion Rifle Brigade to help improve the trenches.

Chapter 20

Preparations

The British Tommies marching past the Cloth Hall in Ypres on the night of the 15th June 1915 on their way to Bellewaarde. Illustration by Dawn Monks http://www.dawnmonksillustrations.co.uk/

The Royal Saxon Reserve Jager Battalion No. 26

'Following the German attack of 25th May 1915 the frontline activity became greatly reduced and finally it was possible to allow troops time to rest and also to focus on training again.

The entire 53th Reserve-Division (R.D.), responsible for the right-hand of the XXVII. Reserve-Korps' (R.K.) sector had been pulled out as army reserve. The 54th R.D. took over the whole Korps' sector and they were also able to assign troops to reserves. During the nights of 6th-7th and 7th-8th June Reserve-Jäger-Battalion 26 was relieved by R.I.R. 248 and drawn back to Molenhoek to become divisional reserve.

Besides enjoying boozy beer evenings, the spare time was mainly spent to regain combat readiness. Alas, this included alarm practice during inconvenient hours, nobody's favourite occupation, but this became part of our daily routine.'

Heinz Lehmann. The Royal Saxon Reserve
Jager Battalion No. 26. Dresden 1923

Monday 14 June

At the close of the Battles of Ypres, the German trenches between the Menin Road and the Ypres-Roulers railway formed a salient. The British front line was positioned on the longest part of the copse that lay north of the Menin Road and crossed open land to bisect the wood immediately south of Ypres. From opposite Hooge it ran just south of the Menin Road to just east of Birr Cross Road, then turned sharply northwards skirting the eastern edges of the Cambridge Road to the angle formed by the latter and the railway, where, for some 300 yards, it followed the latter eastwards, turning again sharply northwest.

In the previous month the Germans had taken Chateau Wood, Bellewaarde Lake and Farm and, more importantly perhaps, Bellewaarde Ridge. This lay behind British lines and gave the enemy a good observation point over the British lines. The German front line ran along the farthest edge of Y Wood to the top of Railway Wood and was linked by a web of communication trenches leading to two heavily defended trench lines, one halfway up the slope, the other on the top of the ridge itself.

Hooge Chateau was in German hands, but the chateau stables were occupied by the British as was the battered ruined village of Hooge which lay at the southern point of this salient. Just south of the Ypres-Roulers railway the eastern edges of Railway Wood were held by the enemy, and the western edges by British troops of the 3rd Division. It would be their task to straighten the line and capture it. The area between the two woods was open with little or no cover and this would make the assault difficult.

On 14 June the Commanding Officer of the Honourable Artillery was summoned to a Brigade conference. Rumours had already been circulating that an attack by 13th Division was imminent and this confirmed it. The plan was to straighten the line between Hooge Chateau and Railway Wood, a front of around 1,000 yards. The assault was to be delivered by 9th Brigade supported by 7th Brigade with 8th Brigade in reserve. As soon as the German front line and support line had been captured the HAC was to follow the 1st Lincolns into the assault.

Their advance would be through Y Wood with three Companies of the HAC to occupy and reconstruct the captured trenches and one Company to dig a communication trench back from the captured trenches in Y Wood to the original line. It was impressed on them the importance of not allowing themselves to be deflected from their role or diverted by any other side shows. The artillery bombardment would start at 2.50 am and lift at 4.15 am which was when the assault would take place. The date was to be 16 June 1915.

There was considerable optimism about the impending assault. To ensure communications were not interrupted the lines back to Brigade HQ were laid in triplicate, a system of signals was organized and a pigeon service arranged. Meanwhile, 6 Squadron RFC were allotted for reconnaissance and artillery spotting. No 6 Squadron RFC was formed on 31 January 1914 at Farnborough and its first Squadron Leader was Major J. H. W. Becke. Its motto was *Oculi Exercitus –*

'the eyes of the army' – and one of its more famous members was Hugh Dowding, Commander of RAF Fighter Command in the 1940 Battle of Britain.

Eight rows of jumping off trenches were to be prepared to allow succeeding troops to advance quicker. The assault would be helped by the guns of the French 36th Corps who would fire towards Pilken to prevent German reinforcements coming up to the line.

The King's (Liverpool) Regiment

> 'On the evening of 14th June Major A.S. Anderson proceeded to Railway Wood (which is situated West of Bellewaarde Farm and North of Hooge) from which point the 9th Brigade were to attack on the morning of the 16th. He took with him 2 men per Company to act as markers and also 2 Cyclists.'

Tuesday 15 June

1st Battalion Honourable Artillery Company

On 15 June the CO of HAC held a Battalion conference and explained the orders to all the officers and NCOs. Each Company had its sector of trench in Y Wood marked on the map with D Company on the right, B Company in the centre, C Company on the left and A Company detailed to make the communication trench. This was a very dangerous job as it meant digging in the open under continuous fire so the Company Commanders drew lots and it fell to Captain Lankester.

They left their bivouac at 5.30 pm and marched to Kreustaat which was just south of Ypres. While resting near the Chateau the Adjutant, Captain Walsh, was injured for the third time after receiving three wounds to the head. Captain Carnwath made sure he was treated by the dressing station and then dispatched in an ambulance while the rest of the Battalion moved on. Captain C.F. Osmond was appointed acting Adjutant by the OC.

They reached Lille Gate at about 10.30 pm and collected their guides from the 4th Middlesex. As the shelling did not appear to be too bad around Hell Fire Corner, Colonel Treffy decided it would be safer to use the road rather than across country so he gave the order to 'close up and step out'. To their relief the shelling stopped altogether and they marched in fours straight down the Menin Road until they met their Battalion guides who led the Companies into their correct positions in the trenches. Unfortunately, B Company, which was the rear Company, was delayed by another battalion for some minutes and Lieutenant Ayscough and four men were hit.

2nd Battalion South Lancashire

> '… these two companies had to work very hard as the trenches were required for immediate occupation by Units who were moving East of YPRES to take

part in operations near HOOGE. 'B' and 'C' Companies remained in reserve at YPRES. During this evening the whole of the Units of 3rd Division moved from their bivouacs, marching in an Easterly direction through YPRES, in preparation for the attack on enemy's line in vicinity of HOOGE. Beyond this moment there was very little activity in the sector.

The work on which 'A' and 'B' Companies were occupied was completed soon after midnight, when they withdrew to reserve at YPRES. Casualties – 4 other ranks wounded, 2 of whom died of wounds during the night.'

Battalion Diary

1st Battalion Lincolnshire Regiment

'The Battalion remained in bivouac resting during the day. The Battalion paraded at 4:15pm ready to march to the assembly trench Cambridge Rd south end. The order of march was D.C. Mgn. A and B companies. The machine gun detachment accompanied the left column of the brigade: – (5th Fusiliers, R Scots Fusiliers, Liverpool Scottish). The right 4th Royal Fusiliers formed the right column. The right column marched off from road junction H18 Central at 5:00pm and proceeded by the road through H13 H14 H15 H16 H17 & H23 to Kruisstraat, crossed the canal at bridge 13, thence through YPRES to the Lille Gate at 8:30pm continuing via railway track to x 10 x 02 Thence by MENIN Rd. Casualties 4 OR [other ranks] wounded. Fine summer weather.'

Battalion Diary

1/1st Cheshire Field Company R.E

'Day was spent preparing for attack on 16th. A guard of 1 NCO and 6 men which was on the pontoon bridge was relieved by 56 Company. As they were returning through Ypres a shell burst on the square and wounded 5 of the sappers and 1 sapper suffered from shell shock. Company left billets at 8 p.m. to take their place in the line of march into Assembly Trenches. No 1 section was attached to 1st Lincolns, No 3 to Liverpool Scottish, No's 2 and 4 to Royal Irish Rifles for the purpose of digging a CT (Communication Trench) from our present front to the captured trenches.'

Battalion Diary

2nd Battalion Royal Irish Rifles

'The Battalion paraded at 5.30 p.m. and marched to the Assembly Trenches between WITTEPOORT FARM and railway to support 9th Infantry Brigade in an attack on BELLWAARDE FARM SPUR. Strength:- 21 officers, 630 other ranks.'

Battalion Diary

At the King's (Liverpool) Regiment's camp the trench stores were laid out at various intervals around the field and after breakfast the men formed a long line and began collecting them from the two men at each pile of provisions. The line moved slowly, a platoon at a time. They all had two extra bandoliers of ammunition slung cross wise across their shoulders, two empty sandbags, a waterproof sheet and an extra days' food ration. Wire cutters were distributed, hand grenades to the bombers and shovels to the unlucky platoon detailed to carry them. Overcoats were rolled up and stowed on a waggon and packs were dumped as 'light order' was the order of the day. As they lined up to take their place in the Battalion they were in high spirits, mouth organs were played while others sung along or made jokes. The field cookers had already left when the Liverpool Scottish made their way to the line. Their QM had arranged a hot meal for his men on the far side of Ypres while they waited for the cover of darkness to hide their progress to the front. As darkness fell they began moving into the trenches in front of Y Wood. In the Battalion Diary, Lieutenant G. Wall, who commanded 10th Scottish Battalion, the King's (Liverpool Regiment) recorded:

> '4.00 pm on the afternoon of the 15th the Battalion left the camping ground near Busseboom and proceeded via Ypres to Railway Wood. The attack was made on a frontage of about 1,000 yards, the Northumberland, Royal Scots and Royal Fusiliers were detailed to take the first line and we, in conjunction with the Lincolns, were to take the 2nd Line, the 7th Brigade being in Reserve.'

3rd Battalion Worcestershire Regiment

> 'The 3rd Worcestershire left their bivouac at Busse Boom on the evening of June 15th, marched forward by Kruisstraat and the Lille Gate of Ypres and reached the Assembly Trenches south of Witte Poort Farm just before midnight. The Battalion was to be in the fourth line of the attack. In front of them the H.A.C. were in immediate support of the 9th Brigade.'
>
> Battalion Diary

Sergeant Bernard Joseph Brookes, Queen's Westminster Rifles

> 'On Tuesday 15th June we were told to be in readiness for an attack which we were to make up on a line of the German trenches near Hooge, and as this was our first attack we were rather excited, and we had a swim to cool down.
>
> We were to be in the second line, and half of the Battalion were to move into the trench as soon as the line was taken.
>
> The battalion moved up at 8.30 pm, but as I was detailed to wait until relieved by a Brigade signaller, I went forward at 10.30 pm with the Colonel and Adjutant.

246 Regiment near Bellewaarde June 1915. Kind permission of Rob Schäfer, Military Historian.

It was a terribly dark night, and we made our away over a number of fields containing many shell holes, and we occasionally came to earth. The Germans, star shells however, helped us considerably to see our way, and after traversing about three miles of fields we arrived on the left of the village of Hooge at midnight.

With another signaller, I had to open a new station about a hundred yards away from headquarters in case the battalion got cut off, so that as soon as I arrived I had to lay a wire and get connected up. This work was completed in about half an hour and it consisted of a great deal of travelling on the stomach as the Germs were firing rather heavily, and the line was made above the trenches. After completing we managed each to get an hour's sleep before operations commenced.'[21]

Reserve Infanterie Regiment 246

'On 14 June 1915 an aerial photograph was received by the regiment. Clearly visible on it was the fact that south of the Menin – Ypres road between Hooge and 3rd Borne and east and west of the track between Eierwäldchen [Egg Copse = Railway Wood] the enemy had dug a complex of trenches (a so-called trench honeycomb) with four parallel lines of trenches arranged one behind the other. It was estimated that six battalions could be assembled

---

21. Kind permission of Bob Brookes.

within them ready to launch a quick succession of assaulting waves. The regiment realized at once that an attack was imminent and had the artillery increase its rate of firing. Stocks of ammunition and hand grenades were increased. In the main battle trench the firing points along the parapet were completed. The gunners of the machine gun platoon tested their weapons and inspected their ammunition. The artillery was briefed in fullest detail and kept completely up to date with the results of all observations.

The regimental battle sector, which ran from Eierwäldchen to the Bellewaarde stream, had been under heavy fire for eight days; two or three times per day the enemy hammered our trenches with an iron fist. It seemed to be merely some sort of overture. Our patrols, pushed forward, reported nothing more specific which would have led to the conclusion that an attack was actually imminent. During the evening of 14 May all commanders and subordinate commanders received copies of all the information collected thus far and were warned that it was assumed that an enemy attack would take place within the next two or three days. The forward position was occupied by 3rd Battalion under Hauptmann Kölle. 10th, 11th and 12th manned the battle positions, whilst 9th Company was back in reserve in the Storchschnabel [Stork's Beak]. 1st Battalion, commanded by Hauptmann Keiper-Knorr was in support and 2nd Battalion led by Hauptmann Baumann was in reserve in the valley of the Hanebeek and in Polygon Wood.

At midnight and 2.00 am during the night 15/16 June 1915 regimental headquarters demanded over the telephone reports concerning enemy activity from the commander of the forward battalion and reminded him once more about the need for watchfulness. The engineers were also ordered to bring down mortar fire on the enemy trenches. Following this, the three company commanders in the front line reported that their companies were battle ready, that hand grenades had been prepared and that the machine crews were stood to behind their weapons. At 2.00 am regimental headquarters received a report that the enemy was strikingly quiet. At 3.00 am the [artillery?] observation officer and the officer commanding 11th Company reported simultaneously, 'The enemy have opened gaps [in their wire] ready to assault. Noise and movement can be clearly detected in the enemy trenches. Strangely the enemy artillery is completely silent.'

The regimental adjutant immediately passed this information on to the artillery and caused artillery fire, both light and heavy, to be brought down on the enemy infantry positions, but the intensity of the fire soon died away. The entire regiment was brought to the highest state of alert.'[22]

---

22. Extract from Leutnant der Reserve Louis Orgeldinger *Das Württembergische Reserve-Infanterie-Regiment Nr. 246* (1931) Stuttgart , 97–107. Translation © Dr Jack Sheldon 2012.

Part Two

The Battle

Chapter 21

The Battle Begins

As previously mentioned, in the fighting on the Bellewaarde Ridge the British line had been thrust back between the Menin road and the Roulers railway. The 3rd Division had been given the task of reducing the salient which had developed by the capture of the German positions between the southwest corner of Bellewaarde Lake and the Roulers railway to the north of Railway Wood. The 8th Brigade was to take over the position of the line from which the attack was to start; the 9th Brigade to carry out the assault, and the 7th Brigade (less one battalion) to stand in reserve in trenches west of Cambridge Road.

The attack was to be delivered in three stages. The first objective was to take the German front line. The second was to take the line of the road from Hooge to Bellewaarde Farm and the final objective, the trench on the edge of the lake.

The attacking troops for the first phase were (from right to left) the 4th Royal Fusiliers, 1st Royal Scots Fusiliers and the 1st Northumberland Fusiliers. As soon as the German front was taken the Royal Fusiliers were to bomb down the trench from Y.16 to Y.17, while the Royal Scots Fusiliers, in conjunction with the 1st Battalion Northumberland Fusiliers, (The Fifth) were to seize the hostile trench lying between Y.13 and Y.15 and the second objective, the 5th Fusiliers pushing their bombing parties on towards Y.7.

As soon as the first objective had been gained the guns were to bombard the second objective. This was from the house 100 yards south of Y.17 to Y.11. Bellewaarde Farm lay roughly on the centre of this line. The troops from the first phase would then attack the second objective. The 1st Lincolns and Liverpool Scottish (1/10th King's Regiment), were to move up to the front line vacated by the troops of the first phase, and were then to capture the third objective. In later years this was known as 'leap-frogging'.

The 7th Brigade was to support the 9th, while the 8th was to be held in reserve. On

Pte Patrick Carpenter. Kind permission of Gary Carpenter.

the right of the 3rd Division troops of the 7th Division were ready to support the 9th Brigade by seizing the German trenches from Y.20 to Y.16, and by covering rifle and machine-gun fire from the Menin Road. On the left the 6th Division was to assist the 3rd by opening covering fire with rifles and machine guns.

No 3 section Cheshire Field Company, Royal Engineers had been attached to the Liverpool Scottish to dig a communication trench (CT) from the present front line to the captured trenches.

A rough map showing the enemy's trench system had been issued. Armed with this and with periscopes, company commanders went forward on 13 June to the front line to reconnoitre the front of attack. Following this reconnaissance the final orders for the attack were issued. A hedge about 125 yards south of Railway Wood, marked on the map, and plainly recognizable on the ground, was selected as the boundary between the Northumberland Fusiliers and the Royal Fusiliers. North of this the attack of the Northumberland Fusiliers would be delivered astride a sunken road situated immediately south of Railway Wood. This road had been observed to be full of British dead, and was noted as a place to be avoided.

Preliminary to the infantry assault, an artillery bombardment of the enemy's trenches and wire was to be opened at 2.50 am and, with three pauses of ten minutes at 3.10 am, 3.40 am and 4.00 am, to continue till 4.15 am., when the guns would lift from the German front line, and the infantry advance to the capture of the first objective. Thereafter, the artillery support to the attack would be by observation. To facilitate this, distinctive screens were to be carried by infantry units to indicate to the gunners the progress of the attack.

The Divisional Artillery had sixty-six 18-pounders with a total of 12,000 rounds of ammunition, twelve 4.5-inch howitzers with 2,000 rounds, six 5-inch Howitzers with 500 rounds and four 2.75-inch howitzers with 400 rounds. The 2 Group Heavy Artillery had three 9.2-inch howitzers with 300 rounds, two 6-inch guns with 100 rounds, eight 6-inch howitzers with 450 rounds, eight 60-pounders with 1,200 rounds and six 4.7-inch howitzers with 2,000 rounds.

Lieutenant Colonel Elkington was commanding A Group which consisted of 23rd, Battery 45th Battery and 49 Battery. Their task was to destroy the wire entanglements on the front, map reference I.12c.2.1. to I.11d.8.7. Each Battery was to concentrate on the two points that had been earlier selected during the consultation between brigade, battery and battalion commanders. They had fifteen rounds per gun, the intention being to allow them to find the range before the howitzers began. Once they had obtained the correct line the guns would be anchored and the platforms prepared.

Lieutenant Colonel Philpotts commanded B Group, consisting of 38th Brigade RFA and 65th Forward Howitzer Battery which were to destroy the wire at map reference 1.11d.8.8 to 1.13a.0.8 taking care to omit the 100 yards that were screened by the trees of Railway Wood. Commanded by Lieutenant Colonel Stockley, C Group Company consisted of the 4th Durham Howitzer Brigade (less one section) and the 61st Forward Howitzer Battery.

The eight lines of jumping-off trenches were ready. Four had been dug behind the front trenches and four behind the support line. But as the ground was under continual observation by the Germans it wasn't long before they were spotted and ranged on by the enemy. To save the troops from being heavily shelled whilst waiting for the assault it was decided to attack at dawn.

The first Line consisted of 9th Brigade: 4th Royal Fusiliers, 1st Royal Scots Fusiliers, and the 1st Northumberland Fusiliers, with the 1st Wiltshire (7th Brigade) to cover the right of the attack; the second Line was the 1/10th King's (Liverpool Scottish) and 1st Lincolnshire. In the third and fourth Lines were the 7th Brigade: H.A.C. and 2nd Royal Irish Rifles; 3rd Worcestershire and 1/4th South Lancashire. They were under orders not to advance unless ordered.

In the German trenches, across no man's land, were Reserve Infanterie Regiment (RIR) 246, Reserve Infanterie Regiment (RIR) 248 and Unter-Elsässisches Infanterie-Regiment Nr.132.

With Reserve Infanterie Regiment 246 were Leutnant Adolf R. Burry, Leutnant Karl Schellhorn and Leutnant Eduard Haüssler – all killed on 16 June 1915 – and Gefreiter Christian Wirth (*covered in more detail in Chapter 10*).

Reserve Infanterie Regiment 246

> 'On 16th June in the morning the troops' rest was disturbed by a serious alarm. To our surprise the enemy had attacked and taken Hooge Chateau as well as the trenches occupied by R.I.R. 247 around T-Wäldchen (Y. Wood) on the 24th May. Bellewaarde Farm also fell.'[23]

Brigadier General Alexander Johnston

> 'Up at two o'clock by which time the day had begun to break and at 2.30 am the bombardment started and lasted till 4.15 am. We had something like 200 guns firing and the noise was deafening; I think we cannot fail to have knocked the Germans about a good deal. High explosive was turned on to the German 1st and 2nd line trenches, shrapnel over the communication trenches and ground behind, and the big 9.2 gun fired on Bellewaarde Farm and the various redoubts and strong points in the German 3rd line.'[24]

The British shelling began as scheduled at 2.50 am and continued with three brief interruptions at 3.10 am, 3.40 am and 4.00 am until 4.15 am. The opposing

---

23. Heinz Lehmann. *The Royal Saxon Reserve Jager Battalion No. 26*, Dresden 1923. Translated by: Sebastian Laudan. (Heinz Lehmann, Das Königlich Sächsische Reserve-Jäger-Bataillon Nr. 26, Dresden 1923).
24. By kind permission of Edwin Astill. Naval & Military Press.

trenches were between thirty to 150 yards apart, so close the men in the front line could see clods of earth rising in the air together with heads and bodies of the enemy. After a brief pause the Germans replied. To start with they used shrapnel, but later began using heavy shell. Their fire was mainly aimed at Railway Wood and they also fired a number of gas shells. Because of the close proximity to the enemy trenches and the need to fire low bursts to cut through the barbed wire entanglements it was inevitable that the British artillery caused several casualties to its own troops before the assault began.

Unter-Elsässisches Infanterie-Regiment Nr. 132

> 'On the morning of 16th of June, at 0415 am. the enemy directed heavy artillery fire on the right wing of the regiment and onto the positions of RIR246. It soon increased in intensity and within the next two hours it crushed the positions on the right, engulfing everything in a cloud of smoke, dust and debris. Losses were inflicted and some of the men were buried alive.'[25]

The 9th Brigade was positioned on the left of 3rd Division with instructions to attack the Germans in the direction of Bellewaarde Farm. The 9th Infantry Brigade attacked the German lines immediately on the right of the 1st Battalion West Yorkshire Regiment, the right of which nested on the railway with 2 platoons of B Company on the southern side. The Battalion, together with two Companies of Westminsters and one section No 12 Coy R.E. under the orders of Lieutenant Colonel F.W. Towsey, were ordered to protect the left flank of the 9th Infantry Brigade. If the attack succeeded, they were to support and assist the attack as opportunity offered.

The troops had left their packs and greatcoats behind and were carrying their waterproof ground sheets on their backs. Each man carried two bandoliers of rifle ammunition, one day's rations in addition to the iron ration and two sandbags fastened through the belt at the back. One Platoon also carried shovels securely slung on their backs. Each of the first line Battalions had fifty wire cutters and 400 bombs including 150 Mills grenades, which at the time were a new invention. They also carried ten small flags for the bombers to mark their positions. The Lincolns and Liverpool Scottish had twenty-five wire cutters each and 150 Mills grenades. The Brigade Reserve only had 1,200 bombs in all while the enemy had considerably more at their disposal. This would prove to play a decisive part in the outcome.

The front line of 9th Brigade was distributed as follows: The 4th Battalion Royal Fusiliers were on the right with the 1st Battalion Royal Scots Fusiliers in

---

25. Translation courtesy of Rob Schäfer, Military Historian.

the centre, and the Northumberland Fusiliers (The Fifth) on the left. In support were the Liverpool Scottish on the left, the Wiltshire on the right and the Lincolns in the centre.

9th Brigade was to capture three successive objectives. The first of these was the edge of the wood Y16 – Y15, and the German front line as far as the northeast corner of Railway Wood; the second, the line of the road from a house one hundred yards south of Y17, through Y17 to Bellewaarde Farm, and the third and final objective, through Y14 and Y11 to Y7.

Three Companies of the 1st Northumberland Fusiliers (9th Brigade) were detailed to make the first assault. Those involved included:

- Captain Gerard Orby Sloper – wounded in three places and taken prisoner. After several attempts to escape from Germany he was transferred to Holland early in 1918, and was eventually repatriated to England in December 1918.
- Lieutenant George. H. Fearnley-Whittingstall – transferred from ASC in May 1915 and wounded on 16 June 1916. He was on sick leave until January 1916 when he was attached to the 3rd Battalion in July 1916 and joined the 11th (Service) Battalion. He was killed by a shell while doing transport work in August and buried at Albert.
- Lieutenant Graham John – killed in action on 16 June 1015.
- Lieutenant Benjamin Gunner – survived the battle but was killed in action on 7 October 1915. He was one of the witnesses at the trial of Herbert Burden.
- Second Lieutenant Charles James Shelly Dalbiac – killed in action on 16 June 1915.
- Second Lieutenant Hugh Urquhart Scrutton – awarded the MM for his actions during the 16th June 1915. He led his platoon with great dash under heavy fire against the enemy's line, and later, though wounded in the head, continued to direct the work of a bombing party. Although again wounded in the head, knocked down and rendered deaf, he returned to his trench after his wounds had been bound up, and remained at his post till dark.
- Sergeant Francis Frederick Casey – killed in action on 16 June 1915.
- Private Albert Rowley – later transferred to the Machine Gun Corps and demobbed after the war.
- Private James Miller – killed in action on 16 June 1915. He left a wife, Margaret Jane and four children, James, Elizabeth Mary, Jane Peel and Margaret Jane who was born on 27 July 1915.
- Private Thomas Henderson – killed in action on 16 June 1915, leaving a wife, Maggie, and nine children.
- Private Herbert Burden – aged 17 and went absent the following month. He was shot for desertion on 21 July 1915.

Under Captain Leonard Vale Bagshawe, X Company included:

- Corporal James Elliott Mavin – killed in action on 16 June 1915 and left a wife Miranda Amelia (Vairy) and four children, James, Richard Elliott and Emmanuel David .
- Private Arthur Lloyd – killed in action 16 June 1915.
- Private William Player William – captured on 16 June 1915 and confirmed as a Prisoner of War on 8 August 1915. He was interned at Sennelager III in Germany. After three years and 179 days in captivity he was repatriated back to England on 12 December 1918.

Under Captain Sandilands W Company included:

- Corporal Austin Frank Broughton – listed as wounded but not killed. Another soldier may have seen him wounded and reported what he saw, or he was killed, possibly by a shell, together with the men en route to a dressing station. He was never found.
- Lance Corporal Edward Beech – killed in action on 16 June 1915.
- Lance Corporal James Morris – initially reported as missing at evening roll call but later returned to his unit. He was discharged on 10 May 1919 with a gunshot wound on his left thigh.

Captain Robert Roddam was in command of Y Company which was on the left. He was killed in action on 16 June 1915. Lieutenant Dorman-Smith[26] commanded Z Company which included Private William Carr – who was also to die in action that day after the support trenches for Zoave Wood were heavily shelled. (His elder brother also died in the Great War.) This Company was to remain in reserve while X and W Companies were ordered to assemble for the attack in specially constructed trenches to the south of the sunken road. Meanwhile, Y Company was to assemble to the north of the road, in the British front line on the west side of Railway Wood.

At the east corner of Railway Wood were three German trenches in the shape of a triangle. The west side of the triangle was part of the German front line but this was to be avoided in the initial attack. After taking the front line south of the wood W Company would then push a party north until they reached point Y13 to clear the west and east faces of the triangle. The orders for Y Company were to advance through Railway Wood and to direct the right of their attack on the junction of the northern and western faces of the triangle. Once this was secured they were

---

26. Dorman-Smith was nicknamed 'Chink' after the regimental mascot, the Chinkara antelope. He served throughout the First World War during which he was wounded three times, and he was awarded the Military Cross. He attained the rank of Major by the end of the war. While in Italy he met American writer Ernest Hemingway and they became close friends. Hemingway based many of his characters on Dorman-Smith, these included 'Colonel Richard Cantwell', the hero of Hemingway's novel *Across the River and into the Trees*.

to push forward until they made contact with W Company at its eastern apex; Y Company would also direct bombing parties north to clear the trench towards Y7. As they gained their objectives all companies, if not already in contact with those on their flanks, were to push bombers right and left to clear the trench of the enemy and to gain contact with each other. They were also to gain ground by bombing up communication trenches on their own individual fronts.

The limited number of officers available did not allow a Second-in-Command to stay with Battalion Headquarters. If Colonel Yatman became a casualty, command would fall to Captain Sandilands. Lieutenant Heyder, the senior subaltern, and two others were assigned to W Company. This was in contrast to X and Y Companies who only had two officers and Z Company who only had one officer, Lieutenant Dorman-Smith.

At 4.45 pm on 15 June, the 1st Battalion Northumberland Fusiliers paraded in its bivouac area in readiness to move forward to the designated Assembly Trenches. The dress was marching order, without packs. Each man carried his two extra bandoliers of SAA, one day's rations (in addition to the iron ration); two empty sand-bags (for consolidation) and one water-proof sheet. Four hundred grenades (mostly Mills pattern) had been distributed among the Companies to be carried in canvas carriers. Two platoons of Z (reserve) Company carried shovels, slung on their backs.

It was an eight-mile march to the assembly positions. Just before 5pm they set off through Vlamertinghe towards Ypres. After a two-hour halt just west of the town, they marched through Ypres and arrived at the Menin Gate. It was almost the shortest night of the year, and it was important the companies should be established in their Assembly Trenches before the remaining hours of darkness had passed. Marching by the Menin Road, the Battalion finally reached Hell Fire Corner. This was the point where the Roulers railway crossed the road and where the companies were to turn northeast and, at ten-minute intervals, move independently across country to their assembly positions. Unfortunately they were halted by the movement of other Battalions of the Brigade. This was the last place in the Ypres Salient that troops would wish to remain still so the next few minutes were very tense. Luckily the German guns were inactive and after fifteen minutes the men were able to continue. However, the delay had left them with little spare time and they were relieved to reach the Assembly Trenches. But their relief was short-lived as there was a misunderstanding about the assignment of the trenches. This caused considerable confusion and delay and it was almost dawn before W Company moved into its positions. The enemy front line was only 100 yards away and the early light allowed the Germans to spot their movement. For the next fifteen minutes they came under intense bombardment and took several casualties.

Eventually the guns fell silent and the men settled down into the narrow cramped Assembly Trenches which were sometimes only three and a half feet deep. It was a long wait. The companies were to attack in columns, leaving their trenches platoon by platoon. Punctually at 2.50 am, the field artillery opened. To the disappointed infantry it sounded rather thin and weak to start with. But it gradually grew louder and more intense as the heavier guns joined in and they could hear the shells of the heavy howitzer, known as mother, bursting over Bellewaarde Farm.

Although the German guns made little reply initially there were still casualties among the crouching men as the air was filled with flying shrapnel, shells fell short or whistled perilously close to their heads. During the two pauses in the bombardment there was almost complete silence on the enemy front lines. But it was now broad daylight, and when, at 4.00 am, the British artillery ceased fire for the third time, the Germans manned their parapet and began retaliating with intense rifle and machine gun fire.

Unteroffizier Schönfelder, 1st Battalion Reserve Infantry Regiment 246

'We were at readiness in the Strohhäuschen [Straw Shed] on 16 June 1915 and awaited the enemy attack, because the artillery fire went on all night. Nobody dared emerge from the dugout, because the fire was so heavy. Everyone's thoughts were concentrated on the probability of his escaping with his life during the coming enemy attack. Suddenly the door opened and my platoon commander entered. He gave the order, "Unteroffizier Schönfelder you are to detail one man from your Korporalschaft [A group of men of roughly two section strength] to go to battalion headquarters and find out what is happening to our front. All links forward are broken and we need to know what the situation is there".

The eyes of all my comrades were directed at me. They knew that it would be hard for me to send one of my lads to almost certain death. On whom was the order to fall? There was complete silence. I felt as though my throat had been cut. Finally I pulled myself together and said, "Gotthilf, off you go!" He looked at me knowing that the order I had given had to be obeyed. "Gotthilf", I said, "you'll get back". He picked up his rifle and left, accompanied by the thoughts of all who remained behind.

The communication trench was totally shot up, so our runner had to work his way forwards in bounds. He succeeded in reaching battalion headquarters unwounded. Major von Natzmer was utterly amazed that it had proved possible to get forward through this hellish fire. He was not allowed to return, because it appeared to be completely impossible to get through. We now awaited our good Gotthilf Schoch with the utmost concern. Finally the enemy artillery fire eased somewhat and after several nerve wracking hours Gotthilf mit Gottes Hilfe [German pun: Gotthilf, with God's help] returned to us unhurt. The joy at his return was enormous. He then went forward in the attack with his company, as described at another place and shortly afterwards was awarded the Iron Cross. He later attended a potential officers' course, returning as a Vizefeldwebel. He was killed near Ripont in March 1917.'[27]

At 4.10 am the British guns opened up again bringing down an intense bombardment on the exposed Germans causing many casualties. The whole of the German front line was covered in black and yellow clouds and sandbags, shattered bodies and barbed wire flew into the air. In the Assembly Trenches the word was passed down the line to prepare for the assault.

Sergeant 2820, John Keith Forbes, 1/4th Gordon Highlanders

'At length the position was ready for the attack which all had expected. The British, owing to excessive strain and arduous labour, were ready first, and the attack was planned for 16th June, 1915, the hundredth anniversary of the battle of Quatre Bras. The object of the attack was to capture the German lines in and beyond a strip of trees called Y wood, about half a mile long and two or three hundred yards deep, the idea being to link up the trenches on the right – just west of Hooge – with the British position on the left, some distance north of the Menin road. Early in the morning our artillery opened, and for a full hour and a half rained shells of every calibre, transforming a fresh green wood into a few withered and scorched tree-trunks.

While this was taking place, J. K. Coolly began to "drum-up," saying, "we must have a good meal while yet there is time and opportunity". At the moment due the attack went over and was forthwith a great success.'[28]

Brigadier General Alexander Johnston

'At 4.15 am the 9th Inf Brigade assaulted the German line in Y Wood which they carried with little loss, and about 150 prisoners were taken. In the same rush the German 2nd line was carried and eventually the 1st Scots Fusiliers actually got within 30 yards of the lake and captured Bellewaarde Farm. Then followed the same old trouble which has so often occurred before, and which seems so terribly difficult to prevent; namely our men got heavily shelled by our own guns, our foremost people perhaps had gone too fast or too far? We got several messages back about it, and the guns were told to lengthen, which I think in most cases they did, but at the same time the Germans then turned

---

27. Extract from Leutnant der Reserve Louis Orgeldinger *Das Württembergische Reserve-Infanterie-Regiment Nr. 246* Stuttgart 1931, 97–107. Translation © Dr Jack Sheldon 2012.
28. Extract from *Student and Sniper Sergeant. A Memoir of J.K. Forbes, M.A* (1916) William Taylor, M.A. and Peter Diack, M.A. Hodder and Stoughton.

their guns on to them also and they had a very bad time of it, some of them had to come back though till quite late in the day a few gallant men held on.'[29]

Five minutes later the leading platoons sprang from the trenches, relieved the waiting was finally over. They rushed forward followed almost immediately by the remaining platoons. Though the artillery had ceased firing the smoke from the shells still hung over the front line. Through this the Germans could be seen still firing over their parapet, mowing down the assaulting troops all along the front line as they moved at the double across no man's land. It was only a short distance but casualties were heavy. Four officers were killed: Captain Bagshawe on the right, Captain Roddam and Second Lieutenant Carter on the left and in the centre, Second Lieutenant Dalbiac, whose platoon led W Company attack. As W Company's rear platoon began to advance its commander, Lieutenant Heyder, was shot through the chest. Several senior NCOs and other ranks also fell in this narrow stretch including Lance Corporal Austin Frank Broughton.

Lance Corporal Albert Joynson on the right of the attack was one of the few men to get across while the machine gun was still in action. However he did not come through altogether unscathed. One of the bullets chipped a piece of flesh from his right thumb and carried away part of the stock of his rifle, although it did not damage the barrel. Joynson was later awarded the DCM for his actions that day.

Despite these losses the rest of the three companies, with the five remaining officers, stormed forward and took the German front line. As they leaped into the trench, the majority of the German garrison fled up communication trenches to the rear. The few who had been unable to escape were too demoralized to offer further resistance. The rest of the enemy who remained were either dead or seriously wounded. The Battalion had been given to understand it would be facing a Saxon regiment, but it later transpired from the two unwounded officers captured in the front lines that they were from Wurttemburg.

At 3.00 am in the German trenches across no man's land the artillery observation officer from Reserve Infanterie Regiment 246 and the Officer commanding 11th Company both reported that the British had opened gaps in their wire and were ready to begin an assault. They could hear movement in the enemy trenches and they believed an assault was imminent, although at that time the British artillery was strangely quiet.

The Regimental adjutant immediately passed the information back to the German artillery who responded by bombarding the British trenches with a short violent burst of light and heavy fire. The rest of the Regiment was immediately bought to the highest level of alert. At 3.10 am the Germans in the frontline trenches came

---

29. *The Great War Diaries of Brigadier General Alexander Johnston (2008)* Pen & Sword Military. By kind permission of Edwin Astill. Naval & Military Press.

under shrapnel and light shelling which gradually increased in intensity. Twenty five minutes later the heavier shells began raining down, damaging both trenches and parapets. Trees were uprooted and fell into the trenches and large numbers of men were buried under mountains of earth as the trench walls collapsed on top of them. On the left flank the machine gun was completely buried.

Feldwebel-Leutnant Gastel

'A short time later heavy shells began landing on the trench and, after approximately fifteen minutes, it was completely flattened. Sandbags and loopholes flew through the air, landing up to fifty metres behind the trench. I could see that the machine gun on the left flank was totally buried and had disappeared from view. It would have been about 3.30 am and because of all the destruction caused by the heavy shells, about fifty of which had impacted on the parapet or in the trench itself, to say nothing of countless light shells and shrapnel rounds, it could be assumed with certainty that the two machine guns in the centre had also been buried. The smoke from the shells was so thick that it was impossible to see more than ten metres, but those who could still fire shot into the clouds. The lungs did not suffer as much from the effect of the gases, as the eyes, which ran tears of such burning pain that it was hard even to open them.

At exactly 3.30 am the enemy artillery fire fell silent but, simultaneously, numerous machine guns opened fire on our position. The garrison, unable to spot any enemy, fired blindly into the thick smoke clouds. About seven minutes later the enemy renewed the bombardment of our position, but lifted the heavy shell fire more to the rear, directing it against communication trenches and alternative positions. To the south from the direction of Hooge came [the sound] of heavy small arms fire.

Under the impression that the garrison was firing at us, a patrol was immediately dispatched to the frontline trench of Infantry Regiment 132. After about an hour, at approximately 5.30 am, the patrol returned and reported to me that Infantry Regiment 132 was holding the edge of the wood. Hearing this report and being aware of the risk of being cut off, I pulled back with my platoon to the area of Bellewaarde Farm where two companies of the support battalion were already in position. There I received confirmation of what my patrol had reported, namely that Infantry Regiment 132 was holding the edge of the wood southwest of Bellewaarde Lake'[30]

---

30. *Extract from Leutnant der Reserve Louis Orgeldinger Das Württembergische Reserve-Infanterie-Regiment Nr. 246* Stuttgart 1931, 97–107 Translation © Dr Jack Sheldon 2012.

The Germans had no idea what had happened to the centre and right of the regiment, but could only assume that the whole trench had collapsed and all the men there had been buried. Those at the rear were unable to see what was happening because of the smoke from the numerous exploding shells, but before long it was obvious that the British had overrun their flattened right flank, and, after some fierce hand to hand fighting, had overwhelmed the few surviving members of the trench garrison.

The 4th Battalion Royal Fusiliers were in position east of the Cambridge Road trench at 1.30 am on 16 August. Among them were:

- Lieutenant Brian Edmund Douglas Warde – the only remaining officer of his company who remained unhurt in the initial attack. He had helped in the capture of three lines of German trenches and had fallen back to the German second line where his wounded Captain saw him quite unconcerned and leading a group of men down the trench for its defence. He jumped on to the parapet to fire on and bomb a party of the advancing enemy when he was hit in the head by a sniper. He died an hour later having not regained consciousness and was buried in the trench where he fell.
- Lieutenant Robert West Thornton – killed in action on 16 June 1915, aged nineteen.
- Lieutenant Norman Frederick Hunter – killed in action on 16 June 1915 aged thirty-six. A well-known Cambridge University amateur golfer, he was captain of Sunningdale Golf Club and was a familiar figure at North Berwick playing with Freddie Tait and Harold Hilton.
- Sergeant John Harvey – killed in action on 16 June 1915.
- Fusilier Richard Parrish – killed in action on 16 June 1915.

They were on the right of the British Front. Immediately in front of them lay the wood with a German trench guarding its western edge. The 4th Battalion Royal Fusiliers were off the mark immediately the shelling stopped at 4.15 am. Two Companies advanced in half company columns and soon captured the German trench with little loss of life. They too met little resistance and those who did survive surrendered willingly. They found the wire had been cut so effectively that they had no difficulty in climbing through and scaling the German parapets. In some places it had been swept away as if it had never existed.

Back on the British front line the trenches of the Royal Scots Fusiliers had only been slightly damaged by the counter bombardment and at 4.15 am, as the shelling ceased, they too had advanced. Among the Royal Scots were Second Lieutenant Philip Margetson who was wounded during the battle (he was later promoted to Lieutenant on 25 December 1915 and awarded the Military Cross for gallantry in action in the 1916 King's Birthday Honours) and Private Albert John Holland who was to be among the 479 casualties (dead or wounded). In February 1916 he was declared killed in action. On the left, B Company under Captain Wigham rushed their objective under heavy shell and rifle fire. Second Lieutenant Webster and CSM Gardiner were killed but they took the first line of trenches and began consolidating them.

On the right, under Captain Utterson-Kelso, A Company reached their objective with practically no casualties. Fifteen minutes later, together with the Liverpool Scottish and Lincolns, they pushed on and seized Y15 Communication trench at 4.45 am.

Reserve Infanterie Regiment 246

'In the meantime Hauptmann Kölle and 9th Company Reserve Infantry Regiment 246, which was acting as his battalion reserve, had occupied a counter-penetration position at the Storchschnabel. All contact with the three forward companies had been lost. The telephone lines were broken and no runners could get through the fire. Not a single one returned. The increased confusion and uncertainty forced him to decide to give up trying to defend the ground between the front line and the Storchschnabel. His intention was to replace the previous junction point with Infantry Regiment 132 with another next to the lake, off to the right contact had been roughly established.'[31]

---

31. Extract from Leutnant der Reserve Louis Orgeldinger *Das Württembergische Reserve-Infanterie-Regiment Nr. 246* Stuttgart 1931, 97–107. Translation © Dr Jack Sheldon 2012.

Chapter 22

Early Success

British Tommies going 'over the top' at the Battle of Bellewaarde. Illustration by Dawn Monks http://www.dawnmonksillustrations.co.uk/

Diary of the 1st Battalion West Yorkshire Regiment

'The Artillery bombardment commenced at 2.50 a.m. and ceased at 4.15 a.m. when the 9th Infantry Brigade assaulted and took the 1st and 2nd line of German trenches and also part of the 3rd line on a front of 1000 yards. About 300 German prisoners were taken.'

Once the first line was captured the Liverpool Scottish on the left, the Lincolns in the centre and the Wiltshire on the right were to go through and capture the second line from a house 100 yards south of Y17 to Y11. The dividing line between the Battalions was a hedge 150 yards south of Railway Wood, running east from Cambridge Road and to the track leading to Bellewaarde Farm.

The flanks during the second phase were to be secured on the right by 7th Brigade who were to work under Y20 and on the left by the Northumberland Fusiliers who were to work up Y7 and Y8 by bombing parties. The Royal Fusiliers and Royal Scots Fusiliers were to reorganize and support the second phase if necessary. The

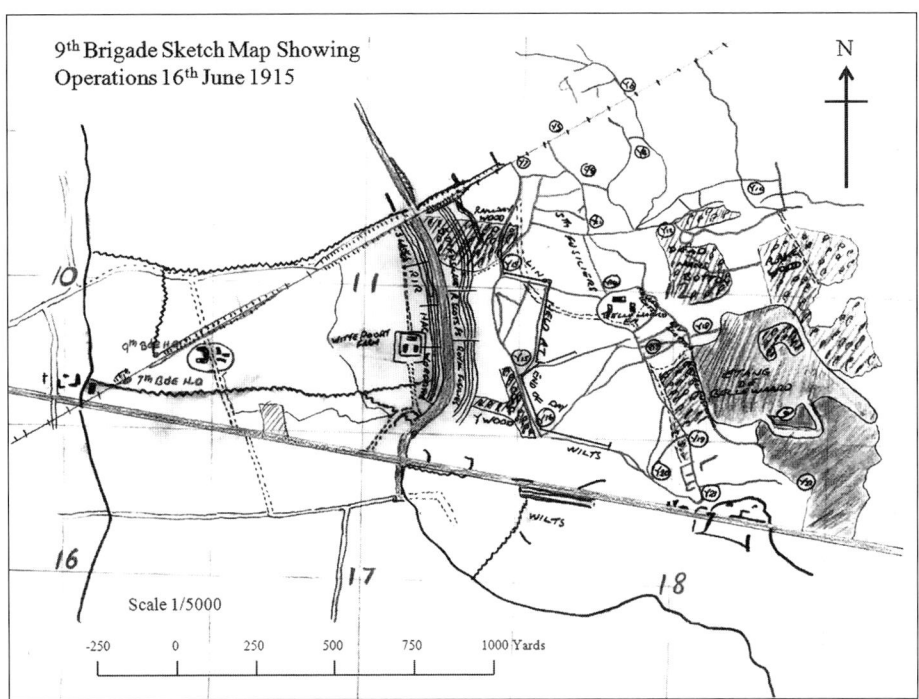

9th Brigade Sketch Map showing ops 16th June 1915. Courtesy of Martin Clift

7th Brigade were to support 9th Brigade by occupying trenches vacated by them, digging communication trenches to link the enemy's trench system with their own and, after the third objective had been gained, by consolidating the line. No 3 Machine Gun Company would also support the attack from the Menin Road.

The whole operation was a double leap frog for the Battalions involved. First the Lincolns and Liverpool Scottish would pass through the other battalions to attack the second objective and then the Royal Fusiliers, Royal Scots Fusiliers and Northumberland Fusiliers would go through and attack the third objective.

The Liverpool Scottish disposition was, from right to left X, Y and V Companies each with two platoons in the first wave and two supporting; Z Company would support the whole. Each of the front companies had seven shovels and Z Company had thirty.

The Battalion had left Busseboom at 4.00 pm on 15 June. Among them were:

- Captain George Fryer Dickinson – severely wounded. He was to suffer from his wounds until his death, aged forty-six, in 1932.
- Captain Noel Godfrey Chavasse – a captain with the Royal Army Medical Corps, attached to the 1/10th (Scottish) Battalion of the King's (Liverpool Regiment). Awarded the Military Cross for gallantry during the battle.
- Lieutenant Kenneth Alexander Gemmell – killed in action on 16 June 1915.

- Lieutenant William Stewart Turner – died while leading his men in the advance on Bellewaarde Farm on 16 June 1915. They had just captured a German trench when a heavy shell burst. He and Sergeant J.B. Jones were killed instantly.
- Second Lieutenant John Christian Barber – killed in action on June 16 1915.
- Second Lieutenant Christian Dalrymple Hamilton Dunlop – killed in action on 16 June 1915.
- Second Lieutenant James Pringle White – killed in action on 16 June 1915.
- Corporal Gordon Bartlett – killed in action on 16 June 1915. His body was never found. (*There is more about Corporal Bartlett at the end of this book.*)
- Private William Black – enlisted on 12 January 1915 and killed in action on 16 June.
- Private James Clarkson – posted missing after the battle.
- Private Wilfred Coop – fatally wounded on 16 June 1915.
- Private Thomas A. Dickson – posted missing after action on 16 June 1915.
- Private Oswald Evans – with the Machine-Gun Section, Liverpool Scottish. Killed in action on 16 June 1915.
- Private J. E. Haugh – listed as missing after the battle.
- Private James Thomas Johnstone – fatally wounded.
- Private Brisco Francis MacSwiney – killed in action on 16 June 1915. Previously with the Cheshire Engineers, he enlisted in the Liverpool Scottish at the outbreak of war.
- Private Thomas McAteer – killed in action on 16 June 1915, aged twenty-three.
- Private John Reginald Morris – embarked for France on 10 March 1915 and killed in action on 16 June.
- Private Michael John O'Connor – killed in action on 16 June 1915 aged 20.
- Private John Godwin Raschen – killed in action on 16 June 1915.
- Private William H Short – awarded the French Croix de Guerre on 6 November for conspicuous gallantry on 16 June 1915. With two corporals he attacked a trench held by thirty Germans with a machine gun. They killed all the occupants, captured the gun and used it in repelling a counter-attack. Private Short was nineteen. He joined the Liverpool Scottish in November 1914 and was sent out to the front in February 1915.
- Private William Webster Stark – killed in action on 16 June 1915.
- Private George Alexander Wright – posted as missing after the battle.

Having spent several months in the trenches the men went forward laughing and joking, delighted that they would finally be able to have a go at the enemy. The march was very slow with several stops, but eventually they reached their assembly position in the Cambridge Road around midnight. Unfortunately the Germans had soon noticed the unusual concentration of British troops and the number of new trenches that had been dug in the area and within moments of their arrival the Germans began shelling the Cambridge Road steadily with 5.9-inch and 8-inch shells, causing many casualties.

As they expected the bombardment began at 2.50 am with pauses to confuse the Germans as to when the actual assault would take place. The men had spent many months suffering heavy German shelling. Due to the acute shortage of shells which left the British artillery with an inadequate supply, the Germans had not suffered anything like as much. Hearing the enemy on the receiving end for once was very satisfying.

At 4.15 am the front battalions left their trenches and began the attack against the enemy front line. There was little resistance and soon they were sticking coloured screens into the enemy parapets to let the gunners know which section of the trenches had been taken. These screens were made of canvas, about six feet long and three feet deep and were coloured red and yellow. They were nailed to two coloured poles. Each Company carried six of them and they were singularly ineffective. In places there was a thick mist, others a morning haze. This, combined with the smoke of the shelling, completely obscured them from view. Time after time the British artillery shelled trenches that had been taken, killing and wounding many of their own men. The situation was made worse by the enemy counter bombardment which was so heavy that it was continually blowing up the telephone lines laid by the gunner signallers who, together with the Forward Observation officers, were close up behind the attacking troops. The runners were too slow and unreliable to be much assistance, it was a long time before creeping barrages came into being and, at this time, the Royal Flying Corps were unable to distinguish between infantry once a battle was under way. This meant the artillery were essentially working in the dark and it was impossible for the men on the ground to avoid being fired on by their own artillery.

As soon as they saw the frontline trenches had been taken the Liverpool Scottish left their assembly position in Cambridge Road and moved forward of the British Front line to just short of the parapet of the enemy trench. Here they lay down to reorganize and await the signal to go onto the second objective. With them were Sections 1–3 of the 1/1st Cheshire Company RE including Sapper Percy Richmond Byrne (who was to die when hit by shrapnel at Bellewaarde on 16 June) and his brother Corporal A. J. Byrne who was wounded in the same incident. They were there to help to consolidate the captured positions as quickly as possible. The remainder stood by awaiting orders to dig communication trenches from the British front line to the captured trenches. As they went over the top Sapper Walter Smith, twenty-three, was shot through the heart and killed instantly. His friend John Williams, twenty-two, who was busy cutting barbed wire entanglements, was mortally wounded when a shell burst nearby showering him with shrapnel. He died of his wounds in hospital the following day.

The Lincolnshire Regiment were in the Assembly Trenches by 1.15 am. Those waiting to go over the top included Lieutenant Colonel Hugh Edward Richard Boxer who was to die that day while leading the Regiment in advance. Also killed in action were Lieutenant Allan Dixon Walker, Sergeant Thomas Andrew Fuller, Private Edward James Backlog, Private Harry Essam, Private Harry Lawson and

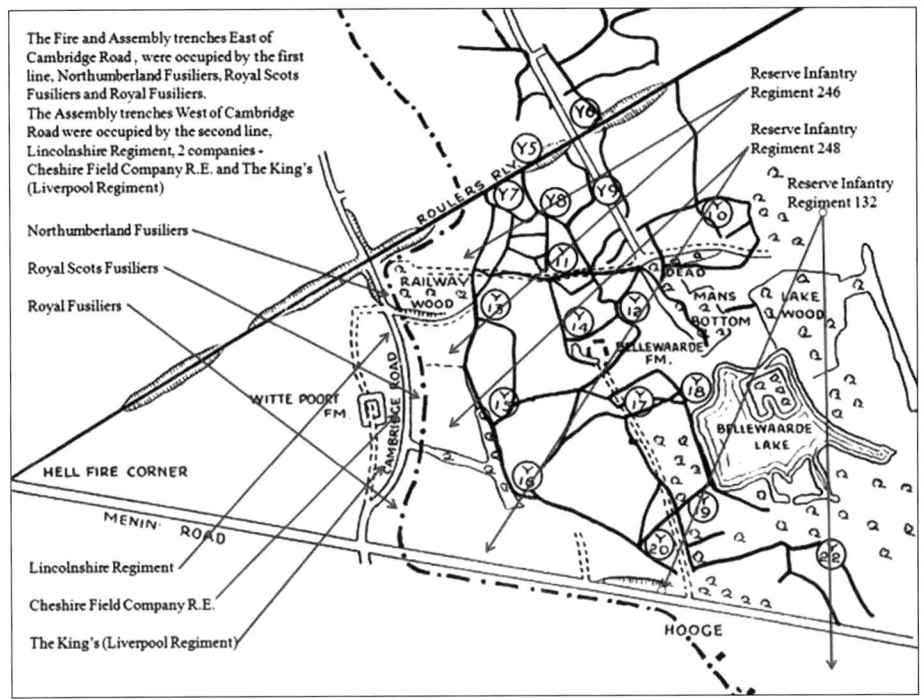

Map which regiment was where. Courtesy of Martin Clift.

Private Frederick Pittaway. Corporal George William Boyall was wounded but survived. He was later killed in action.

The British artillery bombarded the enemy trenches and barbed wire entanglements and the Germans retaliated. The bursting of the shells from both sides lit up the sky, the noise was deafening and the Lincolnshire took its first casualties before even leaving the trenches.

The Queen's Westminsters also took casualties before leaving their trenches as the Germans pounded them relentlessly. Those waiting in the trenches included Sergeant Bernard Joseph Brookes. Within an hour the telephone line, which was alongside a farm, had been broken three times after the Germans shelled the farm suspecting it to hold ammunition.

As the British guns fell silent the men from the Lincolnshire Regiment fixed bayonets and, after climbing out of the trenches, charged the two hundred yards to the first line of German trenches, from the east edge of the wood Y16–Y15– northeast corner of Railway Wood. The wire in front of the British trenches had been cut and removed during the night and the knife-rests placed at right angles so as not to hinder the advance. As they crossed no man's land they were met with hostile rifle and machine gun fire and heavy shelling. But the enemy wire had been cut by the Divisional artillery and the troops got through with little difficulty and were soon over the parapet.

Early Success   153

The sight that met them was one of devastation. The shells had blown the trenches and dugouts in on themselves, burying the Germans underneath. There were dying and dead everywhere and the dazed survivors offered little resistance, holding up their hands and surrendering. The troops immediately began consolidating the trench. This meant turning everything round. Parapets became parados and vice versa and wire had to be placed in front of the new parapet which now faced east. The land between the German first and second line trenches now became 'no man's land'. The old British trenches were then connected to the German trenches by means of a communication trench.

Once they had finished the initial bombardment of the Phase 1 objective at 4.15 am the Royal Artillery had moved on to bombarding the Phase 2 objective. They could see that 9th Brigade had been successful in taking the German front line with little difficulty and their orders were to concentrate the shelling on the second line. However, the infantry allotted to Phase 2 and Phase 3 moved so quickly they became caught up under their own bombardment.

Together with the Royal Fusiliers, the 1st Battalion Lincolns had forced their way along the communication trenches pushing the enemy back to his second line trenches. The attack was covered on the right by rifle and machine gun fire from the 1st Wiltshires from 7th Division. Their trenches were on the Menin Road, halfway between the ruins of Hooge and the Birr Cross roads. On the left troops from the 6th Division were also covering them.

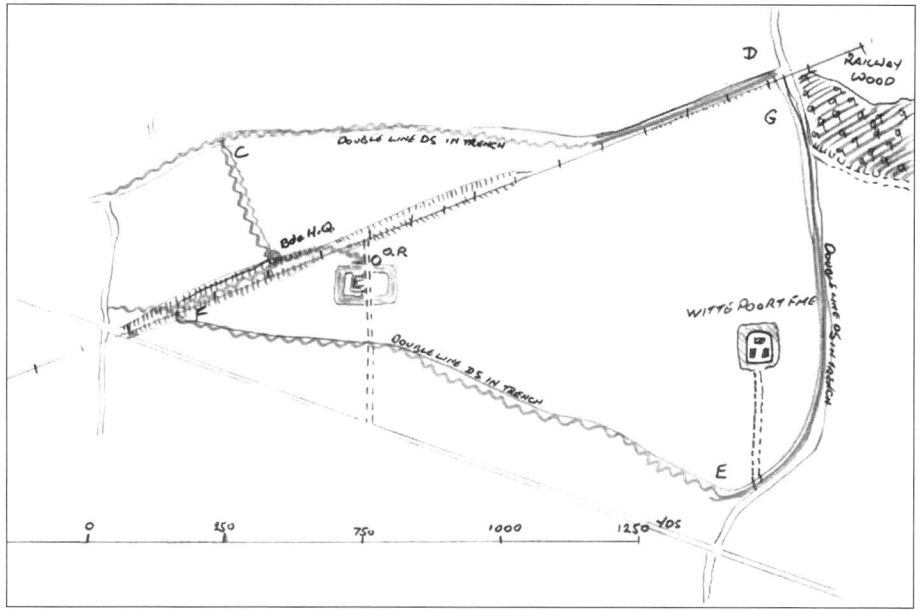

Sketch Map of Communications 16th June 1915. Courtesy of Martin Clift.

The next trench they took was full of dead Germans, the barbed wire entanglements were completely destroyed and the trenches were unusable. The few survivors were taken prisoner and passed back along the line.

The next stage of the attack now took place. The artillery had done their job well and the surviving Germans were ejected at the point of bayonets. The trench had been taken by 4.30 am. Although the infantry were working to the artillery timed programme they were told to push on if resistance was not too strong and that a message would be sent back to the artillery to stop bombarding that area.

They were then ordered onto their final objective, a split-locked trench on the western edge of Bellewaarde Lake. On the right the two supporting Companies pushed through the wood to the trench, but as they advanced the telephone line wire was cut.

The British artillery lifted from the second objective and aimed for the third. This was supplemented by the German guns and they took heavy losses despite several attempts to correct the range by the use of their coloured screens.

Reserve Infanterie Regiment 246

'At 4.30 am the battalion in support was ordered to thrust forward with two companies to link up with the elements of 3rd Battalion Reserve Infantry Regiment 246 which had been forced backwards. It then transpired that Hauptmann Kölle had already given orders to retire. On regimental orders, Hauptmann Baumann assumed responsibility for command of the front line.'[32]

As the Westminsters waited anxiously in their trenches wondering what was happening they were heartened to see a batch of German prisoners under guard coming down the Menin Road. For some reason the Germans fired on them and the prisoners and guard scattered to the edge of the road but none tried to escape and when the danger was over they stood up and marched off uncomplainingly under guard.

As dawn broke over the battlefield the Honourable Artillery Company moved forward in support and the Worcestershire moved up from their reserve positions across the Cambridge Road into the original British Line. With the Honourable Artillery Company was Captain Thomas Carnwath the Medical Officer to the 1st Battalion. Also there were Lieutenant Cautley Tatham who would be fatally wounded, Private Harry Dunkinfield Jones, Private Roger Harwicke Ballard, Private George Ivor Neal and Private Arthur Harry Wigg who were all killed in action. Second Lieutenant Lawrence William McArthur was severely wounded but when the troops were forced to retire from the third line of German trenches

---

32. Extract from Leutnant der Reserve Louis Orgeldinger *Das Württembergische Reserve-Infanterie-Regiment Nr. 246* Stuttgart 1931, 97–107. Translation © Dr Jack Sheldon 2012.

he rallied part of the retiring troops and re-occupied and held the vacated trench under heavy fire until he was forced to withdraw. Private John Thompson was wounded and later received the D.C.M. he joined the Royal Flying Corps and was the fifth pilot to be shot down by Manfred von Richthofen – the Red Baron.

Following the battle on 16 June, Colonel Treffry of the 1st H.A.C. wrote this tribute:

> 'During this action no one behaved with more steadfast courage or showed a greater devotion to duty than our Medical Officer, Captain Carnwath. He had his aid post in our original front line and from the time of the first assault when the wounded commenced to come in, in fact even before that time, he was at his post and remained there all through the 16th, all through the night of 16-17th, and all through the 17th, on the latter day searching about for any who might have been overlooked and wanted aid. His unit had been relieved and gone down but he still carried on until no further wounded could be found. This had been the spirit in which Carnwath had worked ever since the Battalion came out and I am sure all ranks of the H.A.C. will agree that no more sympathetic, human or devoted medical officer was ever attached to a unit'.

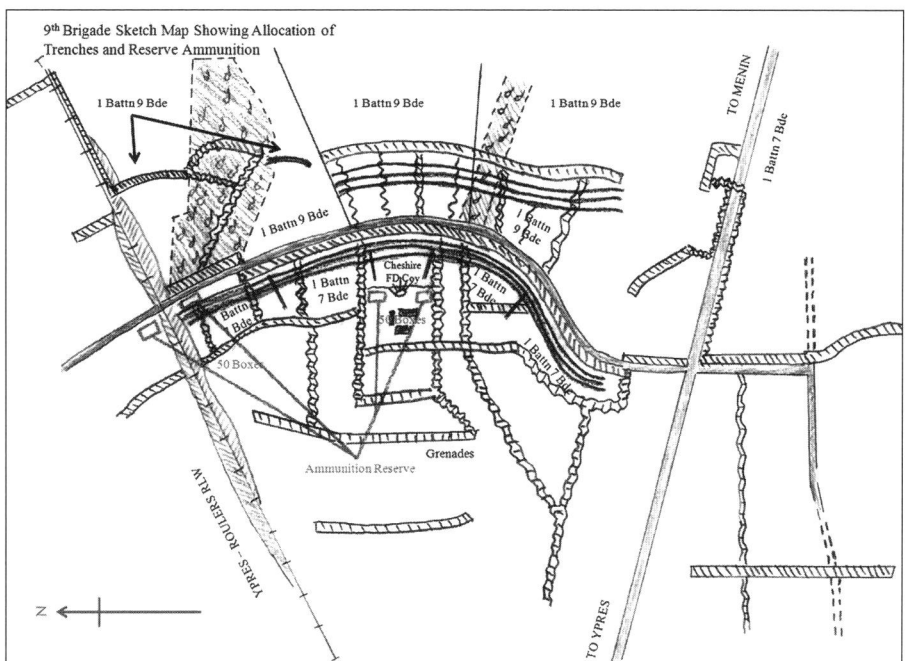

Sketch Map Showing Allocation of Trenches and Reserve Ammunition. Courtesy of Martin Clift.

The grass in the field was knee high and it was split diagonally by an old footpath. On the other side of the field was a belt of trees. This was known as Y Wood and it was here that the first German trenches lay. To their delight the flags soon went up indicating it had been captured and that the troops were going on the next line. The whistle blew and the HAC scrambled over the parapet and across the field. They were so weighted down that it was impossible to run and many took the diagonal path across the field as it was easier.

The German trench was made of white sandbags, back and front and was three feet wide and at least eight feet deep. In some places there was no damage from the shelling, but there were a number of dead Germans in the bottom of the trench. There was a sniper's post which was fitted with seats, shelves, bottles of beer and tinned meats. There was even a helmet hanging from a hook.

The first task was to turn the trench round and put out some wire. To do this they used the wire that was already there although most of it was loose coils and the knife rests were only a couple of feet high. They had only just finished when they were told to move further down the trench as their diagonal advance had bought them too far to the right.

They moved down the narrow belt of woodland to where other members of their company were already digging a communication trench back to the old front line. At this point there was virtually no trench left as a large artillery shell had completely demolished it burying several Germans. As some of the men dug out the buried Germans others began repositioning the wire. Unlike the previous area it was in much better condition and took some time to move it. As they worked they were passed by a constant stream of wounded on stretchers on their way back to the field hospital and occasionally by demoralized prisoners, hands raised.

2nd Battalion South Lancashire

> 'The whole of the "Assembly Trenches" which had been constructed during the past few nights were occupied by various units before 2 a.m. Shortly after that hour the whole of our guns East and West of Ypres opened a heavy fire on enemy's line in vicinity of Hooge, and about an hour later the infantry of 7th, 8th and 9th Brigades moved forward. The enemy's trenches were successfully carried and a number of prisoners taken. The Battalion still in reserve at Ypres was detailed to take over and dispose of all prisoners, in accordance with special orders issued on the subject.'

The Wiltshire Regiment of the 7th Brigade, including Second Lieutenant John Hugh Vaudrey Barker-Mill[33] and Private John Carey (who died on 27 June 1915

---

33. Second Lieutenant John Hugh Vaudrey Barker-Mill, 1st Battalion The Duke of Edinburgh's (Wiltshire Regiment). He was honoured for conspicuous gallantry on 16 June, 1915, at Hooge,

after being severely wounded at the battle) were detailed to support the right flank of 9th Brigade and had made considerable progress. As the artillery bombardment stopped at 4.15 am, 1 Platoon of C Company had assaulted the trench at the southern edge of Y Wood and taken it with little difficulty, capturing sixty prisoners. They had continued forward by bombing up communication trenches from Y20 to Y16 and made rapid progress. The rest of C and D Company followed with the leading men reaching a point some 100 yards from Hooge village by 5.00 am.

Meanwhile a communication trench was dug from the culvert under the Menin Road to the southern edge of Y Wood and attempts were made to join up the two pieces of German trench which ran east towards Hooge. By now the Germans were retaliating with machine-gun fire against the Honourable Artillery Company and a steady stream of bullets was strafing the trench. They were taking serious casualties so the troops quickly started digging out the trench and building a shelter in front of it.

At this point the Honourable Artillery Company could see very little in front of them other than a wide grassy field which stretched upwards to a low mound of earth several hundred yards away. But they were told that the attacking battalions were still advancing and they were to consolidate and hold the trench at all costs. The Germans were continuing to rain down machine-gun and rifle fire on them and casualties began to mount including a Captain who was standing on the parapet directing operations. Two men were detailed to take him back to the field hospital; one came back and was killed later in the day. The other took a bullet on the way and ended up in the hospital too.

The men began frantically digging deeper in an attempt to protect themselves against the continuing gun fire which was mercilessly accurate. As they dug they found bodies of dead Germans or even more disturbing, body parts that were almost unrecognisable. But there was no time to be squeamish, no time to think. If they didn't dig deeper they would be dead.

Diary of the 1st Battalion West Yorkshire Regiment

'The Northumberland Fusiliers were unable to take the trenches immediately south of the railway – the artillery not having destroyed the wire on the front of the trenches. The enemy commenced to heavily shell our trenches at about 5.00 a.m. and continued to do so very heavily with short intervals throughout the day. The shelling prevented any reinforcements being brought up and also held up the attack compelling the 9th Brigade to retire from the 2nd and third line of trenches and fall back to the 1st line of German trenches which they strengthened and continued to hold.

---

when, after leading an assault with great dash, he succeeded in taking some 300 yards of the enemy's trench, capturing many prisoners and two machine guns. Although wounded he remained with his company consolidating the position gained.

The Battalion were able, from their position, to assist the attack by rifle and enfilade fire, the Machine guns also getting some excellent targets.

Very useful information by Captain Huffman commanding C Coy was sent back which enabled the Artillery to prevent counter-attacking. Captain Hoffman was assisted by 2 officers' servants who got across open ground to the artillery with the message, all the communications having been cut by the violent shell fire. These servants, L Cpl Tyson and L Cpl Wilson were both mentioned in despatches for their gallantry.

The new stick rifle-grenade was used very successfully on this occasion. The enemy machine gun was holding up the whole of the line but Cpl Atkinson placed 7 stick grenades in quick succession into the midst of the hostile gun team and killed them all.'

Having reached the first line with little difficulty the 1st Battalion Northumberland Fusiliers had paused briefly. The enemy were as yet unaware that their front line had been over run so were not firing on them. The trench was littered with German helmets, gas respirators and other equipment. Having survived the initial assault the men were still high on adrenaline and immediately began hunting for souvenirs and had to be restrained by the officers and NCOs who ordered them to consolidate their position and prepare for the predictable counter-attack.

Although the Germans were unaware of the loss of their front line they did know about the British advance as this had been signalled to them as soon as the infantry advanced. In retaliation they had immediately started bombarding the Assembly Trenches which were now full of Z Company who had moved forward as soon as Y Company had begun their assault. They began to suffer heavy casualties until they too were pushed up the line to the captured position.

At this time air photography was just starting and the map they had been issued was a poor guide to the German trench system which was a labyrinth. Fortunately the main triangle of trenches east of Railway Wood which W Company were tasked to clear, were clearly identified. However the Sergeant who had initially set out to map the trenches had been wounded and his party scattered. Therefore the mapping was never finished. This meant that while the inner flanks of W and X Companies were in contact, W and Y were not.

It was imperative to clear the triangle and Captain Sandilands immediately started to organize a party to do just that. But before the men could be gathered they came under attack from their own artillery. At this point the Companies were occupying the whole of the enemy front line along the Battalion front, and had parties forward in the communication trenches. They had planted artillery screens throughout but the smoke from the earlier shelling, the dust and the continuing German barrage completely obscured the artillery observers' view. Uncertain of the success of the first phase the gunners continued to fire.

It was at this point that the Liverpool Scottish rushed forward. Unable to continue to the second objective because of the British artillery bombardment they halted and became inextricably mixed up with the Northumberland Fusiliers in the captured trenches.

As they advanced, V Company of the Liverpool Scottish, whose path was through Railway Wood, found that the attack here had been held up by machine gun fire and the enemy still held the front line.

There was a pause while part of Z Company came forward to reinforce them and then they thrust forward, bayonetting the remaining enemy and soon taking the position. They took about forty prisoners. Other parts of the front line were also holding on and Corporal W. E. Blackburne, Corporal S. Smith and Lance Corporal A. Moir of Y Company bombed their way into the trench captured a machine gun and killed several of the enemy. Corporal Smith was awarded a DCM for this action.

The artillery was still bombarding the second objective and the men waited for fifteen minutes before pushing forward. Again the line gave way with little resistance except at one point. In the vicinity of the railway cutting at Y6 there was withering machine gun fire. Despite this they captured the line from Bellewaarde Farm to Y11. The trench here proved to be very shallow, only three feet deep in places and was not occupied by the enemy. It was also indefensible without time to deepen and improve it. There was no time for this so Lieutenant Colonel E. G. Thin gave the orders to carry on to the final objective. He was wounded almost immediately afterwards.

Most of the Liverpool Scottish, with a few men from the Royal Scottish Fusiliers and Northumberland Fusiliers moved forward. Some went over the open ground, others used the communication trenches. Unfortunately, a number of men from the Liverpool Scottish arrived at the second line and did not carry on with the rest. Instead they began digging in where they were. They were virtually all killed or wounded when their own artillery began bombarding the line under the mistaken impression the Germans were still occupying it.

The Northumberland Fusiliers joined the Liverpool Scottish in the assault on the Second Line and Z Company now came forward to the front line from its supporting position having suffered heavy casualties from the German artillery bombardment.

Companies W and Y bore to the left and began bombing down the enemy trenches. The fierce fighting was hand-to-hand and ebbed and flowed as first the Germans then the British gained the upper hand. But eventually the Germans bought up fresh reinforcements and more bombs and this, together with strategically placed machine guns, finally forced the Battalion to abandon the idea of any further advance.

Meanwhile some of Z and X Companies, together with some Liverpool Scottish had advanced and had made good the line just west of Bellewaarde Farm. Finding themselves exposed to continuous sniping from both sides and machine gun fire from the left, they stopped near an old French trench and dug in. But there were very few men left to hold it.

The strength of the 2nd Battalion Royal Irish Rifles going into action was 21 officers and 630 other ranks. These included 19-year-old Second Lieutenant

Edwin Blow Kertland, CSM, James Joseph McGibney, Sergeant Jackson Clarke, Corporal George Morgan, 23-year-old Corporal Hugh Murray, Corporal Robert Platt, Lance Corporal William McIlroy, Lance Corporal Thomas Brady, Rifleman William Cotter, Rifleman Francis Dunne, 19-year-old Rifleman Hugh Johnston, 18-year-old Rifleman James Mayes and Rifleman Patrick Fitzsimmons, 35. All died in action that day.

They had been ordered to support the left flank of 9th Brigade and consolidate the first German line south of the Ypres–Roulers railway. From their viewpoint it appeared the initial bombardment had been very effective with the 9th Brigade easily taking their first objective. Delighted at their success, the Royal Irish didn't wait for their orders; instead they rushed into action through the first line and onto the second. Unfortunately the second line soon had to be abandoned after taking heavy fire from the British artillery. But before they abandoned the second line, C and D Companies, carried away by a wave of enthusiasm, advanced to the third line causing chaos as they became mixed up with other regiments. They had to be reorganized and bought back. B Company never got up at all as they were caught by very heavy enfilade fire as they moved forward and lost over forty of their men.

But the German front line through Ypres Wood and Railway Wood was taken, although several smaller parties continued to hold on, including the one near Bellewaarde Farm.

By 5.00 am the results of 9th Brigade's attack were reasonably satisfactory. The units had been disorganized by the slow advance of the artillery barrage but they had taken a considerable number of prisoners and the second objective had been achieved as far as Y11. But, apart from the portion of the line taken by Y Company in the first assault, the trenches between this point and the railway were still full of Germans.

Chapter 23

The Attack Falters

Sergeant James Fraser 'D' Coy, 4th Gordon Highlanders

> '16th: Beautiful sunny morning. Our bombardment started at 2.50a.m. and continued until 4.15. German trenches fairly flying. British attack began at 4.15 and we watched the first wave go over and saw troops dancing round each other with their bayonets. Some German prisoners came along; they looked quite human, but about eight o'clock the German guns began to hit back.'[34]

At 5.00 am the Royal Scots Fusiliers under Captain Wigham and the Liverpool Scottish seized the trench southwest of the pond at Bellewaarde Farm, consolidated the trench and were preparing to take their next objective. But the shelling at the farm by their own artillery was so heavy they were unable to go any further forward. The CO returned back to the telephone that had now been established in Y15 and informed the OC of 9th Brigade of the situation. It made no difference, the artillery continued to shell the men causing severe casualties.

Despite this, Captain Wigham decided to push on and they took the German trench flow. Together with thirty men from the Royal Scots Fusiliers and twenty men from Liverpool Scottish they held this until 6.30 am when they had no option but to retire as there was no support. They returned back to the original trench south west of the farm. Here they received reinforcements at midday under CSM Taylor and remained until 3.00 pm.

At 5.30 am the Germans began shelling the HAC and the new communication trench quickly became a death trap. At the rear of the trench there was a constant stream of wounded coming back from another trench and the Germans made a point of shelling both areas. The wounded were hit several times and the communication trench began to fill with bodies, so many that it soon became easier to pass it on open ground.

---

34. Kind permission of John Blomfield.

Unter-Elsässisches Infanterie-Regiment Nr. 132

'At about 6 am the barrage was lifted and followed by an attack of English infantry directed against the sections A and B. Sections C and D were put under suppressive fire by machine-guns. The enemy managed to break into the positions of 11th company, overwhelming our men in close combat at the point of the bayonet. Another attack was directed at 9th company which managed to defend itself successfully. The "Eclusette trench", which was not fully manned and still under construction was also taken by the English. The left wing of the neighbouring regiment was pushed out of the front line, enabling the enemy to take hold of the communication trench. The regimental reserve, alarmed by the sound of the fighting, was moved forward but did not manage to intervene in time.'[35]

The 1st Battalion the Wiltshire Regiment had made more progress in the German trench they had captured. They had moved nearer Hooge eventually reaching a point only fifty yards from the village. For the next three hours the situation remained the same and they used their time reversing the parapets, and in general consolidating and reinforcing the trench ready for the expected counter- attack.

Unter-Elsässisches Infanterie-Regiment Nr. 132

'Being severely wounded, the commander of 11th company made his back towards the rear, meeting the section commander Hauptmann Hoffmann on the way. After listening to his report, Hauptmann Hoffmann gave command of the company to Leutnant Bartenstein. Taking a platoon of 12th company (Leutnant Grasser) with him, Bartenstein moved forward to retake the lost position. A small group of Pioneers of R.PI.R.22 went with them and distinguished themselves in support of the attack.'[36]

Reserve Infanterie 248

'At 6.15 am the English attacked near the (Eier-)Wäldchen (Railway Wood) and south of it. On our left flank and near T-Wäldchen (Y Wood) the Reserve-Infanterie-Regiment 246 withdraw towards Storchschnabelwald due to the shelling. Offizierstellvertreter Hertle's platoon near Gierwäldchen became encircled by superior forces despite its fierce resistance with hand grenades and rifle butts; who didn't fall became prisoner.

---

35. Translation courtesy of Rob Schäfer, military historian.
36. Translation courtesy of Rob Schäfer, military historian.

According to witnesses' statements Hertle was shouting, "Comrades, we fight to the last, no one may yield." The English entered RIR 246's sector, endangering the left flank of our II Battalion, although company Schwarzkopf held out bravely, rejecting the enemy from both front and flank with hand grenades.'[37]

By 6.30 am the centre and right of the Battalion's front of attack had secured their second objective. However, although the centre of this trench provided reasonable cover on the right it was barely three feet deep and not a continuous trench. It was also open to enfilade machine gun fire which caused several casualties. The attack on the left had floundered and all attempts to remedy this had also failed. It was decided the only way was to begin a new frontal assault across the open.

Sergeant Bernard Joseph Brooks, Queen's Westminster Rifles

'For 4 hours this ceaseless bombardment continued, and at 6.40 am we received the following message: "All goes well. AAA. We have captured the enemies' first line".

Just before receiving this message we were wondering how things were progressing in front, and were rather worried about having no news, when we saw a batch of German prisoners under our guard coming appalling the Menin road. This informed us that we had at least been successful in paraded through.

For some reason or other the Germs fired on their prisoners coming along the road, and the prisoners and our guard had to scatter and lie down for a time, but none tried to escape, but hurried to a place of safety where they paraded together and marched off under the guard.

It is possible that the Germs fired on their own men on the principle that "dead men tell no tales", but whether this is the case or not, they did it intentionally for they could distinguish the Germs from the British and could have held their fire from the spot where they were.'[38]

At 8.30 am Reserve Jaeger Battalion 26 was moved to Eksternest, and closer to the front. Further to the right, at 9.00 am, the Wiltshire also came under heavy attack. The Germans had advanced down the two communication trenches from the north and under cover of intense artillery fire started bombing heavily. The Wiltshires replied with grenades and the fighting continued for an hour and a half.

The 1/4th Battalion South Lancashire Regiment had already sent parties forward to support the elements of 7th and 9th Brigade under fierce attack in

---

37. Translated by Sebastian Laudan.
38. Kind permission of Bob Brookes from *The Diaries of Sgt Bernard J. Brookes*.

between the first and third German lines. Among those involved were Lieutenant Edmund Lionel Frost, Corporal Sidney Thomas Ince, Private Arthur Alldred, Private Gilbert Harding, Private Samuel Pierce, Private John Henry Carter, Private Frank Williams and Private James Sharp were all killed in action on 16 June 1915. Second Lieutenant Trafford Leigh-Mallory was wounded in the leg during an attack on the German trenches at Ypres. He was sent to a hospital in Oxford and was determined not to return to the Western Front. (When he recovered he joined the Royal Flying Corps in July 1916. He was later mentioned in dispatches several times and was awarded the Distinguished Flying Cross. In 1931 Leigh-Mallory became deputy director of staff studies in the Air Ministry and commander of No. 2 Flying School. He also served as a senior staff officer in Iraq before becoming commander of No.12 Fighter Group in 1937.)

At 9.30 am the attackers, having no bombs left, fell back to the German front line which was being held by a detachment of the Battalion.

Major Egerton Fairclough decided to advance and, after calling the men to follow him, he managed to occupy part of the enemy's second line trenches, south of Bellewaarde Farm, before he could regain possession of them. All through the day, despite severe shelling and a counter-attack at dusk, they hung on and prevented the enemy retaking this important locality. Meanwhile, the remainder of the 1/4th South Lancashire Battalion was still in its original assembly position, where it suffered heavy casualties from hostile artillery fire, and B Company, which was sent forward to reinforce the forward troops, was caught by a concentration of high explosive and nearly wiped out.

By now all pre-arranged plans had been abandoned and it was left to Company officers to improvise ways to achieve their objectives. Captain Sandilands together with a mixed party of Liverpool Scottish and his own men cleared the triangle east of Railway Wood. They had still not made contact with Y Company so they consolidated their position against counter-attack and continued eastwards to Point Y11. Their own artillery barrage had now lifted and the German counter bombardment was erratic. Slowly but surely they drove the enemy back and eventually established themselves at Y11.

On the right was X Company and the Liverpool Scottish were still occupying the trench west of Bellewaarde Farm, north and south of Point Y14. 2nd Lt Fearnley-Whittingstall had been wounded leaving them with only one officer, 2nd Lt John, a young officer attached from the Special Reserve of the York and Lancaster Regiment. Between Y14 and Y11 the left flank of the Company was in contact with a party of Liverpool Scottish who had accompanied W Company to Y11. They had been directed to occupy the trench running south from that point.

While the Northumberlands and Liverpool Scottish had fought their way forward on the left, the centre and the right of 9th Brigade had not been idle. The Royal Scots Fusiliers, the Royal Fusiliers together with parties of Liverpool Scottish and Lincolns had succeeded in taking the second objective.

Reserve Infanterie Regiment 246

'Between 7.00 and 8.00 am the battle slowed to a halt. Elements of 2nd and 3rd Battalions occupied the front line at the Storchschnabel, upon which the enemy was bringing down heavy fire. To the front dense lines of enemy infantry were pinned down by our heavy small arms fire and suffered serious casualties. The regiment then caused artillery fire to be brought down there. This had a visible, successful, effect. Once more it is not known how the enemy managed to close up to the Storchschnabel position. Of the frontline trench garrison only Gastel's platoon manning the left flank returned. From the remaining garrison, neither leaders nor led returned; all the officers were killed. The pathetic remnants of the men who did get back had almost all been wounded during the bombardment, so they were not involved in the actual infantry battle for the trenches.

It appeared that the enemy had broken into the front in three places: opposite the southern edge of Eierwäldchen, at the northern tip of T-Wäldchen [T Copse = Y Wood] and along the Bellewaarde stream. The trench garrisons which survived the bombardment were taken in the flank and rear. They had no ability to manoeuvre, their weapons had been destroyed by shells and their ammunition was buried and so a few went into captivity.

It appears that the first attacking waves closed up very near to our front line during the artillery bombardment. Their rate of advance after that must have been very slow, because it was quite late when they arrived in front of the Storchschnabel position. It also seems as though the British artillery was unsure about the progress of the attack. For a long time it shot at the unoccupied German trenches in the Second Position, causing casualties among its own infantry and holding them up.'[39]

Major W. A. Murray (in command of the 119th Battery, 27th Brigade, 5th Division)

'My dear Claudine,
    I am writing this in the middle of a battle. We started bombarding at 3 am this morning, and at 4.15, the Infantry (which included the Northumbrian folk) went in, and took a lot of German trenches. They are at this moment held up on the right, but we are expecting every moment to hear they have got through and established the whole line. The Germans were not prepared and made a poor show, but they are waking up now, and we are beginning to feel the effects of their wrath, and moreover, the wind is blowing lightly in

---

39. Extract from Leutnant der Reserve Louis Orgeldinger *Das Württembergische Reserve-Infanterie-Regiment Nr. 246* Stuttgart 1931, 97– 107. Translation © Dr Jack Sheldon 2012.

our faces, and we are expecting to get a dose of gas, but our new helmets are proof against it, I believe.

At the same time the 1st Army has gone through further South, and I hear they have the Germans on the run. I hope it is true. At all events we have given them a busy day. I am off to get a little sleep, as things are quiet at the moment, and I was up all last night and will be again tonight.

Goodbye, and love – Bill'[40]

By 9.30 am the British had taken and were holding the old German Front Line, Y16 – Y17 – Y13. It was now time for the third phase of the attack for the Lincolns. A party of fifty NCOs and men led by Major H.E R. Boxer succeeded in occupying the line Y17–Y18. However their own artillery was still shelling this area so they found it impossible to remain there. Major Boxer was wounded as the men retired back to Y17–Y20. Meanwhile the 1st Northumberland Fusiliers were still fighting their way to the German second line, Y7 and Y8.

Captain Sloper, the Battalion MG officer, arrived at Point Y11 and reported that although the enemy were in strength between Y11 and Y8 he was convinced the trench further east was unoccupied. This was part of the third objective and could provide the breakthrough they needed. But there were insufficient troops available to clear the left of the second line and push forward to occupy the third so Captain Sandilands went back to the original German front line to talk to the Commanding Officer and Adjutant. Meanwhile Lieutenant Scrutton had arrived at Y11 with his platoon from Y Company. He had been wounded and his face was covered in blood. It would seem that after the deaths of Captain Roddam, Lieutenant Carter, two other platoon commanders and the Company Sergeant Major, the rest of the platoon had become lost in the labyrinth of the trenches and had veered to the right. This explained the difficulties being faced on the left flank.

Captain Gerard Orby Sloper

'At 4.15 am the 9th Brigade attacked. As machine-gun officer I went with the first wave to choose positions for the guns. When I reached a sunken road I found that a boche machine gun, which had been reported as laid on the road, had not been silenced. I was hit in the left hand. Across the road I turned to the left and was hit in the nose by a piece of grenade. I stumbled into a gap & silenced the gun & shot three of the team. Presently a bombing party came down the trench from my right – which I joined. About five minutes later I was hit on the back of the neck by a piece of shrapnel shell.

I went up to the second line of trenches, collected about twenty men of the Liverpool Scottish under an officer & one of my machine guns proceeded

---

40. With kind permission of Alan Whitworth.

to the 3rd line. I collected and sent back to the O.C. 9th Brigade all papers in this trench with a memo stating that the trenches on my left had not been taken & asked for 200 men to do it with. I then placed the machine-gun in position to cover my left flank & just as I had arranged this a piece of a heavy shell hit me on the top of the head.'

Captain Sloper and a small reconnaissance party pushed forward towards the third objective and as soon as reinforcements from the Liverpool Scottish arrived, they were able to clear the line northwards to point Y8. At the same time Captain Sandilands cleared the second objective between Y11 and the same point.

They managed to push the Germans back after a fierce bombing fight in the trench between Y11 and Y8. Having taken the trench they positioned their coloured screens to ensure they were not bombarded by their own artillery again. But they had now run out of bombs and enemy reinforcements could be seen swarming along the railway line. Reluctantly they withdrew until they received some more bombs and then attacked again, succeeding in pushing the Germans back. Again they ran out of bombs and again they were forced back to Y11 by a counter-attack.

This time they barricaded the trench junction at Y11 and mounted a machine gun on the parapet of the communication trench west of the junction. Three times the Germans counter-attacked, rushing up the trench shouting, bayonets drawn and three times they drove them back under intense rifle and machine-gun fire despite the fact that the machine gunner, Private Marsden, was wounded.

There was a brief lull in the battle as the Germans withdrew and the men braced themselves for their imminent return. Suddenly Private Homer leapt over the barricade. He had spotted a man, abandoned as dead after the bombing and fighting, crawling towards the barricade. He was helped by a Lance Corporal and the two men began lifting the man to the top of the barricade. As the others rapidly helped him over the two men stood guard and then the Lance Corporal followed by Private Homer coolly climbed back over the barricade.

The forward Companies had now been reinforced by Z Company. Lieutenant Dorman-Smith had led the majority of his company to support X Company while Second Lieutenant Lawson took his platoon across the open ground to where W Company were still holding the trench south of point Y11. As he arrived at the trench Lawson was seriously wounded and had to be evacuated.

The Liverpool Scottish and Lincolns continued to advance, crossing the first line of captured trenches and onto the second line but soon found themselves under attack from their own artillery. The red and yellow screens which had been supplied to the troops to display when they had captured the objectives still could not be seen by the artillery, so they continued to shell the same positions. This meant that despite reaching the third line and the hostile trenches east of Bellewaarde Lake the men had to withdraw because they were taking too many casualties from their own fire. The whole area was also under fire from the enemy artillery, there were counter-attacks and bombing attacks and a great deal of hand to hand fighting.

Reserve Infanterie Regiment 246

'At 9.00 am the regiment seized the initiative once more and pushed forward to the eastern edge of Bellewaarde Farm. One company of the reserve battalion deployed along Bellewaarde Lake. The line reached ran via Eclusette, to the track running north past the eastern edge of Bellewaarde Farm. There was no connection with Reserve Infantry Regiment 248 and nothing could be seen of Infantry Regiment 132 to the left.'[41]

---

41. Extract from Leutnant der Reserve Louis Orgeldinger *Das Württembergische Reserve-Infanterie-Regiment Nr. 246* Stuttgart 1931, 97–107. Translation © Dr Jack Sheldon 2012.

Chapter 24

The Tide Turns

Sergeant James Fraser 'D' Coy. 4th Gordon Highlanders

'We led on from the support trench at 10 am and filed up a communication trench which had been dug this morning. It was only about three feet deep and not much protection. Just before we reached the German line a shrapnel shell burst about twenty feet in the air and sprayed us. A lump about the size of a fist hit me on the left of my chest, but I had my Sergeant's whistle in my breast pocket and it deflected the missile, I was knocked down entirely unhurt. Poor Cpls. McIver and McSween both got it in the head and one or two others were wounded. All I had to show was a blue mark on the left side of my chest.

I went on to the German trench where a Staff major was directing the traffic. He asked who I was, I replied "4th Gordons" and he said "GO there" and I went there. I saw my platoon commander and went to him. We got into a small wood between the first and second German lines. We lined up along the wood parallel to the German line and proceeded to make some defence. No one knew we were there and we stayed put.'[42]

At 10.00 am the Commander of 7th Brigade took control of the Royal Fusiliers. He ordered Major Hely Hutchinson to go into the wood which had been captured by the Battalion and organize the men who remained. But the damage done by both the enemy and the British artillery was too much and having lost several officers and men they had no option but to withdraw to a line in a communication trench that Captain de la Perrelle had taken up and turned into a fire trench. They consolidated this and held against all counter-attacks and frontal attacks, as well as a bomb attack on the right until they were finally told to leave the trench. They had been subjected to heavy shelling all day and casualties were appalling. The Adjutant, Captain G. Thomas O'Donel, was killed as were Lieutenants Thornton, Harter, Warde and Rogers and Second Lieutenants Dudley and Bannister by a high explosive shell. Major Hely Hutchinson was badly wounded.

---

42. Kind permission of John Blomfield.

Private Robert Patrick Gordon, 1/4th Gordon Highlanders

'At 10.30am 'D' Coy advanced to 'Y' Wood from trenches across the Menin road near Birr Cross Roads undergoing heavy shelling from shrapnel. No room could be found in 'Y' Wood as the trenches were all occupied, with more men being driven back by German bombs, shrapnel and machine gun fire from 'Y' Wood.'

At 10.30am, after orders to occupy a portion of the German trenches that had been captured that morning, D Company from the 1/4th Gordon Highlanders, advanced to Y Wood with shovels. Among them was Sergeant James Fraser. They came under continuing heavy shrapnel fire and on arrival at Y Wood found all the trenches occupied and more men retreating under heavy German bombing.

Unable to find an unoccupied trench they dug themselves in and waited. There was considerable confusion and no orders of any sort. The severe bombing of the wood lasted for three quarters of an hour but the shelling of the trenches went on all day.

By 10.30 am the Wiltshires' supply of grenades had become exhausted and the Germans succeeded in slowly driving them back down the trench. They took heavy casualties as they retired back pursued by the rapidly advancing Germans. At 11.00 am they evacuated the eastern portion of the German trench and retired into the open losing a considerable number of men in doing so. A counter charge was organized about this time to check the enemy's advance, but without success, as the officer and many men were shot down and the remainder made no progress.

The 3rd Worcestershire had moved up from their reserve positions across the Cambridge road and taken positions in the original British front line. In front of them there was a confused struggle going on. The assault troops of the 9th Brigade had broken through the first line and rushed onto the confused tangle of defences around Bellewaarde Farm. Here they had been halted by their own artillery and eventually had withdrawn back to the German first line which was now full of inter mixed men from the various frontline battalions. The fierce fighting around the Farm had continued all morning with German reinforcements pushing their way through to join in the struggle.

Unter-Elsässisches Infanterie-Regiment Nr. 132

'Soon the "Eclusette trench" was retaken and the reminder of 11th company and the platoon of 12th company moved towards section A. In the meantime 2nd company had managed to link itself to the RIR246. By 11 am the brigade intelligence officer was able to report that the communication trench and a good part of Section A was back in German hands. At 2 pm the work was done and everything was firmly under control of the regiment'.[43]

---

43. Translation courtesy of Rob Shäfer, military historian.

By 11.00 am the 1st Battalion the Wiltshire Regiment had evacuated the eastern portion of the German trench and, although they counter-attacked in an attempt to halt the enemy advance, this was unsuccessful. The officer and men who took part were shot down and the remainder made no progress at all.

The rest of the Liverpool Scottish had now reached the third line, taken it and were busy consolidating it. Others, carried away by excitement and over enthusiasm, carried on towards Dead Man's Bottom and were never seen again.

For a short while it seemed that the Battalion would be able to hold on as the third line was a well-made deep trench. But they were very few men and they urgently needed reinforcements.

Messages were sent back urgently requesting reinforcements and three small parties of Liverpool Scottish managed to make their way up to the most advanced trench. They were followed some time later by a platoon of Northumberland Fusiliers.

But the enemy shelling was very heavy and in places the communication trenches were completely destroyed. They were also choked with dead and wounded so that movement through them was very difficult. The leap frogging and moving up of the supporting Brigade as it relieved the 9th Brigade caused serious congestion and men became badly mixed up with each other. Some of the Royal Irish Rifles from 7th Brigade had actually taken part in the attack on the third line and had to be returned to their correct position. Despite this chaos it might have been possible for them to hold the third line if all of it had been captured. But a section on the right of the Liverpool Scottish had not been captured leaving their right flank open to counter-attack.

The fighting went on all morning in the network of trenches between Y8 and Y11. The enemy had a covered access to his part of the system from the railway cutting, Y5 to Y6. This enabled them to launch continuous counter-attacks, sometimes across the open but mostly by bombing parties. These were all repulsed and the left flank temporarily secured. The defence of this flank was by the Northumberland Fusiliers and some of the Liverpool Scottish. Captain Sandilands of the Northumberland Fusiliers detailed Corporal Bartlett and Private W. Short of V Company to join the bombing squads which were engaged in clearing the enemy out of the trenches on the left onto which he was still clinging. After much heavy fighting Corporal Barlett was killed, but Private Short continued to take part in the continuing attack and counter-attack which went on well into the afternoon. He would subsequently receive the DCM and the French Croix de Guerre for this.

The remainder of the Liverpool Scottish who had reached the final objective remained there for several hours. There were no serious attacks but they did break up an assault from the northerly side of Dead Man's Bottom. They were under continual fire from the machine guns in the railway cutting between Y5 and Y6. These were able to enfilade parts of their trench and a number of men were hit. In an attempt to counter this Captain W. J. H. Renison organized a defensive flank in the communication trench immediately north of Bellewaarde Farm. At the same time the enemy began developing an enveloping movement of the left flank and on the right the British troops began retiring.

Threatened on both sides they were now in an impossible position and they withdrew back to the second line where they made a stand. However the enemy had already reoccupied his second line of trenches south of Bellewaarde Farm and his bombing parties began making their way northwards. The Royal Scots Fusiliers had used all their bombs and were forced to withdraw back to the German first line trenches:

> 'During this action Sergeant William Nash was the last man to retire. He remained in a demolished communication trench with an officer of another battalion who was wounded and unable to move, and then rallied some of the men who had retired, getting them to open fire from the communication trench in order to make the enemy think that the section of trench just vacated was still occupied. In doing this he had to pass repeatedly up and down the ruined trench with less than three feet of cover and exposed to close rifle fire and machine gun fire.'[44]

Sergeant Nash was later warded the DCM for 'conspicuous gallantry' on 16 June 1915.

At about 11.00 am, General Ballard, Officer Commanding 7th Brigade, had come up to the front to attempt reorganization. In the German frontline trenches men from no less than nine Battalions of the 7th and 9th Brigade had become mixed up. The trench was overcrowded, the communication trenches leading to it were choked with wounded and dead bodies and all the telephone wires had been cut. The Germans were bombarding the front line very heavily and there was little response from the British artillery, apparently because they had already used up their daily ammunition allowance and shells and ammunition were scarce. While he was struggling to sort out the various units he received orders from Allenby to launch another attack at 3.30 pm by the troops of 7th and 42nd Brigade to secure the final objective, the line Y18 –Y8.

Brigadier General Alexander Johnston

> 'Losses were heavy and the 7th Inf Brigade were ordered up to support. Our original frontline trenches and the German trenches which we had captured along the edge of Y and Railway Woods were therefore now very crowded.

---

44. Sergeant Nash later became Company Quartermaster Sergeant in the 8th Battlion Royal Scots Fusiliers and was transferred to Salonika. He died of his wounds on 10 November 1918 and is buried in Mikra British Cemetery in Kalamaria, Greece. With kind permission of his grandson.

The German shell fire increased and caused a lot of casualties in these trenches which were full of all sorts of regiments hopelessly mixed up who wanted sorting out a lot. We wanted our artillery to keep the German guns quiet but were told that we had shot away our allowance of ammunition for the day, and that ammunition was scarce. It's too sickening for words that numbers of brave men are losing their lives just because they cannot turn out enough ammunition for us.'[45]

General Ballard immediately requested that no extra troops were sent forward because the trenches were already blocked with dead and wounded men who could not be evacuated. Cramming two fresh battalions in the trench would mean that every enemy shell would kill someone as there was no room to move and no elbow room between the men. However the orders for the attack were repeated and he was informed that the attack was to be preceded by an artillery bombardment from 3.00 pm to 3.30 pm.

General Ballard again pointed out that it was impossible for commanding officers to reach their units, and that owing to the mist no detailed objectives for close support could be given to the artillery. It would also take time to tell all the batteries and many of the telephone lines to the gunners had been cut. It was therefore impossible for the guns to prepare the way for the attack. He was ignored and the main assault was allotted to the 3rd Worcestershires and 2nd Royal Irish Rifles with the Battalions of 42nd Brigade in support. Among the 3rd Worcestershires were Lance Corporal Allen Savage and Sergeant Henry Freeman who were killed in action that day, Lieutenant Colonel Burleigh Francis Brownlow Stuart[46], Captain Samuel Alwyne Gabb, Private George Albert Reynolds and Private John Henry Pitt.[47]

Brigadier General Alexander Johnston

'Well, as some of our people were still holding out about Bellewaarde Farm, it was naturally decided to make another attack and to employ the 7th Inf Brigade to do it; but of course time was required to organize it. Besides the fact that the guns wanted time to get ready for the show, everybody wanted sorting out in the trenches which were already fully crowded and which were being heavily shelled. Unfortunately Allenby arrived at our HQ, and as usual we were then incessantly interfered with. We were told that we had got to attack at once, and that he was sending up the whole of the 42nd Inf

---

45. From *The Great War Diaries of Brigadier General Alexander Johnston*. By kind permission of Edwin Astill. Naval & Military Press.
46. Lieutenant Colonel Burleigh Francis Brownlow Stuart had led the Battalion throughout the Retreat from Mons and the Battle of Le Cateau. He was wounded in the action on 16 June 1915.
47. Private Pitt survived the battle. If you would like to know more about John please visit http://www.bellewaarde1915.co.uk/.

Brigade, a brigade of the New Army, to support. It was simply too wicked for words, and to my mind nothing short of murder.

The attack was to be preceded by an artillery bombardment from 3–3.30 pm: yet at five minutes past three, the orders were only just being written out, lots of the gunner communications were cut, and in any case it would take some time to tell all the batteries their objectives. It was impossible therefore for the guns to adequately pave the way for the attack. Moreover Gen Ballard had 3 times sent back word imploring that no more troops should be sent up to him. Suddenly having 2 fresh battalions crammed into the trenches merely made it impossible to reorganize, the communication trenches were blocked with dead and wounded who could not be evacuated; and passage along them, apart from the enemy's fire, was made impossible by all these extra men being pushed up. The result was that there was no elbow room anywhere, the men were like sardines in a box, and every enemy shell could not fail to hit somebody: one could only move outside the trenches, and then one was almost certain to get hit.

When the attack did take place, the Regiment led the way but it was very difficult to get out of the trenches even, and the enemy's shell and machine gun fire had not been beaten down, so that our front line was simply mown down, and the attack failed; the Regiment lost 13 officers and over 250 men all told, though not all actually in this last attack. Given a fair chance I think the attack would have succeeded; as it was, it was a useless waste of life. It was wicked too shoving this brigade of the New Army in their initial fight into such a rotten situation. They are probably excellent troops, full of keenness, and would have done splendidly, if they had been given a chance. As it was, they realized that they were only in the way, lost a lot of lives, and probably have had their dash impaired.'[48]

Reserve Infanterie Regiment 246

'At 11.20 am [54th Reserve] Division ordered that the line which had been secured was to be defended at all costs and that there was to be reconnaissance forward. Above all, however, there was to be no further advance for the time being and in no circumstances whatsoever if there was no link up with Infantry Regiment 132. However the regiment was determined to take possession of Hill 44 forward of Bellewaarde Farm. An attack order was hastily prepared. The written order, complete with sketches, arrived in the forward area by 11.40 am.'[49]

---

48. From *The Great War Diaries of Brigadier General Alexander Johnston*. By kind permission of Edwin Astill. Naval & Military Press.
49. Extract from Leutnant der Reserve Louis Orgeldinger *Das Württembergische Reserve-Infanterie-Regiment Nr. 246* Stuttgart 1931, 97–107. Translation © Dr Jack Sheldon 2012.

The German gun fire grew heavier by the hour and although the 3rd Worcestershires were not actively engaged they took several casualties under the rain of shells. Midday arrived and the battle for Bellewaarde Spur hung in the balance.

Private Robert Patrick Gordon, 1/4th Gordon Highlanders

'At 12.00 'D' Coy, having failed to find unoccupied trenches, start to dig new trenches in 'Y' Wood amid considerable confusion and poor communications. The trenches in 'Y' Wood were severely shelled during the afternoon and evening. At 3pm 42nd Brigade arrive in the frontline trenches but are unable to advance due to heavy German shell fire and GAS shells.'

The men from the Honourable Artillery Company were still sheltering in the communication trench. As the day wore on the shelling had grown worse as the Germans threw everything at them. It was scorching hot, the air was filled with grit, dust and smoke and the troops began to feel sick and dehydrated. Most only had one water bottle which they sipped from sparingly not knowing how long it would be before they could obtain fresh supplies.

For hour upon hour, shells fell every few minutes showering them in dust, clods of earth and human detritus. The smell of the explosives was overpowering adding to their discomfort. The troops could do nothing to defend themselves, only crouch down against the parapet panting in the heat and lack of oxygen and pray that each breath would not be their last.

At midday an alarm sounded and they raised their heads warily in a brief pause in the shelling. To their horror they could see scores of men running towards them, retreating from the trench in front. They ran right over the Honourable Artillery Company, many dropping to the ground and into the trench as they came under continuing enemy rifle and machine-gun fire and artillery. Some of the retreating men shouted that gas had been used but it later transpired that all the officers in the two frontline trenches had been killed and someone had shouted gas and the rest had panicked and run.

Many of the retreating men gathered by the hedge situated behind their trench. Several troops from Honourable Artillery Company warned them it was too dangerous to stand there but were ignored. Soon they were taking large numbers of casualties.

In the brief lull the troops examined their rifles. They were clogged with dirt and utterly useless and the men set to cleaning them. The enemy artillery was still shelling them but the British artillery was quiet. The retreating men had gradually begun returning and began to crowd into the communication trench until there was virtually no room to move. It was so hot no one could eat and they were constantly covered in debris from the shells. The wounded began to mount up and the men cowered lower into the trench. The less seriously wounded were taken back to the field hospital, but the more serious cases were left as it was too dangerous to risk more lives in moving them.

Sergeant Bernard Joseph Brookes, Queen's Westminster Rifles

'We received the following message about midday:-
"Each Third Division reports situation rather obscure. After reaching the enemies of second line of trenches on a line running up from a point J.13 A 4.5 in a S. S. E. direction through BELLEWAARD FARM to about J 12 D 1.2 the Germs shell them very heavily and our line had to retire in places. The Germs commenced a counter-attack against centre of line. Aah. This counter-attack appears to have been driven back by the observation of the F. O. O. (Forward Observation Officer) who could see enemy retiring and losing heavily from our rifle and gunfire about a hundred prisoners belonging to the 27 reserve division and 15th Corps have been taken."[50]

Reserve Infanterie Regiment 246

'By 12.15 pm the regiment (246) was once more master of Bellewaarde Farm and had thrown the British back over the hill. There was an advance on the left flank and Infantry Regiment 132 also gained some round, [so that] the junction point to the left could be re-established. During this operation the enemy was subjected to concentrated fire and suffered very heavy casualties in the process. By now the companies were completely intermingled so, to re-establish the normal chain of command, the regiment divided the front into three sectors. The right hand sector, north of the farm, was commanded by Hauptmann Baumann, the central sector by Hauptmann Kölle, with Hauptmann Keiper Knorr on the left. Each sector commander immediately [created and] withdrew a reserve.'[51]

At 1.00 pm, with the pressure mounting on the Germans to recapture the lost trenches, the 1st and 3rd Companies, Reserve Jaeger Battalion 26 were assigned to Reserve Infanterie Regiment 246.

Meanwhile Captain Dickinson, OC of X Company, Liverpool Scottish, was severely wounded in the second line and it was impossible to move him to safety. With him were twelve to fifteen other men of the Battalion; most were wounded. They refused to leave the Captain, instead choosing to remain where they were and fight it out despite having virtually no bombs left. It was only when the Germans were right on top of them that they finally obeyed the Captain's order to retire. By that time it was too late and only one or two succeeded in getting back to the first line of trenches, the rest were killed.

---

50. Kind permission of Bob Brookes from the 'Diary of Sergeant Bernard Brooks'.
51. Extract from Leutnant der Reserve Louis Orgeldinger *Das Württembergische Reserve-Infanterie-Regiment Nr. 246* Stuttgart 1931, 97–107. Translation © Dr Jack Sheldon 2012.

Chapter 25

A Desperate Situation

Sergeant 2820, John Keith Forbes, 1/4th Gordon Highlanders

'Success favoured us till the afternoon, when in desperate and repeated counter-attacks the Germans swarmed on our lines and would fain have thrust back. It was at this point that part of the 4th Gordons, though originally meant for reserve, was called up as supporting reinforcements, and at this part of the day Forbes displayed the utmost coolness and alertness, observing with his glasses the Germans' every movement and picking off the enemy as they showed themselves a target for his rifle. He escaped himself without a scratch, but lost one of his closest friends, one who had been with him since the Bedford days, of whom he writes, "I knew not until he was gone how close he had actually come to me".'[52]

The Northumberland Fusiliers were struggling from lack of officers. Captain Herbert, the Adjutant was wounded and Lieutenant Colonel Yatman was back at Battalion HQ without either a second in command or an Adjutant. The situation was just as bad in the forward positions.

Other than Captain Sandilands who was also Battalion Second in Command, there was only one officer with each of the companies: Second Lieutenant Cunningham with W Company, Second Lieutenant John with X Company, Second Lieutenant Scrutton with Y Company and Lieutenant Doman-Smith in Z Company. There was also the Machine Gun Officer, Captain Sloper who had assumed command of a mixed party of Fusiliers and Liverpool Scottish. They were all with the troops in the second objective and unable to advance because of fierce opposition from the opposing trenches which were being steadily reinforced. Although there were supporting troops from each Company in the original German front line many were wounded and there had been heavy casualties amongst the NCOs leaving them virtually leaderless. The old no man's land was still full of wounded and the area behind that was being heavily bombarded to prevent reinforcements being bought up.

---

52. This is an extract from *Student and Sniper Sergeant. A Memoir of J.K. Forbes*, M.A. (1916) by William Taylor, M.A. and Peter Diack, M.A. Hodder and Stoughton.

Captain Sandilands left Second Lieutenant Cunningham in charge at Y11 and Second Lieutenant Scrutton in charge of the trench south of that point and went back to report the situation to Lieutenant Colonel Yatman. However, the 2nd Royal Irish Rifles had managed to get forward and their commanding officer had taken over the NF original Battalion HQ. He had no idea where Lieutenant Colonel Yatman was but was in touch with 9th Brigade so Captain Sandilands delivered his report to him instead. He then made his way forward to the right of X Company who were just south of Y14. The situation here was desperate. Large numbers of men had been killed and those remaining had appointed their own leaders as all the NCOs were dead. The trench was so shallow that in order to move along it under cover of the parapet, he had to crawl over the men, including the wounded, who were lying in the bottom.

As the trench ran north it gradually improved and became deeper and there were fewer breaks. He found Second Lieutenant John (now wounded in the arm) Captain Sloper (wounded in the face and in considerable pain) and Lieutenant Dorman-Smith. He had reached the third objective east of Y11 virtually unopposed. But he had been unable to progress towards Y8 although he had succeeded in holding his position south of the trench junction for nearly an hour. As a threat developed on his right flank he had withdrawn his party back to the portion of the second objective held by the left and centre of X Company.

They were completely pinned down by the enemy. The slightest exposure drew immediate heavy rifle and machine-gun fire from the opposing trench. The only way they would be able to go forward would be after a heavy artillery bombardment directed on the enemy trenches opposite them. Without this it would be impossible and lead to massive loss of life. For the moment all they could do was to cling to their positions and wait for some support.

Having viewed the seriousness of their position Captain Sandilands moved to re-join Second Lieutenants Scrutton and Cunningham on the left. But he never made it. Before he could reach them he was hit by a sniper and had to be evacuated. Captain Sloper was now only the senior officer with the forward troops but he was unaware of this.

Captain Gerard Orby Sloper

> 'Owing to my wounds I am rather vague about the subsequent proceedings until a Sergeant of the Liverpool Scottish came to report that his officer said the boches were in the trench on his right & that he would have to retire. I went to fix things up & found that he had retired. Instead of sending a message for him to come back again I took the machine-gun back to the second line. I now consider that was a mistake although our left flank was in the air, but I was not in a fit state to decide at the time.'

By now much of the ground won by the right and centre of 9th Brigade had been lost. The Royal Fusiliers, supported by the Lincolns had gained the west bank of Bellewaarde Lake and some of the Royal Scots Fusiliers, supported by the Liverpool Scottish, had secured a toehold in the third objective to the south of Captain Sloper's position. However, yet again they had been forced to withdraw after the failure of the artillery screens to prevent their own men shelling them as well as those of the enemy. This had exposed Captain Sloper's right flank and led to his withdrawal. Fortunately the enemy did not seem to be aware of the difficulties facing the Northumberland Fusiliers. Although they were fired on continually by the German forward troops they were not shelled by enemy artillery for several hours.

Even further right the Royal Fusiliers were so heavily bombarded that they too were forced to retire falling back as far as the original German front line. The German bombardment on Railway Wood, the old no man's land and the Assembly Trenches had not stopped since it had begun at 4.15 am. It was so intense that it was impossible for stretcher-bearers to take the wounded back to the dressing stations and field hospitals. They lay on the ground all day impeding the advance of the desperately needed reinforcements.

Reserve Infanterie Regiment 248

> 'III Battalion (Major von Flatlow) was given the task to support the line and recapture lost ground. According to this, Major von Flatlow was put in charge of the southern sector; Hauptmann Nuber was given the northern one. North of the railway small groups of advancing English and a battery acting in the open became scattered by our artillery, infantry and machine gun fire. At the left flank of the regimental area the fight was surging for a long time within the maze of the trenches.'[53]

The Northumberland Fusiliers HQ in Cambridge Road which had also been occupied by the Royal Irish Rifles had been obliterated. This left Lieutenant Colonel Yatman to share the HQ of the 1st West Yorkshire Regiment, 6th Division. This was situated in a dugout where the Cambridge Road crossed Roulers Railway.

Units of 7th Brigade were rushed forward to reoccupy the line between Y17 and Bellewaarde Farm but the artillery bombardment was too intense and all attempts to do this broke down. The Germans were still in their trenches northeast of Railway Wood and this left the Northumberland Fusiliers in the line between Y14 and Y11 with both flanks exposed.

The situation for the Northumberland Fusiliers grew steadily worse as the hours went by. They only had one officer left, Lieutenant Dorman-Smith. The

---

53. Translated by Sebastian Laudan.

remaining officers of Y Company and W Company, Second Lieutenants Scrutton and Cunningham had both been wounded and evacuated.

Captain Gerard Orby Sloper

> 'The next event I remember was a message being passed up that I could not have the men I asked for, but the 7th (I think) Brigade would attack. I therefore considered it my duty to hold on until the attack began although my left flank was still in the air & we were suffering losses. Soon after this the boches counter-attacked.
>
> We held them up until a bombing party came up the communication-trench my left rear. I was then hit by a grenade which burst behind me while I was trying to collect a party to drive them out, & wounded me in the back & left arm & cut a large blood-vessel below my neck. I lost a great quantity of blood but managed to squeeze the blood-vessel below the cut & the last thing I remember was a boche kicking me on the head at the other end of the trench. Two years later a Sergeant informed me that I had run down the trench.'

Captain Sloper (X Company) had been shot through the lungs and Second Lieutenant John (Z Company) was too seriously wounded to be moved. The enemy had been strongly reinforced and was now massing for an assault on the trenches east and northeast of Bellewaarde Farm. In contrast there were only a handful of Northumberland Fusiliers and Liverpool Scottish who were still able to hold a rifle.

At about 2.30 pm all hell broke loose for the Northumberland Fusiliers. The enemy began subjecting the trenches between Y14 and Y11 to a continuous stream of machine-gun and rifle fire. Every foot of the parapet was blasted as they simultaneously charged up the communication trench to Y11, grenades and bombs flying as they advanced. The Fusiliers tried in vain to stem the advance by manning the barricade and throwing bombs at the attackers. Every man was killed and the trench junction carried by the enemy.

On the right flank the Germans were steadily advancing east of Bellewaarde Farm towards Y14 and virtually all the men were now wounded or dead. Lieutenant Dorman-Smith began to think he was the only survivor until a young soldier from the Liverpool Scottish came up to tell him the Germans were working their way along the trench and were barely sixty yards off where they stood. As he finished speaking he too was shot dead.

There was little to do other than to withdraw. The one remaining officer was nowhere near the few remaining troops so there was no question of giving orders to that effect. The communication trench was completely blocked by the shelling so it was obvious to the few remaining men that the only way to avoid death or capture was to risk crossing open ground. Having held the position for nine hours

Lieutenant Dorman-Smith and a handful of survivors escaped back to the shelter of the old German front line. He found Second Lieutenant Scrutton who'd had his wounds dressed and returned to action. He had taken charge of several groups of leaderless men from the Northumberland, Liverpool Scottish and Scots Fusiliers and was busy consolidating the trench for defence.

The other Battalions of 9th Brigade had lost most of their officers too and were completely exhausted. The Royal Fusiliers had also suffered as the Germans had begun using gas shells freely. By the end of the day only a small amount of ground still remained in the hands of the Battalion who had taken losses of fifteen officers and 376 men.

Private A. Beckett was killed while assisting a wounded colleague along a trench. Private McGee was wounded in two places but continued to carry messages through the shell swept area until sent to a dressing station by his Captain. Lance Corporal Filter stuck to his machine gun all through the day though wounded; the Machine Gun Sergeant, Sergeant Jones, also remained at his gun throughout the day until sent to the Dressing Station to have his wounds dressed – he was wounded early in the day. Sergeant H. Smith bandaged two wounded men and then carried them to cover all the time under heavy fire.

Meanwhile No 2 and No 4 sections of the 1/1st Cheshire Field Company RE had been told by the CO of the Royal Irish Rifles to standby and await orders. A digging party of 150 which was supposed to be at their disposal had advanced with the initial attack and had not returned. The situation appeared uncertain on their left and it was not until 2.00 pm that the officers of 2 and 4 sections were sent for to discuss the digging of a communication trench. An officer went to reconnoiter and found that the sunken road leading forward from the old line to the captured first line was covered from view and rifle fire. He considered this would be secure for anyone going up to the lines.

At 3.00 pm the Royal Engineers were told that a minor assault on the left was being contemplated. The question of the communication trench was finally shelved as they considered that the sunken road was secure enough for both good communication and for moving troops up to the front.

At the same time the Germans had started a heavy bombardment of Y Wood and the trenches which had been captured in the morning. The British guns replied by shelling the Germans in the Bellewaarde Lake area. For the Wiltshires the situation remained unchanged and the men stayed in their trenches as the battle raged elsewhere.

At 3.35 pm, five minutes after the fixed hour, 7th Brigade received a message postponing the attack till 3.50 pm. This message never reached the troops, who were left assuming the attack was to start when the bombardment finished.

The 3rd Worcesters and the Royal Irish Rifles waited for their orders to advance. As they did so, the overflowing trenches behind them were further crowded by the arrival of the two new battalions from the 14th Division who had just arrived in France. They had received orders to advance into the Assembly Trenches at

1.00 pm but had been delayed by a particularly heavy German barrage put down specifically to prevent reinforcements being bought up.

At 9.45 pm on the 15 June, 9th Battalion Kings Royal Rifle Corps (KRRC) had marched out on the Ypres road round the outskirts of Ypres to the railway embankment just north of the Lille Gate. With them were the Adjutant, Lieutenant Eustace George Bourke, 19-year-old Lance Corporal Edwin Lofthouse, 23-year-old Rifleman Ernest Reader, 30-year-old Rifleman Edward Presswell, Rifleman James Weir and Rifleman George Alfred Silvers – all died on 16 June. Lieutenant J. Stowe was wounded.

They spent the night digging themselves in on the embankment and at dawn lay down to try and catch a little sleep. But two batteries of the artillery were close to their dugouts so at 2.50 am they were woken by the ensuing bombardment. When the Germans replied the men watched as the shells soared over their heads and hit the ramparts of Ypres 100 yards behind them. As they waited the shelling grew more intense and the road was clogged with wounded men and German prisoners as they streamed past on their way to the advance dressing stations near the Lille Gate.

The 9th Battalion Rifle Brigade had settled into dugouts near the Lille Gate on 15 June. With them were 26-year-old Rifleman Gilbert Sanoby and 25-year-old Rifleman Alfred Abraham. (Both were to die the next day.) At 1.00 am they received orders to move up to the Assembly Trenches on the north of the Menin Road behind Witte Poort Farm. But they were seen as they advanced and subject to heavy bombardment. The Companies were ordered to dump their packs and advance in two lines either side of the railway embankment. The intention was to occupy the trenches vacated by the 9KRRC.

But when they arrived they found they were already occupied by the 7th Battalion KRRC from 41st Brigade. 7th Battalion Rifle Brigade were Corps Reserve and as such had marched at 9.15 pm on 15 June to Vlamertinghe where they had gone into huts. On 16 June at 10.30 am they had marched to a position south of Ypres and taken shelter along the southwest of the railway. They were still Corps Reserve and would remain there until 8.30 pm that night.

The 5th (Service) Battalion Ox and Bucks were in trenches at Vlamertinghe south of Ypres on 15 June. With them were 27-year-old Lieutenant Charles M. Berlein and Lance Corporal Henry Tills who were to be killed in action the following day. Second Lieutenant Curry and Captain Carfrae were wounded. At 10.00 pm the men, with 200 round of ammunition each, went by train to Poperinghe. Once there they marched in two columns by the main road to Ypres and went into trenches south of the Lille Gate. On arrival the two sand bags each man carried were filled and they set to work improving the cover.

The 5th Battalion King Shropshire Light Infantry from 42nd Brigade had dug itself in on the night of 15 June near the Ypres-Roulers railway line southeast of and just outside the walls of Ypres. With them were Lieutenant Basil Herbert Ellis, Captain Avery and Second Lieutenant Valentine Douglas French – all killed in action on June 16. (French's brother was wounded in the same action.)

On the morning of 16 June they had listened to the sound of the guns for several hours before marching at 10.00 am to support the attack. They were intended to support the centre but, on leaving the railway cutting at Hell Fire Corner and coming out into the open, they came under heavy fire from high explosive and other shells. This led them to divert to the right. The two leading platoons of A Company did not receive the order to retire and so continued under heavy fire to the sunken road which had been the original objective.

The remainder of the 5th Battalion King's Shropshire Light Infantry finally reached the high ground at Gordon House. But here they came under such intense gun fire from the direction of Hill 60 that the platoons lost touch with each other. They eventually found the trench and most of them entered it and tried to pass through. But it was already packed with men of the various different regiments taking part in the attack and progress was agonisingly slow. They finally ground to a halt after reaching the low ground near and across the Menin Road. Here it was so crowded it was impossible to move.

The 1/4th Gordon Highlanders now found themselves sharing their already overflowing fire trench with men from 42nd Brigade so trenches in Y Wood were visited with a view to moving two Companies there to support D Company. However the trenches here were also congested with more men from 42nd Brigade and no move was made.

Sergeant James Fraser 'D' Coy. 4th Gordon Highlanders

'The German artillery made excellent shooting on their captured line and the Honourable Artillery Company were having a bad time. All the shells passed over our heads and apart from knocking branches off trees, did us no harm. A Royal Artillery Forward Observation officer joined us and when he saw the Germans were showing signs of coming out of their trench, by good fortune his telephone wire was not cut, he got on to his battery and they soon stopped any aggressive ideas.

Three of us had an extraordinary escape. Sergeant. Major Low, Sergeant. McKenzie and myself were having some food when suddenly a small field gun shell dropped between McKenzie's knees. I'll never forget the look of horror on our faces and after a few seconds of paralysis we scrambled away. It never went off, but we did not touch it. Stayed in the wood for the rest of the day.'[54]

---

54. Kind permission of John Blomfield.

Chapter 26

Gas and Counter-Attack

The 9th KRRC were delighted to hear that the attack was succeeding and that the British had soon captured the second line of German trenches. With the 5th Shropshire leading the way, closely followed by the 9th KRRC, 5th Oxfordshire and Buckinghamshires and 9th Rifle Brigade, they began to advance. They moved carefully along the railway with 100 yards between platoons. Their orders were to get into the Assembly Trenches due north of the Menin Road and east and west of a track leading north from there to the railway.

At 11.00 am A Company, the 5th (Service) Battalion Ox and Bucks in the north end of the trench moved out to occupy dugouts on the railway bank. They moved up a communication trench that was three feet deep in water in places and blocked with the wounded near the recently captured German front line. They were then told that the Assembly Trenches into which they were to move were still full of the 9th KRRC so they had to remain outside.

The 5th Shropshire left the railway and headed in a south easterly direction towards their objective but immediately came under heavy shrapnel fire as they went over the ridge. Seeing this, the OC of the King's Royal Rifle Corps (Major Hennessey) decided to take his Battalion by the railway along the lower ground. He went with the leading Company, B Company, under Captain E. Benson and succeeded in reaching the point where the Menin Road crossed the railway without taking any casualties.

He waited there with B Company until A Company under Captain Christie came up. However, the German observation balloon had spotted the move and at once the guns opened up on the railway. The Adjutant, Lieutenant E. W. Bourke, was killed and as the shrapnel continued to burst with dreadful accuracy a number of men were killed and wounded. Realizing there was no point staying where they were, and unable to advance because of congestion caused by stretcher-bearers collecting and bringing back wounded, Major Hennessey turned right into a communication trench. This was apparently in the direction of the trenches they had been ordered to occupy. They were closely followed by D Company.

After only a few hundred yards they found the trench was blocked by a fatigue party carrying bombs and despite several attempts to pass them they were unable to do so. Eventually the OC decided the only option was to climb out and cross the ridge a little further left from where the Shropshires had tried earlier.

Each platoon calmly left the trench and began doubling across the open plain followed by D Company. The guns rained fire down on them but despite this they took surprisingly few casualties and eventually reached a trench running parallel to their advance. At one end they found a communication trench which led directly to their objective. Meanwhile A and B Companies had also advanced to the north side of the Menin Road and C and D Companies were on the south so the whole Battalion had managed to reach their assigned positions.

The Germans then began bombing them and further movement was impossible. The men lay close together, unable to move as the shelling went on for an hour and a half. Gas and gas shells were also used. The British guns finally opened up with a furious barrage about half an hour before the German guns ceased. By then it was getting dark and they could see by the flashes from the guns that the Germans were on three sides of them.

The 9th Battalion RB had been ordered to follow the 5th Ox and Bucks into the Assembly Trenches built on the Y15 and Y16 position. But 1,000ft from Sally Port they received the message that the trenches were too crowded and they were not needed. Like the 5th Ox and Bucks they too were left with no option but to lie out in the open. But this time it was along the railway where they were shelled continuously with high explosive from 3.15 pm to 6.45 pm.

Despite the non-appearance of the units from 42nd Brigade, back in the front line the order had been given for the assault. The plan was for the Royal Irish Rifles and the 3rd Worcestershire to push through the captured positions and storm the enemy third line of defences on the edge of Bellewaarde Lake. To pave the way for the attack the British artillery had already begun bombarding the enemy, eventually stopping at 3.50 pm. As the guns fell silent, B Company, under Captain Maitland, followed by C Company, under Captain Buckler, got ready to go over the top. But they had trouble leaving the trench.

Having made their way through the crowds of wounded and disorganized troops who blocked the trenches they had emerged on the other side. Here they were met with a wall of fire which killed the two Commanding officers and virtually all the men instantly. The machine guns and rifles of the enemy had not been blown apart by the artillery bombardment so the men on the front assault line were simply mown down. The survivors threw themselves to the ground and took cover among some trees until support arrived. The Battalion stretcher-bearers managed to rescue some of the wounded and Sergeant F. E. Lamb was awarded the DCM for rescuing five wounded men. The 3rd Worcestershire continued to wait for support which never came. Thirteen officers and 250 men were killed and wounded in the attack.

For the Royal Irish Rifles, the attack was launched by C and D Companies led by Captain Farran and Lieutenant Eales. They had already spent thirty hours without sleep and been subjected to the unceasing pounding of German shells all day, yet they still went forward. But the odds against them were too great. They met a wall of fire from the front and from the flank, the railway line. The few survivors managed to get back to the trench exhausted and dazed. Meanwhile A Company on the extreme left flank, worked hard at consolidating their position and their bombers managed to prevent the Germans from succeeding in their counter-attack.

Reserve Infanterie regiment 246

'Hardly had the new line been established than the British launched another attack. However it was beaten off completely around 3.30 pm. The Tommies received a bloody nose once more during this attack. The newly deployed reserve machine guns played an active part in defeating this thrust. By 4.00 pm the entire regiment was engaged. The regimental commander only had two companies of the 2nd Battalion in reserve at his disposal. Following a request, two companies of Jäger Battalion 26 were made available. Contradictory reports from the front made it impossible to evaluate either the overall situation or the line reached. As a result General von Roschmann[55] went forward personally to the position where he discussed the future shape of the counter-attack with the battalion commanders. In the Storchschnabel he fired up the men and, for a while, directed the battle himself. He took no account of the shells, though Leutnant Pfister, adjutant of 3rd Battalion Reserve Infantry Regiment 246 who was standing next to him, was wounded, as were some runners. The personal appearance of the general in the firing line, in the turmoil of battle, made an indescribable impression on the men. There he was, right in the middle of the regiment with his red collar insignia clearly visible from a distance.

Once more the enemy artillery fire increased to such an extent that an advance was out of the question for the time being. The British, too, suffered severely as a result of their own high explosive shells and shrapnel fire. To the west of Bellewaarde Farm, they had hoisted an artillery recognition flag, but apparently it was not visible from the rear.'[56]

At 3.50 pm it was decided to abandon the attack and to consolidate the line from Y16–Y15–Y13 and from there to the railway. The Royal Scots Fusiliers were already back in their original trench southwest of the farm. Shelling continued all day from both sides and at 5.00 pm the second bombardment took place. It was here that most of the Royal Scottish Fusilier casualties were sustained.

It was obvious to the 3rd Worcestershires that success was impossible in the face of the superior German artillery which was dominating the battle. The German batteries which ringed the Ypres Salient from east, south and north had turned

---

55. Generalmajor Alfred von Roschmann, Commander 107 Reserve Infantry Brigade 54th Reserve Division. He was fatally wounded on 13 September 1916 at Manancourt Chateau.
56. Extract from Leutnant der Reserve Louis Orgeldinger *Das Württembergische Reserve-Infanterie-Regiment Nr. 246* Stuttgart 1931, 97–107. Translation © Dr Jack Sheldon 2012.

their batteries to fire on the attack and the spur made an easy target. The seven thousand troops crammed into a space of not more than a thousand square yards were shelled incessantly and casualties were appalling.

Finally, at 4.00 pm, orders filtered through to the Honourable Artillery Company that they were to retire, but no one was sure if the orders were real as they were passed from person to person.

By now a heavy, but fortunately fairly inaccurate bombardment, was being directed at the crowded trenches. Unable to move, some of the men from the 5th Battalion Shropshire Light Infantry climbed out and tried to escape across the open ground. They died instantly, mowed down by the intense rifle fire from the counter-attacking Germans.

At 4.00 pm the 4th Gordon Highlanders began collecting their wounded. They had received orders that the Battalion was to go with the Brigade into reserve at GHQ line.

The 9th Rifle Brigade communication with Brigade had been cut so they did not receive any further orders. At 7.00 pm one Company from the Oxfordshire and Buckinghamshire separated from its own battalion and put itself under 9th Battalion Rifle Brigade orders. By 7.00 pm the area was clogged with wounded and other soldiers coming back from the front lines and the shelling was growing nearer. Without orders the Battalion took up a new position in some fields south of the railway and dug themselves in under heavy shrapnel fire. At 8.15 pm they received orders to retire back to the original trenches. They found these were already occupied by troops from 41st Brigade (7th KRRC), so they dug fresh ones behind them.

By 6.00 pm orders were given that there would be no further attacks. They had gained the German front line and this would be consolidated by fresh reinforcements while the attacking battalions would be withdrawn. The orders reached the beleaguered men at 7.30 pm and the 1/4th Battalion South Lancashire Regiment moved up to help in the consolidation of the new line. Men from the various regiments began to slowly crowd together and eventually they were sorted out and reorganized into groups. They then began making their way back to their starting places.

Unaware of the British orders, at 7.00 pm the remaining Companies from Reserve Jaeger Battalion 26 were transferred to Reserve Infanterie Regiment 246.

Reserve Jaeger Battalion 26

> 'Sergeant Schmidt was ordered to take the position with 3 MG near Klavierhaus in order to cover any further hostile advances towards Bellewaarde Farm. Later in the evening he was ordered to proceed to the frontline, in an area that was unfamiliar to him, and find convenient positions for his guns.
>
> Fortunately the enemy did not take advantage of the considerable confusion at R.I.R. 246's frontline battalion, nor did they exploit the gains

won at Bellewaarde Farm. During the rest of the day and evening the enemy withdrew from the conquered positions, without being seriously counter-attacked.

1st company R.J.B. 26 under command of Leutnant Duckart took part in the mopping-up during the evening and night of the 16th. 3rd company took over and held the trench near the Storchenschnabel wäldchen (Stork's beak Wood) and acted as back-up. By next morning the enemy had withdrawn to the west of Bellewaarde Farm.'[57]

At around the same time as the orders were given to halt the attack, the Germans began pounding the Honourable Artillery Company with a different kind of shell. To the troops it sounded like a gigantic firecracker with two clearly separate explosions. They came over much quicker than normal shells and were much closer together. These were gas shells and it took them by surprise, having not experienced this before. Their first warning was when there was a sudden crash in the trench, blinding everyone with dust. As the dust cleared they looked down at what appeared to be dead bodies mingling with sandbags on the bottom of the trench. Then they smelt the gas. Most of them hurriedly put on their respirators but others were slower to react. The gas made them violently sick while others began coughing uncontrollably. After the longest day many of them had ever spent under constant shelling, this was the final straw and many lay there waiting for the end. But it was not to be.

After about fifteen minutes the gas shells stopped and the surviving troops were able to take off their respirators. The trench was badly damaged and they set about rebuilding the parapet, but the smell of the gas lingered making them feel sick.

Sergeant Bernard Joseph Brookes, Queen Westminster Rifles

'The afternoon was somewhat quieter, but the battle commenced again at six o'clock when the Germs subjected us to a very severe bombardment for an hour, which they followed up with a strong attack, and our men had to retire. We now held only one line.

For some purpose-the reason of which I cannot say-during this counter-attack our guns were practically silent.

The Germans were bombarding us terribly, and all our men were falling over like ninepins, but not one of our guns as far as we could tell, belched forth their death dealing missiles until the Germs were about to attack, when they opened up with shrapnel practically making a curtain of fire. This

---

57. Heinz Lehmann, *The Royal Saxon Reserve Jager Battalion No. 26* Dresden 1923. Translated by Sebastian Laudan. (Heinz Lehmann, Das Königlich Sächsische Reserve-Jäger-Bataillon Nr. 26, Dresden 1923).

procedure may be the best if the signalling wires are not broken and the S. O. S. message (the call sent when the enemy is seen to leave the trench to attack) can be got through to the Batteries Artillery, but if the lines are broken, which invariably is the case, it has to be left to the infantry to repel the attack after they have been subjected to a severe bombardment.

    I do not think that at this time it was a case of shortage of shells for we saw tremendous stocks of ammunition in certain places before the attack, and some artillerymen to whom we were speaking said that it had been brought up for attack, and that we had more handy.'[58]

The German counter-attack started almost as soon as the shelling ceased. The weary men stood up ready to put up the best defence they could. But the men in the front trench had been badly affected by the gas attack and it seemed unlikely they would be able to hold on. There was a big gap in the parapet that could not be manned so four men were detailed to lie behind what was left of the parados and cover the gap with their rifles. It was very uncomfortable as the trench was full of dead bodies and the smell of the gas still lingered. The men prepared themselves and then, just as the Germans began massing for the assault, the British artillery started up and the counter-attack crumpled.

    By now most of the branches had been blown off the trees and many of the trees were nothing more than splintered shapes punctuating the landscape. The thick hedge behind the trench had completely disappeared, blown away by the tornado of gas shells that had scythed through it.

---

58. Kind permission of Bob Brookes from *The Diary of Sgt Bernard J. Brookes*.

Chapter 27

The Battle Ends

Reserve Infanterie Regiment 248

'The adversaries fought each other with hand grenades over open ground as well. Companies Fassbender and Bommas particularly distinguished themselves. The Battalion's aide-de-camp, Leutnant Gehweiler, carried several hand grenade parties along. It was in part thanks to Leutnant Fassbender that Battalion Flatlow had been able to throw the English out of our trenches by nightfall, completely regaining the regimental sector except a small bit within the Gierwäldchen.

Bataillon LEGL – initially being in brigade reserve – was ordered to support Reserve-Infanterie-Regiment 246, which made an advance up to Bellewaarde farm.'[59]

Reserve Infanterie Regiment 246

'Towards evening the right flank also managed to gain ground astride the Roschmannweg [presumably named after the commander 107 Reserve Infantry Brigade] and to emerge via Bellewaarde Farm. Here the remainder of the 3rd Battalion was still fighting, together with 8th Company [commanded by] Leutnant Hoffmann and the 6th Company [under] Hauptmann Seeger. During this advance a platoon of 6th Company, commanded by Feldwebelleutnant Castel of 12th Company, captured a British machine gun, together with thirty unwounded prisoners.

Following a heavy preliminary bombardment a further thrust was launched from the area of the Storchschnabelwäldchen against the British position by Bellewaarde Lake. Reserve Infantry Regiment 248 supported this attack and drove forward between Bellewaarde Farm and Eierwäldchen in a southwesterly direction. Infantry Regiment 132 was to have participated and so was Jäger Battalion 26 but, because the time for preparation was so short, the attack was not developed fully. In view of the gathering darkness and the contrary wishes of neighbouring regiments, a further advance had to be abandoned. The troops remained in the line they had reached and turned it

---

59. Translated by Sebastian Laudan.

into a defensive position overnight. In order to reorganize the units, 1st and 2nd Battalions were withdrawn from the line of battle. This meant that the front line was now manned by 3rd Battalion and Jäger Battalion 26, which had been completely under command of the regiment since the morning.'[60]

The 1st Battalion the Wiltshire Regiment remained in their trenches until 6.30 pm when another heavy bombardment started which lasted about an hour. They also fired a considerable number of gas shells at the area around the Menin Road but these only caused temporary inconvenience.

As the night wore on, scores of men returned from the front line. Many were wounded or suffering from the gas attacks. They stumbled wearily across the open ground but very few were hit. The shelling continued, but gradually became more intermittent. It was much cooler now and the men took the opportunity to eat some of their rations.

It was past midnight when a long line of men in kilts, the Gordon Highlanders, appeared from the rear. The relief had finally arrived. As the men began to retire they passed through the old British front line which was full of wounded waiting to see doctors. Half a mile further back was the dressing station. The fields were dotted with small parties of men who had been withdrawn and because the ground was lower a smell of gas pervaded the whole area.

At 2.00 am on 17 June Private Edward Sprunt, 1510, 1st Battalion Honourable Artillery Company, (Stretcher-Bearer Section) was helping a wounded comrade back near Chateau Hooge. He was only fifteen yards from the dressing station when a shell came over and exploded beneath the stretcher killing him and two others and wounding the remaining two stretcher-bearers.

As they withdrew further back along the road the intermittent shelling continued and at intervals their way was blocked by fallen trees adding to the general confusion as men rushed to escape the continuing bombardment.

Everywhere they looked along the road and the railway they saw discarded ammunition, food, tins, and clothing. Anything that added to the weight of the exhausted men had been thrown away as they tried to put themselves out of range of the guns. Some found water at abandoned houses; others kept going until they reached a wayside watering place. Others stopped to eat food while some just fell asleep in ditches and on piles of sacks outside deserted cottages. As they reached the transport fields they were given tea and then fell asleep where they were without even taking their boots off.

---

60. Extract from Leutnant der Reserve Louis Orgeldinger *Das Württembergische Reserve-Infanterie-Regiment Nr. 246* Stuttgart 1931, 97–107. Translation © Dr Jack Sheldon 2012.

2nd Battalion South Lancashire

'During the whole day fire from our guns and those of the enemy was heavy – many of the enemy's shells pitched into YPRES and there, together with falling buildings, placed the battalions in very considerable danger. Whole battalions moved forward from YPRES about 9 p.m. to consolidate the ground won and still held by Units of 8th Brigade. As companies moved up to the positions they were exposed to enemy's fire of shrapnel; high explosions, and gas shells, sustaining a number of casualties, and the move was really slow. On arrival at the position there was a certain amount of companies amongst the Units in occupation and it was found impossible to carry out the work intended.'

Later that afternoon the shelling died down, but it was not possible to remove the wounded until it was dark. Many had been wounded in the first assault and had lain there all day.

At 6.00 pm the Lincolns, under the command of Major D. H. F. Grant received orders to fall back to the first line of captured trenches, Y16 – Y17 and Y16 – Y15. Here they were ordered to reorganize and hold the line at all costs. At the same time the Germans bombarded them with gas shells and the men had to use their respirators.

The German shelling reached its height between 7.00 pm and 8.30 pm that evening. During that time it was estimated that about 100 shells a minute fell on the Brigade front. The Germans continued to make desperate attempts to win back their trenches, but they were unsuccessful. At 8.00 pm 42 Brigade received its orders to return to Vlamertinghe. Each Battalion was to move independently under cover of darkness. The weary men prepared for the long walk back to their bivouacs.

At about 9.30 pm the 1st Battalion the Lincolnshire Regiment was relieved by the 4th Gordon Highlanders and arrived back at their bivouacs (18b45) at about 5.00 am on 17 June.

The Liverpool Scottish also withdrew back to the captured German front line where they helped consolidate it. The Liverpool Scottish remained in the old German front line until just before midnight when they and other units of 9th Brigade were relieved by troops of 8th Brigade. Their stretcher-bearers remained in the line after the Battalion had been relieved. On the night of 16/17 June they continued to make sure all the wounded were brought in.

During the night the Northumberland Fusiliers were relieved by the 2nd Royal Scots of 8th Brigade.

For the Worcesters the approach of sunset bought no relief. The German gunners began redoubling their fire power determined to destroy the attackers before they could reorganize. Before the bombardment ceased at midnight more than half the attacking troops had been killed or wounded. They were finally able to withdraw at 11.00 pm when they handed over their positions to the Royal Scots from 8th Brigade. The exhausted survivors reassembled near Hell Fire Corner and marched wearily back down the Menin Road through Ypres and back to Vlamertinghe.

At midnight the 2nd Royal Irish Rifles handed over their trench intact to the Royal Scots, of the 8th Brigade.

Sergeant Bernard Joseph Brookes, Queen's Westminster Rifles

> 'As evening fell the firing became a more normal and the night passed without any further attack, we holding one line on a ridge on the left of the village of Hooge.
>
> Twice during the night the Germs broke our wire, and I had to go out and mend it, but although it is more difficult to trace the break, it is not such a bad job as when it had to be mended in daylight under observation of the Bosches.
>
> The importance of keeping up communications cannot be exaggerated, for if the line is broken messages have to be taken by hand, and apart from the length of time this method takes, it is very dangerous for the signaller who may not get through.'[61]

After nearly twelve hours of fighting all that remained in the hands of the British were the positions they had captured as their first objective.

The net result of the first Battle of Bellewaarde was the gain of 250 yards upon a front of 800 yards, over 200 prisoners, and three machine guns. Heavy losses were also inflicted on the enemy, but probably not more than half those of the British. These numbered about 3,800 killed, wounded and missing. The British line had been carried forward to just north of the Menin road, but the enemy remained in possession of Bellewaarde ridge and the observation posts on it.

---

61. Kind permission of Bob Brookes from *The Diary of Sergeant Bernard J. Brookes.*

Part Three

Summing Up

Chapter 28

The Aftermath

During the rest of the night of 16/17 June U Company, The 1/4th Gordon Highlanders, held on to the trenches captured the previous day. They carried out the wounded and ate their iron rations. Sentries were posted every few yards while the others tried to snatch what little sleep they could. In the distance they could hear the Germans repairing their trenches and strengthening their battered front line.

Sergeant James Fraser 'D' Coy, 4th Gordon Highlanders

'17th: *Got out of the wood at 2a.m. and got back to the support trench, everyone had thought we were all scuppered as no one had heard of us since 11 o'clock.*
18th: *Back to old line by Hell Fire Corner, everything quiet.*
19th: *Quiet day, had one blast of shelling which killed three of us. Gordon, McLean and Donald. Relieved that night.*
20th: *In bivouacs at Ouderdohm, slept most of the day.*
21st: *Battalion parade, Col. Ogilvie had tears in his eyes as he looked at his battalion now about half strength. In afternoon went Poperinghe for baths and delousing, our shirts and kilts were put through some sort of oven, but when we looked at our shirts again the lice seemed a bit stunned. Back we went to bivvies.*'[62]

Having survived the incidents before the battle and the battle itself, Sergeant Fraser would be regarded as lucky or one who had a Guardian Angel as even at the Battle of Loos in September the same year he received a 'Blighty' wound (allowing a man to be sent home for recuperation) which ensured he would be away from frontline duties indefinitely.

A tour of the area the following morning showed that the area south of Birr Crossroads and up towards Witt Poort Farm had taken a heavy pounding and was badly chewed up. South of the farm and Y Wood were in a terrible state. All the trees had been knocked down although many of the German trenches had survived intact. These were well dug, very deep and narrow with formidable gun

---

62. Kind permission of John Blomfield.

emplacements and very strong dugouts. Very little of the barbed wire remained and any that did was torn up and coloured bright yellow from the lyddite fumes. Many of the German prisoners also had yellow hair suggesting the content of the large British howitzer shells was extremely unpleasant.

The old German communication trench which ran to Bellewaarde Farm had now been turned into a fire trench and the British were finally able to look down into the German line that ran up towards Hooge. They were also able to enfilade it from the side. West of the farm a sap ran out to the east at the end of which the British were building a fire trench.

At Railway Wood the area was completely devastated and the German trenches were only about fifteen yards away. But looking back toward Ypres the British could see all the ground. In theory this would allow them more movement. That afternoon a burial party of about sixty-nine men arrived and began to clear the bodies in preparation for the arrival of 14th Division who were going to take over the trenches. There would be a couple of small attempts to improve the British line over the next few weeks but the next serious attempt to extend the front line here would not take place until 25 September.

Private John Thomson Allan

> 'On 16th June 1915, the 3rd Division had taken part in a disastrous diversionary attack on Bellewaarde Ridge, which aimed to deprive the enemy of observation and at the same time straighten out the British line between Hooge and Railway Wood. Although some ground had been won, and quickly held by battalions of the 8th Brigade following up behind, the cost had been high. Heavy and concentrated German artillery fire, well directed onto lines until recently held by their own troops, cut swathes through the attacking British forces and by the end of the operation the 3rd Division had lost 140 officers and 3,391 men. The 9th Brigade suffered particularly heavily, losing 73 officers out of 96 and 2,012 men out of 3,663.'

Private John Thomson Allan was a Territorial from Aberdeen. He quickly volunteered for overseas service and arrived with a draft in March 1915, scarcely more than a month after the battalion had landed at Havre.

Corporal Robert Platt, Portglenone, County Antrim 2nd Battalion Royal Irish Rifles

This letter was written by Corporal Platt to his father John. It describes the battle in which the rifles distinguished themselves and lost a large number of men:

> 'Since last I wrote to you we were in a charge and it was awful. We started out the night before and marched 13 miles. We arrived at the place about

half past one in the morning so that we were put into an old trench and told to await orders so you can have an idea that our nerves were strung to the highest pitch. So, the Germans started to rain shells into us but then our artillery opened fire on the German trenches. The row was awful. the whole sky was just in one great blaze with bursting shells.

Sharp at three o'clock the order came down our lines to fix bayonets and to load our rifles and 10 minutes later down came the order to charge so we all rushed over the trench but a good few of our boys fell on the parapet as the Germans had their machine guns trained on us but on we went and as one fell, another took his place.

We arrived at the German trench and when it came to the steel they could not match us and I am proud to say that I put a few out with the bayonet myself. Although one does not think of it at the time, one does think of it after the excitement is over.

We took over 200 prisoners and a couple of machine guns. I sent home a German sword. But we were not satisfied with one trench we went on and took two more lines of them. They shelled us the whole day after we took them and they eventually sent loads of gas but we stuck on for what we had so dearly won.

I was to be recommended for the DCM for fetching in wounded under fire but the officer that took my name was killed shortly afterwards and I do not know how it will go now but I was promoted on the field by our own officer to Corporal. I was buried three times by shells and had to be dug out and I got a slight bullet wound in the thigh but I am out of hospital again and expect to go into action in a couple of day's time.

The battle took place on 16th June. It was even worse than the charge we made at Hill 60. The Germans lost a good deal more than we did. The Brigade officer says the Rifles have made a name for themselves out here that will go down in history. All the English Regiments out here are very fond of the Rifles since we came out of the charge.'[63]

Private Samuel Pierce, 1st/4th Prince of Wales' Volunteers (South Lancashire Regiment)

'Mr. Pierce, of 11, Stanley-street, Earlestown, has received the following from his son, Private Sam Pierce, who along with his brother Percy, is doing trench work at the front:

"We have been fairly through it since I wrote last. Talk about hell with the lid off! The other night – Tuesday in fact – we were expecting an attack on our position, and only twenty-five yards separated us from the enemy. Percy

---

63. Kind permission of *The Royal Irish Rifles 1914–1918*.

was in the first line, and I in the reserve. They started rapid firing, and we thought they were coming, so off I bolt to Percy and said "Buck up, kid, I am with you." And we were on top of the trench together, and our bayonets glittered as we fired. You would have been proud of your two little lads had you seen them then.

I am pleased to tell you that we are both in the best of health, and what do you think, when I first saw Percy he did not know me until I spoke to him. He said I looked better than I had done for years.

I am sending you a pair of cufflinks which I got from Ypres. I should have been able to send you a helmet, only I broke it – with the head inside. I gave one a "clough" with the butt, and it was heavier than I ever struck in the smithy.

I was sent to the dumping ground for a box for headquarters, and a sniper nearly had me. The bullet struck the back of my cap, but "a miss is as good as a mile". It shook me for a while, but I soon got over it. I went up with water for Percy the other day, and when I was coming back I saw one of our chaps, named Thomas, shot through the chest on the same road as I had just gone over. They had a machine gun trained on the road.

We have been examined by the doctor this morning, and you know what that means. You will be reading great things shortly now. Have you heard that Joe Betts has been killed? Only a few hours before he shouted to me, "How goes it, Piercy," and waved his hand. He was a good soldier, and he died a soldier's death with his rifle to his shoulder, sniping from a sap. Two of them were waiting for him, and one got him in the cheek and the other in the neck".'

Private Pierce wrote this letter home a few days before the battle and it was published in the *Newtown and Earlstown Guardian* on 18 June 1915. Two days before it was published Private Pierce was killed in action. He was married with two young children. His brother Private Percy Pierce wrote home after hearing of the death of his brother. On 25 June 1915, his letter too was printed in the *Newton and Earlstown Guardian:*

'Dear Father,
Just a few lines to let you know that I have the painful duty to let you know that our Sam was killed in action this morning. I am very glad to tell you that he died without any pain. He had a very peaceful smile on his face, and he is buried on the ground where the battle of Waterloo was fought ….. (censored) …..

Now, dear dad, I don't want you to take this too much to heart, for we are only one family out of about 8,000 that is fixed in the same position. We got the order to capture four lines of trenches, and when we were charging the last line he got hit in the neck with what they call a "Wizz Bang".

Dear dad, you might keep it from Mamma for a short time, and tell her that he has been wounded, and when she is strong enough, break it to her gently. Dear dad, you don't know what a blow it has been for me, for he did more for me out here than anybody, and I thought the world of him, and to think that I should lose him now. Would to God that it was all over. We were under artillery fire for over 24 hours, and that we have come out alive is a miracle. I have no more to say this time, my heart is too full.

Your loving son, Percy

Corporal Gordon Bartlett

'My dear Lady

I will gladly tell you what I know about your fallen son. I fulfil this Christian duty with special feeling as it is done by one soldier to a fellow soldier. Your son fell on June 16th 1915 about 3 kilometres east of Ypres. According to what I remember of the day of the fight in which your son died the events were as follows.

It was on the 16th June at 2 a.m. that the English artillery suddenly began to shell our trenches north and south of the Ypres– Roulers road, from the small wood as far as Bellewaarde farm a murderous artillery fire had battered our trench forces, the English Infantry succeeded in penetrating into our trenches. I myself with the Battalion was then sent forward to strengthen the front trench garrison and recapture the lost ground.

The fight to capture the trench streamed backwards and forwards for a long time. Towards evening the last portion of trench was again in our hands.

In this section which I had captured with my platoon three fallen English soldiers lay close to each other dressed in the uniform of Highlanders. These in the night of 16–17 June were placed behind our trenches.

One of the fallen, according to the letter he had with him, was Corporal Bartlett. The tragedy which lay therein, namely that his father was saved from shipwreck, but that he had fallen after receiving the news from his Mother, made at the time a very deep impression on me.

This explains why in the course of many events of the long war I have never forgotten Corporal Bartlett. I can today see the three dead men before me. They were big fine men lying on top of the trench as if they were sleeping. There were no visible wounds on them. I cannot tell you how your son died; it must be supposed that he and his two comrades were killed outright through a bomb exploding in the neighbourhood.

Near by the bodies was also found an Oxford University circular, I picked it up on account of its contents and sent it to my parents with the two telegrams and letter.

I do not know to this day whether the Oxford University circular was your son's or one of his comrades. Should it have belonged to your son I shall be glad to send it to you. In a sheltered spot close by the dead men lay a wounded English soldier. This soldier was carried back during the night to the casualty clearing station by our R.A.M.C. men. If I remember rightly however, this soldier was not wearing Scottish uniform.

You would like to have more detailed information concerning your son's grave. I have marked the place where I found your son with a small cross in the enclosed map. At the spot outside the trench he was buried with his two comrades just as we also in the changing fight were forced to bury our comrades quickly not far from the trench. It was not until autumn of 1915 that my regiment went out to rest in order to lay out its own cemetery in Polygon wood. Your son, therefore found his last resting place where he fell in the fight for his country. For the soldier there is happiness, for his relatives, pain, because they do not know where he lies.

I scarcely think it probable that the grave is still marked. The fight before Ypres went on bitterly for such a long time and I doubt whether any of the graves in the immediate neighbourhood of the front remained recognisable as such.

I myself went away in January 1916 from the Ypres front to another war area. Since that time I have not been to Ypres and I do not know therefore whether the many graves are all preserved.

That is all that I can tell you of your son to whom I rendered the last service and whose letter and telegrams now find their way to his Mother in England.

Yours obediently
P. Schwirzke,
Dr. Med. Vet.
Tierarzt.
Lagow.'[64]

Corporal Bartlett was first described as missing in action. In 1927 his family received a letter from German Medical Officer Dr Schwirze who enclosed papers found on the corporal's body including a telegram from his mother stating that his father had been rescued from the liner Lusitania after it was sunk by a German submarine in the Irish Sea. His father had previously been reported as missing.

---

64. By kind permission of Perce. See http://www.bellewaarde1915.co.uk/ for more information about this story.

Captain John Baber

'19th June 1915.
Dear Frank,

I expect you want to hear a little of our scrap. First of all, I did not fire the M.G. as the Germans had had enough and did not counter attack where we were. We got up to the trenches on the evening of the 15th, and began to dig ourselves in and put the railway lines in a state of defence. Sharp at 2.59 A.M. when it was growing light, swish, swish went our heavy shells, & wump, wump at the other end. Bang, whiz etc went the smaller fry and that continued till 4.30 A.M. when the first assault was made; there was little left to resist.

In the meantime the Hun guns got to work, and their Heavies gave us gyp till about 10.30. Those eight hours were the longest I have ever spent, and our trench was so narrow that we had to sit without a possibility of moving, with our knees up to our chins. I tried Demon Patience but could not get the beastly thing out.

Between 10.30 A.M. and about 4.30 P.M. everyone shelled everyone else intermittently, but at teatime the Huns thought they would like to counter attack. So their guns began to fire rapid. I've never heard such a noise. After an hour of that, the message was sent down for two of our guns, so I made my way up a communication trench with 2 guns.

It was melodrama in the best Lyceum style. Wounded men hobbling down the communication trench, harassed orderlies, "Machine guns, thank God, – hurry up guns, you're wanted badly up there, etc." I couldn't help laughing. When we got up, German prisoners were being passed back, and the trenches were full of their casualties and ours but I chose two positions and waited but nothing happened.

Our field guns had caught the Germans collecting in a wood and had broken them up all by themselves. The Germans whom I saw seemed delighted that they were captured with the exception of one Prussian boy aged 19, wounded in hip and leg. He thought we were going to shoot him, but was consoled with cigarettes and chocolate. A kiltie had tried to comfort him, but Gaelic and beard and kilt almost frightened the poor kid off his head.'[65]

This letter from Captain Baber to his sister was describing events from just outside the main attack. He then took part in the consolidation after the battle and witnessed the aftermath. He was immediately on the left of the 3rd Division. At the time he was serving with the Machine Gun Section of the Queen's Westminster

---

65. By permission of Nick Balmer.

Rifles, who were apparently under the orders of Lieutenant Colonel F.W. Towesy of the West Yorks, tasked with protecting the flank of the 9th Infantry Brigade.

Private W. Day, 1st Lincolns

Private W. Day of the 1st Lincolns wrote to the wife of Pte Lawson giving a graphic account of the battle in which he had been killed. It was published in the *Gainsborough News* on 2 July 1915.

> 'Our Colonel told us that we had to give the enemy "beans" and to make them retire. We got the order to fix bayonets and charge, and we went with a swing over the two hundred yards to the German trenches. The sights were terrible. Our shells had blown in their trenches and dug-outs, and had buried the Germans underneath. There were dying and dead everywhere: others were running wild and trying to escape, but none got away free. One tried to get away near me, but two of us headed him off, and we were just about to give him cold steal when he dropped back dead, and so saved us the trouble of killing him. We got the trenches all right, and we kept the enemy from retaking them. Then they shelled us and blew the trenches in on top of us, but we stuck to it until the ********* started with the gas, and we gave up the third trench we had taken. The gas affected our eyes and I got a whiff of it.
>
> After that we made another bayonet charge and retrieved the third trench. We were sights, all black and bleeding and covered with blood. Our clothes were torn and in tatters. Mine were with getting through the barbed wire. I had 100 cuts on my hands and legs. While we were running across the open in the charges shells were bursting everywhere. In the trenches I was buried with earth and sandbags three times, and the last time I thought my end had come. I had to be dug out for only the top of my head was not buried. We found the Germans dead in the trenches in good numbers, and the stench was awful.
>
> I used 200 rounds of ammunition, and I've seen 20 fall dead from my gun. The rifles were red hot. I never thought I should live to write this letter."[66]

Major W. A. Murray in command of the 119th Battery, 27th Brigade, 5th Division

> '22nd June, 1915.
> Dear Father,
>
> I haven't written for some days, as we have been having a very quiet time since the fight of the 16th. There was some desperate hand-to-hand work there. When our Infantry got the first line German trenches they found the

---

66. Contributed by Stephen Knox.

Germans panic-stricken and our Tommies bayonetted them like pigs by the dozen. One officer told me he couldn't bear it, and ordered his men to stop, as they were such miserable creatures.

When the Germans counter-attacked, our guns completely wiped them out before they got to grips. The German Staff Officers could be seen riding up and trying to get their men to go on, but they were absolutely annihilated. We had to leave the advanced trenches at nightfall, because the Germans brought a terrific gunfire to bear on them. It was rather sad, as their Infantry were absolutely beaten, and couldn't put up any sort of fight.

There was one rather curious incident. The Colonel of the Lincolns was wounded in the assault, and the Orderly who was with him ran up to the Second in Command and said "the Colonel is hit and is lying over….". At that moment a bullet went through his head and he fell dead. So they never heard where the Colonel was laying and he has never been found although they searched everywhere for him.

We made a "feint" attack here the night before last, as they thought the Germans had nearly all gone, and as we got no reply I believe there are very few in front. I shouldn't be surprised if we had a try to go through shortly.

The King told our General that there would be plenty of ammunition in 6 weeks.

Love to all,
I hope you are well. Yours ever – Bill'[67]

Major Murray survived the war and was decorated with the CMG, DSO Croix de Guerre. The Colonel referred to was Lieutenant Colonel H.E.R. Boxer Commanding 1st Battalion Lincoln Regiment. He is mentioned on panel 21 of the Ypres (Menin Gate) Memorial.

---

67. With kind permission of Alan Whitworth.

Chapter 29

The British

438th 1/1st Cheshire Field Company RE

Relieved at dusk by 56 Company and returned to billets. Their casualties for the day were six NCOs and twelve Sappers wounded and two Sappers killed; one NCO and one Sapper missing. In 1916 they took part in the Actions of the Bluff and St Eloi Craters then moved to The Somme for The Battle of Albert, The Battle of Bazentin helping to capture Longueval, The Battle of Delville Wood and The Battle of the Ancre. In 1917 they were at Arras, seeing action at Battles of the Scarpe and The Battle of Arleux. They moved north to the Flanders and were in action during The Battle of the Menin Road and Battle of Polygon Wood during the Third Battle of Ypres. After this they moved south and were in action at The Battle of Cambrai. In 1918 they were in action on The Somme, in the Battles of the Lys, the Battles of the Hindenburg Line and the Battle of the Selle. After the Armistice they remained with 3rd Division as it advanced into Germany as part of the Occupation Force.

1st Battalion Northumberland Fusiliers

Casualties suffered on 16 June by the three companies in the front line of attack amounted to almost seventy-five per cent of their strength. They had started the battle with 15 officers and 645 other ranks. By the end of the day their casualties totalled 15 officers and 386 other ranks. Of these, two officers, Lieutenant Colonel Yatman and Lieutenant Dorman-Smith, and twenty other ranks had been only slightly wounded and remained at duty. Second Lieutenant Scrutton was awarded the DSO and Lance Corporal A. Joynson a DCM. Lieutenant Dorman-Smith was awarded the Military Cross in the following New Year's List. Sergeant Alfred

Panorama 16th June 1915. Image by Private F.A. Fyfe 16th June 1915 spliced.

Bellewaarde from the air 1917 kind permission of Lesley Fusiliers Museum of Northumberland
http://www.northumberlandfusiliers.org.uk/index.php

Hobday was first listed as wounded and missing but was confirmed dead in December 1915. Having fought with the Battalion since their arrival in France, he had rescued a wounded officer while under fire and been promoted to Sergeant. He had also been awarded the Légion D'Honneur and was even recommended for the Victoria Cross.

All four machine guns were knocked out during the day. They moved back to the bivouac they had left on 15 June. It would be four weeks before what was left of the Battalion would be able to take to the field again.

4th Battalion Royal Fusiliers
Of the 22 officers and 820 men who had entered the battle,15 officers and 376 men were casualties; 37 killed, 211 wounded and 202 missing. Those killed included Captain and Adjutant O'Donel, Lieutenants Thornton, Harte, Warde and Rogers, Second Lieutenants Dudley and Bannister. Major Hely Hutchinson was badly wounded and Captain de la Peverelle took over the Battalion. Eventually they retired back to Y13–14 where they held the line until the Brigade was relieved at 11.00 pm. After a day's rest on 17 June they were visited by General Allenby who told them they had done the finest bit of work in the campaign.

1/10th Battalion King's (Liverpool) Regiment
Went into battle with 21 officers and 519 other ranks. Only two officers and 140 men came through untouched. At the end of 16 June their casualties were four officers and seventy-five men killed. Eleven officers and 201 men were wounded and six officers and 103 men were missing. With very few exceptions these were later confirmed as dead. Most of their casualties were taken in or near the second German line. After the Battalion returned to camp at Busseboom Brigade HQ asked for a list of those recommended for decoration or mention and this was sent. However, it never arrived, possibly destroyed by a fire in Brigade HQ. When this was realized another list was sent, but they were told that all the decorations for the battle had already been allocated so no member of the Liverpool Scottish was decorated by recommendation of his own unit.

The three men who received the DCM did so on the recommendation of COs from other Regiments. Eventually in 1916 ten men were awarded the Military medal in recognition of conspicuous gallantry at Hooge – Sergeants J. Briggs, W. Sloss, and P. J. Thompson, Lance Corporal A. F. Foden and J. M. Thomkinson, Private B. G. Barnshaw, J.C. Darroch, W. Fitton, J. R. Pollock and D. Williams. Captain Noel Chavasse was with the Royal Army Medical Corps, attached to the 1/10th (Scottish) Battalion of the King's (Liverpool) Regiment. He was awarded the Military Cross for gallantry at the Battle of Hooge.

1st Battalion the Lincolnshire Regiment
Rested throughout 17 June at Red Wine Camp. Their casualties were 24 killed, 269 wounded and 76 missing. Among those killed were Lieutenant Colonel Hugh Richard Boxer who led the Battalion in its advance, Lieutenant Allan Dixon Walker and Private Edward Backlog. After this, they spent a period back in the trenches, some in the Ypres theatre of Operations, and others in the trenches at Sanctuary Wood. On 30 June they were relieved by the 5th and 6th Battalion Lincolnshire Battalions.

1st Battalion West Yorkshire Regiment

'During this action the fire of the artillery was most effective, the prisoners testifying to its destructiveness and accuracy. It also prevented the delivery of counter-attacks which were paralysed at the outset.
   Casualties: 2nd LT. O. Tennent, Machine Gun officer, was killed. Wounded: LT. E.R. Chomeley and LT. N.E. Atkinson. Other Ranks 8 Killed and 45 Wounded,*2 suffering from gas.
   *Caused by gas shells. CPT Scott RAMC, Sergeant Burke and the stretcher-bearers rendered invaluable assistance throughout the days and nights of the 16th and 17th in helping to evacuate the great number of wounded of the 9th Bde in addition to our own. This work was carried out very often under heavy shell fire.'

On 18 June the Battalion was relieved by the Royal East Kent Regiment at 10.00 am and marched seven miles back to a camp in a wood about one and a half miles northwest of Vlamertinghe.

1st Battalion Royal Scots Fusiliers
Took heavy casualties. Second Lieutenant Webster and 36 OR had been killed, 12 officers and 199 OR were wounded and there were 202 men missing.

3rd Battalion the Worcestershire Regiment
Spent 17 June resting at Busseboom east of Ypres. Then 7th Brigade moved back into the line again. On 19 June it took over its former front line at Hooge. They continued to hold the trenches facing Sanctuary Wood until 8 July with brief respites when they were relieved by the Royal Irish Rifles and the Honourable Artillery Company. They were under heavy artillery fire for much of the time and took many casualties.

South Lancashire Regiment
Also took heavy casualties. Other than the party under Major Egerton Fairclough, who had occupied part of the enemy's second line trenches, south of Bellewaarde Farm, the rest of the Battalion had remained in its original assembly position. Here it suffered heavy casualties from enemy artillery fire, and B Company, which was sent forward to reinforce the forward troops, was caught by a concentration of high explosive and nearly wiped out. Later that evening the Battalion moved up to help in the consolidation of the new line, but only stayed there a short while as they were relieved at midnight. One famous member of the South Lancashire Regiment was Second Lieutenant Trafford Leigh-Mallory who is perhaps better known for coming into conflict with Vice Marshal Keith Park during the Battle of Britain in 1940.

5th Battalion King's Shropshire Light Infantry
Arrived back in their billets in Vlamertinghe a few hours after daybreak on 17 June. Their brief sortie had cost them thirteen dead; two officers, Captain T. Avery and Lieutenant B. H. Ellis, and eleven OR. Second Lieutenant V. D. French died the following day of his wounds. Second Lieutenant R. G. W. Stark and fifty-seven OR were wounded and one OR missing. They spent 17 June resting and refitting. On 19 June a new draft of eighty-two men arrived from England and the Battalion went into the trenches for the first time on their own, taking over from the Suffolks.

5th Battalion The Oxfordshire and Buckingham Light Infantry
Suffered two deaths – Lieutenant C.M. Berlein and Lance Corporal Henry Tills. Two other officers and thirty OR were wounded.

9th Service Battalion KRRC
Relieved at midnight by the 4th Gordon Highlanders and they too made their way back to Vlamertinghe. They found 9th Battalion Rifle Brigade in their quarters and so had no option but to sleep in the open. They had suffered sixty-six casualties, with one officer killed another wounded and five OR ranks killed; one died of his wounds and another fifty-eight were wounded.

9th Battalion The Rifle Brigade
Sustained forty-eight OR casualties including two dead. Arrived back exhausted at Vlamertinghe twenty-four hours after setting out. They had not eaten for virtually the whole period and had taken nineteen casualties – two killed and seventeen wounded – all from shrapnel.

1st Battalion the Wiltshire Regiment
Suffered several casualties. Two Officers were killed and a further five were wounded. One was wounded and captured. Twenty OR were killed, three were missing believed killed, 103 wounded, three wounded and prisoners and 54 missing with six slightly wounded. At 12.30 am on 17 June they were relieved by the Suffolks and at 1.30 am the whole Battalion left and marched to billets between Ypres and Vlamertinghe. On 18 June they marched to Hooge and took over the trenches from the Durham Light Infantry. Back in the Wiltshire trenches the Suffolks started digging a trench parallel to the communication trench from the corner of Y Wood to the culvert. The trench running eastwards from the corner of Y Wood was abandoned and completely blocked over a distance of thirty yards.

4th Gordon Highlanders
Lost four officers and fifty-three OR, killed or wounded, with one missing.

2nd Battalion Royal Irish Rifles
Not clear of the trenches till 2.00 am on 17 June. Two officers dead, another two wounded and missing. A further 9 wounded and 300 OR were also casualties. On 23 June Colonel Morris departed and Captain Goodman took temporary command. That day they went into the trenches near Hooge. The area was completely unrecognizable after suffering such a heavy bombardment. Major G. A. Weir DSO from the 3rd Dragoon Guards assumed command the next day and on the night of 27 June the Battalion was relieved by the 3rd Worcestershires. During the month a new draft of 15 officers and 160 men arrived to reinforce the depleted Battalion.

1st Battalion the Honourable Artillery Company
Lost almost half the Battalion and nearly all their officers, including the Colonel and Second in Command. They were relieved by the 1st Battalion the Gordon Highlanders at about 1.00am on 17 June and returned to the transport field near Branthoec where they had three days' rest.

Queen's Westminster Rifles
Did not take an active part in the battle but were exposed to considerable shelling especially near the railway where a continuous stream of wounded and prisoners poured along the road heading to the rear. Lieutenant Donald Herbert Hutchison and Captain John Baber of the Battalion Machine Gun Section were both killed. One Company moved forward to occupy the railway barrier and fire trench south of the railway, relieving a Company of West Yorkshires. On 17 June the Battalion stretcher-bearers and volunteer parties from D Company who were then in reserve spent the day collecting and clearing casualties from the battlefield. During the night they returned to the canal bank as Brigade Reseve. Their casualties on 16/17 June were four OR and one officer, Captain P. M. Glasier, killed and forty-six OR wounded. On 18 June the Brigade went into hutments northeast of Poperinghe for a week's rest.

3rd Division
Lost 140 Officers and 3,391 men. It remained on the Western Front throughout the rest of the war and took part in most of the major actions including the actions at Hooge in July 1915 and the second Battle of Bellewaarde (25 September to 30 September 1915) in support of the opening attack in the Battle of Loos. At the end of the war 3rd Division was selected to march into Germany and was part of the Occupation Force.

7th Brigade
Lost 13 officers and 250 men. On 18 October 1915 it left 3rd Division and joined 25th Division. In exchange, 76th Brigade transferred across to 3rd Division. The 1/4th South Lancashire Regiment left 7th Brigade to become Pioneers 12 October 1915.

8th Brigade
On 17 June 1915, under Brigadier General A. R. Hoskins, took over the line that had been won the previous day. The 1/4th Battalion the Gordon Highlanders left 8th Brigade for 76th Brigade 19 October 1915.

9th Brigade
Lost 78 out of their 98 Officers and 2,012 men out of 3,663. One of the officers wounded was General Sir Archibald Wavell, the great Second World War soldier. He lost his left eye while serving as GSO 111 9th Infantry Brigade. The 1st Battalion the Lincolnshire Regiment left 9th Brigade in November 1915; the 1st Battalion the Royal Scots Fusiliers left the 9th Brigade for 8th Brigade on 5 April 1916 and the 1/10th Battalion the King's (Liverpool) Regiment left in January 1916.

14th Light Division
Served on the Western Front throughout the war, taking part in actions at Ypres, Hill 60, the Somme, and Arras.

42nd Brigade
The 5th Battalion the Oxfordshire and Buckinghamshire Light Infantry left as cadres in June 1918 as did the 9th Battalion KRRC and the 9th Battalion Rifle Brigade. The 5th Battalion the King's Shropshire Light Infantry were disbanded in February 1918. On 24 February 1916 the 42nd Machine Gun Company joined the Brigade leaving on 1 March 1918 to move into the 14th Machine Gun Battalion. The 42nd Trench Mortar Battery joined the Brigade on 15 April 1916 and on 6 June 1918 the 6th Battalion Wiltshire Regiment, the 16th Battalion the Manchester Regiment and the 14th Battalion the Argyll and Sutherland Highlanders all joined as cadres and rebuilt.

Bellewaarde 1924. By kind permission of Sue Holmes.

Chapter 30

The Germans

Several hundred Germans were taken prisoner[68] during the battle and they suffered numerous casualties, although considerably less than the British. (I have been unable to determine how many Germans died exactly and figures of prisoners also seem to vary. 3rd Division history mentions 195 prisoners.)

Unter-Elsässisches Infanterie-Regiment Nr. 132

'The losses on the 16th had been severe. On the 17th the regiment reported 46 NCOs and men killed, 170 wounded and 38 missing. A total of 254 men. Three officers had been wounded. The soldiers in the trenches had put up a gallant and spirited defence. When the trenches were retaken many of the dead were still holding their weapons. The machine gun crews had spent all of their ammunition continuing the fight with their pistols and disabling their guns before they could be captured.

The brave officer in command of the counter attack, Leutnant Bartenstein, received the Iron Cross 1st Class. Feldwebel Noack of 11th company, who had distinguished himself in the attack, was promoted to Leutnant. The Gefreiter Kolb of 1st company was promoted to Unteroffizier. He had, throughout the day and under constant fire, carried messages and dispatches and on the 24th of November he received the Iron Cross 1st Class which was presented to him by General Deimling himself.

The enemy had paid in blood for his temporary success. Not only did he lose a large number of dead and wounded on the field, the regiment also managed to take a number of men of the Lincoln and 1st Wiltshire Regiment prisoner. Three enemy machine guns were captured.'[69]

---

68. In Niall Ferguson's book *The War of the World* he quotes a Private in the Honourable Artillery Company who states that after eight hours of constant shelling he witnessed the shooting of 300 German prisoners by 'The Royal Scots'. 2nd Battalion The Royal Scots were part of 8th Brigade but, as far as I am aware, they were not directly involved in the battle so I am not sure who he is referring to. It is also possible the battle referred to is The Third Division's action between the 25–30 September 1915 which was fought at the same place. This was quite a Scottish affair with 4th Gordon Highlanders, 1st Royal Scots Fusiliers and 2nd Royal Scots bearing the brunt of the fighting, and all suffering very heavy casualties.
69. Translation courtesy of Rob Schäfer, Military Historian.

Reserve Infanterie Regiment 246

'Day dawned on 17 June. Protected by early morning fog, Hauptmann Kölle and a detachment of Jägers launched a raid on the enemy position. The attempt failed, however, because it was spotted at once by the British and lacerating small arms fire was opened. Hauptmann Kölle and most of the Jägers fell and the arrival of complete daylight ruled out any further attempts at surprise. Tactical considerations and the heavy cost in blood of 16 June meant that the chain of command abandoned any thought of renewing the attack. The line which had been secured on 17 June was much more favourable than that occupied on 16 June, in that it offered far fewer attackable places than the old one. The regiment was grateful that the General decided to yield a small part of the position to the British. During the winter it appeared ever more clearly that the Tommies could take no joy in their positions. They were almost drowned by the water in T-Wäldchen [T Copse = Y Wood] and had constant difficulties with this poor position, which had been bought by them at so high a price in blood.

The outcome of the battle saw the regiment left holding a position on the 50 metre contour to the west of Bellewaarde Farm and running more or less from northwest to southeast, with the left flank at Schleusenhäuschen (Eclusette) [Hut by the lock] on the Bellewaarde stream. The enemy position essentially comprised our former Second Position. At their closest the lines were about eighty metres apart. Regimental casualties were nineteen officers, seventeen senior NCOs, forty two junior NCOs and 662 other ranks. 3rd Battalion was worst hit, being reduced to the strength of a single company. The enemy only captured about seventy five men.

Almost all the regimental dead were buried by the chapel in Eksternest [= Westhoek], near the well-known Linde [Lime Tree]. A large number was laid to rest together in the centre of the Storchschnabel, where the Roschmannweg crossed it. From then on this place was known as the Schwabengrab [Schwabian Grave]. A raised mound was built up, planted and decorated with wreathes. On a cross was neatly inscribed the names of the fallen heroes and the place was fenced in. From then on it was holy ground for the men of the 246th and was always passed quietly and with thoughts of our dear comrades. The grave was still undisturbed when the regiment moved to occupy new positions in September; it was not until 25 September 1915 that shells buried the cross, the flowers and the fence with earth and even then the point was still known as the Schwabengrab.

Those who had been there always spoke of 16 June in hushed tones as an elemental event when the infantry, reduced by a third due to artillery fire, nevertheless for an entire summer morning lay their bodies on the line to hold back the enemy until, at last reinforced, they were able in undiminished force to press back the enemy, who were significantly stronger, in a counter-action lasting an hour. There were no theoretical lessons, no practical rehearsal, no technical pamphlet which came anywhere near to providing preparation for the general difficulties of the trench warfare and the particularly unfavourable aspects of that day. Yet, in the final analysis, to regard the ultimate outcome of 16 June as a success is correct – despite the fact that long afterwards nobody who had fought there could think of T- and Eierwäldchen without a heavy heart.

It is simply impossible to speak of 16 June 1915 without the question arising as to how this catastrophe could have occurred. Inevitably the impression is given that the German side simply let the three companies in the front line be shot to pieces without doing anything to help them. Unfortunately that is correct in the sense that for hours during the morning our artillery hardly stirred themselves at all. If a veteran of the battle was asked about it, he would immediately launch into a bitter complaint about the artillery, saying they had simply abandoned the troops to their fate. In the regimental history of Reserve Field Artillery Regiment 54 is stated, 'The enemy fire came down at 4.00 am, but was not correctly identified because contact was lost at once with our observation posts in the front line, whilst an unfavourable wind meant that the backup observation posts could not obtain a clear idea about what was happening. So each battery fired on its main defensive task and, as a result, the weight of fire was correspondingly thin. Not until the regiment gave instructions could fire be concentrated and even then there was no exact information coming from any point. As a result it was impossible to say which sectors of the front could be left without fire. The infantry positions which could be reached by telephone were unable to give sufficient information, because they too lacked links forward.'

This attempt at justification by the artillery cannot be entirely correct. According to the battle log of Reserve Infantry Regiment 246, the regimental adjutant, Oberleutnant Sautter, had already informed the artillery during the night 13/14 June that something was about to happen. At the regiment's instigation, that night the artillery engaged the enemy exactly as they had during the day of 13 June when they had also been prompted by the regiment. The artillery was briefed again on 15 June and they were informed about what the trench garrison had observed. The artillery must have been made aware about the aerial photography, on which the network of jumping off trenches for the assault force could clearly be seen. These trenches ought to have been brought under heavy fire no later than the start of the operation. In the same way the enemy artillery ought to have been harassed during the bombardment, but neither of these things happened.

A further factor is that the enemy attacked with very strong forces and the main thrust was directed against the regiment. It later transpired from an examination of the report of the British commander General [sic] French that we were attacked by the entire British V Corps. French's report states,

'On 16 June V Corps attacked the Bellewaarde Ridge to the east of Ypres. The enemy front line was captured and numerous enemy dead and wounded were found there. The assaulting troops pushed on to a point to the east of Bellewaarde Lake, but could not hold on to this forward position. Nevertheless it was possible to retain the sector of the front which had been captured in the initial phase of the attack. This sector was some 1,000 paces long and included the section of enemy trench which jutted forward north of the Menin – Ypres road. During the attack the artillery fire was extraordinarily effective. Its accuracy and destructive effect was confirmed by prisoner statements.'

So this was the attack of a complete corps directed against a few companies. One success of 16 June, which later worked in favour of the regiment, was the recognition by the artillery how important close cooperation with the infantry was. From that day forward the regiment never had occasion to complain about the gunners of the 54th.'[70]

One of the more infamous members of Reserve Infanterie Regiment 246 was Gefreiter Christian Wirth. Wirth was born on 24 November 1885 in Oberbalzheim Laupheim in Wurttemberg. He was married to Maria and had two children, Eugen and Kurt. He was no stranger to war having joined Grenadier Regiment 123 'Koenig Karl' in Ulm in 1905. Wirth only served two years before re-enlisting in the same regiment in 1908 and becoming an instructor. By June 1915 he was a Lance Corporal in RIR 246. He was promoted to Sergeant in 1915 and Acting Officer in 1917. He was awarded the Iron Cross I and II Class, Gold Wurttemberg Military Services Medal, Military Service Decorations, Frontline Troop Medal and Black Wound Badge.

At the end of the war he joined the police in Stuttgart, rising gradually through the ranks until in 1938 he was Head of Kommissariat 5. Wirth joined the Nazi Party and by 1933 was Sturmfuhrer on the staff of SA Sturm 119 in Stuttgart. In 1937 he joined the SD and in August 1939 he was Untersturmfuhrer SS. He was promoted in October 1939 to SS-Obersturmfuhrer and was attached to the Chief of SIPO/SD Prague staff Olomouc Czechoslovakia.

Between October and December 1939 he worked in the Fuhrer's Chancellery in Berlin working on the planning and euthanasia operation, later called T4. Between January and February 1940 he personally participated in the first gassing experiments. He was eventually appointed Lauterungsinsektor of the T4 Euthanasia killing centres for Greater Germany and was believed to have overseen operations in Lublin and Chelmo between September and December 1941. He accompanied Adolf Eichman and Herman Julius Hofle on an inspection

---

70. Extract from Leutnant der Reserve Louis Orgeldinger *Das Württembergische Reserve-Infanterie-Regiment Nr. 246* Stuttgart 1931, 97–107. Translation © Dr Jack Sheldon 2012.

Sturmbannführer C Wirth. Holocaust Education & Archive Research Team.

Gefreiter Christian Wirth.

of the death camp at Belzec and commanded the camp between January 1941 and February 1942 supervising the first gassing experiments with Zyklon B and the first large transport of Jews from Lublin. He went on to reorganize the death camp at Treblinka in September 1942 and played a leading role in the Harvest Festival Massacre of Jewish workers in Lublin in November 1943.

Wirth was shot dead by Yugoslav partisans near Kozina, Istria and was buried with full military honours in the German cemetery near Trieste. His remains were exhumed in 1959 and reburied in the German Military Cemetery at Costermano on the south eastern shore of Lake Garda, Verona province, northern Italy 1959.

Reserve Infanterie Regiment 248

> 'So, 16th June became another glorious day. Our enemy was mainly Highlanders, some carrying iron-enhanced clubs with them. By dawn on 20th June the English sent over clouds of gas, provoking nothing but irritation of the throat and the eyes and some headache.'[71]

---

71. Translated by Sebastian Laudan.

54th Reserve Division

After the battle, the 54th Reserve Division remained in the line along the Yser into 1916. After two months in army reserve in the winter of 1916, the Division returned to the trenches again in the Flanders and Artois region. It was heavily engaged in the Battle of the Somme in 1916 and returned to the line in Flanders and the Artois again until the end of the year. In December 1916 and January 1917 it saw action in Verdun and then went into the line in the Champagne region. In May 1917 it fought in the Second Battle of the Aisne, also known as the Third Battle of Champagne. The Division then went back to Verdun in August 1917 in response to the French offensive here.

In late October it went back to Flanders and took part in the Battle of Passchendaele, also known as the Third Battle of Ypres. It remained in Flanders until March 1918 and then participated in the German Spring Offensive.

BERLIN REPORT OF FIGHTING IN THE WEST
FRENCH SUCCESSES ADMITTED
AMSTERDAM, June 17.

To-day's official German communiqué, published in Berlin, says:-

'North of the lake at Bellewaarde we have recaptured the greater part of the trenches which we lost the day before yesterday.

The British and French yesterday continued their attempts to break through. To the north of La Bassée Canal the British, in hand-to-hand fighting, were overpowered by our Westphalian troops and were forced to beat a hasty retreat from their positions.

The French are continually directing fresh attacks against our front from west of Liévin to Arras. On the Lorette height a trench which had been completely destroyed was abandoned to the French. South of Souchez they succeeded in gaining a footing in our position on a front of 850 yards. Fighting there is proceeding.

Yesterday's attacks, which were conducted regardless of the waste of ammunition and of very heavy losses, thus again terminated with the defeat of the British and French. The hand-to-hand fights, in which we were victorious, again prove the brilliant bravery and the dauntless perseverance of our troops.

French attacks near Moulin-sous-Touvent also failed. Here we captured five officers and 300 men.

In the Vosges vigorous fighting was proceeding yesterday between the valleys of Fecht and the Lauch, but it came to an end in the evening. Apart from a slight loss of ground to the north-west of Metzeral, we maintained our positions. We also captured 100 prisoners.

The assertion made in the French official report of yesterday that the Cathedral of Reims has been bombarded with incendiary shells is untrue. Our fire was directed against the eastern barracks and the battery near the railway triangle, north of Reims, which had vigorously bombarded our positions.'

Reuter.

Chapter 31

Conclusion

The attack on Bellewaarde on 16 June 1915 only lasted one day but it clearly demonstrated the strengths and weaknesses of the British Army in 1915. The objective was achievable and given the parameters of the time, the planning was sound. However, the assault failed to achieve its objectives for two main reasons.

The first was the total lack of communication between the attacking troops and the rear command elements. The use of the red and yellow artillery screens was an attempt to give more flexibility to the artillery. However, the screens were obscured by the thick mist and the smoke from the shelling so they couldn't be seen by the artillery. This forced them to stick to the prearranged timetable which in turn led to the shelling of their own troops. This problem was to dog the British Army until the development of the creeping barrage in late 1916.

The second reason was the high rate of officer casualties. The high casualty rate before this battle had decimated the officer corps. This had left the British forces with an inadequate number of proficiently trained officers and a dearth of sufficiently trained NCOs who were capable of taking over from fallen officers.

That the ordinary soldier carried out his orders with the characteristic courage and determination of the British soldier is not in doubt, the high casualty rate is demonstrable proof of this. But as officer casualties mounted, the attack lost its impetus. The attacking troops then became mixed up and disorganized. Some of this could have been avoided if NCOs had been better trained and the men themselves had received more detailed briefings.

This problem of communications and lack of control would continue to cause the BEF problems throughout the war. Although some of these were caused by the Generals and the technology of the time, the main reason for the difficulties was the parsimony of the British Government.

The British Government has always been loath to give sufficient resources to the Forces. This can clearly be seen in virtually all wars and conflicts the British forces have been sent to. Unfortunately, politicians, past and present, never appear to learn the lessons of the past. The army that was sent to Europe in 1914 was much too small and ill-equipped for the task it was expected to carry out. Although the army did eventually overcome these difficulties and achieve success, this was not thanks to a more enlightened attitude of the wartime government. It was a tribute to its senior officers who guided improvements during the war and to the tenacity and sheer bloody mindedness of the British soldier, very much as it is today.

The following is an extract from a special Order by Major General Haldane Commanding 3rd Division published on 17 June:

'The Major General Commanding cannot adequately express his admiration for the gallant manner in which the attack was carried out yesterday. The dash and determination of all ranks was beyond praise, and that some actually reached the objective in the first rush and remained there under most trying circumstances is a proof of their superiority over the German Infantry. That the captured ground could not all be held is disappointing, more especially as the losses incurred were heavy. But these casualties have not been in vain. The 3rd Division carried out a fine piece of work and fought splendidly, and their commander is deeply proud of them.'

Appendix A

The Fallen – The British

Full name	Rank	Service	Unit	Regiment	Date	Age	Additional	Grave	Cemetery	Locality
ABBOTT, REGINALD FREDERICK WILLIAM	Private	2694	1st Bn.	Honourable Artillery Company	16-Jun-15	33	Son of John Octavius and Mary Jane Abbott.	Panel 9.	Ypres (Menin Gate) Memorial	Ieper, West-Vlaanderen
BALLARD, ROGER HARDWICKE	Private	1926	1st Bn.	Honourable Artillery Company	16-Jun-15	unknown		Panel 9.	Ypres (Menin Gate) Memorial	Ieper, West-Vlaanderen
BARRETT, ERIC	Private	2034	1st Bn.	Honourable Artillery Company	16-Jun-15	19	Son of Herbert Thomas and the late Maude Alice Barrett, of 34, Vicarage Rd., Tottenham, London.	Panel 9.	Ypres (Menin Gate) Memorial	Ieper, West-Vlaanderen
CAPEL, GEORGE HERBERT	Private	2052	1st Bn.	Honourable Artillery Company	16-Jun-15	24	Son of Herbert C. Capel and Clara Capel, of 260, Green Lanes, Finsbury Park, London.	Panel 9.	Ypres (Menin Gate) Memorial	Ieper, West-Vlaanderen
CLARE, DENIS JOHN	Private	1144	1st Bn	Honourable Artillewry Company	16-Jun-15	19	Son of Capt. William Ernest Clare (H.A.C.) and Henrietta Clare, of 61, New Church Rd., Hove, Brighton.	Panel 9.	Ypres (Menin Gate) Memorial	Ieper, West-Vlaanderen
DE WECK, LOUIS IGNATIUS ALBERT	Private	2565	1st Bn.	Honourable Artillery Company	16-Jun-15	29	Son of Albert Joseph and Marguerite Christine Marie de Weck, of 61, Melbury Gardens. Wimbledon, London.	Panel 9.	Ypres (Menin Gate) Memorial	Ieper, West-Vlaanderen
DERRY, FRANCIS THOMAS	Lance Corporal	2399	1st Bn.	Honourable Artillery Company	16-Jun-15	32	Son of Thomas and Edith Derry, of 106, Osbaldeston Rd., Stamford Hill, London.	Panel 9.	Ypres (Menin Gate) Memorial	Ieper, West-Vlaanderen
FISENDEN, FRANCIS HEREWARD	Private	1201	1st Bn.	Honourable Artillery Company	16-Jun-15	unknown		Panel 9.	Ypres (Menin Gate) Memorial	Ieper, West-Vlaanderen
GODFREE, TOM HATCHER	Private	2585	1st Bn.	Honourable Artillery Company	16-Jun-15	25	Son of Alfred and the late Kate Godfree, of "Kingswood," Burnt Ash Rd., Lee, London.	Panel 9.	Ypres (Menin Gate) Memorial	Ieper, West-Vlaanderen

Name	Rank	Number	Battalion	Regiment	Date	Age	Family	Cemetery/Memorial	Panel	Location
GRIX, SIDNEY LIONEL	Private	2718	1st Bn.	Honourable Artillery Company	16-Jun-15	unknown		Ypres (Menin Gate) Memorial	Panel 9.	Ieper, West-Vlaanderen
HATTON, HENRY HATTON	Lance Corporal	2259	1st Bn.	Honourable Artillery Company	16-Jun-15	unknown		Ypres (Menin Gate) Memorial	Panel 9.	Ieper, West-Vlaanderen
HENRY, CYRIL LLOYD	Lance Corporal	759	1st Bn.	Honourable Artillery Company	16-Jun-15	unknown		Ypres (Menin Gate) Memorial	Panel 9.	Ieper, West-Vlaanderen
HOARE, WILLIAM GEORGE	Second Lieutenant			Honourable Artillery Company	16-Jun-15	29	Son of A. P. Hoare and J. Hoare, of Town Farm, Amersham, Bucks.	Ypres (Menin Gate) Memorial	Panel 9.	Ieper, West-Vlaanderen
JOBLING, JOSEPH CECIL	Corporal	2350	1st Bn.	Honourable Artillery Company	16-Jun-15	22	Son of Elizabeth Jobling, of 86, Malford Grove, South Woodford, Essex, and the late Joseph Christopher Jobling.	Hooge Crater Cemetery	III. J. 6.	Ieper, West-Vlaanderen
JONES, HARRY DUKINFIELD	Private	2504	1st Bn.	Honourable Artillery Company	16-Jun-15	unknown		Ypres (Menin Gate) Memorial	Panel 9.	Ieper, West-Vlaanderen
KENT, REGINALD FREDERICK	Corporal	1308	1st Bn.	Honourable Artillery Company	16-Jun-15	25	Son of W. Gipps Kent, of The Myrtles, Hockley, Essex, and the late Adelaide Rebecca Kent.	Ypres (Menin Gate) Memorial	Panel 9.	Ieper, West-Vlaanderen
LASHMORE, FRANK	Lance Corporal	1588	1st Bn.	Honourable Artillery Company	16-Jun-15	26	Son of George and Catherine Lashmore, of Market Drayton, Salop.	Ypres (Menin Gate) Memorial	Panel 9.	Ieper, West-Vlaanderen
LEWIS, OSMOND HENRY	Private	2205	1st Bn.	Honourable Artillery Company	16-Jun-15	unknown	Son of Henry James and Alice Lewis, of 40, Great Tower St., London.	Ypres (Menin Gate) Memorial	Panel 9.	Ieper, West-Vlaanderen
MONEY, SIDNEY AUBREY KYRLE	Sergeant	1416	1st Bn.	Honourable Artillery Company	16-Jun-15	unknown		Ypres (Menin Gate) Memorial	Panel 9.	Ieper, West-Vlaanderen

Full name	Rank	Service	Unit	Regiment	Date	Age	Additional	Grave	Cemetery	Locality
MOORAT, BERNARD JOSEPH	Corporal	1238	1st Bn.	Honourable Artillery Company	16-Jun-15	unknown		Panel 9.	Ypres (Menin Gate) Memorial	Ieper, West-Vlaanderen
MUNT, ELLIOT ROY	Lance Corporal	1695	1st Bn.	Honourable Artillery Company	16-Jun-15	22	Son of W. Edsall Munt and Bessie Munt, of The Coppice, Coppice Lane, Reigate.	Panel 9.	Ypres (Menin Gate) Memorial	Ieper, West-Vlaanderen
NEAL, GEORGE IVOR	Private	1976	1st Bn.	Honourable Artillery Company	16-Jun-15	unknown		Panel 9.	Ypres (Menin Gate) Memorial	Ieper, West-Vlaanderen
OPENSHAW, FREDERICK AMBROSE	Lance Corporal	1369	1st Bn.	Honourable Artillery Company	16-Jun-15	unknown		Panel 9.	Ypres (Menin Gate) Memorial	Ieper, West-Vlaanderen
PEARSE, GERALD ENRICO	Private	2181	No. 4 Coy. 1st Bn.	Honourable Artillery Company	16-Jun-15	26	Son of Albert E. and Jane Pearse, of 85, Princes' Crescent, Ditchling Rd., Brighton.	Panel 9.	Ypres (Menin Gate) Memorial	Ieper, West-Vlaanderen
PITTS, HAROLD BERTRAM	Company Sergeant Major	688	"B" Coy. 1st Bn.	Honourable Artillery Company	16-Jun-15	24	Son of Mr. and Mrs. J. Berry Pitts, of Children's Homes, Aldersbrook, Wanstead, London.	Panel 9.	Ypres (Menin Gate) Memorial	Ieper, West-Vlaanderen
REID, JOHN BLANFORD	Lance Corporal	485	1st Bn.	Honourable Artillery Company	16-Jun-15	30	Son of William Crewe Reid and Fanny Elizabeth Reid, of 17, Amhurst Park, Stoke Newington, London. Livery of Poulters Company.	Panel 9.	Ypres (Menin Gate) Memorial	Ieper, West-Vlaanderen
RUSSELL, EVAN HARLEY	Private	1543	1st Bn.	Honourable Artillery Company	16-Jun-15	unknown		Panel 9.	Ypres (Menin Gate) Memorial	Ieper, West-Vlaanderen
SIMS, ALBERT CHARLES	Private	2675	1st Bn.	Honourable Artillery Company	16-Jun-15	19	Son of Charles and Alice Sims, of 332, Hither Green Lane, Lewisham, London.	Panel 9.	Ypres (Menin Gate) Memorial	Ieper, West-Vlaanderen

Name	Rank	Number	Bn.	Regiment	Date	Age	Details	Panel	Memorial	Location
SMITH, WILLIAM ALBERT	Lance Corporal	744	1st Bn.	Honourable Artillery Company	16-Jun-15	unknown		Panel 9.	Ypres (Menin Gate) Memorial	Ieper, West-Vlaanderen
SNOW, ERIC JOHN	Private	1405	1st Bn.	Honourable Artillery Company	16-Jun-15	unknown		Panel 9.	Ypres (Menin Gate) Memorial	Ieper, West-Vlaanderen
SOUTHWELL, WILFRID ALAN GLANVILLE	Private	2292	1st Bn.	Honourable Artillery Company	16-Jun-15	unknown		Panel 9.	Ypres (Menin Gate) Memorial	Ieper, West-Vlaanderen
SPRUNT, EDWARD LAWRENCE	Private	1510	1st Bn.	Honourable Artillery Company	16-Jun-15	22	Son of J. D. and Jane Naismith Sprunt, of Montgomerie, Berkhamsted, Herts.	Panel 9.	Ypres (Menin Gate) Memorial	Ieper, West-Vlaanderen
TINDALL, HUGH	Lance Corporal	1550	1st Bn.	Honourable Artillery Company	16-Jun-15	33	Son of Henry Edward and Nelly Tindall, of Arnside. Chislehurst, Kent.	Panel 9.	Ypres (Menin Gate) Memorial	Ieper, West-Vlaanderen
WHITEHEAD, SYDNEY NORMAN COOPER KEATS	Serjeant	765	1st Bn.	Honourable Artillery Company	16-Jun-15	25	Son of Sydney Whitehead, of "Grasmere," Effingham Rd., Surbiton, Surrey. B.Sc. London.	Panel 9.	Ypres (Menin Gate) Memorial	Ieper, West-Vlaanderen
WIGG, ARTHUR HARRY	Private	2685	1st Bn.	Honourable Artillery Company	16-Jun-15	24	Son of Mrs H O Wigg and the late Mr Wigg. An old Etonian.	XVI. B. 11.	Cement House Cemetery	Langemark-Poelkapelle, West-V.
WITHERS, EDMUND ROY	Private	1729	1st Bn.	Honourable Artillery Company	16-Jun-15	unknown		Panel 9.	Ypres (Menin Gate) Memorial	Ieper, West-Vlaanderen
BAGSHAWE, I. V.	Captain		3rd Bn.	King's Own Scottish Borderers	16-Jun-15			Panel 22	Ypres (Menin Gate) Memorial	Ieper, West-Vlaanderen
ANDERSON, JOHN	Private	14612	1st Bn.	Lincolnshire Regiment	16-Jun-15	unknown		Panel 21.	Ypres (Menin Gate) Memorial	Ieper, West-Vlaanderen

Full name	Rank	Service	Unit	Regiment	Date	Age	Additional	Grave	Cemetery	Locality
ANDERTON, JAMES	Lance Corporal	14527	1st Bn.	Lincolnshire Regiment	16-Jun-15	20	Son of James William and Caroline Anderton, of 2, Bedford Court, Lincoln.	Panel 21.	Ypres (Menin Gate) Memorial	Ieper, West-Vlaanderen
ANDREWS, GEORGE	Private	13887	1st Bn.	Lincolnshire Regiment	16-Jun-15	21	Son of James S. and Annie Andrews, of 3, Balfour St, East Kirkby, Notts.	Panel 21.	Ypres (Menin Gate) Memorial	Ieper, West-Vlaanderen
ATKINS, ANTHONY ALFRED	Private	15470	1st Bn.	Lincolnshire Regiment	16-Jun-15	18	Son of Mrs. Louisa Atkins, of "The Green," Thornham, King's Lynn.	Panel 21.	Ypres (Menin Gate) Memorial	Ieper, West-Vlaanderen
ATTENBOROUGH, JOSEPH CECIL	Serjeant	9290	1st Bn.	Lincolnshire Regiment	16-Jun-15	26	Son of the late Edward and Mary Attenborough.	Panel 21.	Ypres (Menin Gate) Memorial	Ieper, West-Vlaanderen
BACKLOG, EDWARD JAMES	Private	11945	1st Bn.	Lincolnshire Regiment	16-Jun-15	37	Son of John Edward and Sarah Ann Backlog, of 30, Bury Rd., Thetford, Norfolk.	Panel 21.	Ypres (Menin Gate) Memorial	Ieper, West-Vlaanderen
BALDWIN, HARRY	Private	10294	1st Bn.	Lincolnshire Regiment	16-Jun-15	unknown	Husband of Mrs. H. Baldwin, of Masonic Lane, Spilsby, Lincs.	Panel 21.	Ypres (Menin Gate) Memorial	Ieper, West-Vlaanderen
BALDWIN, WALTER EDWIN	Lance Corporal	9436	1st Bn.	Lincolnshire Regiment	16-Jun-15	22	Son of Ada Baldwin, of 4, Grove Rd., Abbey Wood, London and the late Staff S.M. W. Baldwin (R.A.S.C.).	Panel 21.	Ypres (Menin Gate) Memorial	Ieper, West-Vlaanderen
BENNETT, SAMUEL	Private	6237	1st Bn.	Lincolnshire Regiment	16-Jun-15	30	Husband of Mary Elizabeth Bennett, of 14, D Block, Queen's Buildings, Birkenhead.	Panel 21.	Ypres (Menin Gate) Memorial	Ieper, West-Vlaanderen
BILLINGER, WILLIAM	Corporal	6334	1st Bn.	Lincolnshire Regiment	16-Jun-15	unknown		Panel 21.	Ypres (Menin Gate) Memorial	Ieper, West-Vlaanderen
BLANCHARD, JOSEPH	Lance Corporal	7768	1st Bn	Lincolnshire Regiment	16-Jun-15	18	Son of Foster and Mary Ann Blanchard, of 86 Patrick St., Grimsby.	Panel 21.	Ypres (Menin Gate) Memorial	Ieper, West-Vlaanderen

Name	Rank	Number	Battalion	Regiment	Date	Age	Details	Panel	Memorial	Location
BOXER, HUGH EDWARD RICHARD	Lieutenant Colonel		Cdg. 1st Bn.	Lincolnshire Regiment	16-Jun-15	44	Son of Edith Graham Le Grice (formerly Boxer), of Thorpe Lodge, Sandown, Isle of Wight, and the late Lieut. E. W. F. Boxer, R.N.	Panel 21.	Ypres (Menin Gate) Memorial	Ieper, West-Vlaanderen
BREWERTON, GEORGE	Lance Corporal	6249	1st Bn.	Lincolnshire Regiment	16-Jun-15	unknown		Panel 21.	Ypres (Menin Gate) Memorial	Ieper, West-Vlaanderen
BROUGHTON, CHARLES	Private	7966	1st Bn.	Lincolnshire Regiment	16-Jun-15	unknown		Panel 21.	Ypres (Menin Gate) Memorial	Ieper, West-Vlaanderen
BURNHAM, CHARLES	Private	13910	1st Bn.	Lincolnshire Regiment	16-Jun-15	unknown		Panel 21.	Ypres (Menin Gate) Memorial	Ieper, West-Vlaanderen
BURT, JAMES	Private	15273	1st Bn.	Lincolnshire Regiment	16-Jun-15	unknown		Panel 21.	Ypres (Menin Gate) Memorial	Ieper, West-Vlaanderen
CARR, ROBERT SYDNEY	Private	9424	1st Bn.	Lincolnshire Regiment	16-Jun-15	unknown		Panel 21.	Ypres (Menin Gate) Memorial	Ieper, West-Vlaanderen
CHARLES, JOSEPH	Private	7024	"B" Coy. 1st Bn.	Lincolnshire Regiment	16-Jun-15	30	Son of the late Mr. and Mrs. Elijah Charles; husband of Harriett Charles, of 34, Sherwood Rise, Nuncar Gate, Nottingham.	Panel 21.	Ypres (Menin Gate) Memorial	Ieper, West-Vlaanderen
CLARK, ALFRED	Private	8086	1st Bn.	Lincolnshire Regiment	16-Jun-15	30	Son of Esther Clark, of 216, High St., Homerton, London.	Panel 21.	Ypres (Menin Gate) Memorial	Ieper, West-Vlaanderen
CLARK, STANLEY	Private	13979	1st Bn.	Lincolnshire Regiment	16-Jun-15	21	Son of Mrs. Elizabeth Clark, of II, North St., Sutton-in-Ashfield, Notts.	Panel 21.	Ypres (Menin Gate) Memorial	Ieper, West-Vlaanderen
CLARKE, HERBERT	Private	14567	1st Bn.	Lincolnshire Regiment	16-Jun-15	18	Son of George and Eliza Clarke, of Wilsford Heath, Grantham.	Panel 21.	Ypres (Menin Gate) Memorial	Ieper, West-Vlaanderen
CLARKE, WILLIAM	Private	14437	1st Bn.	Lincolnshire Regiment	16-Jun-15	21	Son of Henry Thomas and Eliza Clarke, of Northfield Farm, Messingham, Gainsborough.	Panel 21.	Ypres (Menin Gate) Memorial	Ieper, West-Vlaanderen

Full name	Rank	Service	Unit	Regiment	Date	Age	Additional	Grave	Cemetery	Locality
CLAYTON, GEORGE	Private	7641	1st Bn.	Lincolnshire Regiment	16-Jun-15	unknown		Panel 21.	Ypres (Menin Gate) Memorial	Ieper, West-Vlaanderen
COCKLIN, WILLIAM	Private	6205	1st Bn.	Lincolnshire Regiment	16-Jun-15	unknown		Panel 21.	Ypres (Menin Gate) Memorial	Ieper, West-Vlaanderen
COLES, LEVI	Private	12805	1st Bn.	Lincolnshire Regiment	16-Jun-15	17	Son of Mrs. S. E. Coles, of 67, Heavy Gate Avenue, Sheffield.	Panel 21.	Ypres (Menin Gate) Memorial	Ieper, West-Vlaanderen
COLLARD, HERBERT FRED GEORGE	Private	14839	1st Bn.	Lincolnshire Regiment	16-Jun-15	18	Son of George and Ada Collard, of 19, Hartfield Crescent, Wimbledon, London.	Panel 21.	Ypres (Menin Gate) Memorial	Ieper, West-Vlaanderen
COULSON, WILLIAM	Corporal	9183	1st Bn.	Lincolnshire Regiment	16-Jun-15	unknown		Panel 21.	Ypres (Menin Gate) Memorial	Ieper, West-Vlaanderen
CROOKS, WILLIAM	Private	15183	1st Bn.	Lincolnshire Regiment	16-Jun-15	unknown		Panel 21.	Ypres (Menin Gate) Memorial	Ieper, West-Vlaanderen
DAVIS, FREDERICK JAMES	Company Serjeant Major	7970	1st Bn.	Lincolnshire Regiment	16-Jun-15	unknown		Panel 21.	Ypres (Menin Gate) Memorial	Ieper, West-Vlaanderen
DEMPSEY, FRANK	Private	8114	1st Bn.	Lincolnshire Regiment	16-Jun-15	unknown		Panel 21.	Ypres (Menin Gate) Memorial	Ieper, West-Vlaanderen
DREW, EDWARD ROBERT	Private	7849	1st Bn.	Lincolnshire Regiment	16-Jun-15	unknown		Panel 21.	Ypres (Menin Gate) Memorial	Ieper, West-Vlaanderen
DUNN, JOHN GEORGE	Private	14008	1st Bn.	Lincolnshire Regiment	16-Jun-15	unknown	Son of Elijah and Fanny Dunn, of 46, Market St., Shirebrook, Notts; husband of Elizabeth Mattock (formerly Dunn), of 11, First Avenue, Brownhills, Walsall, Staffs.	Panel 21.	Ypres (Menin Gate) Memorial	Ieper, West-Vlaanderen
ELLIS, JOHN	Private	8515	1st Bn.	Lincolnshire Regiment	16-Jun-15	35	Husband of Edith May Ellis, of 8, Hart St., New Cleethorpes, Grimsby.	Panel 21.	Ypres (Menin Gate) Memorial	Ieper, West-Vlaanderen

Name	Rank	Service No.	Battalion	Regiment	Date	Age	Family	Panel	Memorial	Location
ESSAM, HARRY	Private	8227	1st Bn.	Lincolnshire Regiment	16-Jun-15	35	Son of the late Jesse Essam; husband of Minnie Essam, of 48, Tooley St., Gainsborough.	Panel 21.	Ypres (Menin Gate) Memorial	Ieper, West-Vlaanderen
EVETTS, GEORGE	Private	6819	1st Bn.	Lincolnshire Regiment	16-Jun-15	28	Son of the late Frederic Evetts.	Panel 21.	Ypres (Menin Gate) Memorial	Ieper, West-Vlaanderen
FEATHERSTONE, G S	Private	9318	1st Bn.	Lincolnshire Regiment	16-Jun-15	unknown		XIII. A. 10.	Harlebeke New British Cemetery	Harelbeke, West-Vlaanderen
FRANKLIN, SYDNEY	Corporal	9092	1st Bn.	Lincolnshire Regiment	16-Jun-15	22	Son of Mr. A. J. Franklin, J.P. and Mrs. A. H. Franklin, of "Lairseat," Parkhurst Rd., Bexley, Kent.	Panel 21.	Ypres (Menin Gate) Memorial	Ieper, West-Vlaanderen
FULLER, THOMAS ANDREW	Serjeant	9114	1st Bn.	Lincolnshire Regiment	16-Jun-15	26	Son of Gillson Fuller, of 1, Potts Yard, New Town, Ramsey, Hunts.	Panel 21.	Ypres (Menin Gate) Memorial	Ieper, West-Vlaanderen
GOSLING, GEORGE	Private	13747	1st Bn.	Lincolnshire Regiment	16-Jun-15	19	Son of Mr. George D. and Amelia Gosling, of Algarkirk, Boston, Lincs.	Panel 21.	Ypres (Menin Gate) Memorial	Ieper, West-Vlaanderen
GOY, WILLIAM	Private	9514	1st Bn.	Lincolnshire Regiment	16-Jun-15	21	Nephew of Robert Goy, of 3, Norfolk Row, Eastfield Rd., Louth, Lincs.	Panel 21.	Ypres (Menin Gate) Memorial	Ieper, West-Vlaanderen
GREEN, FRANK CLIFFORD	Second Lieutenant		1st Bn.	Lincolnshire Regiment	16-Jun-15	unknown		Panel 21.	Ypres (Menin Gate) Memorial	Ieper, West-Vlaanderen
GREEN, LEWIS	Private	16215	1st Bn.	Lincolnshire Regiment	16-Jun-15	unknown		Panel 21.	Ypres (Menin Gate) Memorial	Ieper, West-Vlaanderen
HARRIS, EDGAR	Private	13729	"D" Coy. 1st Bn.	Lincolnshire Regiment	16-Jun-15	30	Son of Major and Ann Harris, "Bickmarsh," Bidford-on-Avon; husband of Annie Elizabeth Houghton (formerly Harris), of Barton, Bidford-on-Avon. Warwickshire.	Panel 21.	Ypres (Menin Gate) Memorial	Ieper, West-Vlaanderen

Full name	Rank	Service	Unit	Regiment	Date	Age	Additional	Grave	Cemetery	Locality
HODKINSON, THOMAS	Private	9451	1st Bn.	Lincolnshire Regiment	16-Jun-15	39	Son of Mrs. E. Hodkinson, of 13, Trent St., Gainsborough.	Panel 21.	Ypres (Menin Gate) Memorial	Ieper, West-Vlaanderen
HORNE, EDMUND	Private	7720	1st Bn.	Lincolnshire Regiment	16-Jun-15	unknown		Panel 21.	Ypres (Menin Gate) Memorial	Ieper, West-Vlaanderen
HORRY, FRANK	Corporal	5519	1st Bn.	Lincolnshire Regiment	16-Jun-15	33	Son of Mary Jane Horry, of 21, White Horse Yard, Gainsborough, and the late John Horry.	Panel 21.	Ypres (Menin Gate) Memorial	Ieper, West-Vlaanderen
HUTCHINSON, GEORGE	Private	14090	1st Bn.	Lincolnshire Regiment	16-Jun-15	19	Son of John Jabez Holworthy Hutchinson and A. Elizabeth Hutchinson, of 8, William St., Eckington, Sheffield.	Panel 21.	Ypres (Menin Gate) Memorial	Ieper, West-Vlaanderen
JACKSON, HAROLD	Private	13768	"B" Coy. 1st Bn.	Lincolnshire Regiment	16-Jun-15	18	Ward of David Markham, of Helpringham, Sleaford, Lincs.	Panel 21.	Ypres (Menin Gate) Memorial	Ieper, West-Vlaanderen
JENNINGS, TOM	Lance Corporal	7299	1st Bn.	Lincolnshire Regiment	16-Jun-15	unknown		Panel 21.	Ypres (Menin Gate) Memorial	Ieper, West-Vlaanderen
JOHNSON, THOMAS HARRY	Private	9358	1st Bn.	Lincolnshire Regiment	16-Jun-15	20	Son of Mr. G. and Emma Johnson, of 37, Manor St., Wigston Magna, Leicester.	Panel 21.	Ypres (Menin Gate) Memorial	Ieper, West-Vlaanderen
JONES, JOSEPH ALFRED	Serjeant	14103	"A" Coy. 1st Bn.	Lincolnshire Regiment	16-Jun-15	24	Son of Joseph Morris Jones and Mary Jones.	Addenda Panel 57.	Ypres (Menin Gate) Memorial	Ieper, West-Vlaanderen
KETTLE, EDWARD BARKER	Private	14108	1st Bn.	Lincolnshire Regiment	16-Jun-15	unknown		Panel 21.	Ypres (Menin Gate) Memorial	Ieper, West-Vlaanderen
KIME, GEORGE	Private	11700	1st Bn.	Lincolnshire Regiment	16-Jun-15	unknown		Panel 21.	Ypres (Menin Gate) Memorial	Ieper, West-Vlaanderen
KITSON, ROBERT	Private	7861	1st Bn.	Lincolnshire Regiment	16-Jun-15	unknown		Panel 21.	Ypres (Menin Gate) Memorial	Ieper, West-Vlaanderen

LAVELL, THOMAS	Lance Corporal	8424	1st Bn.	Lincolnshire Regiment	16-Jun-15	0		Ypres (Menin Gate) Memorial	Panel 21.	Ieper, West-Vlaanderen
LAWSON, HARRY	Private	7676	1st Bn.	Lincolnshire Regiment	16-Jun-15	23	Son of James and Mary Jane Lawson, of Crooked Billet St., Morton, Gainsborough.	Ypres (Menin Gate) Memorial	Panel 21.	Ieper, West-Vlaanderen
LINFORD, TOM	Private	15345	1st Bn.	Lincolnshire Regiment	16-Jun-15	unknown		Ypres (Menin Gate) Memorial	Panel 21.	Ieper, West-Vlaanderen
McNEE, HERBERT	Private	8167	1st Bn.	Lincolnshire Regiment	16-Jun-15	18	Brother of William Jess McNee, of 19, Fotherly St., Grimsby.	Ypres (Menin Gate) Memorial	Panel 21.	Ieper, West-Vlaanderen
MELTON, JOSEPH HENRY	Private	15221	"C" Coy. 1st Bn.	Lincolnshire Regiment	16-Jun-15	21	Son of Emmanuel and Frances Melton, of Bloxholm Cottages, Dorrington, Lincoln.	Ypres (Menin Gate) Memorial	Panel 21.	Ieper, West-Vlaanderen
MITCHELL, ALFRED	Private	8109	1st Bn.	Lincolnshire Regiment	16-Jun-15	unknown		Ypres (Menin Gate) Memorial	Panel 21.	Ieper, West-Vlaanderen
MOLLOY, WILLIAM	Private	9942	1st Bn.	Lincolnshire Regiment	16-Jun-15	unknown		Ypres (Menin Gate) Memorial	Panel 21.	Ieper, West-Vlaanderen
MUMBY, NAYLOR	Private	8308	1st Bn.	Lincolnshire Regiment	16-Jun-15	40	Brother of Mr. W. Mumby, of 15, Fraser St., Grimsby.	Ypres (Menin Gate) Memorial	Panel 21.	Ieper, West-Vlaanderen
NEEDHAM, J. R.	Lance Corporal	5943	1st Bn.	Lincolnshire Regiment	16-Jun-15	unknown		Tyne Cot Cemetery	LXVI. H. 10.	Zonnebeke, West-Vlaanderen
PATTERSON, ALFRED	Private	14650	1st Bn.	Lincolnshire Regiment	16-Jun-15	17	Son of Mrs. A. M. Davison (formerly Patterson), of 22, Abney St., Sheffield, and the late Vincent Patterson (2nd Bn. Lincolnshire Regt.).	Ypres (Menin Gate) Memorial	Panel 21.	Ieper, West-Vlaanderen
PEACH, WILLIAM	Private	13881	1st Bn.	Lincolnshire Regiment	16-Jun-15	20	Son of George and Mahalah Peach, of Holbeach St. John's, Holbeach, Lincs.	Ypres (Menin Gate) Memorial	Panel 21.	Ieper, West-Vlaanderen

Full name	Rank	Service	Unit	Regiment	Date	Age	Additional	Grave	Cemetery	Locality
PEARSON, REGINALD OSWALD	Second Lieutenant		1st Bn.	Lincolnshire Regiment	16-Jun-15	unknown		Panel 21.	Ypres (Menin Gate) Memorial	Ieper, West-Vlaanderen
PENN, WALTER	Lance Corporal	8091	1st Bn.	Lincolnshire Regiment	16-Jun-15	unknown		Panel 21.	Ypres (Menin Gate) Memorial	Ieper, West-Vlaanderen
PICKWELL, JOHN	Private	9376	1st Bn.	Lincolnshire Regiment	16-Jun-15	unknown		Panel 21.	Ypres (Menin Gate) Memorial	Ieper, West-Vlaanderen
PITTAWAY, FREDERICK	Private	14408	1st Bn.	Lincolnshire Regiment	16-Jun-15	18	Son of Mr. Henry and Mrs. Lucy Pittaway, of 8, The Brooklands, Broughton, Brigg, Lincs.	Panel 21.	Ypres (Menin Gate) Memorial	Ieper, West-Vlaanderen
PRATT, JOHN THOMAS	Private	5725	1st Bn.	Lincolnshire Regiment	16-Jun-15	38	Son of the late William and Sarah Pratt, of Ewerby, Sleaford; husband of Ann Pratt, of 52, Ewerby, Sleaford, Lincs.	Panel 21.	Ypres (Menin Gate) Memorial	Ieper, West-Vlaanderen
PRESCOTT, FRANK	Corporal	6167	1st Bn.	Lincolnshire Regiment	16-Jun-15	32	Son of Eliza Ann Page (formerly Prescott), of 12, Stapley Rd., Belvedere, Kent.	Panel 21.	Ypres (Menin Gate) Memorial	Ieper, West-Vlaanderen
PRITCHARD, THOMAS HENRY	Lance Corporal	14174	1st Bn.	Lincolnshire Regiment	16-Jun-15	unknown		Panel 21.	Ypres (Menin Gate) Memorial	Ieper, West-Vlaanderen
REDMILE, FRANK	Private	14185	1st Bn.	Lincolnshire Regiment	16-Jun-15	19	Son of Mark and Mary Elizabeth Redmile, of 126, Westfield Lane, Mansfield.	Panel 21.	Ypres (Menin Gate) Memorial	Ieper, West-Vlaanderen
RHODES, EDMUND	Private	14384	1st Bn.	Lincolnshire Regiment	16-Jun-15	18	Son of Hannah Rhodes.	Panel 21.	Ypres (Menin Gate) Memorial	Ieper, West-Vlaanderen
SELBY, GEORGE EDWARD	Private	5477	1st Bn.	Lincolnshire Regiment	16-Jun-15	unknown		Panel 21.	Ypres (Menin Gate) Memorial	Ieper, West-Vlaanderen
SENGER, EDWIN	Private	9765	1st Bn.	Lincolnshire Regiment	16-Jun-15	unknown		Panel 21.	Ypres (Menin Gate) Memorial	Ieper, West-Vlaanderen

Name	Rank	Number	Bn.	Regiment	Date	Age	Details	Panel	Memorial	Location
SHIPMAN, CHARLES WILLIAM	Private	14209	1st Bn.	Lincolnshire Regiment	16-Jun-15	20	Son of Mrs. Elizabeth A. Warrener, of White Lion Square, Bidworth, Mansfield.	Panel 21.	Ypres (Menin Gate) Memorial	Ieper, West-Vlaanderen
SHIPP, HARRY ERNEST	Serjeant	8034	1st Bn.	Lincolnshire Regiment	16-Jun-15	37	Son of Mary Shipp, of 70, Malton Rd., Upton Park, London.	Panel 21.	Ypres (Menin Gate) Memorial	Ieper, West-Vlaanderen
SMITH, WILLIAM HENRY	Private	8047	1st Bn.	Lincolnshire Regiment	16-Jun-15	32	Son of William Henry and Rebecca Smith, of 63, Tonning St., Lowestoft.	Panel 21.	Ypres (Menin Gate) Memorial	Ieper, West-Vlaanderen
STAFFORD, HARRY	Private	11439	1st Bn.	Lincolnshire Regiment	16-Jun-15	33	Son of Harry and Julia Stafford, of The Green, Ketton, Stamford, Lincs. Served in the South African War.	Panel 21.	Ypres (Menin Gate) Memorial	Ieper, West-Vlaanderen
STEBBING, HENRY THOMAS	Private	8051	1st Bn.	Lincolnshire Regiment	16-Jun-15	22	Husband of Edith Taylor (formerly Stebbing), of 55, Cassiobury Rd., Coppermill Lane, Walthamstow, London.	Panel 21.	Ypres (Menin Gate) Memorial	Ieper, West-Vlaanderen
SWAIN, JOHN	Private	14205	1st Bn.	Lincolnshire Regiment	16-Jun-15	unknown		Panel 21.	Ypres (Menin Gate) Memorial	Ieper, West-Vlaanderen
SYLVESTER, WILLIAM HENRY	Private	14370	1st Bn.	Lincolnshire Regiment	16-Jun-15	20	Son of William Sylvester, of Calceby, Alford, Lincs.	Panel 21.	Ypres (Menin Gate) Memorial	Ieper, West-Vlaanderen
TANN, JOHN GEORGE	Serjeant	9519	1st Bn.	Lincolnshire Regiment	16-Jun-15	unknown		Panel 21.	Ypres (Menin Gate) Memorial	Ieper, West-Vlaanderen
TODD, JOHN EDWARD	Private	7690	1st Bn.	Lincolnshire Regiment	16-Jun-15	unknown		Panel 21.	Ypres (Menin Gate) Memorial	Ieper, West-Vlaanderen
TOLLERTON, ALBERT ERNEST	Private	7770	1st Bn.	Lincolnshire Regiment	16-Jun-15	22	Son of Mr. and Mrs. E. Tollerton, of 9, Carr St., Lincoln.	Panel 21.	Ypres (Menin Gate) Memorial	Ieper, West-Vlaanderen
TOMLIN, GEORGE	Private	14353	1st Bn.	Lincolnshire Regiment	16-Jun-15	unknown		Panel 21.	Ypres (Menin Gate) Memorial	Ieper, West-Vlaanderen
TONKS, MARK	Private	14225	1st Bn.	Lincolnshire Regiment	16-Jun-15	unknown		Panel 21.	Ypres (Menin Gate) Memorial	Ieper, West-Vlaanderen

Full name	Rank	Service	Unit	Regiment	Date	Age	Additional	Grave	Cemetery	Locality
WALKER, ALFRED JAMES	Private	8044	1st Bn.	Lincolnshire Regiment	16-Jun-15	unknown		Panel 21.	Ypres (Menin Gate) Memorial	Ieper, West-Vlaanderen
WALKER, ALLAN DIXON	Lieutenant		2nd Bn.	Lincolnshire Regiment	16-Jun-15	unknown		Panel 3.	Ploegsteert Memorial	Comines-Warneton, Hainaut
WALTON, CHARLES WILLIAM	Private	14715	1st Bn.	Lincolnshire Regiment	16-Jun-15	17	Son of Eliza Marshall (formerly Walton), of Wilsford Lane, Ancaster, Grantham, and the late Mr. R. Walton.	Panel 21.	Ypres (Menin Gate) Memorial	Ieper, West-Vlaanderen
WARD, WILLIAM	Private	9784	1st Bn.	Lincolnshire Regiment	16-Jun-15	unknown		Panel 21.	Ypres (Menin Gate) Memorial	Ieper, West-Vlaanderen
WATSON, JOHN HENRY	Private	9737	1st Bn.	Lincolnshire Regiment	16-Jun-15	unknown		Panel 21.	Ypres (Menin Gate) Memorial	Ieper, West-Vlaanderen
WEDD, REUBEN JOHN	Private	7994	1st Bn.	Lincolnshire Regiment	16-Jun-15	19	Son of Reuben John and Rose Wedd, of 36, Grange Rd., St. James's St., Walthamstow, London.	Panel 21.	Ypres (Menin Gate) Memorial	Ieper, West-Vlaanderen
WELLS, GEORGE WILLIAM	Private	9522	1st Bn.	Lincolnshire Regiment	16-Jun-15	unknown		Panel 21.	Ypres (Menin Gate) Memorial	Ieper, West-Vlaanderen
WHITTAKER, JOSEPH	Lance Corporal	15264	1st Bn.	Lincolnshire Regiment	16-Jun-15	24	Son of Joseph Whittaker, of Stapenhill, Burton-on-Trent; husband of Ellen Whittaker, of 225, Hewitt St., Warsop Vale, Mansfield.	Panel 21.	Ypres (Menin Gate) Memorial	Ieper, West-Vlaanderen
WILKINSON, FRANK	Private	13406	1st Bn.	Lincolnshire Regiment	16-Jun-15	unknown		Panel 21.	Ypres (Menin Gate) Memorial	Ieper, West-Vlaanderen
WILLERTON, ARTHUR	Private	13606	1st Bn.	Lincolnshire Regiment	16-Jun-15	unknown		Panel 21.	Ypres (Menin Gate) Memorial	Ieper, West-Vlaanderen

Name	Rank	Number	Bn.	Regiment	Date	Age	Details	Panel	Memorial	Location
WILSON, ALLAN	Private	7925	1st Bn.	Lincolnshire Regiment	16-Jun-15	19	Son of Allan and Christina Wilson, of 89, Eleanor St., Grimsby.	Panel 21.	Ypres (Menin Gate) Memorial	Ieper, West-Vlaanderen
WISE, THOMAS	Private	14421	1st Bn.	Lincolnshire Regiment	16-Jun-15	27	Husband of Lily V. Wise, of 6, Pearson's Court, Stamford, Lincs.	Panel 21.	Ypres (Menin Gate) Memorial	Ieper, West-Vlaanderen
YOUNG, ANDREW ALBERT	Private	9152	1st Bn.	Lincolnshire Regiment	16-Jun-15	39	Son of Mrs. Kezia Young, of 41, Foster St., Lincoln.	Panel 21.	Ypres (Menin Gate) Memorial	Ieper, West-Vlaanderen
GREENOUGH, BENJAMIN	Private	G/8706	4th Bn	London Regiment (Royal Fusiliers)	16-Jun-15	unknown		Panel 52.	Ypres (Menin Gate) Memorial	Ieper, West-Vlaanderen
ABBOTT, GEORGE	Private	4338	1st Bn.	Northumberland Fusiliers	16-Jun-15	unknown		Panel 8 and 12.	Ypres (Menin Gate) Memorial	Ieper, West-Vlaanderen
ALVINE, ALFRED	Private	7668	1st Bn.	Northumberland Fusiliers	16-Jun-15	unknown		Panel 8 and 12.	Ypres (Menin Gate) Memorial	Ieper, West-Vlaanderen
ANDREWS, EDWARD	Lance Corporal	9894	1st Bn.	Northumberland Fusiliers	16-Jun-15	37	Son of George Andrews, of 24, Richardson Terrace, Cowpen, Bebside, Northumberland; husband of Jane Ann Hewitt (formerly Andrews), of 71, Pitt St., Newcastle-on-Tyne.	Panel 8 and 12.	Ypres (Menin Gate) Memorial	Ieper, West-Vlaanderen
ANDREWS, WILLIAM EDWIN	Private	8808	1st Bn.	Northumberland Fusiliers	16-Jun-15	unknown	Son of William Andrews, of 59, Caevelen St., Llanhilleth, Newport, Mon.	Panel 8 and 12.	Ypres (Menin Gate) Memorial	Ieper, West-Vlaanderen
ASHMORE, SAMUEL	Serjeant	8148	1st Bn.	Northumberland Fusiliers	16-Jun-15	35	Son of Mrs. Mary Ann Ashmore, of 23, Hedderley St., Union Rd., Nottingham.	Panel 8 and 12.	Ypres (Menin Gate) Memorial	Ieper, West-Vlaanderen
BAGBROUGH, BENJAMIN	Lance Corporal	7472	1st Bn.	Northumberland Fusiliers	16-Jun-15	unknown		Panel 8 and 12.	Ypres (Menin Gate) Memorial	Ieper, West-Vlaanderen

Full name	Rank	Service	Unit	Regiment	Date	Age	Additional	Grave	Cemetery	Locality
BARRETT, WILLIAM	Private	8861	1st Bn.	Northumberland Fusiliers	16-Jun-15	30	Son of Herbert and Ellen Barrett, of 58, Light Pipe Hall Rd., Stockton-on-Tees.	Panel 8 and 12.	Ypres (Menin Gate) Memorial	Ieper, West-Vlaanderen
BEECH, EDWARD	Private	9285	1st Bn.	Northumberland Fusiliers	16-Jun-15	unknown		Panel 8 and 12.	Ypres (Menin Gate) Memorial	Ieper, West-Vlaanderen
BELL, HENRY	Private	1371	1st/4th Bn.	Northumberland Fusiliers	16-Jun-15	unknown		Panel 8 and 12.	Ypres (Menin Gate) Memorial	Ieper, West-Vlaanderen
BLACK, JOHN	Private	Mar-52	1st Bn.	Northumberland Fusiliers	16-Jun-15	47	Son of the late William and Mary Black.	Panel 8 and 12.	Ypres (Menin Gate) Memorial	Ieper, West-Vlaanderen
BORTHWICK, GEORGE	Private	1396	1st/7th Bn.	Northumberland Fusiliers	16-Jun-15	19	Son of Mrs. C. M. Young (formerly Borthwick), of 100, Juliet St., Ashington, Northumberland, and the late Serjt. George Borthwick (R.G.A.).	Panel 8 and 12.	Ypres (Menin Gate) Memorial	Ieper, West-Vlaanderen
BRADLEY, WILLIAM HENRY	Lance Serjeant	7769	1st Bn.	Northumberland Fusiliers	16-Jun-15	27	Son of Waller and Matilda Bradley; husband of Catherine Davenport Bradley, of 91, Preston Rd., South Yardley, Birmingham.	Panel 8 and 12.	Ypres (Menin Gate) Memorial	Ieper, West-Vlaanderen
BRENNAN, JAMES EDWARD	Private	7892	1st Bn.	Northumberland Fusiliers	16-Jun-15	unknown	Brother of John Brennan, of 25, Roseberry View, Thornaby-on-Tees, Yorks.	Panel 8 and 12.	Ypres (Menin Gate) Memorial	Ieper, West-Vlaanderen
BRINE, WALTER CLARENCE	Lance Corporal	1146	1st Bn.	Northumberland Fusiliers	16-Jun-15	28	Son of Francis Brine, of 9, Bryan St., Caledonian Rd., King's Cross, London.	Panel 8 and 12.	Ypres (Menin Gate) Memorial	Ieper, West-Vlaanderen
BROADBENT, JACK	Private	3908	1st Bn.	Northumberland Fusiliers	16-Jun-15	unknown		Panel 8 and 12.	Ypres (Menin Gate) Memorial	Ieper, West-Vlaanderen
BROUGHTON, AUSTIN FRANK	Private	3555	"W" Coy. 1st Bn.	Northumberland Fusiliers	16-Jun-15	19	Son of William C. and Ellen E. Broughton, of 9, Rosebery Avenue, Gloucester.	Panel 8 and 12.	Ypres (Menin Gate) Memorial	Ieper, West-Vlaanderen

Name	Rank	Service No.	Regiment	Battalion	Date	Age	Details	Panel	Memorial	Location
BUCKLEY, JAMES	Private	3/95	Northumberland Fusiliers	1st Bn.	16-Jun-15	22	Son of Mrs. Bridget Buckley, of 5, Mill Square, Morpeth, Northumberland.	Panel 8 and 12.	Ypres (Menin Gate) Memorial	Ieper, West-Vlaanderen
CAMPBELL, JOHN	Private	6351	Northumberland Fusiliers	1st Bn.	16-Jun-15	31	Husband of Elizabeth Campbell, of 25, West Wear St., Sunderland.	Panel 8 and 12.	Ypres (Menin Gate) Memorial	Ieper, West-Vlaanderen
CARR, DAVID	Private	8129	Northumberland Fusiliers	1st Bn.	16-Jun-15	unknown		Panel 8 and 12.	Ypres (Menin Gate) Memorial	Ieper, West-Vlaanderen
CARR, WILLIAM	Private	1610	Northumberland Fusiliers	1st/7th Bn.	16-Jun-15	20	Son of John and H. Carr, of Ellingham Home Farm, Chathill, Northumberland.	Panel 8 and 12.	Ypres (Menin Gate) Memorial	Ieper, West-Vlaanderen
CARTER, HENRY	Second Lieutenant		Northumberland Fusiliers	1st Bn.	16-Jun-15	39	Son of the late Henry and Sarah Carter; husband of Jessie Carter, of 154, Warley Rd., Brentwood, Essex.	Panel 8 and 12.	Ypres (Menin Gate) Memorial	Ieper, West-Vlaanderen
CASEY, FRANCIS FREDERICK	Serjeant	4169	Northumberland Fusiliers	1st Bn.	16-Jun-15	33	Husband of Georgina Lilian Lukes (formerly Casey), of 2, Gordon Place, Gravesend.	LVI. E. 9.	Poelcapelle British Cemetery	Langemark-Poelkapelle, West-V.
CAVANAGH, THOMAS	Private	7968	Northumberland Fusiliers	1st Bn.	16-Jun-15	26	Son of Francis and Ann Cavanagh, of 48, Back, Ouse St., Ouseburn, Newcastle-on-Tyne.	Panel 8 and 12.	Ypres (Menin Gate) Memorial	Ieper, West-Vlaanderen
CHAPMAN, WILLIAM ERNEST	Lance Corporal	9544	Northumberland Fusiliers	1st Bn.	16-Jun-15	unknown		Panel 8 and 12.	Ypres (Menin Gate) Memorial	Ieper, West-Vlaanderen
CHERRY, ROBERT	Private	8831	Northumberland Fusiliers	1st Bn.	16-Jun-15	46		Panel 8 and 12.	Ypres (Menin Gate) Memorial	Ieper, West-Vlaanderen
CLARKE, WILLIAM JAMES	Private	306	Northumberland Fusiliers	1st Bn.	16-Jun-15	unknown		Panel 8 and 12.	Ypres (Menin Gate) Memorial	Ieper, West-Vlaanderen
COATES, EDWIN	Private	7357	Northumberland Fusiliers	1st Bn.	16-Jun-15	36	Son of the late Robert and Catherine Coates. Served in the South African Campaign.	Panel 8 and 12.	Ypres (Menin Gate) Memorial	Ieper, West-Vlaanderen

Full name	Rank	Service	Unit	Regiment	Date	Age	Additional	Grave	Cemetery	Locality
COLES, FRANCIS	Private	942	1st Bn.	Northumberland Fusiliers	16-Jun-15	32	Son of the late Thomas Coles.	Panel 8 and 12.	Ypres (Menin Gate) Memorial	Ieper, West-Vlaanderen
COOPER, SAMUEL	Lance Corporal	1941	1st Bn.	Northumberland Fusiliers	16-Jun-15	29	Son of Mrs. Mary Elliott (formerly Cooper), of 148, Weedon St., Brightside, Sheffield.	Panel 8 and 12.	Ypres (Menin Gate) Memorial	Ieper, West-Vlaanderen
COSER, GEORGE	Lance Corporal	8043	1st Bn.	Northumberland Fusiliers	16-Jun-15	unknown		Panel 8 and 12.	Ypres (Menin Gate) Memorial	Ieper, West-Vlaanderen
COX, ALBERT ARTHUR	Private	1967	1st Bn.	Northumberland Fusiliers	16-Jun-15	unknown		Panel 8 and 12.	Ypres (Menin Gate) Memorial	Ieper, West-Vlaanderen
COXON, JOSEPH	Private	2166	1st Bn.	Northumberland Fusiliers	16-Jun-15	unknown		Panel 8 and 12.	Ypres (Menin Gate) Memorial	Ieper, West-Vlaanderen
CRAINE, J.J.	Private	8866	1st Bn.	Northumberland Fusiliers	16-Jun-15	unknown		LXV. K. 9.	Tyne Cot Cemetery	Zonnebeke, West-Vlaanderen
CURRY, J.THOMAS	Private	1569	1st/5th Bn.	Northumberland Fusiliers	16-Jun-15	unknown		Panel 8 and 12.	Ypres (Menin Gate) Memorial	Ieper, West-Vlaanderen
DALBIAC, CHARLES JAMES SHELLEY	Second Lieutenant		1st Bn.	Northumberland Fusiliers	16-Jun-15	19	Son of Col. Philip Hugh Dalbiac, C.B., and Lilian Dalbiac, of "The Elms," Seal, Sevenoaks, Kent. Prize Cadet, Sandhurst.	Panel 8 and 12.	Ypres (Menin Gate) Memorial	Ieper, West-Vlaanderen
DALEY, WILLIAM	Private	3914	1st Bn.	Northumberland Fusiliers	16-Jun-15	20	Son of Mrs. Elizabeth Daley, of 63, Upperhead Row, Huddersfield.	Panel 8 and 12.	Ypres (Menin Gate) Memorial	Ieper, West-Vlaanderen
DALGARNO, WILLIAM DUNCAN	Lance Corporal	11105	1st Bn.	Northumberland Fusiliers	16-Jun-15	35	Husband of Elizabeth Dalgarno, of 50, Victoria Rd., West Back, Hebburn New Town, Co. Durham.	Panel 8 and 12.	Ypres (Menin Gate) Memorial	Ieper, West-Vlaanderen
DALTON, GEORGE	Private	2423	1st/7th Bn.	Northumberland Fusiliers	16-Jun-15	unknown		Panel 8 and 12.	Ypres (Menin Gate) Memorial	Ieper, West-Vlaanderen

Name	Rank	Service No	Bn.	Regiment	Date	Age	Notes	Panel	Memorial	Location
DEDMAN, REGINALD	Private	3811	1st Bn.	Northumberland Fusiliers	16-Jun-15	unknown	Son of Herbert Dedman, of 211, Beeston Rd., Leeds.	I. D. 3.	Kemmel No. 1 French Cemetery	Heuvelland, West-Vlaanderen
DEVLIN, JOHN JAMES	Private	Mar-26	1st Bn.	Northumberland Fusiliers	16-Jun-15	43	Son of the late Daniel and Agnes Devlin.	Panel 8 and 12.	Ypres (Menin Gate) Memorial	Ieper, West-Vlaanderen
DIGGINS, JAMES	Private	318105	1st Bn.	Northumberland Fusiliers	16-Jun-15	21	Son of James Diggins, of 47, Raglan St., South Shields.	Panel 8 and 12.	Ypres (Menin Gate) Memorial	Ieper, West-Vlaanderen
DOBSON, WILLIAM	Private	Mar-42	1st Bn.	Northumberland Fusiliers	16-Jun-15	unknown		Panel 8 and 12.	Ypres (Menin Gate) Memorial	Ieper, West-Vlaanderen
DOWSE, THOMAS	Private	Mar-41	1st Bn.	Northumberland Fusiliers	16-Jun-15	unknown		Panel 8 and 12.	Ypres (Menin Gate) Memorial	Ieper, West-Vlaanderen
ELLIOTT, JOHN	Lance Corporal	Mar-47	1st Bn.	Northumberland Fusiliers	16-Jun-15	unknown		Panel 8 and 12.	Ypres (Menin Gate) Memorial	Ieper, West-Vlaanderen
FITZPATRICK, EDWARD	Private	16781	1st Bn.	Northumberland Fusiliers	16-Jun-15	unknown		Panel 8 and 12.	Ypres (Menin Gate) Memorial	Ieper, West-Vlaanderen
FITZPATRICK, THOMAS	Private	8582	1st Bn.	Northumberland Fusiliers	16-Jun-15	38	Brother-in-law of Annie Fitzpatrick, of 284, Church St., Walker, Newcastle-on-Tyne.	Panel 8 and 12.	Ypres (Menin Gate) Memorial	Ieper, West-Vlaanderen
FLANIGAN, ARTHUR	Private	1026	1st/7th Bn.	Northumberland Fusiliers	16-Jun-15	19	Son of George and Mary Flanigan, of 88, High Street, Berwick-on-Tweed.	Panel 8 and 12.	Ypres (Menin Gate) Memorial	Ieper, West-Vlaanderen
FLATT, WILLIAM ALFRED	Private	17058	1st Bn.	Northumberland Fusiliers	16-Jun-15	unknown		Panel 8 and 12.	Ypres (Menin Gate) Memorial	Ieper, West-Vlaanderen
FLOOD, ALBERT EDWARD	Serjeant	9121	1st Bn.	Northumberland Fusiliers	16-Jun-15	31	Husband of Ellen Flood, of 26, Abbott St., Gateshead.	Panel 8 and 12.	Ypres (Menin Gate) Memorial	Ieper, West-Vlaanderen
FULLERTON, ARTHUR ROBERT	Corporal	666	1st/7th Bn.	Northumberland Fusiliers	16-Jun-15	unknown	Brother of Mrs. Jeanie Dunbar, of 28, Narrowgate, Alnwick, Northumberland.	Panel 8 and 12.	Ypres (Menin Gate) Memorial	Ieper, West-Vlaanderen

Full name	Rank	Service	Unit	Regiment	Date	Age	Additional	Grave	Cemetery	Locality
GILCHRIST, WILLIAM	Private	16863	1st Bn.	Northumberland Fusiliers	16-Jun-15	unknown		Panel 8 and 12.	Ypres (Menin Gate) Memorial	Ieper, West-Vlaanderen
GODFREY, HENRY	Lance Serjeant	9724	1st Bn.	Northumberland Fusiliers	16-Jun-15	unknown		Panel 8 and 12.	Ypres (Menin Gate) Memorial	Ieper, West-Vlaanderen
GOLIGHTLY, DAVID	Private	17035	1st Bn.	Northumberland Fusiliers	16-Jun-15	unknown		Panel 8 and 12.	Ypres (Menin Gate) Memorial	Ieper, West-Vlaanderen
GRANTHAM, FREDRICK WILLIAM	Private	8631	1st Bn.	Northumberland Fusiliers	16-Jun-15	30	Son of the late George and Sarah Grantham.	Panel 8 and 12.	Ypres (Menin Gate) Memorial	Ieper, West-Vlaanderen
GRAY, ANDREW GEORGE	Corporal	2263	1st/7th Bn.	Northumberland Fusiliers	16-Jun-15	25	Son of Jane Oliver Gray, of 23, Green Batt, Alnwick, Northumberland, and the late Robert Gray.	Panel 8 and 12.	Ypres (Menin Gate) Memorial	Ieper, West-Vlaanderen
GREATHEAD, CLARENCE	Private	1850	1st/4th Bn.	Northumberland Fusiliers	16-Jun-15	unknown		Panel 8 and 12.	Ypres (Menin Gate) Memorial	Ieper, West-Vlaanderen
GREEN, JAMES HENRY	Private	2828	1st Bn.	Northumberland Fusiliers	16-Jun-15	unknown		Panel 8 and 12.	Ypres (Menin Gate) Memorial	Ieper, West-Vlaanderen
GRIMES, WILLIAM	Private	4644	1st Bn.	Northumberland Fusiliers	16-Jun-15	21	Son of Annie L. Grimes, of 42, Willow St., Leicester, and the late James Grimes.	Panel 8 and 12.	Ypres (Menin Gate) Memorial	Ieper, West-Vlaanderen
HALL, JOSEPH	Private	3738	1st Bn.	Northumberland Fusiliers	16-Jun-15	unknown	Son of the late Thomas and Mary Hall.	Panel 8 and 12.	Ypres (Menin Gate) Memorial	Ieper, West-Vlaanderen
HARDING, JAMES HENRY	Private	7973	1st Bn.	Northumberland Fusiliers	16-Jun-15	19	Son of Mr. and Mrs. Harding, of 14, Duke St., Jarrow, Co. Durham.	Panel 8 and 12.	Ypres (Menin Gate) Memorial	Ieper, West-Vlaanderen
HARRINGTON, HERBERT	Private	8436	1st Bn.	Northumberland Fusiliers	16-Jun-15	unknown		Panel 8 and 12.	Ypres (Menin Gate) Memorial	Ieper, West-Vlaanderen

Name	Rank	Service No.	Battalion	Regiment	Date of Death	Age	Biographical Notes	Panel	Memorial	Location
HARRIS, ABEL	Private	17040	1st Bn.	Northumberland Fusiliers	16-Jun-15	39	Husband of Maria Harris, of 33, Ravensworth Terrace, Bedlington Station, Bedlington Colliery, Northumberland.	Panel 8 and 12.	Ypres (Menin Gate) Memorial	Ieper, West-Vlaanderen
HARRIS, HENRY WILLIAM	Corporal	3806	1st Bn.	Northumberland Fusiliers	16-Jun-15	29	Son of the late William Alfred and Charlotte Harris.	Panel 8 and 12.	Ypres (Menin Gate) Memorial	Ieper, West-Vlaanderen
HEALEY, GEORGE	Private	623	1st Bn.	Northumberland Fusiliers	16-Jun-15	unknown		Panel 8 and 12.	Ypres (Menin Gate) Memorial	Ieper, West-Vlaanderen
HENDERSON, THOMAS	Private	8937	1st Bn.	Northumberland Fusiliers	16-Jun-15	unknown		Panel 8 and 12.	Ypres (Menin Gate) Memorial	Ieper, West-Vlaanderen
HILL, GEORGE WILLIAM	Lance Corporal	596	"D" Coy. 1st Bn.	Northumberland Fusiliers	16-Jun-15	28	Son of Joseph and Hannah Hill, of 113A, Edinburgh St., Hull; husband of Beatrice Harrison (formerly Hill), of 266, St. George's Rd., Hessle Rd., Hull.	Panel 8 and 12.	Ypres (Menin Gate) Memorial	Ieper, West-Vlaanderen
HOBDAY, ALFRED	Serjeant	377	1st Bn.	Northumberland Fusiliers	16-Jun-15	unknown		Panel 8 and 12.	Ypres (Menin Gate) Memorial	Ieper, West-Vlaanderen
HODGSON, WILLIAM	Private	8368	1st Bn.	Northumberland Fusiliers	16-Jun-15	unknown		Panel 8 and 12.	Ypres (Menin Gate) Memorial	Ieper, West-Vlaanderen
HOLMES, WILLIAM	Private	7873	1st Bn.	Northumberland Fusiliers	16-Jun-15	unknown	Husband of Mrs. W. Scott (formerly Holmes), of 18, Pearson Place, Jarrow, Northumberland.	Panel 8 and 12.	Ypres (Menin Gate) Memorial	Ieper, West-Vlaanderen
HOLT, WILLIAM	Private	6455	1st Bn.	Northumberland Fusiliers	16-Jun-15	38	Son of the late John and Annie Holt.	Panel 8 and 12.	Ypres (Menin Gate) Memorial	Ieper, West-Vlaanderen
HOPE, LESLIE	Private	4886	1st Bn.	Northumberland Fusiliers	16-Jun-15	22	Son of William and Dorothy Hope, of 1, New Row, Cowpen Square, Blyth, Northumberland.	Panel 8 and 12.	Ypres (Menin Gate) Memorial	Ieper, West-Vlaanderen
HOWARD, WILLIAM	Private	16837	1st Bn.	Northumberland Fusiliers	16-Jun-15	24	Son of John and Ada Howard, of Dogdyke Bank, Dogdyke, Lincoln.	Panel 8 and 12.	Ypres (Menin Gate) Memorial	Ieper, West-Vlaanderen

Full name	Rank	Service	Unit	Regiment	Date	Age	Additional	Grave	Cemetery	Locality
IBBITSON, GEORGE	Private	5633	1st Bn.	Northumberland Fusiliers	16-Jun-15	40		Panel 8 and 12.	Ypres (Menin Gate) Memorial	Ieper, West-Vlaanderen
JARVIS, JOHN WILLIAM	Private	11204	1st Bn.	Northumberland Fusiliers	16-Jun-15	36	Son of the late Ishmael and Margaret Janis; husband of Elizabeth Park Jarvis, of 29, Albion St., Middlestone Moor, Spennymoor, Co. Durham.	Panel 8 and 12.	Ypres (Menin Gate) Memorial	Ieper, West-Vlaanderen
JENNINGS, PETER	Private	8314	1st Bn.	Northumberland Fusiliers	16-Jun-15	21	Son of Christopher and Elizabeth Jennings, of 33, Benson Rd., Byker, Newcastle-on-Tyne.	Panel 8 and 12.	Ypres (Menin Gate) Memorial	Ieper, West-Vlaanderen
JOHNSON, ALEXANDER	Private	4133	1st Bn.	Northumberland Fusiliers	16-Jun-15	unknown		Panel 8 and 12.	Ypres (Menin Gate) Memorial	Ieper, West-Vlaanderen
JOHNSON, ARTHUR	Lance Corporal	8226	1st Bn.	Northumberland Fusiliers	16-Jun-15	30	Son of Mrs. Elizabeth Johnson, of 81, Laurel St., Wallsend, Northumberland.	Panel 8 and 12.	Ypres (Menin Gate) Memorial	Ieper, West-Vlaanderen
JOHNSON, JOHN	Private	3872	1st Bn.	Northumberland Fusiliers	16-Jun-15	22	Son of James and Winifred Johnson, of 48, Haig St., Dunston, Gateshead.	Panel 8 and 12.	Ypres (Menin Gate) Memorial	Ieper, West-Vlaanderen
JONES, JOHN EDWARD	Lance Corporal	7324	1st Bn.	Northumberland Fusiliers	16-Jun-15	unknown		Panel 8 and 12.	Ypres (Menin Gate) Memorial	Ieper, West-Vlaanderen
JORDAN, JESSE FREDERICK	Serjeant	2303	1st Bn.	Northumberland Fusiliers	16-Jun-15	unknown		Panel 8 and 12.	Ypres (Menin Gate) Memorial	Ieper, West-Vlaanderen
JOYCE, JAMES	Private	8309	1st Bn.	Northumberland Fusiliers	16-Jun-15	unknown		Panel 8 and 12.	Ypres (Menin Gate) Memorial	Ieper, West-Vlaanderen
KNOX, JOHN	Private	1998	1st Bn.	Northumberland Fusiliers	16-Jun-15	unknown		Panel 8 and 12.	Ypres (Menin Gate) Memorial	Ieper, West-Vlaanderen
LAMB, JOHN JOSEPH	Private	7369	1st Bn.	Northumberland Fusiliers	16-Jun-15	unknown		Panel 8 and 12.	Ypres (Menin Gate) Memorial	Ieper, West-Vlaanderen

Name	Rank	Service No.	Unit	Regiment	Date	Age	Details	Panel	Memorial	Location
LATIMER, WILLIAM	Private	8565	"W" Coy. 1st Bn.	Northumberland Fusiliers	16-Jun-15	30	Son of Joseph Latimer, of 51, Walker Rd., Newcastle-on-Tyne.	Panel 8 and 12.	Ypres (Menin Gate) Memorial	Ieper, West-Vlaanderen
LEONARD, JOHN	Private	4789	1st Bn.	Northumberland Fusiliers	16-Jun-15	38	Son of Mrs. Jane Lennard, of 1613, Walker Rd., Walker, Newcastle-on-Tyne.	Panel 8 and 12.	Ypres (Menin Gate) Memorial	Ieper, West-Vlaanderen
LLOYD, ARTHUR	Private	8853	1st Bn.	Northumberland Fusiliers	16-Jun-15	36	Son of John and Sarah Ann Lloyd, of 8, Cottage St., Stafford.	Panel 8 and 12.	Ypres (Menin Gate) Memorial	Ieper, West-Vlaanderen
LONG, ALBERT	Private	7946	1st Bn.	Northumberland Fusiliers	16-Jun-15	unknown		Panel 8 and 12.	Ypres (Menin Gate) Memorial	Ieper, West-Vlaanderen
LUKE, ARTHUR	Private	6083	1st Bn.	Northumberland Fusiliers	16-Jun-15	unknown		Panel 8 and 12.	Ypres (Menin Gate) Memorial	Ieper, West-Vlaanderen
MACKEY, JOSEPH	Private	11195	1st Bn.	Northumberland Fusiliers	16-Jun-15	unknown		Panel 8 and 12.	Ypres (Menin Gate) Memorial	Ieper, West-Vlaanderen
MAHONEY, PATRICK	Private	9669	1st Bn.	Northumberland Fusiliers	16-Jun-15	32	Son of the late Patrick and Mary Ann Mahoney.	Panel 8 and 12.	Ypres (Menin Gate) Memorial	Ieper, West-Vlaanderen
MASON, JAMES	Private	8005	1st Bn.	Northumberland Fusiliers	16-Jun-15	unknown	Son of Mr. R. and Mrs. E. Mason, of 42, Union Rd., Southwark, London.	Panel 8 and 12.	Ypres (Menin Gate) Memorial	Ieper, West-Vlaanderen
MAVIN, JAMES ELLIOTT	Private	5938	1st Bn.	Northumberland Fusiliers	16-Jun-15	36	Son of the late Robert and Sarah Mavin; husband of Miranda A. Mavin, of 23, North St., Milburn Place, North Shields. Served in the South African Campaign.	Panel 8 and 12.	Ypres (Menin Gate) Memorial	Ieper, West-Vlaanderen
McCALLUM, JOHN ROBERT	Private	16827	1st Bn.	Northumberland Fusiliers	16-Jun-15	19	Son of Isabella and the late J. McCallum.	Panel 8 and 12.	Ypres (Menin Gate) Memorial	Ieper, West-Vlaanderen
McCANN, PETER	Private	10129	1st Bn.	Northumberland Fusiliers	16-Jun-15	unknown		Panel 8 and 12.	Ypres (Menin Gate) Memorial	Ieper, West-Vlaanderen

Full name	Rank	Service	Unit	Regiment	Date	Age	Additional	Grave	Cemetery	Locality
McCLARENCE, JAMES	Private	5165	1st Bn.	Northumberland Fusiliers	16-Jun-15	unknown		Panel 8 and 12.	Ypres (Menin Gate) Memorial	Ieper, West-Vlaanderen
McKIBBIN, ARTHUR	Private	8874	1st Bn.	Northumberland Fusiliers	16-Jun-15	unknown		Panel 8 and 12.	Ypres (Menin Gate) Memorial	Ieper, West-Vlaanderen
McNALLY, JOHN PATRICK	Private	3632	1st Bn.	Northumberland Fusiliers	16-Jun-15	unknown	Nephew of Rose Ann McNally, of 15, Centre St., Newcastle-on-Tyne.	Panel 8 and 12.	Ypres (Menin Gate) Memorial	Ieper, West-Vlaanderen
MELVILLE, ALBERT	Private	9307	1st Bn.	Northumberland Fusiliers	16-Jun-15	unknown		Panel 8 and 12.	Ypres (Menin Gate) Memorial	Ieper, West-Vlaanderen
MIDDLETON, JOSEPH	Lance Corporal	6465	1st Bn.	Northumberland Fusiliers	16-Jun-15	33	Husband of Emily Middleton, of Riccall Lane, Helfield, York.	Panel 8 and 12.	Ypres (Menin Gate) Memorial	Ieper, West-Vlaanderen
MILLER, JAMES	Private	9266	1st Bn.	Northumberland Fusiliers	16-Jun-15	unknown		Panel 8 and 12.	Ypres (Menin Gate) Memorial	Ieper, West-Vlaanderen
MOFFATT, WILLIAM HENRY	Private	9581	1st Bn.	Northumberland Fusiliers	16-Jun-15	unknown		Panel 8 and 12.	Ypres (Menin Gate) Memorial	Ieper, West-Vlaanderen
MOONEY, EDWARD	Private	7970	1st Bn.	Northumberland Fusiliers	16-Jun-15	unknown		Panel 8 and 12.	Ypres (Menin Gate) Memorial	Ieper, West-Vlaanderen
NELSON, WILLIAM ERNEST	Private	9335	1st Bn.	Northumberland Fusiliers	16-Jun-15	unknown		Panel 8 and 12.	Ypres (Menin Gate) Memorial	Ieper, West-Vlaanderen
NETTLETON, ARTHUR	Private	3065	1st Bn.	Northumberland Fusiliers	16-Jun-15	22	Son of J. W. and Jane E. Nettleton, of Main St., Thorner, Leeds.	LXV. K. 14.	Tyne Cot Cemetery	Zonnebeke, West-Vlaanderen
NICHOLSON, JAMES	Private	8551	1st Bn.	Northumberland Fusiliers	16-Jun-15	unknown		Panel 8 and 12.	Ypres (Menin Gate) Memorial	Ieper, West-Vlaanderen
O'DONNELL,	Private	6993	1st Bn.	Northumberland Fusiliers	16-Jun-15	44	Son of John O'Donnell.	Panel 8 and 12.	Ypres (Menin Gate) Memorial	Ieper, West-Vlaanderen

Name	Rank	Number	Bn.	Regiment	Date	Age	Details	Panel	Memorial	Location
ONICHAM, EDWARD	Private	17982	1st Bn.	Northumberland Fusiliers	16-Jun-15	unknown		Panel 8 and 12.	Ypres (Menin Gate) Memorial	Ieper, West-Vlaanderen
PARKIN, RICHARD	Private	8155	1st Bn.	Northumberland Fusiliers	16-Jun-15	21	Son of Magdalen Parkin, of 11, Eversleigh Place, Newburn, Northumberland, and the late Richard Parkin.	Panel 8 and 12.	Ypres (Menin Gate) Memorial	Ieper, West-Vlaanderen
PARRINGTON, WILLIAM SIDNEY	Private	953	1st Bn.	Northumberland Fusiliers	16-Jun-15	38	(Served as OSBORN). Son of the late William and Mary Parrington, of Elder Villa, Batley, Yorks.	Panel 8 and 12.	Ypres (Menin Gate) Memorial	Ieper, West-Vlaanderen
PEARSON, WILLIAM FREDERICK	Private	2313	"A" Coy. 1st/6th Bn.	Northumberland Fusiliers	16-Jun-15	27	Son of William and Mary Ann Pearson, of The Post Office, Allenheads, Allendale, Northumberland.	Panel 8 and 12.	Ypres (Menin Gate) Memorial	Ieper, West-Vlaanderen
PERRY, EDWARD	Private	8498	1st Bn.	Northumberland Fusiliers	16-Jun-15	35	Son of John Perry, of 46, Harriet St., Byker, and the late Elizabeth Perry; husband of Hannah Perry, of 22, Brough's Buildings, Byker, Newcastle-on-Tyne.	Panel 8 and 12.	Ypres (Menin Gate) Memorial	Ieper, West-Vlaanderen
PINDER, JAMES	Serjeant	392	1st Bn.	Northumberland Fusiliers	16-Jun-15	unknown		Panel 8 and 12.	Ypres (Menin Gate) Memorial	Ieper, West-Vlaanderen
POPPLEWELL, WILLIAM	Private	8375	1st Bn.	Northumberland Fusiliers	16-Jun-15	39	Son of James Popplewell; husband of Evelyn M. Johnson (formerly Popplewell), of 42, Thornton St., Kempston, Bedford.	Panel 8 and 12.	Ypres (Menin Gate) Memorial	Ieper, West-Vlaanderen
POULTNEY, FRANK	Private	7319	1st Bn.	Northumberland Fusiliers	16-Jun-15	32	Husband of Agnes V. Graham (formerly Poultney), of 8, Lansdowne Terrace, Goodman St., Burton-on-Trent.	Panel 8 and 12.	Ypres (Menin Gate) Memorial	Ieper, West-Vlaanderen
PURTON, JOHN	Lance Corporal	3765	1st Bn.	Northumberland Fusiliers	16-Jun-15	unknown		Panel 8 and 12.	Ypres (Menin Gate) Memorial	Ieper, West-Vlaanderen

Full name	Rank	Service	Unit	Regiment	Date	Age	Additional	Grave	Cemetery	Locality
QUIGLEY, JOHN	Private	6502	1st Bn.	Northumberland Fusiliers	16-Jun-15	unknown		Panel 8 and 12.	Ypres (Menin Gate) Memorial	Ieper, West-Vlaanderen
RAILTON, THOMAS	Private	9328	1st Bn.	Northumberland Fusiliers	16-Jun-15	42	Son of the late John and Mary Railton, of Alston, Cumberland; husband of Isabella Railton, of 28, Cookson St., Newcastle-on-Tyne.	Panel 8 and 12.	Ypres (Menin Gate) Memorial	Ieper, West-Vlaanderen
RAINE, THOMAS HENRY	Private	9915	1st Bn.	Northumberland Fusiliers	16-Jun-15	unknown		Panel 8 and 12.	Ypres (Menin Gate) Memorial	Ieper, West-Vlaanderen
RICHARDSON, GEORGE	Private	8048	1st Bn.	Northumberland Fusiliers	16-Jun-15	41	Son of William Richardson, of 5, Victoria St., Crook, Co. Durham; husband of Agnes Jane Richardson, of 11, Lintzford, Rowland Gill, Co. Durham.	Panel 8 and 12.	Ypres (Menin Gate) Memorial	Ieper, West-Vlaanderen
RIDLEY, THOMAS	Private	6637	1st Bn.	Northumberland Fusiliers	16-Jun-15	unknown		Panel 8 and 12.	Ypres (Menin Gate) Memorial	Ieper, West-Vlaanderen
ROBERTSON, WILLIAM JOHN	Private	8106	1st Bn.	Northumberland Fusiliers	16-Jun-15	23	Son of Daniel and Sarah Robertson, of 91, Beaumont St., Newcastle-on-Tyne; husband of Theresa Taylor (formerly Robertson), Or 4, Glue Terrace, Elswick, Newcastle-on-Tyne.	Panel 8 and 12.	Ypres (Menin Gate) Memorial	Ieper, West-Vlaanderen
ROBINSON, HENRY	Private	8846	1st Bn.	Northumberland Fusiliers	16-Jun-15	unknown		Panel 8 and 12.	Ypres (Menin Gate) Memorial	Ieper, West-Vlaanderen
ROBSON, JOHN	Private	1652	1st/4th Bn.	Northumberland Fusiliers	16-Jun-15	unknown		Panel 8 and 12.	Ypres (Menin Gate) Memorial	Ieper, West-Vlaanderen
RODDAM, R. C.	Captain		3rd Bn. attd. 1st Bn.	Northumberland Fusiliers	16-Jun-15	25	Son of Lt. Col. Roddam John Roddam, O.B.E., and Helen, his wife, of Roddam Halt, Alnwick, and Greenfield House, Powburn, Northumberland.	Panel 8 and 12.	Ypres (Menin Gate) Memorial	Ieper, West-Vlaanderen

Name	Rank	Service No.	Battalion	Regiment	Date	Age	Details	Panel	Memorial	Location
ROOKE, FRANCIS WILLIAM	Private	3160	1st Bn.	Northumberland Fusiliers	16-Jun-15	23	Son of John Rooke, of 18, Mitchell St., Musselburgh, Midlothian; husband of Elizabeth Ann Rooke, of 9, Beall's Square, Camden Lane, North Shields.	Panel 8 and 12.	Ypres (Menin Gate) Memorial	Ieper, West-Vlaanderen
SCULLEY, WILLIAM	Private	8283	1st Bn.	Northumberland Fusiliers	16-Jun-15	unknown		Panel 8 and 12.	Ypres (Menin Gate) Memorial	Ieper, West-Vlaanderen
SEMOUR, ALBERT	Private	16826	1st Bn.	Northumberland Fusiliers	16-Jun-15	unknown		Panel 8 and 12.	Ypres (Menin Gate) Memorial	Ieper, West-Vlaanderen
SIDDLE, WILLIAM	Private	20942	1st Bn.	Northumberland Fusiliers	16-Jun-15	22	Son of Lancelot and Rachel Bell, of Rosedale House, St. Helen's, Auckland, Bishop Auckland, Co. Durham.	Panel 8 and 12.	Ypres (Menin Gate) Memorial	Ieper, West-Vlaanderen
SMITH, FRANK	Corporal	8548	1st Bn.	Northumberland Fusiliers	16-Jun-15	30	Son of Charles and Kate Smith, of 80, Garfield Rd., Nottingham; husband of H. Ada Florence Elliott (formerly Smith), of 10, Vincent Terrace, Randal St., Hyson Green, Nottingham.	Panel 8 and 12.	Ypres (Menin Gate) Memorial	Ieper, West-Vlaanderen
SMITH, ROBERT	Private	3010	1st Bn.	Northumberland Fusiliers	16-Jun-15	unknown		Panel 8 and 12.	Ypres (Menin Gate) Memorial	Ieper, West-Vlaanderen
SMYTHE, ROBERT	Private	16876	1st Bn.	Northumberland Fusiliers	16-Jun-15	18	Son of Robert and Mary Smythe, of 17, George St. Willington Quay, Northumberland.	Panel 8 and 12.	Ypres (Menin Gate) Memorial	Ieper, West-Vlaanderen
STANLEY, JOSEPH JOHN	Private	3638	1st Bn.	Northumberland Fusiliers	16-Jun-15	20	Son of Thomas and Minnie J. Stanley, of 11, Drayton Terrace, Clayton Rd., Saltley, Birmingham.	Panel 8 and 12.	Ypres (Menin Gate) Memorial	Ieper, West-Vlaanderen
STOBBART, MATTHEW	Private	1975	1st/4th Bn.	Northumberland Fusiliers	16-Jun-15	17	Son of Joseph Stobbart, of Stublic Bog, Langley-on-Tyne, Northumberland.	Panel 8 and 12.	Ypres (Menin Gate) Memorial	Ieper, West-Vlaanderen

Full name	Rank	Service	Unit	Regiment	Date	Age	Additional	Grave	Cemetery	Locality
TAIT, W	Private	6490	1st Bn.	Northumberland Fusiliers	16-Jun-15	35	Husband of Caroline A. Lambird (formerly Tait), of 57, Wellington St., Gravesend, Kent. Served in the South African War.	Panel 8 and 12.	Ypres (Menin Gate) Memorial	Ieper, West-Vlaanderen
TEMPLEMAN, WILLIAM ROBERTS	Lance Corporal	9757	1st Bn.	Northumberland Fusiliers	16-Jun-15	36	Son of the late William and Elizabeth Templeman; husband of Margaret Templeman, of 2, Sunny Terrace, South Shields.	Panel 8 and 12.	Ypres (Menin Gate) Memorial	Ieper, West-Vlaanderen
THOMPSON, JOHN	Private	20941	1st Bn.	Northumberland Fusiliers	16-Jun-15	25	Son of the late Ralph and Annie Thompson.	Panel 8 and 12.	Ypres (Menin Gate) Memorial	Ieper, West-Vlaanderen
TRINDER, ARNOLD JAMES	Lieutenant		7th Bn.	Northumberland Fusiliers	16-Jun-15	unknown		Panel 8 and 12.	Ypres (Menin Gate) Memorial	Ieper, West-Vlaanderen
TULLEY, GEORGE HENRY	Private	3668	1st Bn.	Northumberland Fusiliers	16-Jun-15	22	Son of James Tulley, of 32, St. Giles Cottage, Madehurst, Arundel, Sussex.	Panel 8 and 12.	Ypres (Menin Gate) Memorial	Ieper, West-Vlaanderen
TURNBULL, ANDREW	Private	20943	1st Bn.	Northumberland Fusiliers	16-Jun-15	20	Son of William Turnbull, of 69, Clasper St., Teams, Gateshead.	Panel 8 and 12.	Ypres (Menin Gate) Memorial	Ieper, West-Vlaanderen
TURNBULL, THOMAS	Private	7945	1st Bn.	Northumberland Fusiliers	16-Jun-15	27	Son of Thomas and Annie Turnbull, of 16, Temple St., Newcastle-on-Tyne; husband of Sarah Jane Llewellyn (formerly Turnbull), of 47, Grosvenor St., Gateshead.	Panel 8 and 12.	Ypres (Menin Gate) Memorial	Ieper, West-Vlaanderen
WALKER, EDWARD ROTCHFORD	Private	8836	1st Bn.	Northumberland Fusiliers	16-Jun-15	45	Husband of Sarah Walker, of 134, Barnsbury Rd., Islington, London.	Panel 8 and 12.	Ypres (Menin Gate) Memorial	Ieper, West-Vlaanderen
WALLACE, WILLIAM	Private	4491	1st Bn.	Northumberland Fusiliers	16-Jun-15	unknown		Panel 8 and 12.	Ypres (Menin Gate) Memorial	Ieper, West-Vlaanderen

Name	Rank	Service No.	Battalion	Regiment	Date	Age	Family/Details	Panel	Memorial	Location
WHITFIELD, JOSEPH	Private	8980	1st Bn.	Northumberland Fusiliers	16-Jun-15	31	Son of Joseph Whitfield, of The Age d Miners Cottages, Woodhorn, Ashington, Northumberland; husband of Emma Swindells (formerly Whitfield), of 13, Wellington St., Goldthorpe Rotherham, Yorks.	Panel 8 and 12.	Ypres (Menin Gate) Memorial	Ieper, West-Vlaanderen
WILKINSON, HARRY	Private	7555	1st Bn.	Northumberland Fusiliers	16-Jun-15	18	Son of Mrs. Martha Wilkinson, of 23, Lupton St., Cornwall Rd., Bradford, Yorks.	Panel 8 and 12.	Ypres (Menin Gate) Memorial	Ieper, West-Vlaanderen
WILSON, WALTER	Private	3644	1st Bn.	Northumberland Fusiliers	16-Jun-15	unknown		Panel 8 and 12.	Ypres (Menin Gate) Memorial	Ieper, West-Vlaanderen
WOOD, ROBERT	Private	8935	1st Bn.	Northumberland Fusiliers	16-Jun-15	21	Son of Fred and Emma Wood, of Brick Row, Commondale, Grosmont, York.	Panel 8 and 12.	Ypres (Menin Gate) Memorial	Ieper, West-Vlaanderen
WOODALL, ERNEST WILLIAM	Private	16844	"Y" Coy. 1st Bn.	Northumberland Fusiliers	16-Jun-15	31	Husband of Eliza Elizabeth Woodall, of 319, Taylor St., South Shields.	Panel 8 and 12.	Ypres (Menin Gate) Memorial	Ieper, West-Vlaanderen
YATES, THOMAS	Lance Corporal	1023	4th Bn.	Northumberland Fusiliers	16-Jun-15	19	Son of John George and Bridget Yates, of Haltwhistle, Northumberland.	I. C. 3.	Brandhoek Military Cemetery	Ieper, West-Vlaanderen
ABRAHAM, ALFRED	Rifleman	B/1219	9th Bn	Rifle Brigade	16-Jun-15	25	Son of Alfred Phillip Abrahams, of Lacklands Cottage, Bishop's Sutton, Alresford, Hants.	Panel 46 - 48 and 50.	Ypres (Menin Gate) Memorial	Ieper, West-Vlaanderen
SAVORY, GILBERT	Rifleman	B/1711	9th Bn	Rifle Brigade	16-Jun-15	26	Son of the late Robert and Margaret Jane Savory; husband of Milly Savory, of 4, New Rd., Latchford, Warrington.	Panel 46 - 48 and 50.	Ypres (Menin Gate) Memorial	Ieper, West-Vlaanderen
BALINARI, CHRISTOPHER UMBERTO	Private	G/3341	4th Bn.	Royal Fusiliers	16-Jun-15	22	Son of Mrs. Eliza Elizabeth Balinari, of 3, Porteus Rd., Paddington, London.	Panel 6 and 8.	Ypres (Menin Gate) Memorial	Ieper, West-Vlaanderen

Full name	Rank	Service	Unit	Regiment	Date	Age	Additional	Grave	Cemetery	Locality
BANISTER, CHARLES WILFRED	Second Lieutenant		4th Bn.	Royal Fusiliers	16-Jun-15	22	Son of Howard Cottrell Banister, of St. Catherine's, Cadogan Gardens, Tunbridge Wells, Kent.	Panel 6 and 8.	Ypres (Menin Gate) Memorial	Ieper, West-Vlaanderen
BARKER, CHARLES EDWARD	Private	L/15912	4th Bn.	Royal Fusiliers	16-Jun-15	unknown		Panel 6 and 8.	Ypres (Menin Gate) Memorial	Ieper, West-Vlaanderen
BATT, JOSEPH	Lance Corporal	L/14644	4th Bn.	Royal Fusiliers	16-Jun-15	unknown		Panel 6 and 8.	Ypres (Menin Gate) Memorial	Ieper, West-Vlaanderen
BATTEN, JOHN	Private	SR/258	4th Bn.	Royal Fusiliers	16-Jun-15	unknown		Panel 6 and 8.	Ypres (Menin Gate) Memorial	Ieper, West-Vlaanderen
BECKETT, ALBERT GEORGE	Private	SR/8488	4th Bn.	Royal Fusiliers	16-Jun-15	22	Son of John Thomas and Annie Susan Beckett, of 4, Cross St., Hampton Hill, Middx.	Panel 6 and 8.	Ypres (Menin Gate) Memorial	Ieper, West-Vlaanderen
BERRY, WILLIAM JAMES	Serjeant	L/13446	4th Bn.	Royal Fusiliers	16-Jun-15	20	Son of Mrs. Alice Berry, of 96, Martindale Rd., Hounslow, Middlesex.	Panel 6 and 8.	Ypres (Menin Gate) Memorial	Ieper, West-Vlaanderen
BESTER, ARTHUR BANNARD	Private	9658	4th Bn.	Royal Fusiliers	16-Jun-15	30	Son of William and Elizabeth Ann Bester; husband of Isabella H. Bester, of 28, Cavendish St., New North Rd., Hoxton, London. Born at Blisworth, Northants.	XIII. B. 11.	Harlebeke New British Cemetery	Harelbeke, West-Vlaanderen
BIRCHER, ARTHUR SIDNEY	Private	T/8662	4th Bn.	Royal Fusiliers	16-Jun-15	28	Son of Albert Thomas and Sarah Ann Bircher, of 133, Carlyle Rd., Ealing, London.	Panel 6 and 8.	Ypres (Menin Gate) Memorial	Ieper, West-Vlaanderen
BLACKMORE, CHARLES THOMAS	Private	2628	4th Bn.	Royal Fusiliers	16-Jun-15	unknown		Panel 6 and 8.	Ypres (Menin Gate) Memorial	Ieper, West-Vlaanderen

Name	Rank	Service No.	Battalion	Regiment	Date	Age	Details	Panel	Memorial	Location
BLANKS, ALFRED WALTER	Private	L/16418	4th Bn.	Royal Fusiliers	16-Jun-15	27	Son of Mr. R. C. and Mrs. Emma Blanks, of 10, Cavendish St., Chichester, Sussex.	Panel 6 and 8.	Ypres (Menin Gate) Memorial	Ieper, West-Vlaanderen
BOURDON, BENJAMIN	Private	SR/7881	4th Bn.	Royal Fusiliers	16-Jun-15	24	Son of Mrs. Bourdon, of 39, Tidy St., Brighton; husband of Rose Louisa Bourdon, of 92, Torriano Avenue, Kentish Town, London.	Panel 6 and 8.	Ypres (Menin Gate) Memorial	Ieper, West-Vlaanderen
BOURNE, FREDERICK ERNEST	Corporal	G/2386	4th Bn.	Royal Fusiliers	16-Jun-15	29	Son of George and Mary Jane Bourne, of 8, West Hill Avenue, Hednesford, Staffs.	Panel 6 and 8.	Ypres (Menin Gate) Memorial	Ieper, West-Vlaanderen
BOUSFIELD, ARTHUR THOMAS	Private	L/11866	14th Bn.	Royal Fusiliers	16-Jun-15	26	Son of Thomas and Ada Bousfield, of 28, Percival Rd., Enfield, Middx.	Panel 6 and 8.	Ypres (Menin Gate) Memorial	Ieper, West-Vlaanderen
BRAHAM, VICTOR GEORGE	Corporal	L/11875	4th Bn.	Royal Fusiliers	16-Jun-15	unknown		Panel 6 and 8.	Ypres (Menin Gate) Memorial	Ieper, West-Vlaanderen
BROCK, ERNEST	Private	G/9667	4th Bn.	Royal Fusiliers	16-Jun-15	19	Son of Edward Henry and Caroline Rebecca Brock, of 16, Brook St., Silverdale, Stoke-on-Trent.	Panel 6 and 8.	Ypres (Menin Gate) Memorial	Ieper, West-Vlaanderen
BROWN, THOMAS	Private	SR/6983	4th Bn.	Royal Fusiliers	16-Jun-15	33	Son of the late Thomas and Mary E. Brown; husband of Mary Margaret Brown, of 73, Rayleigh Rd., West Kensington, London.	Panel 6 and 8.	Ypres (Menin Gate) Memorial	Ieper, West-Vlaanderen
BURNS, HENRY CHARLES	Private	12627	4th Bn.	Royal Fusiliers	16-Jun-15	36	Husband of Rose Ellen Burns, of 125, Wilmot St., Bethnal Green Rd., London.	Panel 6 and 8.	Ypres (Menin Gate) Memorial	Ieper, West-Vlaanderen
CADREMAN, FREDERICK GEORGE	Private	G/9620	4th Bn.	Royal Fusiliers	16-Jun-15	28	Son of Susan Cadreman, of 151, Lewisham Rd., Lewisham, London, and the late Thomas Cadreman. Enlisted Nov., 1914.	Panel 6 and 8.	Ypres (Menin Gate) Memorial	Ieper, West-Vlaanderen

Full name	Rank	Service	Unit	Regiment	Date	Age	Additional	Grave	Cemetery	Locality
CAMPBELL, COLIN	Private	L/16343	4th Bn.	Royal Fusiliers	16-Jun-15	unknown		Panel 6 and 8.	Ypres (Menin Gate) Memorial	Ieper, West-Vlaanderen
CASTLEDINE, MONTAGU CYRIL	Private	G/9261	4th Bn.	Royal Fusiliers	16-Jun-15	26	Son of Mr. G. H. and Mrs. E. E. Castledine, of SS, Lyndhurst Grove, Peckham, London.	Panel 6 and 8.	Ypres (Menin Gate) Memorial	Ieper, West-Vlaanderen
CLARK, JACK	Lance Corporal	L/12170	4th Bn.	Royal Fusiliers	16-Jun-15	unknown		Panel 6 and 8.	Ypres (Menin Gate) Memorial	Ieper, West-Vlaanderen
CLOWES, TIMOTHY	Private	G/8822	4th Bn.	Royal Fusiliers	16-Jun-15	21	Son of Timothy and Mary Clowes, of 29, Colclough Lane, Goldenhill, Stoke-on-Trent.	Panel 6 and 8.	Ypres (Menin Gate) Memorial	Ieper, West-Vlaanderen
COLLINS, HENRY W.	Private	SR/2339	4th Bn.	Royal Fusiliers	16-Jun-15	20	Son of Mrs. Amelia M. Collins, of 6, Haddon House, Haddonhall St., Tower Bridge Rd., London.	Panel 6 and 8.	Ypres (Menin Gate) Memorial	Ieper, West-Vlaanderen
COLLINS, JOHN	Private	SR/2279	4th Bn.	Royal Fusiliers	16-Jun-15	unknown		Panel 6 and 8.	Ypres (Menin Gate) Memorial	Ieper, West-Vlaanderen
CONNOR, WILLIAM	Private	G/8820	4th Bn.	Royal Fusiliers	16-Jun-15	unknown		Panel 6 and 8.	Ypres (Menin Gate) Memorial	Ieper, West-Vlaanderen
COOK, HARRY	Private	L/16012	4th Bn.	Royal Fusiliers	16-Jun-15	unknown		Panel 6 and 8.	Ypres (Menin Gate) Memorial	Ieper, West-Vlaanderen
COOLING, RICHARD	Private	SR/8319	4th Bn.	Royal Fusiliers	16-Jun-15	unknown		Panel 6 and 8.	Ypres (Menin Gate) Memorial	Ieper, West-Vlaanderen
COOPER, BLANCHARD JOSEPH	Lance Corporal	G/4233	4th Bn.	Royal Fusiliers	16-Jun-15	unknown		Panel 6 and 8.	Ypres (Menin Gate) Memorial	Ieper, West-Vlaanderen
COX, NORMAN WILFRED	Private	G/2375	"W" Coy. 4th Bn.	Royal Fusiliers	16-Jun-15	22	Son of William Henry and Alice Mary Cox, of Llwyn-onn, Glan Conway, Denbighshire.	Panel 6 and 8.	Ypres (Menin Gate) Memorial	Ieper, West-Vlaanderen

Name	Rank	Service No.	Unit	Regiment	Date	Age	Next of Kin	Panel	Memorial	Location
CULLIS, FRANK	Private	G/1415	"C" Coy. 4th Bn.	Royal Fusiliers	16-Jun-15	23	Son of the late Thomas and Annie Cullis, of 59, Sandy's Rd., Worcester.	Panel 6 and 8.	Ypres (Menin Gate) Memorial	Ieper, West-Vlaanderen
DANIELS, WALTER ARTHUR	Private	G/9356	4th Bn.	Royal Fusiliers	16-Jun-15	unknown		Panel 6 and 8.	Ypres (Menin Gate) Memorial	Ieper, West-Vlaanderen
DAVISON, WILLIAM H.E.	Private	SR/390	4th Bn.	Royal Fusiliers	16-Jun-15	unknown		Panel 6 and 8.	Ypres (Menin Gate) Memorial	Ieper, West-Vlaanderen
DERBYSHIRE, JAMES	Private	SR/8726	4th Bn.	Royal Fusiliers	16-Jun-15	unknown		Panel 6 and 8.	Ypres (Menin Gate) Memorial	Ieper, West-Vlaanderen
DIGBY, F.	Private	SR/8455	4th Bn.	Royal Fusiliers	16-Jun-15	unknown		Panel 6 and 8.	Ypres (Menin Gate) Memorial	Ieper, West-Vlaanderen
DUDLEY, WALTER JOSEPH	Lieutenant		4th Bn.	Royal Fusiliers	16-Jun-15	unknown		Panel 6 and 8.	Ypres (Menin Gate) Memorial	Ieper, West-Vlaanderen
DYE, JOHN EDWARD	Private	SR/7959	4th Bn.	Royal Fusiliers	16-Jun-15	23	Son of Mrs. Mary Flowers, of 2, Lucas St., Bethnal Green, London.	Panel 6 and 8.	Ypres (Menin Gate) Memorial	Ieper, West-Vlaanderen
EDWARDS, CHARLES JOHN	Private	L/15977	4th Bn.	Royal Fusiliers	16-Jun-15	21	Son of Rosetta Edwards, of 54, Grange Walk, Bermondsey, London, and the late John Edwards.	Panel 6 and 8.	Ypres (Menin Gate) Memorial	Ieper, West-Vlaanderen
EMERY, GEORGE	Private	SR/8010	4th Bn.	Royal Fusiliers	16-Jun-15	unknown		Panel 6 and 8.	Ypres (Menin Gate) Memorial	Ieper, West-Vlaanderen
FISHER, SAMUEL	Private	G/1928	4th Bn.	Royal Fusiliers	16-Jun-15	23	Son of Samuel and Mary Ann Fisher, of 23, West St., Evesham. Worcs.	Panel 6 and 8.	Ypres (Menin Gate) Memorial	Ieper, West-Vlaanderen
FITZGERALD, WILLIAM	Private	L/12838	4th Bn.	Royal Fusiliers	16-Jun-15	27	Son of William and Catherine Fitzgerald, of 50, Marner St., Bromley, Bow, London. A Reservist.	Panel 6 and 8.	Ypres (Menin Gate) Memorial	Ieper, West-Vlaanderen

Full name	Rank	Service	Unit	Regiment	Date	Age	Additional	Grave	Cemetery	Locality
FITZGIBBON, EDWARD WILLIAM	Private	SR/2337	4th Bn.	Royal Fusiliers	16-Jun-15	21	Son of John Fitzgibbon, of 15, Antwerp St., Hackney, London.	Panel 6 and 8.	Ypres (Menin Gate) Memorial	Ieper, West-Vlaanderen
FOLWELL, ALBERT	Private	SR/2423	4th Bn	Royal Fusiliers	16-Jun-15	24	Son of Mrs. Annie Folwell, of 8, Duckett St., Stepney, London.	Panel 6 and 8.	Ypres (Menin Gate) Memorial	Ieper, West-Vlaanderen
GARRETT, GEORGE	Private	L/15224	4th Bn.	Royal Fusiliers	16-Jun-15	unknown		Panel 6 and 8.	Ypres (Menin Gate) Memorial	Ieper, West-Vlaanderen
GILLIES, WALTER	Private	7118	4th Bn.	Royal Fusiliers	16-Jun-15	26		XV. A. 6.	Hooge Crater Cemetery	Ieper, West-Vlaanderen
GOSS, THOMAS	Private	L/12067	4th Bn.	Royal Fusiliers	16-Jun-15	unknown		Panel 6 and 8.	Ypres (Menin Gate) Memorial	Ieper, West-Vlaanderen
GOULD, ALBERT	Private	G/6076	4th Bn.	Royal Fusiliers	16-Jun-15	31	Husband of Mrs. C. Miller (formerly Gould), of 7, Married Quarters, Depot, Dorsetshire Regt., Dorchester.	Panel 6 and 8.	Ypres (Menin Gate) Memorial	Ieper, West-Vlaanderen
GREEN, ALBERT GEORGE	Private	G/5888	4th Bn.	Royal Fusiliers	16-Jun-15	20	Son of Mrs. H. E. Horan (formerly Green), of 21, Chapel St., Uxbridge, Middx., and the late George Green.	Panel 6 and 8.	Ypres (Menin Gate) Memorial	Ieper, West-Vlaanderen
GREEN, GEORGE JAMES	Lance Corporal	G/4059	"B" Coy. 4th Bn.	Royal Fusiliers	16-Jun-15	23	Son of George and Edith Green, of 63, Dijon St., Stepney, London.	Panel 6 and 8.	Ypres (Menin Gate) Memorial	Ieper, West-Vlaanderen
GREENWOOD, JAMES	Private	SR/331	4th Bn.	Royal Fusiliers	16-Jun-15	unknown		Panel 6 and 8.	Ypres (Menin Gate) Memorial	Ieper, West-Vlaanderen
GREENWOOD, THOMAS	Private	SR/9401	4th Bn.	Royal Fusiliers	16-Jun-15	20	Son of Mrs. Greenwood, of 42, Annandale Rd., Chiswick, London.	Panel 6 and 8.	Ypres (Menin Gate) Memorial	Ieper, West-Vlaanderen

Name	Rank	Service No.	Battalion	Regiment	Date	Age	Family	Memorial	Panel	Location
GREGORY, WILLIAM CHARLES	Private	SR/8239	"Y" Coy. 4th Bn.	Royal Fusiliers	16-Jun-15	28	Son of Mr. W. and Mrs. E. Gregory, of 8, Somerford Houses, Somerford St., Bethnal Green, London.	Ypres (Menin Gate) Memorial	Panel 6 and 8.	Ieper, West-Vlaanderen
HADINGHAM, WILLIAM	Private	9966	"X" Coy. 4th Bn.	Royal Fusiliers	16-Jun-15	35	Son of James and Lorina Hadingham, of 2, Shelton Place, St. George's Rd., Beccles, Suffolk; husband of Mary A. Hadingham, of 12, Hudson Rd., Kingston-on-Thames.	Ypres (Menin Gate) Memorial	Panel 6 and 8.	Ieper, West-Vlaanderen
HALLYBONE, B. THOMAS	Private	SR/2243	4th Bn.	Royal Fusiliers	16-Jun-15	unknown		Ypres (Menin Gate) Memorial	Panel 6 and 8.	Ieper, West-Vlaanderen
HAMILTON, WILLIAM WEIR	Serjeant	G/3416	4th Bn.	Royal Fusiliers	16-Jun-15	22	Son of the late William and Mary Weir Hamilton.	Ypres (Menin Gate) Memorial	Panel 6 and 8.	Ieper, West-Vlaanderen
HANKIN, CHARLES HENRY	Private	G/10099	4th Bn.	Royal Fusiliers	16-Jun-15	35	Son of the late Mr. and Mrs. Thomas Hankin; husband of Jane Hankin, of 102, Worple Rd., Isleworth, Middx.	Ypres (Menin Gate) Memorial	Panel 6 and 8.	Ieper, West-Vlaanderen
HARRINGTON, JOSEPH	Private	SR/9405	4th Bn.	Royal Fusiliers	16-Jun-15	unknown		Ypres (Menin Gate) Memorial	Panel 6 and 8.	Ieper, West-Vlaanderen
HARTER, CLEMENT JESSE	Captain		3rd Bn. attd. 4th Bn.	Royal Fusiliers	16-Jun-15	26	Son of Charles B. Hatfield Harter and Violet Harter, of 5, Onslow Houses, South Kensington, London.	Ypres (Menin Gate) Memorial	Panel 6 and 8.	Ieper, West-Vlaanderen
HARVEY, JOHN	Serjeant	L/10434	4th Bn.	Royal Fusiliers	16-Jun-15	unknown		Ypres (Menin Gate) Memorial	Panel 6 and 8.	Ieper, West-Vlaanderen
HAYES, CHARLES GEORGE	Private	G/2823	4th Bn.	Royal Fusiliers	16-Jun-15	20	Son of Charles Hayes, of 110, East Barnet Rd., New Barnet Herts.	Ypres (Menin Gate) Memorial	Panel 6 and 8.	Ieper, West-Vlaanderen
HILL, DANIEL	Private	L/15796	4th Bn.	Royal Fusiliers	16-Jun-15	unknown		Ypres (Menin Gate) Memorial	Panel 6 and 8.	Ieper, West-Vlaanderen

Full name	Rank	Service	Unit	Regiment	Date	Age	Additional	Grave	Cemetery	Locality
HILL, WILLIAM	Private	SR/137	4th Bn.	Royal Fusiliers	16-Jun-15	38	Son of the late Michael John and Caroline Hill.	Panel 6 and 8.	Ypres (Menin Gate) Memorial	Ieper, West-Vlaanderen
HINDLEY, HERBERT	Private	G/5922	4th Bn.	Royal Fusiliers	16-Jun-15	19	Son of Mrs. Elizabeth Hindley, of 24, Weaver St., Hanley, Stoke-on-Trent.	Panel 6 and 8.	Ypres (Menin Gate) Memorial	Ieper, West-Vlaanderen
HOAR, WILLIAM GEORGE	Private	G/3640	4th Bn.	Royal Fusiliers	16-Jun-15	24	Son of Louisa M. Hoar, of 5, Northumberland Row, Colne Rd., Twickenham, Middx., and the late John Thomas Hoar.	Panel 6 and 8.	Ypres (Menin Gate) Memorial	Ieper, West-Vlaanderen
HODGES, CHARLES EDWARD	Second Lieutenant			Royal Fusiliers	16-Jun-15	30	Son of William Davies Hodges and Mary Hodges, of 7, Egerton Mansions, South Kensington, London; husband of Amy Evans.	IV. D. 23.	Zantvoorde British Cemetary	Zonnebeke, West-Vlaanderen
HOODLESS, STANLEY JOHN	Private	G/9342	4th Bn.	Royal Fusiliers	16-Jun-15	22	Son of William James and Ada Hoodless, of The Hollies, Baring Rd., Beaconsfield, Bucks.	Panel 6 and 8.	Ypres (Menin Gate) Memorial	Ieper, West-Vlaanderen
JAMES, JOHN	Private	SR/5451	4th Bn.	Royal Fusiliers	16-Jun-15	38		Panel 6 and 8.	Ypres (Menin Gate) Memorial	Ieper, West-Vlaanderen
JOHNSON, HERBERT LOUIS	Private	SR/8364	4th Bn.	Royal Fusiliers	16-Jun-15	0		Panel 6 and 8.	Ypres (Menin Gate) Memorial	Ieper, West-Vlaanderen
JONES, ARTHUR	Private	G/8832	4th Bn.	Royal Fusiliers	16-Jun-15	19	Son of John and Hannah Jones, of 79, Victoria St., Northwood, Henley, Stoke-on-Trent.	Panel 6 and 8.	Ypres (Menin Gate) Memorial	Ieper, West-Vlaanderen
JONES, GEORGE	Private	L/7559	4th Bn.	Royal Fusiliers	16-Jun-15	36	Husband of Josepha Mary Caroline Jones, of 2, Raynham Rd., Hammersmith, London.	Panel 6 and 8.	Ypres (Menin Gate) Memorial	Ieper, West-Vlaanderen
JONES, GEORGE THOMAS	Private	L/11181	4th Bn.	Royal Fusiliers	16-Jun-15	unknown		Panel 6 and 8.	Ypres (Menin Gate) Memorial	Ieper, West-Vlaanderen

Name	Rank	Service No.	Unit	Regiment	Date of Death	Age	Additional Information	Panel	Memorial	Location
KINGHAM, HENRY CHARLES	Private	SR/923	"A" Coy. 4th Bn.	Royal Fusiliers	16-Jun-15	45	Son of the late Mr. Kingham; husband of Florence Elizabeth Phillips (formerly Kingham), of 16, Story St., Caledonian Rd., King's Cross, London. Served in the South African Campaign.	Panel 6 and 8.	Ypres (Menin Gate) Memorial	Ieper, West-Vlaanderen
LEACH, WILLIAM HENRY	Private	SR/2509	4th Bn.	Royal Fusiliers	16-Jun-15	unknown		Panel 6 and 8.	Ypres (Menin Gate) Memorial	Ieper, West-Vlaanderen
LEE, HENRY DAVID	Private	L/15936	4th Bn.	Royal Fusiliers	16-Jun-15	unknown		Panel 6 and 8.	Ypres (Menin Gate) Memorial	Ieper, West-Vlaanderen
LESTER, CHARLES HENRY	Lance Corporal	G/5031	4th Bn.	Royal Fusiliers	16-Jun-15	unknown		Panel 6 and 8.	Ypres (Menin Gate) Memorial	Ieper, West-Vlaanderen
LEVY, S	Corporal	L/12910	4th Bn.	Royal Fusiliers	16-Jun-15	unknown		Panel 6 and 8.	Ypres (Menin Gate) Memorial	Ieper, West-Vlaanderen
LITTLE, WILLIAM GEORGE	Private	G/13966	4th Bn.	Royal Fusiliers	16-Jun-15	21	Son of Thomas and Mary Little, of Boltons Lane, Bath Rd., Harlington, Hounslow, Middlx.	Panel 6 and 8.	Ypres (Menin Gate) Memorial	Ieper, West-Vlaanderen
MABERLEY, WILLIAM ARTHUR	Private	SR/2453	4th Bn.	Royal Fusiliers	16-Jun-15	19	Son of John Henry and Alice Matilda Maberley, of 9, Church Rd., Iver Heath, Bucks.	Panel 6 and 8.	Ypres (Menin Gate) Memorial	Ieper, West-Vlaanderen
MASON, GEORGE ALFRED	Private	SR/7705	4th Bn.	Royal Fusiliers	16-Jun-15	22	Son of Amelia Mason, of 9, Lesh St., Roman Rd., Barnsbury, London.	Panel 6 and 8.	Ypres (Menin Gate) Memorial	Ieper, West-Vlaanderen
MATTIN, EDWIN	Private	L/16196	4th Bn.	Royal Fusiliers	16-Jun-15	20	Son of John and Eliza Mattin, of 23, St. John's Rd., South Tottenham, London.	Panel 6 and 8.	Ypres (Menin Gate) Memorial	Ieper, West-Vlaanderen
MAXFIELD, JOHN EDWARD	Private	SR/8313	4th Bn.	Royal Fusiliers	16-Jun-15	unknown		Panel 6 and 8.	Ypres (Menin Gate) Memorial	Ieper, West-Vlaanderen

Full name	Rank	Service	Unit	Regiment	Date	Age	Additional	Grave	Cemetery	Locality
MOBBERLEY, ARTHUR	Private	G/4929	4th Bn.	Royal Fusiliers	16-Jun-15	20	Son of George and Mary Ann Mobberley, of 78, Leek Rd., Hanley, Stoke-on-Trent.	Panel 6 and 8.	Ypres (Menin Gate) Memorial	Ieper, West-Vlaanderen
MOORE, CHARLES	Private	L/13383	4th Bn.	Royal Fusiliers	16-Jun-15	unknown		Panel 6 and 8.	Ypres (Menin Gate) Memorial	Ieper, West-Vlaanderen
PARRISH, RICHARD	Private	L/12531	4th Bn.	Royal Fusiliers	16-Jun-15	unknown		Panel 6 and 8.	Ypres (Menin Gate) Memorial	Ieper, West-Vlaanderen
PAYNE, ALBERT DONALD	Private	L/16293	4th Bn.	Royal Fusiliers	16-Jun-15	25	Only son of Albert Edward Horlick Payne, of "Mons," Leinster Walk, Kildare, and the late Mary Ann Payne. Born in London.	Panel 6 and 8.	Ypres (Menin Gate) Memorial	Ieper, West-Vlaanderen
PHILLIPS, RICHARD HURTON	Private	G/9019	4th Bn.	Royal Fusiliers	16-Jun-15	25	Son of Emma Eliza Phillips, of 2, Ballater Rd., Brixton, London, and the late Samuel Phillips.	Panel 6 and 8.	Ypres (Menin Gate) Memorial	Ieper, West-Vlaanderen
PIDDINGTON, CHARLES	Private	SR/2530	4th Bn.	Royal Fusiliers	16-Jun-15	unknown		Panel 6 and 8.	Ypres (Menin Gate) Memorial	Ieper, West-Vlaanderen
PLUMMER, HARRY CHARLES	Private	G/9188	4th Bn.	Royal Fusiliers	16-Jun-15	20	Son of Harry Robert and Emma Plummer, of 20, Somerset Rd., Walthamstow, London.	Panel 6 and 8.	Ypres (Menin Gate) Memorial	Ieper, West-Vlaanderen
POND, BERT	Lance Corporal	SR/11	4th Bn.	Royal Fusiliers	16-Jun-15	unknown		Panel 6 and 8.	Ypres (Menin Gate) Memorial	Ieper, West-Vlaanderen
PORTSMORE, WILLIAM GEORGE	Lance Corporal	G/6064	4th Bn.	Royal Fusiliers	16-Jun-15	31	Husband of Eleanor Smith (formerly Portsmore), of School House, Featherstone Rd., Southall, Middx.	Panel 6 and 8.	Ypres (Menin Gate) Memorial	Ieper, West-Vlaanderen
POXON, GEORGE	Private	G/242	4th Bn.	Royal Fusiliers	16-Jun-15	unknown		Panel 6 and 8.	Ypres (Menin Gate) Memorial	Ieper, West-Vlaanderen
REED WILLIAM	Private	SR/7775	4th Bn.	Royal Fusiliers	16-Jun-15	unknown		Panel 6 and 8.	Ypres (Menin Gate) Memorial	Ieper, West-Vlaanderen

RICHARDSON, THOMAS WILLIAM HENRY	Lance Corporal	G/9652	4th Bn.	Royal Fusiliers	16-Jun-15	29	Husband of Ada Elizabeth Meehan (formerly Richardson), of 53, Stanhope St., Hampstead Rd., London.	Panel 6 and 8.	Ypres (Menin Gate) Memorial	Ieper, West-Vlaanderen
RICHARDSON, WILLIAM	Private	SR/8069	4th Bn.	Royal Fusiliers	16-Jun-15	30	Son of Mrs. Carroll (formerly Richardson), of 44, Aske St., Hoxton; husband of Susannah Richardson, of 4, Boot St., Pitfield St., Hoxton, London.	Panel 6 and 8.	Ypres (Menin Gate) Memorial	Ieper, West-Vlaanderen
ROBINSON, THOMAS WILLIAM	Private	G/4736	"Y" Coy. 4th Bn.	Royal Fusiliers	16-Jun-15	22	Son of Mrs. Alice Maud Robinson, of 22, Colegrove Rd., Peckham, London.	Panel 6 and 8.	Ypres (Menin Gate) Memorial	Ieper, West-Vlaanderen
ROWLAND, WILLIAM	Corporal	SR/8074	4th Bn.	Royal Fusiliers	16-Jun-15	unknown	Son of Mr. and Mrs. Rowland, of Clapham, London; husband of the late Agnes Louise Rowland.	Panel 6 and 8.	Ypres (Menin Gate) Memorial	Ieper, West-Vlaanderen
SANDERSON, WILLIAM RICHARD	Private	G/9870	4th Bn.	Royal Fusiliers	16-Jun-15	32	Son of Mrs. E. Sanderson, of 64, Newton Avenue, Acton; husband of Amelia C. Sanderson, of 16, Packington Rd., Acton, London.	Panel 6 and 8.	Ypres (Menin Gate) Memorial	Ieper, West-Vlaanderen
SMITH, CHARLES	Lance Corporal	SR/4351	4th Bn.	Royal Fusiliers	16-Jun-15	unknown		Panel 6 and 8.	Ypres (Menin Gate) Memorial	Ieper, West-Vlaanderen
SMITH, GEORGE	Private	SR/1341	4th Bn.	Royal Fusiliers	16-Jun-15	22	Son of Robert Woodford Smith and Henrietta Smith, of 6, Gifford St., Caledonian Rd., Islington, London.	Panel 6 and 8.	Ypres (Menin Gate) Memorial	Ieper, West-Vlaanderen
SMITH, GEORGE EDWARD	Private	G/9914	4th Bn.	Royal Fusiliers	16-Jun-15	21	Son of William and Elizabeth Smith, of 4, Rose Cottages, Beacontree Heath, Romford, Essex. His brother Henry Samuel Smith also fell.	Panel 6 and 8.	Ypres (Menin Gate) Memorial	Ieper, West-Vlaanderen
SMITH, JOHN	Private	G/4239	4th Bn.	Royal Fusiliers	16-Jun-15	unknown		Panel 6 and 8.	Ypres (Menin Gate) Memorial	Ieper, West-Vlaanderen

Full name	Rank	Service	Unit	Regiment	Date	Age	Additional	Grave	Cemetery	Locality
SMITHERS, ALBERT EDWARD	Private	G/4141	4th Bn.	Royal Fusiliers	16-Jun-15	30	Son of William T. and Louisa Smithers, of 18, Wheatsheaf Terrace, Bishop's Rd., Fulham; husband of Edith A. Smithers, of 91, Bishops Rd, Fulham, London.	Panel 6 and 8.	Ypres (Menin Gate) Memorial	Ieper, West-Vlaanderen
SNAPES, FREDERICK	Lance Corporal	L/16174	4th Bn.	Royal Fusiliers	16-Jun-15	unknown		Panel 6 and 8.	Ypres (Menin Gate) Memorial	Ieper, West-Vlaanderen
STROUD, CHARLES	Private	L/10668	"E" Coy. 4th Bn.	Royal Fusiliers	16-Jun-15	35	Son of John and Emily Stroud, of 79, Third Goss Rd, Twickenham, Middx.	Panel 6 and 8.	Ypres (Menin Gate) Memorial	Ieper, West-Vlaanderen
THOM, GEORGE HENRY	Corporal	L/12414	4th Bn.	Royal Fusiliers	16-Jun-15	26	Son of James Thom, of 48, Eastbury Grove, Chiswick, London.	Panel 6 and 8.	Ypres (Menin Gate) Memorial	Ieper, West-Vlaanderen
THOMAS-O'DONEL, GEORGE O'DONEL FREDERICK	Captain		Adjt. 4th Bn.	Royal Fusiliers	16-Jun-15	30	Son of Edwin and Milicent Agnes Thomas-O'Donel, of Newport House, Newport, Co. Mayo; husband of Violet Thomas-O'Donel (nee Braddell).	Panel 6 and 8.	Ypres (Menin Gate) Memorial	Ieper, West-Vlaanderen
THOMPSON, FREDERICK	Private	L/12060	4th Bn.	Royal Fusiliers	16-Jun-15	25	Son of Walter and Louisa Thompson, of 61, Lennox Rd., Walthamstow, London.	Panel 6 and 8.	Ypres (Menin Gate) Memorial	Ieper, West-Vlaanderen
THORNTON, ROBERT WEST	Lieutenant			Royal Fusiliers	16-Jun-15	19	Son of Maj. Robert Lawrence Thornton, C.B.E., D.L., J.P. and Charlotte Thornton, J.P., of High Cross, Framfield, Sussex.	Panel 6 and 8.	Ypres (Menin Gate) Memorial	Ieper, West-Vlaanderen
TOUCHARD, CHARLES ALBERT	Private	G/269	4th Bn.	Royal Fusiliers	16-Jun-15	unknown		Panel 6 and 8.	Ypres (Menin Gate) Memorial	Ieper, West-Vlaanderen
TOVEY, HARRY OWEN	Private	L/8739	4th Bn.	Royal Fusiliers	16-Jun-15	20	Son of Frederick Samuel and Elizabeth Ann Tovey, of 41, South	Panel 6 and 8.	Ypres (Menin Gate) Memorial	Ieper, West-Vlaanderen

Name	Rank	Number	Bn.	Regiment	Date	Age	Details	Panel	Memorial	Location
THOMAS HENRY						unknown		Panel 6 and 8.	Ypres (Menin Gate) Memorial	Ieper, West-Vlaanderen
TURNER, FREDERICK RAYNOR	Private	L/7132	4th Bn.	Royal Fusiliers	16-Jun-15	unknown		Panel 6 and 8.	Ypres (Menin Gate) Memorial	Ieper, West-Vlaanderen
VARLEY, FREDERICK ERNEST	Private	G/9250	4th Bn.	Royal Fusiliers	16-Jun-15	20	Son of Thomas Herbert and Alice Varley, of 1, Charles St., Cheadle, Stoke-on-Trent.	Panel 6 and 8.	Ypres (Menin Gate) Memorial	Ieper, West-Vlaanderen
WADE, GEORGE	Private	SR/7189	4th Bn.	Royal Fusiliers	16-Jun-15	unknown		Panel 6 and 8.	Ypres (Menin Gate) Memorial	Ieper, West-Vlaanderen
WALKER, G	Private	G/10001	4th Bn.	Royal Fusiliers	16-Jun-15	unknown		Panel 6 and 8.	Ypres (Menin Gate) Memorial	Ieper, West-Vlaanderen
WALKER, LOUIS FRANK	Private	10604	1st Bn.	Royal Fusiliers	16-Jun-15	29	Son of Mrs. E. Walker; husband of Elizabeth Walker, of 165, Campbell Avenue, Toronto, Canada.	Panel 6 and 8.	Ypres (Menin Gate) Memorial	Ieper, West-Vlaanderen
WARDE, BRIAN EDMUND DOUGLAS	Lieutenant		6th Bn.	Royal Fusiliers	16-Jun-15	20	Son of the late Maj. Charles Aprilis Enthon Warde (Royal Fusiliers and Dragoon Guards) and of Felicia Warde, of 2, Buckingham Mansions, Kensington, London. Educated at Bilton Grange and Lancing College. Joined Aug, 1914, and went to France in the following Dec.	Panel 6 and 8.	Ypres (Menin Gate) Memorial	Ieper, West-Vlaanderen
WARMAN, ALBERT EDWARD	Private	G/8853	4th Bn.	Royal Fusiliers	16-Jun-15	unknown		Panel 6 and 8.	Ypres (Menin Gate) Memorial	Ieper, West-Vlaanderen
WARREN, REUBEN OCTAVIUS	Private	G/4984	4th Bn.	Royal Fusiliers	16-Jun-15	26	Son of the late Robert and Ellen Warren.	Panel 6 and 8.	Ypres (Menin Gate) Memorial	Ieper, West-Vlaanderen
WEBB, CHARLES HENRY	Private	L/10713	4th Bn.	Royal Fusiliers	16-Jun-15	unknown		Panel 6 and 8.	Ypres (Menin Gate) Memorial	Ieper, West-Vlaanderen

Full name	Rank	Service	Unit	Regiment	Date	Age	Additional	Grave	Cemetery	Locality
WELLICOME, LEONARD WHEELER ERIC	Private	G/7089	4th Bn.	Royal Fusiliers	16-Jun-15	unknown		Panel 6 and 8.	Ypres (Menin Gate) Memorial	Ieper, West-Vlaanderen
WELSH, WILLIAM	Private	L/9965	4th Bn.	Royal Fusiliers	16-Jun-15	unknown		Panel 6 and 8.	Ypres (Menin Gate) Memorial	Ieper, West-Vlaanderen
WENHAM, CHARLES WILLIAM	Private	L/14807	4th Bn.	Royal Fusiliers	16-Jun-15	unknown		Panel 6 and 8.	Ypres (Menin Gate) Memorial	Ieper, West-Vlaanderen
WHITEHEAD, ARTHUR JAMES	Sergeant	L/1014	4th Bn.	Royal Fusiliers	16-Jun-15	unknown		Panel 6 and 8.	Ypres (Menin Gate) Memorial	Ieper, West-Vlaanderen
WHITFORD, GEORGE	Private	L/16164	4th Bn.	Royal Fusiliers	16-Jun-15	unknown		Panel 6 and 8.	Ypres (Menin Gate) Memorial	Ieper, West-Vlaanderen
WINTER, WALTER JOSEPH	Sergeant	L/6709	4th Bn.	Royal Fusiliers	16-Jun-15	32	Son of George and the late Mary Winter; husband of Agnes Jane Winter, of 35, Catherine Rd., St. Ann's Rd., South Tottenham, London. Awarded Tibet Medal (1903-4).	Panel 6 and 8.	Ypres (Menin Gate) Memorial	Ieper, West-Vlaanderen
WITHEY, WILLIAM JOHN	Lance Corporal	L/12245	4th Bn.	Royal Fusiliers	16-Jun-15	26	Son of George Edmund John and Annie Louise Withey, of 70, London St., Chertsey, Surrey.	Panel 6 and 8.	Ypres (Menin Gate) Memorial	Ieper, West-Vlaanderen
WOOL, CHARLES	Private	G/76	4th Bn.	Royal Fusiliers	16-Jun-15	unknown		Panel 6 and 8.	Ypres (Menin Gate) Memorial	Ieper, West-Vlaanderen
WRIGHT, ALBERT EDWARD	Private	SR/9399	4th Bn.	Royal Fusiliers	16-Jun-15	23	Son of Mrs. Annie Wright, of 30, Fellbrigg St., Bethnal Green, London.	Panel 6 and 8.	Ypres (Menin Gate) Memorial	Ieper, West-Vlaanderen
WRIGHT, THOMAS	Lance Corporal	L/11024	4th Bn.	Royal Fusiliers	16-Jun-15	29	Son of Henry James and Maria Wright, of 31, Wick Rd., Homerton, London.	Panel 6 and 8.	Ypres (Menin Gate) Memorial	Ieper, West-Vlaanderen

Name	Rank	Number	Battalion	Regiment	Date	Age	Details	Panel	Cemetery/Memorial	Location
				Royal Irish Rifles			Brother of Mrs. Lucy Winifred Schofield, of 446, High St., Lincoln.	Panel 40.	Ypres (Menin Gate) Memorial	Ieper, West-Vlaanderen
BRADLEY, JOHN	Rifleman	10005	1st Bn.	Royal Irish Rifles	16-Jun-15	unknown		Panel 9.	Ploegsteert Memorial	Comines-Warneton, Hainaut
BRADY, THOMAS	Lance Corporal	6980	2nd Bn.	Royal Irish Rifles	16-Jun-15	unknown		Panel 40.	Ypres (Menin Gate) Memorial	Ieper, West-Vlaanderen
COLE, JOHN	Rifleman	10250	2nd Bn.	Royal Irish Rifles	16-Jun-15	19	Foster son of Mrs. Mary Cronin, of 59, Lower Wellington St., Dublin.	Panel 40.	Ypres (Menin Gate) Memorial	Ieper, West-Vlaanderen
CONDON, PATRICK	Lance Corporal	6545	2nd Bn.	Royal Irish Rifles	16-Jun-15	unknown		Panel 40.	Ypres (Menin Gate) Memorial	Ieper, West-Vlaanderen
COTTER, WILLIAM	Rifleman	5849	2nd Bn.	Royal Irish Rifles	16-Jun-15	35	Brother of Mrs. Mary Hunter, of 7, Copperfield St., Belfast.	Panel 40.	Ypres (Menin Gate) Memorial	Ieper, West-Vlaanderen
COUGHLAN, DANIEL	Lance Corporal	9687	2nd Bn.	Royal Irish Rifles	16-Jun-15	unknown		Panel 40.	Ypres (Menin Gate) Memorial	Ieper, West-Vlaanderen
COURTNEY, JAMES THOMAS	Company Serjeant Major	8074	2nd Bn.	Royal Irish Rifles	16-Jun-15	30	Son of Elizabeth Courtney, of 27, Camden Row, Dublin, and the late Richard Courtney.	Panel 40.	Ypres (Menin Gate) Memorial	Ieper, West-Vlaanderen
CREGAN, PATRICK	Rifleman	10287	2nd Bn.	Royal Irish Rifles	16-Jun-15	19	Son of Patrick and Mary Cregan, of 55, Rialto Buildings, South Circular Rd., Dublin.	Panel 40.	Ypres (Menin Gate) Memorial	Ieper, West-Vlaanderen
DALY, FRANCIS	Rifleman	15289	2nd Bn.	Royal Irish Rifles	16-Jun-15	22	Son of James Daly, of Old House, Church Brae, Dunoon, Argyll; husband of Margaret Daly (nee Stewart), of 1561, Paisley Rd. West, Halfwayhouses, Glasgow.	Panel 40.	Ypres (Menin Gate) Memorial	Ieper, West-Vlaanderen
DUNNE, FRANCIS	Rifleman	7335	2nd Bn.	Royal Irish Rifles	16-Jun-15	29	Son of the late John and Anne Dunne.	LVI. F. 14.	Poelcapelle British Cemetery	Langemark-Poelkapelle, West-V.

Full name	Rank	Service	Unit	Regiment	Date	Age	Additional	Grave	Cemetery	Locality
FARRAN, EDMOND CHOMLEY LAMEERT	Captain		3rd Bn. attd. 2nd Bn.	Royal Irish Rifles	16-Jun-15	36	Son of Edmond Chomley Farran and Anne Hume Farran, of Knocklyon House, Templeogue, Co. Dublin. Barrister-at-Law, Kings Inns, Dublin.	Panel 40.	Ypres (Menin Gate) Memorial	Ieper, West-Vlaanderen
FIELDS, PETER	Rifleman	10432	2nd Bn.	Royal Irish Rifles	16-Jun-15	unknown		Panel 40.	Ypres (Menin Gate) Memorial	Ieper, West-Vlaanderen
FITZSIMMONS, JAMES	Rifleman	5510	2nd Bn.	Royal Irish Rifles	16-Jun-15	20	Son of Mrs. Ellen Fitzsimmons, of 37, Skipton St., Belfast.	Panel 40.	Ypres (Menin Gate) Memorial	Ieper, West-Vlaanderen
FITZSIMMONS, PATRICK	Rifleman	6322	"G" Coy. 2nd Bn.	Royal Irish Rifles	16-Jun-15	35	Husband of Bridget Fitzsimmons, of 9, Raphael St., Belfast.	Panel 40.	Ypres (Menin Gate) Memorial	Ieper, West-Vlaanderen
FRASER, THOMAS WILLIS	Rifleman	9488	1st Bn.	Royal Irish Rifles	16-Jun-15	unknown		Panel 9.	Ploegsteert Memorial	Comines-Warneton, Hainaut
GILCHRIST, WILLIAM JOHN	Rifleman	5521	2nd Bn.	Royal Irish Rifles	16-Jun-15	unknown		Panel 40.	Ypres (Menin Gate) Memorial	Ieper, West-Vlaanderen
HARVEY, JOHN	Rifleman	6970	2nd Bn.	Royal Irish Rifles	16-Jun-15	unknown		Panel 40.	Ypres (Menin Gate) Memorial	Ieper, West-Vlaanderen
HENDERSON, WILLIAM ARNOLD	Corporal	6528	"C" Coy. 2nd Bn.	Royal Irish Rifles	16-Jun-15	22	Son of Robert and Mary Henderson, of 19, Eighth St., Shankill Rd., Belfast.	Panel 40.	Ypres (Menin Gate) Memorial	Ieper, West-Vlaanderen
HERON, JAMES	Rifleman	7153	2nd Bn.	Royal Irish Rifles	16-Jun-15	26	Son of William John Heron.	Panel 40.	Ypres (Menin Gate) Memorial	Ieper, West-Vlaanderen
HOLLINGWORTH, ARTHUR	Rifleman	9369	2nd Bn.	Royal Irish Rifles	16-Jun-15	33	Son of the late George William and Catherine Hollingworth. Previously served for nearly six years in India and Ireland.	Panel 40.	Ypres (Menin Gate) Memorial	Ieper, West-Vlaanderen

Name	Rank	Service No.	Battalion	Regiment	Date	Age	Details	Panel	Memorial	Location
HOYSTED, DANIEL	Rifleman	10221	2nd Bn.	Royal Irish Rifles	16-Jun-15	20	Son of Bridget Hoysted, of 43, South William St., Dublin, and the late James Hoysted.	Panel 40.	Ypres (Menin Gate) Memorial	Ieper, West-Vlaanderen
HUDSON, EDWARD	Rifleman	10373	2nd Bn.	Royal Irish Rifles	16-Jun-15	17	Son of Mrs. Margaret McGee, of 9, Lower Clanbrassil St., Dublin.	Panel 40.	Ypres (Menin Gate) Memorial	Ieper, West-Vlaanderen
IRWIN, LEO	Rifleman	17211	"D" Coy. 2nd Bn.	Royal Irish Rifles	16-Jun-15	27	Youngest son of James and Catherine Irwin, of 4, Upper Erne St., Dublin.	Panel 40.	Ypres (Menin Gate) Memorial	Ieper, West-Vlaanderen
IRWIN, SAMUEL	Corporal	8622	2nd Bn.	Royal Irish Rifles	16-Jun-15	unknown		Panel 40.	Ypres (Menin Gate) Memorial	Ieper, West-Vlaanderen
JOHNSTON, HUGH	Rifleman	6467	"C" Coy. 2nd Bn.	Royal Irish Rifles	16-Jun-15	19	Son of Mrs. Sarah Johnston, of 2, Carew St., Ballymacarrett, Belfast.	Panel 40.	Ypres (Menin Gate) Memorial	Ieper, West-Vlaanderen
JOHNSTON, JOHN R.	Rifleman	4717	1st Bn.	Royal Irish Rifles	16-Jun-15	21	Son of Samuel and Mary Johnston, of 5, Linenhall St., Banbridge, Co. Down.	Panel 9.	Ploegsteert Memorial	Comines-Warneton, Hainaut
JONES, JOSEPH	Rifleman	1788	2nd Bn.	Royal Irish Rifles	16-Jun-15	18	Son of Edward and Catherine Ann Jones, of 7, Heelis St., Buckley St., Rochdale Rd., Manchester.	Panel 40.	Ypres (Menin Gate) Memorial	Ieper, West-Vlaanderen
JOY, FREDERICK CHARLES PATRICK	Second Lieutenant		3rd Bn. attd. 2nd Bn.	Royal Irish Rifles	16-Jun-15	23	Son of Robert and Elizabeth Joy. Enlisted 1914, in the 5th Bn. Royal Dublin Fusiliers.	Panel 40.	Ypres (Menin Gate) Memorial	Ieper, West-Vlaanderen
KING, SAMUEL	Rifleman	5559	2nd Bn.	Royal Irish Rifles	16-Jun-15	47	Son of James King, of 35, Eight St., Belfast.	Panel 40.	Ypres (Menin Gate) Memorial	Ieper, West-Vlaanderen
LAIRD, GEORGE	Corporal	8835	2nd Bn.	Royal Irish Rifles	16-Jun-15	unknown		Panel 40.	Ypres (Menin Gate) Memorial	Ieper, West-Vlaanderen
LAPPIN, DANIEL	Rifleman	5047	2nd Bn.	Royal Irish Rifles	16-Jun-15	22	Son of William and Jane Lappin, of 12, Millview, Chapel Hill, Lisburn, Co. Antrim.	Panel 40.	Ypres (Menin Gate) Memorial	Ieper, West-Vlaanderen

Full name	Rank	Service	Unit	Regiment	Date	Age	Additional	Grave	Cemetery	Locality
LOUGHLIN, ROBERT	Rifleman	5921	2nd Bn.	Royal Irish Rifles	16-Jun-15	25	Son of the late Robert and Mary Loughlin; husband of Roseann Loughlin, of 32, Clandeboye St., Belfast.	Panel 40.	Ypres (Menin Gate) Memorial	Ieper, West-Vlaanderen
MALCOMSON, JOSEPH	Rifleman	4894	2nd Bn.	Royal Irish Rifles	16-Jun-15	unknown		Panel 40.	Ypres (Menin Gate) Memorial	Ieper, West-Vlaanderen
MARTIN, WILLIAM	Rifleman	6319	2nd Bn.	Royal Irish Rifles	16-Jun-15	unknown		Panel 40.	Ypres (Menin Gate) Memorial	Ieper, West-Vlaanderen
MAYES, JAMES	Rifleman	5714	1st Bn.	Royal Irish Rifles	16-Jun-15	18	Son of James and Arm Jane Mayes, of 42, Methuen St., Belfast.	Panel 9.	Ploegsteert Memorial	Comines-Warneton, Hainaut
McCARTNEY, MATTHEW	Rifleman	2318	2nd Bn.	Royal Irish Rifles	16-Jun-15	unknown		Panel 40.	Ypres (Menin Gate) Memorial	Ieper, West-Vlaanderen
McCORMICK, ARCHIBALD	Rifleman	7044	"D" Coy. 2nd Bn.	Royal Irish Rifles	16-Jun-15	22	Son of Andrew and Mary Anne McCormick.	Panel 40.	Ypres (Menin Gate) Memorial	Ieper, West-Vlaanderen
McDOWELL, ROBERT	Rifleman	8423	2nd Bn.	Royal Irish Rifles	16-Jun-15	unknown		Panel 40.	Ypres (Menin Gate) Memorial	Ieper, West-Vlaanderen
McGIBNEY, JAMES JOSEPH	Company Sergeant Major	7973	2nd Bn.	Royal Irish Rifles	16-Jun-15	unknown	Son of Mary McGibney of 5 B Block, Piles Buildings, Wood Street, Dublin. His brother John Joseph also fell.	Panel 40.	Ypres (Menin Gate) Memorial	Ieper, West-Vlaanderen
McGREEVY, PATRICK	Corporal	5078	2nd Bn.	Royal Irish Rifles	16-Jun-15	20	Son of Nicholas and Mary McGreevy, of Ballyalton, Downpatriek, Co. Down.	Panel 40.	Ypres (Menin Gate) Memorial	Ieper, West-Vlaanderen
McILROY, JOHN	Corporal	7599	2nd Bn.	Royal Irish Rifles	16-Jun-15	28	Son of David and Catherine Geraldine McIlroy, of Blackstock, South Carolina, U.S.A.; husband of Emily Hester McIlroy, of Cuthbert St., Albany, Western	Panel 40.	Ypres (Menin Gate) Memorial	Ieper, West-Vlaanderen

WILLIAM	Corporal		2nd Bn.	Rifles			husband of Elizabeth McIlroy, of 31, Aberdeen St., Belfast.	Panel 57.	Ypres (Menin Gate) Memorial	Ieper, West-Vlaanderen
McINTOSH, JAMES MARSHALL	Second Lieutenant		2nd Bn.	Royal Irish Rifles	16-Jun-15	unknown	Husband of Margaret McIntosh, of 1, Hurlingham Gardens, Fulham, London.	Panel 40.	Ypres (Menin Gate) Memorial	Ieper, West-Vlaanderen
McKENZIE, THOMAS	Rifleman	10217	2nd Bn.	Royal Irish Rifles	16-Jun-15	18	Son of George McKenzie, of 80, Convention St., Belfast.	Panel 40.	Ypres (Menin Gate) Memorial	Ieper, West-Vlaanderen
McKEOWN, JOHN	Rifleman	5722	2nd Bn.	Royal Irish Rifles	16-Jun-15	22	Son of Douglas McKeown, of 9, Corlig St., Belfast; husband of Ellen McKeown, of 59, Conlon St., Belfast.	Panel 40.	Ypres (Menin Gate) Memorial	Ieper, West-Vlaanderen
McKEOWN, JOHN	Rifleman	6768	2nd Bn.	Royal Irish Rifles	16-Jun-15	41	Son of John and Jane McKeown, of 20, Church St., Newry, Co. Down.	Panel 40.	Ypres (Menin Gate) Memorial	Ieper, West-Vlaanderen
MORGAN, GEORGE	Corporal	7017	2nd Bn.	Royal Irish Rifles	16-Jun-15	30	Son of the late Albert and Elizabeth Morgan; husband of Jane Morgan, of 13, Chamberlain St., Belfast.	Panel 40.	Ypres (Menin Gate) Memorial	Ieper, West-Vlaanderen
MORROW, JAMES	Rifleman	8731	2nd Bn.	Royal Irish Rifles	16-Jun-15	unknown		Panel 40.	Ypres (Menin Gate) Memorial	Ieper, West-Vlaanderen
MULLAN, THOMAS	Rifleman	5542	2nd Bn.	Royal Irish Rifles	16-Jun-15	29	Son of the late Henry and Catherine Mullan; husband of Ellen J. Beattie (formerly Mullan), of 10, Genoa St., Grosvenor Rd., Belfast.	Panel 40.	Ypres (Menin Gate) Memorial	Ieper, West-Vlaanderen
MURRAY, HUGH	Corporal	6095	"C" Coy. 2nd Bn.	Royal Irish Rifles	16-Jun-15	24	Son of Mary Murray, of 20, Seaforde St., Belfast, and the late James Murray.	Panel 40.	Ypres (Menin Gate) Memorial	Ieper, West-Vlaanderen
NICHOLSON, WILLIAM HENRY	Rifleman	5233	2nd Bn.	Royal Irish Rifles	16-Jun-15	19	Son of the late James and Agnes Nicholson.	Panel 40.	Ypres (Menin Gate) Memorial	Ieper, West-Vlaanderen

Full name	Rank	Service	Unit	Regiment	Date	Age	Additional	Grave	Cemetery	Locality
OWENS, JOSEPH	Rifleman	51189	"B" Coy. 2nd Bn.	Royal Irish Rifles	16-Jun-15	32	Long Service and Good Conduct Medal. Son of William and Ellen Owens, of 84, Hill St, Gilford, Co. Down. Served in the South African Campaign.	Panel 40.	Ypres (Menin Gate) Memorial	Ieper, West-Vlaanderen
RODGERS, WILLIAM HERBERT	Corporal	8690	1st Bn.	Royal Irish Rifles	16-Jun-15	unknown		Panel 9.	Ploegsteert Memorial	Comines-Warneton, Hainaut
SMYTH, JOHN JOSEPH	Rifleman	5221	2nd Bn.	Royal Irish Rifles	16-Jun-15	19	Son of Edward and Isabella Smyth, of 49, Edward St., Lurgan, Co. Armagh.	Panel 40.	Ypres (Menin Gate) Memorial	Ieper, West-Vlaanderen
SPRATT, WILLIAM JOHN	Rifleman	5018	1st Bn.	Royal Irish Rifles	16-Jun-15	27	Son of William John Spratt, of 56, Canal St., Lisburn.	Panel 9.	Ploegsteert Memorial	Comines-Warneton, Hainaut
THOMPSON, JOHN	Rifleman	4601	2nd Bn.	Royal Irish Rifles	16-Jun-15	27	Son of Isabella Thompson, of Cromkill, Ballymena, Co. Antrim.	Panel 40.	Ypres (Menin Gate) Memorial	Ieper, West-Vlaanderen
VINT, JAMES	Rifleman	6253	2nd Bn.	Royal Irish Rifles	16-Jun-15	31	Son of James and Mary Ann Vint, of 18, High St., Newry, Co. Down.	Panel 40.	Ypres (Menin Gate) Memorial	Ieper, West-Vlaanderen
WALKER, ARCHIBALD	Rifleman	8097	2nd Bn.	Royal Irish Rifles	16-Jun-15	unknown		Panel 40.	Ypres (Menin Gate) Memorial	Ieper, West-Vlaanderen
WATLING, FREDERICK	Rifleman	2503	2nd Bn.	Royal Irish Rifles	16-Jun-15	unknown		Panel 40.	Ypres (Menin Gate) Memorial	Ieper, West-Vlaanderen
WEST, PETER	Rifleman	10369	2nd Bn.	Royal Irish Rifles	16-Jun-15	18	Son of Patrick and Mary West, of 16, Henrietta St., Dublin.	Panel 40.	Ypres (Menin Gate) Memorial	Ieper, West-Vlaanderen
WINSTANLEY, WILLIAM	Rifleman	1265	2nd Bn.	Royal Irish Rifles	16-Jun-15	19	Son of William Winstanley, of 331, Hale Barns, Altrincham, Cheshire.	Panel 40.	Ypres (Menin Gate) Memorial	Ieper, West-Vlaanderen
WYNNE, PHILIP CAMILLUS	Rifleman	15706	2nd Bn.	Royal Irish Rifles	16-Jun-15	20	Son of the late John and Margaret Wynne.	Panel 40.	Ypres (Menin Gate) Memorial	Ieper, West-Vlaanderen

Name	Rank	Number	Battalion	Regiment	Date	Age	Next of Kin	Grave/Memorial	Cemetery/Memorial	Location
INNES, P	Private	8957	2nd Bn.	Royal Scots	16-Jun-15	unknown		Enclosure No.2 VI. A. 62.	Bedford House Cemetery	Ieper, West-Vlaanderen
POVAH, FRANK	Captain		2nd Bn.	Royal Scots	16-Jun-15	unknown		Panel 11.	Ypres (Menin Gate) Memorial	Ieper, West-Vlaanderen
ANDERSON, DAVID	Private	6731	"B" Coy. 1st Bn.	Royal Scots Fusiliers	16-Jun-15	19	Son of Mrs. M. Anderson, of 20, Fowlds St., Kilmarnock.	Panel 19 and 33.	Ypres (Menin Gate) Memorial	Ieper, West-Vlaanderen
ANDERSON, JAMES JOSEPH	Private	6353	1st Bn.	Royal Scots Fusiliers	16-Jun-15	20	Son of Mrs. Anderson, of 88, St. Andrew St., Leith, Edinburgh.	Panel 19 and 33.	Ypres (Menin Gate) Memorial	Ieper, West-Vlaanderen
BAILLIE, ROBERT	Private	15681	1st Bn.	Royal Scots Fusiliers	16-Jun-15	20	Son of Mr. and Mrs. James Baillie, of Academy St., Dollar, Clackmannanshire.	Panel 19 and 33.	Ypres (Menin Gate) Memorial	Ieper, West-Vlaanderen
BARR, JOHN	Private	7424	1st Bn.	Royal Scots Fusiliers	16-Jun-15	unknown		Panel 19 and 33.	Ypres (Menin Gate) Memorial	Ieper, West-Vlaanderen
BARRY, MALCOLM	Lance Serjeant	8770	1st Bn.	Royal Scots Fusiliers	16-Jun-15	unknown		Panel 19 and 33.	Ypres (Menin Gate) Memorial	Ieper, West-Vlaanderen
BELL, THOMAS	Private	6334	1st Bn.	Royal Scots Fusiliers	16-Jun-15	unknown		Panel 19 and 33.	Ypres (Menin Gate) Memorial	Ieper, West-Vlaanderen
BOYD, HENRY MCPHERSON	Private	9776	"H" Coy. 1st Bn.	Royal Scots Fusiliers	16-Jun-15	27	Son of William and Jeanie McPherson Boyd.	Panel 19 and 33.	Ypres (Menin Gate) Memorial	Ieper, West-Vlaanderen
BRANNEN, WILLIAM	Private	9342	1st Bn.	Royal Scots Fusiliers	16-Jun-15	unknown		Panel 19 and 33.	Ypres (Menin Gate) Memorial	Ieper, West-Vlaanderen
BRIEN, JOHN	Private	13545	1st Bn.	Royal Scots Fusiliers	16-Jun-15	35	Husband of Mary C. Doherty (formerly Brien), of 46, Colinward Street, Springfield Rd., Belfast.	Panel 19 and 33.	Ypres (Menin Gate) Memorial	Ieper, West-Vlaanderen
BROWN, GEORGE	Private	12453	1st Bn.	Royal Scots Fusiliers	16-Jun-15	19	Son of Mr. and Mrs. James Brown, of 37, North St., Armadale, West Lothian.	Panel 19 and 33.	Ypres (Menin Gate) Memorial	Ieper, West-Vlaanderen

Full name	Rank	Service	Unit	Regiment	Date	Age	Additional	Grave	Cemetery	Locality
BROWN, JOHN	Private	A/7439	1st Bn.	Royal Scots Fusiliers	16-Jun-15	unknown		Panel 19 and 33.	Ypres (Menin Gate) Memorial	Ieper, West-Vlaanderen
CANAVAN, ANDREW	Private	7802	1st Bn.	Royal Scots Fusiliers	16-Jun-15	unknown		Panel 19 and 33.	Ypres (Menin Gate) Memorial	Ieper, West-Vlaanderen
CARLIN, PATRICK	Private	6914	1st Bn.	Royal Scots Fusiliers	16-Jun-15	36	Nephew of Mrs. M. Carlin, of 54A, Grassmarket, Edinburgh.	Panel 19 and 33.	Ypres (Menin Gate) Memorial	Ieper, West-Vlaanderen
CASSIDY, J	Private	7746	1st Bn.	Royal Scots Fusiliers	16-Jun-15	unknown		LXV. K. 8.	Tyne Cot Cemetery	Zonnebeke, West-Vlaanderen
CLARK, JOHN	Private	6782	1st Bn.	Royal Scots Fusiliers	16-Jun-15	unknown		Panel 19 and 33.	Ypres (Menin Gate) Memorial	Ieper, West-Vlaanderen
CRAIG, ALEXANDER	Private	15445	1st Bn.	Royal Scots Fusiliers	16-Jun-15	unknown		Panel 19 and 33.	Ypres (Menin Gate) Memorial	Ieper, West-Vlaanderen
CUNNINGHAM, ROBERT	Private	7911	1st Bn.	Royal Scots Fusiliers	16-Jun-15	45	Son of Alexander Cunningham, of 20, Wise St. Eldorado, Illinois, U.S.A.	Panel 19 and 33.	Ypres (Menin Gate) Memorial	Ieper, West-Vlaanderen
CUTHILL, JOHN	Private	12606	1st Bn.	Royal Scots Fusiliers	16-Jun-15	unknown		Panel 19 and 33.	Ypres (Menin Gate) Memorial	Ieper, West-Vlaanderen
DAVIE, GEORGE	Private	12591	1st Bn.	Royal Scots Fusiliers	16-Jun-15	unknown		Panel 19 and 33.	Ypres (Menin Gate) Memorial	Ieper, West-Vlaanderen
DAVISON, ALEXANDER	Private	7339	1st Bn.	Royal Scots Fusiliers	16-Jun-15	39	Son of the late Barry Davison.	Panel 19 and 33.	Ypres (Menin Gate) Memorial	Ieper, West-Vlaanderen
DEVLIN, JAMES	Private	10852	1st Bn.	Royal Scots Fusiliers	16-Jun-15	unknown		Panel 19 and 33.	Ypres (Menin Gate) Memorial	Ieper, West-Vlaanderen
DICKSON, MATTHEW	Private	A/7313	1st Bn.	Royal Scots Fusiliers	16-Jun-15	18	Son of John Dickson, of 147, Thomson St, Dennistoun, Glasgow.	Panel 19 and 33.	Ypres (Menin Gate) Memorial	Ieper, West-Vlaanderen

DICKSON, ROBERT HENDERSON	Corporal	15540	1st Bn.	Royal Scots Fusiliers	16-Jun-15	31	Son of Robert H. and Hannah Dickson, of 8, Brougham St., Greenock.	Panel 19 and 33.	Ypres (Menin Gate) Memorial	Ieper, West-Vlaanderen
DONALD, JOHN	Private	5017	1st Bn.	Royal Scots Fusiliers	16-Jun-15	42	Son of John and Ann Docherty (nee Rush).	Panel 19 and 33.	Ypres (Menin Gate) Memorial	Ieper, West-Vlaanderen
DONNELLY, WILLIAM	Private	8101	1st Bn.	Royal Scots Fusiliers	16-Jun-15	unknown		Panel 19 and 33.	Ypres (Menin Gate) Memorial	Ieper, West-Vlaanderen
DOWNIE, CHARLES	Private	11043	1st Bn.	Royal Scots Fusiliers	16-Jun-15	unknown		Panel 19 and 33.	Ypres (Menin Gate) Memorial	Ieper, West-Vlaanderen
DUFFY, JAMES	Private	6439	1st Bn.	Royal Scots Fusiliers	16-Jun-15	unknown		Panel 19 and 33.	Ypres (Menin Gate) Memorial	Ieper, West-Vlaanderen
DURNION, JAMES	Private	5075	1st Bn.	Royal Scots Fusiliers	16-Jun-15	unknown		Panel 19 and 33.	Ypres (Menin Gate) Memorial	Ieper, West-Vlaanderen
DURWARD, JOHN	Private	10761	1st Bn.	Royal Scots Fusiliers	16-Jun-15	20	Son of Rebecca Durward, of 17, Kerr's Lane, Lochee, Dundee.	Panel 19 and 33.	Ypres (Menin Gate) Memorial	Ieper, West-Vlaanderen
ECCLES, JOHN	Private	6551	1st Bn.	Royal Scots Fusiliers	16-Jun-15	unknown		Panel 19 and 33.	Ypres (Menin Gate) Memorial	Ieper, West-Vlaanderen
ELVIN, JOHN	Private	6957	1st Bn.	Royal Scots Fusiliers	16-Jun-15	unknown		Panel 19 and 33.	Ypres (Menin Gate) Memorial	Ieper, West-Vlaanderen
FAULKNER, FREDERICK	Private	7792	1st Bn.	Royal Scots Fusiliers	16-Jun-15	unknown		Panel 19 and 33.	Ypres (Menin Gate) Memorial	Ieper, West-Vlaanderen
FELL, HERBERT	Private	16763	1st Bn.	Royal Scots Fusiliers	16-Jun-15	19	Son of Sarah Ellen Fell, of 232, Audley Range, Blackburn. and the late Edward Fell.	Panel 19 and 33.	Ypres (Menin Gate) Memorial	Ieper, West-Vlaanderen
FISHER, JOHN	Private	12527	1st Bn.	Royal Scots Fusiliers	16-Jun-15	unknown		Panel 19 and 33.	Ypres (Menin Gate) Memorial	Ieper, West-Vlaanderen
FRANKLAND, ALFRED ALBERT	Lance Corporal	7848	1st Bn.	Royal Scots Fusiliers	16-Jun-15	30	Husband of Ada Frankland, of 28, Victoria Crescent, St. Ann's Rd., South Tottenham, London.	Panel 19 and 33.	Ypres (Menin Gate) Memorial	Ieper, West-Vlaanderen

Full name	Rank	Service	Unit	Regiment	Date	Age	Additional	Grave	Cemetery	Locality
GAFFNEY, JAMES	Private	15623	1st Bn.	Royal Scots Fusiliers	16-Jun-15	18	Son of Thomas and Bridget Gaffney, of 30, High St., Edinburgh.	Panel 19 and 33.	Ypres (Menin Gate) Memorial	Ieper, West-Vlaanderen
GALBRAITH, JOHN WATSON	Private	16696	1st Bn.	Royal Scots Fusiliers	16-Jun-15	18	Son of John and Lizzie Galbraith, of Burnside Cottage, Kingseat, Fife.	Panel 19 and 33.	Ypres (Menin Gate) Memorial	Ieper, West-Vlaanderen
GARDINER, LEONARD GEORGE	Company Serjeant Major	7099	1st Bn.	Royal Scots Fusiliers	16-Jun-15	33	Son of the late G. Gardiner, of 37, Oswin St., Brook St., Kennington, London; husband of Eva Gardiner, of "Axe Vale," Sevington Rd., Hendon, London.	Panel 19 and 33.	Ypres (Menin Gate) Memorial	Ieper, West-Vlaanderen
GARDNER, JAMES	Private	7044	1st Bn.	Royal Scots Fusiliers	16-Jun-15	unknown		Panel 19 and 33.	Ypres (Menin Gate) Memorial	Ieper, West-Vlaanderen
GARLAND, JAMES	Private	6764	1st Bn.	Royal Scots Fusiliers	16-Jun-15	24	Son of Patrick and Mary Garland, of Thomas St., Newbridge, Co. Kildare.	Panel 19 and 33.	Ypres (Menin Gate) Memorial	Ieper, West-Vlaanderen
GAVIN, JOHN	Private	6674	1st Bn.	Royal Scots Fusiliers	16-Jun-15	unknown		Panel 19 and 33.	Ypres (Menin Gate) Memorial	Ieper, West-Vlaanderen
GILMORE, JAMES	Private	12040	1st Bn.	Royal Scots Fusiliers	16-Jun-15	unknown		Panel 19 and 33.	Ypres (Menin Gate) Memorial	Ieper, West-Vlaanderen
GLEW, JOSEPH	Lance Corporal	12501	1st Bn.	Royal Scots Fusiliers	16-Jun-15	unknown		Panel 19 and 33.	Ypres (Menin Gate) Memorial	Ieper, West-Vlaanderen
GRAY, ALEXANDER	Private	10628	1st Bn.	Royal Scots Fusiliers	16-Jun-15	unknown		Panel 19 and 33.	Ypres (Menin Gate) Memorial	Ieper, West-Vlaanderen
GUNTER, JOHN G.	Private	7810	1st Bn.	Royal Scots Fusiliers	16-Jun-15	37	Brother of Mr. T. B. Gunter, of 16, Woodland Row, Briton Ferry, Glam.	Panel 19 and 33.	Ypres (Menin Gate) Memorial	Ieper, West-Vlaanderen
HARRIS, ALBERT	Private	A/7748	1st Bn.	Royal Scots	16-Jun-15	unknown		Panel 19	Ypres (Menin Gate) Memorial	Ieper, West-Vlaanderen

Name	Rank	Service No.	Unit	Regiment	Date	Age	Details	Panel	Memorial	Location
HEBB, JOHN JAMES	Private	7913	1st Bn.	Royal Scots Fusiliers	16-Jun-15	unknown		Panel 19 and 33.	Ypres (Menin Gate) Memorial	Ieper, West-Vlaanderen
HEDGER, ARTHUR	Serjeant	8900	1st Bn.	Royal Scots Fusiliers	16-Jun-15	27	Son of the late Harry and Rosina Hedger.	Panel 19 and 33.	Ypres (Menin Gate) Memorial	Ieper, West-Vlaanderen
HIGGINS, ARTHUR	Private	7334	1st Bn.	Royal Scots Fusiliers	16-Jun-15	unknown		Panel 19 and 33.	Ypres (Menin Gate) Memorial	Ieper, West-Vlaanderen
HOLLAND, ALBERT	Private	15659	1st Bn.	Royal Scots Fusiliers	16-Jun-15	32	Son of Albert and Sarah Holland, of 114, Lancashire Hill, Stockport; husband of Amy Holland, of 6, Morton St., Stockport.	Panel 19 and 33.	Ypres (Menin Gate) Memorial	Ieper, West-Vlaanderen
HUME, WILLIAM	Private	7330	1st Bn.	Royal Scots Fusiliers	16-Jun-15	unknown		Panel 19 and 33.	Ypres (Menin Gate) Memorial	Ieper, West-Vlaanderen
IRONS, JAMES	Private	7383	1st Bn.	Royal Scots Fusiliers	16-Jun-15	unknown		Panel 19 and 33.	Ypres (Menin Gate) Memorial	Ieper, West-Vlaanderen
JACKSON, HENRY	Private	8875	1st Bn.	Royal Scots Fusiliers	16-Jun-15	28	Son of Mrs. Mary Ann Jackson, of 19, Upper Winchester Rd., Catford, London.	Panel 19 and 33.	Ypres (Menin Gate) Memorial	Ieper, West-Vlaanderen
JONES, HENRY	Private	7452	1st Bn.	Royal Scots Fusiliers	16-Jun-15	unknown		Panel 19 and 33.	Ypres (Menin Gate) Memorial	Ieper, West-Vlaanderen
JUDD, PERCY JAMES	Private	12156	1st Bn.	Royal Scots Fusiliers	16-Jun-15	18	Son of Mrs. Elizabeth Judd, of 16, Duncan Rd., Aylestone, Leicester.	Panel 19 and 33.	Ypres (Menin Gate) Memorial	Ieper, West-Vlaanderen
KEITH, DANIEL MACLEAN	Private	9438	1st Bn.	Royal Scots Fusiliers	16-Jun-15	unknown		Panel 19 and 33.	Ypres (Menin Gate) Memorial	Ieper, West-Vlaanderen
KENNEDY, JAMES	Private	14942	1st Bn.	Royal Scots Fusiliers	16-Jun-15	20	Son of Mrs. Jessie Kennedy, of 85, McLean St., Glasgow.	Panel 19 and 33.	Ypres (Menin Gate) Memorial	Ieper, West-Vlaanderen
KETTLES, JAMES	Private	7116	"A" Coy. 1st Bn.	Royal Scots Fusiliers	16-Jun-15	39	Husband of Margaret Penrice McCue (formerly Kettles), of 18, Rossendale Rd., Pollokshaws, Glasgow.	Panel 19 and 33.	Ypres (Menin Gate) Memorial	Ieper, West-Vlaanderen

Full name	Rank	Service	Unit	Regiment	Date	Age	Additional	Grave	Cemetery	Locality
KILPATRICK, DAVID	Private	15978	1st Bn.	Royal Scots Fusiliers	16-Jun-15	23	Husband of Robertina Nixon Kilpatnck, of 3, Regent St., Greenock.	Panel 19 and 33.	Ypres (Menin Gate) Memorial	Ieper, West-Vlaanderen
LAW, WILLIAM ERNEST	Private	6126	1st Bn.	Royal Scots Fusiliers	16-Jun-15	33	Son of John and Sarah Ann Law, of 40, Bethulie Rd., Old Normanton, Derby.	Panel 19 and 33.	Ypres (Menin Gate) Memorial	Ieper, West-Vlaanderen
LEARMONTH, JOHN H.	Private	10893	1st Bn.	Royal Scots Fusiliers	16-Jun-15	21	Son of W. and Alexandra Theresa H. Learmonth, of 26, Gorgie Rd., Edinburgh.	Panel 19 and 33.	Ypres (Menin Gate) Memorial	Ieper, West-Vlaanderen
LEAVER, SAMUEL	Private	17964	1st Bn.	Royal Scots Fusiliers	16-Jun-15	30	Husband of Bertha Leaver, of 15, King's Bridge St., Mill Hill. Blackburn.	Panel 19 and 33.	Ypres (Menin Gate) Memorial	Ieper, West-Vlaanderen
LEES, JAMES	Private	A/6459	1st Bn.	Royal Scots Fusiliers	16-Jun-15	22	Son of Joseph and Jessie Smith Lees, of 19, Tower St., Kinning Park, Glasgow.	Panel 19 and 33.	Ypres (Menin Gate) Memorial	Ieper, West-Vlaanderen
LENNON, WILLIAM	Corporal	16804	1st Bn.	Royal Scots Fusiliers	16-Jun-15	41	Son of Peter Lennon, of Kilwinning, Ayrshire; husband of Margaret Stewart Lennon, of 84 Main St, Menstrie, Clackmannanshire.	Panel 19 and 33.	Ypres (Menin Gate) Memorial	Ieper, West-Vlaanderen
LOCK, ALEXANDER	Lance Corporal	8755	1st Bn.	Royal Scots Fusiliers	16-Jun-15	unknown		Panel 19 and 33.	Ypres (Menin Gate) Memorial	Ieper, West-Vlaanderen
MADDOCK, SAMUEL	Corporal	14771	1st Bn.	Royal Scots Fusiliers	16-Jun-15	unknown		Panel 19 and 33.	Ypres (Menin Gate) Memorial	Ieper, West-Vlaanderen
MATHER, THOMAS	Private	15692	1st Bn.	Royal Scots Fusiliers	16-Jun-15	unknown		Panel 19 and 33.	Ypres (Menin Gate) Memorial	Ieper, West-Vlaanderen
McCREADIE, ROBERT	Private	12647	1st Bn.	Royal Scots Fusiliers	16-Jun-15	unknown		Panel 19 and 33.	Ypres (Menin Gate) Memorial	Ieper, West-Vlaanderen

Name	Rank	Number	Bn.	Regiment	Date	Age	Details	Panel	Memorial	Location
McGHIE, JAMES	Private	12723	1st Bn.	Royal Scots Fusiliers	16-Jun-15	unknown		Panel 19 and 33.	Ypres (Menin Gate) Memorial	Ieper, West-Vlaanderen
McGIBBON, JAMES	Private	7246	1st Bn.	Royal Scots Fusiliers	16-Jun-15	unknown		Panel 19 and 33.	Ypres (Menin Gate) Memorial	Ieper, West-Vlaanderen
McGOLDRICK, EDWARD	Private	6679	1st Bn.	Royal Scots Fusiliers	16-Jun-15	unknown		Panel 19 and 33.	Ypres (Menin Gate) Memorial	Ieper, West-Vlaanderen
McILWRAITH, THOMAS	Private	16047	1st Bn.	Royal Scots Fusiliers	16-Jun-15	21	Son of Mrs. A. McIlwraith, of 184, Crookston St., Glasgow.	Panel 19 and 33.	Ypres (Menin Gate) Memorial	Ieper, West-Vlaanderen
McKENDRICK, THOMAS	Private	15677	1st Bn.	Royal Scots Fusiliers	16-Jun-15	unknown		Panel 19 and 33.	Ypres (Menin Gate) Memorial	Ieper, West-Vlaanderen
McLAREN, JAMES	Private	6543	1st Bn.	Royal Scots Fusiliers	16-Jun-15	18	Son of Mrs. Christina McLaren, of 3, North St. James St., Edinburgh.	Panel 19 and 33.	Ypres (Menin Gate) Memorial	Ieper, West-Vlaanderen
McMILLAN, JOHN	Private	15543	1st Bn.	Royal Scots Fusiliers	16-Jun-15	unknown		Panel 19 and 33.	Ypres (Menin Gate) Memorial	Ieper, West-Vlaanderen
MERRICK, JAMES HENRY	Private	8446	1st Bn.	Royal Scots Fusiliers	16-Jun-15	28	Son of James and Catherine Merrick, of 9, July St., Audley, Blackburn.	Panel 19 and 33.	Ypres (Menin Gate) Memorial	Ieper, West-Vlaanderen
METCALFE, JAMES R.	Lance Corporal	16909	1st Bn.	Royal Scots Fusiliers	16-Jun-15	25	Husband of Augusta Beatrice Metcalfe, of 15, Langstone Rd., Portsmouth.	Panel 19 and 33.	Ypres (Menin Gate) Memorial	Ieper, West-Vlaanderen
MORRIS, JAMES	Private	7317	1st Bn.	Royal Scots Fusiliers	16-Jun-15	39	Son of the late John and Annie Morris, of Craigstonholm, Lugar, Old Cumnock, Ayrshire; husband of Cathrine R. B. Bell Morris, of 68, Dunard St. North, Kelvinside, Glasgow. Served in the Sudan (1898) and the South African Campaigns, with Seaforth Highlanders.	Panel 19 and 33.	Ypres (Menin Gate) Memorial	Ieper, West-Vlaanderen

Full name	Rank	Service	Unit	Regiment	Date	Age	Additional	Grave	Cemetery	Locality
MORTON, THOMAS	Lance Corporal	9044	1st Bn.	Royal Scots Fusiliers	16-Jun-15	33	Son of William Morton; husband of Elizabeth Russell (formerly Morton), of 8, Seanor Lane, Lower Pilsley, Chesterfield.	Panel 19 and 33.	Ypres (Menin Gate) Memorial	Ieper, West-Vlaanderen
MULLEN, EDWARD	Private	8254	1st Bn.	Royal Scots Fusiliers	16-Jun-15	unknown		Panel 19 and 33.	Ypres (Menin Gate) Memorial	Ieper, West-Vlaanderen
MURPHY, JOHN	Private	8268	1st Bn.	Royal Scots Fusiliers	16-Jun-15	unknown		Panel 19 and 33.	Ypres (Menin Gate) Memorial	Ieper, West-Vlaanderen
MURRAY, PATRICK	Private	5614	"C" Coy. 1st Bn.	Royal Scots Fusiliers	16-Jun-15	39	Husband of Mary Ann Murray, of 107, Alexander St., Dundee.	Panel 19 and 33.	Ypres (Menin Gate) Memorial	Ieper, West-Vlaanderen
O'HALLORAN, MATTHEW	Private	11519	1st Bn.	Royal Scots Fusiliers	16-Jun-15	unknown		Panel 19 and 33.	Ypres (Menin Gate) Memorial	Ieper, West-Vlaanderen
PATERSON, JOHN	Private	A/7861	1st Bn.	Royal Scots Fusiliers	16-Jun-15	43	Son of the late Mr. and Mrs. William Paterson; husband of Jane Paterson, of 197, Centre St., South Side, Glasgow. Served in the South African Campaign.	Panel 19 and 33.	Ypres (Menin Gate) Memorial	Ieper, West-Vlaanderen
PAXTON, WILLIAM	Private	10459	1st Bn.	Royal Scots Fusiliers	16-Jun-15	unknown		Panel 19 and 33.	Ypres (Menin Gate) Memorial	Ieper, West-Vlaanderen
PERRYMAN, WILLIAM F.	Private	10351	1st Bn.	Royal Scots Fusiliers	16-Jun-15	19	Son of Mrs. K. Perryman, of 149, Finborough Rd., Kensington, London, and the late Mr. Perryman.	Panel 19 and 33.	Ypres (Menin Gate) Memorial	Ieper, West-Vlaanderen
PETRIE, JAMES	Private	16691	1st Bn.	Royal Scots Fusiliers	16-Jun-15	19	Son of Margaret Petrie, of 149, Toulford Rd., Cowdenbeath, Fife.	Panel 19 and 33.	Ypres (Menin Gate) Memorial	Ieper, West-Vlaanderen
PETTITT, ALBERT	Serjeant	8810	1st Bn.	Royal Scots Fusiliers	16-Jun-15	unknown		Panel 19 and 33.	Ypres (Menin Gate) Memorial	Ieper, West-Vlaanderen

Name	Rank	Number	Battalion	Regiment	Date	Age	Details	Panel	Memorial	Location
POLLOCK, JOHN	Private	7648	1st Bn.	Royal Scots Fusiliers	16-Jun-15	unknown		Panel 19 and 33.	Ypres (Menin Gate) Memorial	Ieper, West-Vlaanderen
QUINN, JOHN	Private	16675	1st Bn.	Royal Scots Fusiliers	16-Jun-15	unknown		Panel 19 and 33.	Ypres (Menin Gate) Memorial	Ieper, West-Vlaanderen
REYNOLDS, HUGH	Private	6760	1st Bn.	Royal Scots Fusiliers	16-Jun-15	unknown		Panel 19 and 33.	Ypres (Menin Gate) Memorial	Ieper, West-Vlaanderen
ROBERTSON, JOSEPH	Lance Corporal	16014	1st Bn.	Royal Scots Fusiliers	16-Jun-15	38	Husband of Christina Robertson, of 105, Standburn, Avonbridge, Stirlingshire.	Panel 19 and 33.	Ypres (Menin Gate) Memorial	Ieper, West-Vlaanderen
RODDIE, DAVID	Private	12433	1st Bn.	Royal Scots Fusiliers	16-Jun-15	unknown		Panel 19 and 33.	Ypres (Menin Gate) Memorial	Ieper, West-Vlaanderen
ROURKE, MICHAEL	Private	6093	1st Bn.	Royal Scots Fusiliers	16-Jun-15	unknown		Panel 19 and 33.	Ypres (Menin Gate) Memorial	Ieper, West-Vlaanderen
RUDKIN, JOSEPH H.	Private	11965	1st Bn.	Royal Scots Fusiliers	16-Jun-15	unknown		Panel 19 and 33.	Ypres (Menin Gate) Memorial	Ieper, West-Vlaanderen
SALMON, THOMAS	Private	9652	"A" Coy. 1st Bn.	Royal Scots Fusiliers	16-Jun-15	28	Son of Mr. and Mrs. W. S. Salmon, of 14, Upper Oxford St., South Bank, Yorks.	Panel 19 and 33.	Ypres (Menin Gate) Memorial	Ieper, West-Vlaanderen
SEGGIE, ROBERT	Private	15988	1st Bn.	Royal Scots Fusiliers	16-Jun-15	21	Son of John Seggie, of 10, Grahamfield Place, Beith, Ayrshire.	Panel 19 and 33.	Ypres (Menin Gate) Memorial	Ieper, West-Vlaanderen
SINCLAIR, JAMES	Lance Corporal	7459	1st Bn.	Royal Scots Fusiliers	16-Jun-15	unknown		Panel 19 and 33.	Ypres (Menin Gate) Memorial	Ieper, West-Vlaanderen
SLADE, ALBERT EDWARD	Private	17114	1st Bn.	Royal Scots Fusiliers	16-Jun-15	24	(Served as BUMSTEAD), Son of William and Louisa Slade, of 10, York Place, Chatham St., Reading.	Panel 19 and 33.	Ypres (Menin Gate) Memorial	Ieper, West-Vlaanderen
SMITH, ARTHUR	Private	16708	1st Bn.	Royal Scots Fusiliers	16-Jun-15	unknown		Panel 19 and 33.	Ypres (Menin Gate) Memorial	Ieper, West-Vlaanderen

Full name	Rank	Service	Unit	Regiment	Date	Age	Additional	Grave	Cemetery	Locality
SMITH, HENRY	Serjeant	95970	1st Bn.	Royal Scots Fusiliers	16-Jun-15	unknown		Panel 19 and 33.	Ypres (Menin Gate) Memorial	Ieper, West-Vlaanderen
SMITH, HUGH JOHN	Corporal	7907	"A" Coy. 1st Bn.	Royal Scots Fusiliers	16-Jun-15	39	Son of the late Hugh and Marion Smith; husband of Cecilia Gray Smith, of 175, Centre St., South Side, Glasgow.	Panel 19 and 33.	Ypres (Menin Gate) Memorial	Ieper, West-Vlaanderen
STEVENS, HENRY	Private	17417	"B" Coy. 1st Bn.	Royal Scots Fusiliers	16-Jun-15	27	Son of Alfred and Harriett Stevens, of 55, Gifford St., Hoxton, London; husband of Caroline Stevens, of 28, Somerford Houses, Brady St., Bethnal Green, London.	Panel 19 and 33.	Ypres (Menin Gate) Memorial	Ieper, West-Vlaanderen
SWINDELLS, JOSEPH	Private	7181	1st Bn.	Royal Scots Fusiliers	16-Jun-15	32	Husband of Ellen Swindells, of 93, Glebe St., Leigh, Lancs.	Panel 19 and 33.	Ypres (Menin Gate) Memorial	Ieper, West-Vlaanderen
THOMPSON, JOHN	Private	16669	1st Bn.	Royal Scots Fusiliers	16-Jun-15	18	Son of Mr. and Mrs. J. B. Thompson, of 8, Rosebank St. Dundee.	Panel 19 and 33.	Ypres (Menin Gate) Memorial	Ieper, West-Vlaanderen
THOMSON, GEORGE	Private	10007	"C" Coy. 1st Bn.	Royal Scots Fusiliers	16-Jun-15	25	Son of George Forbes Thomson and Ellen McFarlane Thomson, of 78, Potterton, Edinburgh.	Panel 19 and 33.	Ypres (Menin Gate) Memorial	Ieper, West-Vlaanderen
THORNTON, FRANK	Private	12673	1st Bn.	Royal Scots Fusiliers	16-Jun-15	22	Son of William and Annie Thornton, of 21, Garnock St., Dalry, Ayrshire.	Panel 19 and 33.	Ypres (Menin Gate) Memorial	Ieper, West-Vlaanderen
WARD, W.	Private	7633	1st Bn.	Royal Scots Fusiliers	16-Jun-15	39	Son of the late Peter and Agnes Ward; husband of Rose Ann Ward, of 14, Bristol St., Edinburgh.	Panel 19 and 33.	Ypres (Menin Gate) Memorial	Ieper, West-Vlaanderen
WATT, WILLIAM JOSEPH	Private	10309	1st Bn.	Royal Scots Fusiliers	16-Jun-15	23	Son of William and Mary Watt, of 5, Gibbs' Entry, Edinburgh.	Panel 19 and 33.	Ypres (Menin Gate) Memorial	Ieper, West-Vlaanderen

Name	Rank	Service Number	Battalion	Regiment	Date	Age	Notes	Panel/Grave	Memorial/Cemetery	Location
WATTERS, ALEXANDER	Private	10124	1st Bn.	Royal Scots Fusiliers	16-Jun-15	unknown		Panel 19 and 33.	Ypres (Menin Gate) Memorial	Ieper, West-Vlaanderen
WEBSTER, GEORGE WILLIAM	Second Lieutenant		"D" Coy. 1st Bn.	Royal Scots Fusiliers	16-Jun-15	32	Son of Mr. and Mrs. Webster, of 12, Lea St., Oldham; husband of Mrs. M. C. Webster, of 7, Killarney Parade, North Circular Rd., Dublin. Served in the South African Campaign.	LXI. C. 15.	Poelcapelle British Cemetery	Langemark-Poelkapelle, West-V.
WHYTE, PETER	Private	A/7770	1st Bn.	Royal Scots Fusiliers	16-Jun-15	unknown		Panel 19 and 33.	Ypres (Menin Gate) Memorial	Ieper, West-Vlaanderen
WILLIAMS, CHARLES	Private	11271	1st Bn.	Royal Scots Fusiliers	16-Jun-15	unknown		Panel 19 and 33.	Ypres (Menin Gate) Memorial	Ieper, West-Vlaanderen
WILSON, SAMUEL	Private	6347	1st Bn.	Royal Scots Fusiliers	16-Jun-15	unknown		Panel 19 and 33.	Ypres (Menin Gate) Memorial	Ieper, West-Vlaanderen
WORDSWORTH, FRED	Private	15734	1st Bn.	Royal Scots Fusiliers	16-Jun-15	18	Son of Ada Wordsworth.	Panel 19 and 33.	Ypres (Menin Gate) Memorial	Ieper, West-Vlaanderen
ALLDRED, ARTHUR	Private	2116	1st/4th Bn.	South Lancashire Regiment	16-Jun-15	24	Son of George Henry and Rose Ellen Alldred, of "The Hollies," Park Rd., Newton-le-Willows, Lancs.	Panel 37.	Ypres (Menin Gate) Memorial	Ieper, West-Vlaanderen
ARMSTRONG, RICHARD	Corporal	3507	2nd Bn.	South Lancashire Regiment	16-Jun-15	32	Husband of Mary Jane Latham (formerly Armstrong), of Bank Cottage, Green Lane, Maghull, Liverpool.	Panel 37.	Ypres (Menin Gate) Memorial	Ieper, West-Vlaanderen
BAILEY, WILLIAM	Serjeant	475	1st/4th Bn.	South Lancashire Regiment	16-Jun-15	38	Husband of Anne Matilda Bailey, of 56, Laira St., Warrington, Lancs.	Panel 37.	Ypres (Menin Gate) Memorial	Ieper, West-Vlaanderen
BAKER, P	Private	3435	2nd Bn.	South Lancashire Regiment	16-Jun-15	21	Son of John and Maria Baker, of 9, Arthur St., Oldham. Born at Hyde.	Enclosure No.2 IV. B. 14.	Bedford House Cemetery	Ieper, West-Vlaanderen

Full name	Rank	Service	Unit	Regiment	Date	Age	Additional	Grave	Cemetery	Locality
BANNISTER, JOHN EDWARD	Private	1785	1st/4th Bn.	South Lancashire Regiment	16-Jun-15	34	Son of George and Margaret Bannister.	Panel 37.	Ypres (Menin Gate) Memorial	Ieper, West-Vlaanderen
BATES, WILLIAM	Private	1328	"D" Coy. 1st/4th Bn.	South Lancashire Regiment	16-Jun-15	21	Brother of Alfred Bates, of 10, Dial St., Warrington, Lancs.	Panel 37.	Ypres (Menin Gate) Memorial	Ieper, West-Vlaanderen
BERRY, EDWARD	Private	1622	1st/4th Bn.	South Lancashire Regiment	16-Jun-15	21	Son of Thomas and Cecelia Berry, of 1, Shaw St., Warrington, Lancs.	Panel 37.	Ypres (Menin Gate) Memorial	Ieper, West-Vlaanderen
BRIMELOW, JOHN	Private	1261	1st/4th Bn.	South Lancashire Regiment	16-Jun-15	22	Son of Richard and Lydia Brimelow, of 22, Pickmere St., Warrington, Lancs.	Panel 37.	Ypres (Menin Gate) Memorial	Ieper, West-Vlaanderen
BROWN, WILLIAM	Private	1926	1st/4th Bn.	South Lancashire Regiment	16-Jun-15	44	Husband of Mary Jane Brown, of 12, Leonard St., Stockton Heath, Warrington, Lancs.	Panel 37.	Ypres (Menin Gate) Memorial	Ieper, West-Vlaanderen
CARTER, J. H.	Private	1593	4th Bn.	South Lancashire Regiment	16-Jun-15	unknown		LVI. F. 16.	Poelcapelle British Cemetery	Langemark-Poelkapelle, West-V.
CATTELL, HARRY	Private	2412	1st/4th Bn.	South Lancashire Regiment	16-Jun-15	unknown		Panel 37.	Ypres (Menin Gate) Memorial	Ieper, West-Vlaanderen
COYNE, JOHN THOMAS	Private	1814	1st/4th Bn.	South Lancashire Regiment	16-Jun-15	21	Son of John T. and Mary Elizabeth Coyne, of 159, Longford St., Warrington, Lancs.	Panel 37.	Ypres (Menin Gate) Memorial	Ieper, West-Vlaanderen
DAVIES, G.	Private	13225	2nd Bn.	South Lancashire Regiment	16-Jun-15	unknown		Enclosure No.2 VI. A. 63.	Bedford House Cemetery	Ieper, West-Vlaanderen
DODD, HENRY	Private	2074	"B" Coy. 1st/4th	South Lancashire	16-Jun-15	39	Husband of Celia Dodd, of 19, Clare St, John St, Warrington,	Panel 37.	Ypres (Menin Gate) Memorial	Ieper, West-Vlaanderen

Name	Rank	Service No.	Battalion	Regiment	Date	Age	Details	Panel	Memorial	Location
...ARTHUR	...	...	... Bn.	South Lancashire Regiment	...	unknown		Panel 37.	Ypres (Menin Gate) Memorial	Ieper, West-Vlaanderen
FROST, EDMUND LIONEL	Lieutenant			South Lancashire Regiment	16-Jun-15	24	Son of Dr. Edmund Frost, of Chesterfield, Eastbourne.	Panel 37.	Ypres (Menin Gate) Memorial	Ieper, West-Vlaanderen
GIBSON, WILLIAM	Private	2352	1st/4th Bn.	South Lancashire Regiment	16-Jun-15	20	Son of Annie Gibson, of 5, Mill St., Warrington, and the late James Gibson.	Panel 37.	Ypres (Menin Gate) Memorial	Ieper, West-Vlaanderen
GILL, THOMAS	Sergeant	533	"B" Coy. 1st/4th Bn.	South Lancashire Regiment	16-Jun-15	28	Husband of Aurora Naylor (formerly Gill), of 52, Forshaw St., Warrington.	Panel 37.	Ypres (Menin Gate) Memorial	Ieper, West-Vlaanderen
HAMBLETON, JOSEPH	Private	1273	1st/4th Bn.	South Lancashire Regiment	16-Jun-15	21	Son of Joseph and Sarah Hambleton, of 5, Bridgewater St., Warrington.	Panel 37.	Ypres (Menin Gate) Memorial	Ieper, West-Vlaanderen
HARDING, GILBERT	Private	2149	1st/4th Bn.	South Lancashire Regiment	16-Jun-15	18	Son of Joseph and Ann Jane Harding, of 14, Manchester Row, Vulcan, Earlestown, Newton-le-Willows, Lancs.	Panel 37.	Ypres (Menin Gate) Memorial	Ieper, West-Vlaanderen
HOLLOWELL, WILLIAM HENRY	Private	1884	1st/4th Bn.	South Lancashire Regiment	16-Jun-15	26	Son of Charlie and Mary Hollowell, of Warrington; husband of May Hollowell, of 2, Jockey St., Winwick Rd., Warrington.	Panel 37.	Ypres (Menin Gate) Memorial	Ieper, West-Vlaanderen
HOLMES, WALTER	Private	2573	1st/4th Bn.	South Lancashire Regiment	16-Jun-15	unknown		Panel 37.	Ypres (Menin Gate) Memorial	Ieper, West-Vlaanderen
HOUGHTON, JOHN JOSEPH	Private	2036	1st/4th Bn.	South Lancashire Regiment	16-Jun-15	unknown		Panel 37.	Ypres (Menin Gate) Memorial	Ieper, West-Vlaanderen
INCE, SYDNEY THOMAS	Corporal	1674	1st/4th Bn.	South Lancashire Regiment	16-Jun-15	26	Son of the late Moses Valentine Ince and Mary Agnes Ince, of 3, Tanner's Lane, Warrington.	Panel 37.	Ypres (Menin Gate) Memorial	Ieper, West-Vlaanderen

Full name	Rank	Service	Unit	Regiment	Date	Age	Additional	Grave	Cemetery	Locality
JACKSON, HENRY	Private	2386	1st/4th Bn.	South Lancashire Regiment	16-Jun-15	23	Son of Mrs. Elizabeth Jackson, of 46, Birchall St., Warrington.	Panel 37.	Ypres (Menin Gate) Memorial	Ieper, West-Vlaanderen
KNOWLES, CHARLES	Private	1736	1st/4th Bn.	South Lancashire Regiment	16-Jun-15	unknown		Panel 37.	Ypres (Menin Gate) Memorial	Ieper, West-Vlaanderen
LIBBITER, CHRISTOPHER	Serjeant	1138	1st/4th Bn.	South Lancashire Regiment	16-Jun-15	25	Son of Thomas and Helen Libbiter, of 104, Hardy St., Warrington.	Panel 37.	Ypres (Menin Gate) Memorial	Ieper, West-Vlaanderen
LIGHTFOOT, ALBERT	Private	1620	1st/4th Bn.	South Lancashire Regiment	16-Jun-15	21	Son of Mr. and Mrs. Enoch Lightfoot, of 58, Winwick St., Warrington.	Panel 37.	Ypres (Menin Gate) Memorial	Ieper, West-Vlaanderen
LITTLER, JOHN	Private	2123	1st/4th Bn.	South Lancashire Regiment	16-Jun-15	unknown		Panel 37.	Ypres (Menin Gate) Memorial	Ieper, West-Vlaanderen
MARSDEN, ELIJAH	Private	1321	"A" Coy. 1st/4th Bn.	South Lancashire Regiment	16-Jun-15	23	Son of Elijah and Elizabeth Ann Marsden, of 21, Alder Lane, Warrington.	Panel 37.	Ypres (Menin Gate) Memorial	Ieper, West-Vlaanderen
MIDDLETON, FRANK	Private	18028	2nd Bn.	South Lancashire Regiment	16-Jun-15	unknown		Panel 37.	Ypres (Menin Gate) Memorial	Ieper, West-Vlaanderen
MONKS, ARTHUR	Private	2309	1st/4th Bn.	South Lancashire Regiment	16-Jun-15	19	Son of James and Mary Jane Monks, of 91, Sharp St., Warrington.	Panel 37.	Ypres (Menin Gate) Memorial	Ieper, West-Vlaanderen
MOONEY, JAMES	Corporal	1127	2nd Bn.	South Lancashire Regiment	16-Jun-15	20	Son of Francis and Margaret Mooney.	I. E. 11.	Ypres Town Cemetery Extension	Ieper, West-Vlaanderen
PIERCE, SAMUEL	Private	91	1st/4th Bn.	South Lancashire Regiment	16-Jun-15	unknown		Panel 37.	Ypres (Menin Gate) Memorial	Ieper, West-Vlaanderen

Name	Rank	Service No.	Bn.	Regiment	Date	Age	Family	Memorial	Panel	Location
...HARRY	...	2213	...Bn.	South Lancashire Regiment	...15	18	Son of William and Rebecca Plumpton, of 81, Knutsford Rd., Warrington.	Ypres (Menin Gate) Memorial	Panel 37.	Ieper, West-Vlaanderen
RHODES, HARRY	Private	2793	1st/4th Bn.	South Lancashire Regiment	16-Jun-15	24	Son of James and Emma Rhodes, of 101, Slater St., Latchford; husband of Annie Rhodes, of 57, Oldham St., Latchford, Warrington.	Ypres (Menin Gate) Memorial	Panel 37.	Ieper, West-Vlaanderen
RYDER, JOHN	Private	125	1st/4th Bn.	South Lancashire Regiment	16-Jun-15	19	Son of George and Maud Ryder, of 25, Grafton St., Warrington.	Ypres (Menin Gate) Memorial	Panel 37.	Ieper, West-Vlaanderen
SHARP, JAMES	Private	1614	4th Bn.	South Lancashire Regiment	16-Jun-15	19	Son of Mr. and Mrs. John Sharp, of 57, West Avenue, Warrington.	Poelcapelle British Cemetery	LVI. F. 20.	Langemark-Poelkapelle, West-V.
SUMNER, GEORGE HENRY	Private	1486	"D" Coy. 1st/4th Bn.	South Lancashire Regiment	16-Jun-15	21	Son of Thomas and Clara Susannah Sumner, of 15, Robson St., Manchester Rd., Warrington.	Ypres (Menin Gate) Memorial	Panel 37.	Ieper, West-Vlaanderen
TAYLOR, GEORGE	Private	1612	1st/4th Bn.	South Lancashire Regiment	16-Jun-15	20	Son of Ann Taylor, of 5, Annie St., Warrington, and the late John Taylor.	Ypres (Menin Gate) Memorial	Panel 37.	Ieper, West-Vlaanderen
TAYLOR, ROBERT	Private	2306	1st/4th Bn.	South Lancashire Regiment	16-Jun-15	23	Son of Mr. and Mrs. R. Taylor, of 27, Leicester St., Warrington.	Ypres (Menin Gate) Memorial	Panel 37.	Ieper, West-Vlaanderen
TURNER, HAROLD	Private	1462	1st/4th Bn.	South Lancashire Regiment	16-Jun-15	20	Son of Joseph and Elizabeth Turner, of 24, Huntley St., Sankey, Warrington.	Ypres (Menin Gate) Memorial	Panel 37.	Ieper, West-Vlaanderen
WILLIAMS, F	Private	1650	4th Bn.	South Lancashire Regiment	16-Jun-15	unknown		Poelcapelle British Cemetery	LVI. F. 12.	Langemark-Poelkapelle, West-V.
WILSON, NORMAN	Private	1754	1st/4th Bn.	South Lancashire Regiment	16-Jun-15	19	Son of Mrs. L. A. Wall, of 283 Leicester St., Warrington.	Ypres (Menin Gate) Memorial	Panel 37.	Ieper, West-Vlaanderen

Full name	Rank	Service	Unit	Regiment	Date	Age	Additional	Grave	Cemetery	Locality
ANDERSON, ANDREW	Private	2824	1st/10th Bn.	The King's (Liverpool Regiment)	16-Jun-15	unknown		Panel 4 and 6.	Ypres (Menin Gate) Memorial	Ieper, West-Vlaanderen
ANDERSON, ANDREW STEWART	Major		10th Bn.	The King's (Liverpool Regiment)	16-Jun-15	unknown		Panel 4 and 6.	Ypres (Menin Gate) Memorial	Ieper, West-Vlaanderen
ANDERSON, JAMES EDWARD	Private	4252	1st/10th Bn.	The King's (Liverpool Regiment)	16-Jun-15	unknown		Panel 4 and 6.	Ypres (Menin Gate) Memorial	Ieper, West-Vlaanderen
ANDERSON, THOMAS COLIN	Private	4206	1st/10th Bn.	The King's (Liverpool Regiment)	16-Jun-15	20	Son of Thomas and Mrs. E. A. Anderson, of 37, Chesterfield Rd., Blackpool.	Panel 4 and 6.	Ypres (Menin Gate) Memorial	Ieper, West-Vlaanderen
ARMSTRONG, FRANK	Private	3748	1st/10th Bn.	The King's (Liverpool Regiment)	16-Jun-15	unknown		Panel 4 and 6.	Ypres (Menin Gate) Memorial	Ieper, West-Vlaanderen
BAILEY, RAMSTON CALMADY	Private	1942	1st/10th Bn.	The King's (Liverpool Regiment)	16-Jun-15	24	Son of Rawston Calmady Bailey and Elizabeth Bailey, of 11, Green Lane, Birkenhead; husband of W. M. Roberts (formerly Bailey), of 47, New Fox St., Birkenhead.	Panel 4 and 6.	Ypres (Menin Gate) Memorial	Ieper, West-Vlaanderen
BARBER, JOHN CHRISTIAN	Second Lieutenant		10th Bn.	The King's (Liverpool Regiment)	16-Jun-15	23	Son of Robert and Alice M. Barber, of The Red House, New Brighton, Wallasey.	Panel 4 and 6.	Ypres (Menin Gate) Memorial	Ieper, West-Vlaanderen
BARTLETT, GORDON	Corporal	3010	1st/10th Bn.	The King's (Liverpool Regiment)	16-Jun-15	21	Son of Mr. and Mrs. E. T. Bartlett, of 1, Sugnall St., Liverpool.	Panel 4 and 6.	Ypres (Menin Gate) Memorial	Ieper, West-Vlaanderen
BEBBINGTON, WILLIAM EDWARD	Private	3842	1st/10th Bn.	The King's (Liverpool Regiment)	16-Jun-15	unknown		Panel 4 and 6.	Ypres (Menin Gate) Memorial	Ieper, West-Vlaanderen
BELL, HERBERT H	Private	3209	1st/10th Bn.	The King's (Liverpool Regiment)	16-Jun-15	unknown		Panel 4 and 6.	Ypres (Menin Gate) Memorial	Ieper, West-Vlaanderen

Name	Rank	Service No.	Battalion	Regiment	Date	Age	Next of Kin	Panel	Memorial	Location
BLACK, WILLIAM	Private	4290	10th Bn.	The King's (Liverpool Regiment)	16-Jun-15	20	Stepson of Emily Black, of 8, Neptune St., Birkenhead, and the late John Charles Black.	Panel 4 and 6.	Ypres (Menin Gate) Memorial	Ieper, West-Vlaanderen
BRELLISFORD, GEORGE	Private	4068	1st/10th Bn.	The King's (Liverpool Regiment)	16-Jun-15	20	Son of the late Edward and Margaret Brellisford.	Panel 4 and 6.	Ypres (Menin Gate) Memorial	Ieper, West-Vlaanderen
BROADFOOT, DAVID	Private	4144	10th Bn.	The King's (Liverpool Regiment)	16-Jun-15	unknown		Panel 4 and 6.	Ypres (Menin Gate) Memorial	Ieper, West-Vlaanderen
BROOKES, ARTHUR ERNEST	Corporal	2722	1st/10th Bn.	The King's (Liverpool Regiment)	16-Jun-15	unknown		Panel 4 and 6.	Ypres (Menin Gate) Memorial	Ieper, West-Vlaanderen
BUCHANAN, ALAN	Private	3186	1st/10th Bn.	The King's (Liverpool Regiment)	16-Jun-15	25	Son of R. and Jeanie R. Buchanan, of Bosbury House, Ledbury, Herefordshire.	Panel 4 and 6.	Ypres (Menin Gate) Memorial	Ieper, West-Vlaanderen
BULLEN, WILLIAM FRANCIS	Second Lieutenant		10th Bn.	The King's (Liverpool Regiment)	16-Jun-15	23	Son of William and Elizabeth Eleanor Bullen, of Bidston, Birkenhead.	Panel 4 and 6.	Ypres (Menin Gate) Memorial	Ieper, West-Vlaanderen
CALLISTER, WILLIAM NELSON	Private	2574	"E" Coy. 1st/10th Bn.	The King's (Liverpool Regiment)	16-Jun-15	21	Son of Charles John Callister, of 42, Trafalgar Rd., Wallasey, and the late Martha Elizabeth Callister.	Panel 4 and 6.	Ypres (Menin Gate) Memorial	Ieper, West-Vlaanderen
CARRUTHERS, SIDNEY	Private	3130	1st/10th Bn.	The King's (Liverpool Regiment)	16-Jun-15	unknown		Panel 4 and 6.	Ypres (Menin Gate) Memorial	Ieper, West-Vlaanderen
CATTERALL, PERCIVAL	Private	3518	1st/10th Bn.	The King's (Liverpool Regiment)	16-Jun-15	unknown		Panel 4 and 6.	Ypres (Menin Gate) Memorial	Ieper, West-Vlaanderen
CHARNLEY, WILLIAM	Private	4242	1st/10th Bn.	The King's (Liverpool Regiment)	16-Jun-15	28	Son of William and Catherine A. Charnley, of 295, Wargrave Rd., Newton-le-Willows, Lancs.	Panel 4 and 6.	Ypres (Menin Gate) Memorial	Ieper, West-Vlaanderen

Full name	Rank	Service	Unit	Regiment	Date	Age	Additional	Grave	Cemetery	Locality
CHEETHAM, JOHN NORMAN	Private	3661	1st/10th Bn.	The King's (Liverpool Regiment)	16-Jun-15	25	Son of William Cheetham, of 56, Lugs More Lane, Toll Bar, St. Helens, and the late Martha Jane Cheetham.	Panel 4 and 6.	Ypres (Menin Gate) Memorial	Ieper, West-Vlaanderen
CLARKSON, JAMES	Private	3624	1st/10th Bn.	The King's (Liverpool Regiment)	16-Jun-15	22	Son of Richard and Lucy Clarkson, of 415, Queen's Drive, Walton, Liverpool.	Panel 4 and 6.	Ypres (Menin Gate) Memorial	Ieper, West-Vlaanderen
CLUNESS, JAMES	Private	4061	1st/10th Bn.	The King's (Liverpool Regiment)	16-Jun-15	24	Son of Elizabeth Cluness, of 52, Berkley St, Liverpool, and the late James Cluness.	Panel 4 and 6.	Ypres (Menin Gate) Memorial	Ieper, West-Vlaanderen
COATES, GEORGE WALLACE	Private	3223	1st/10th Bn.	The King's (Liverpool Regiment)	16-Jun-15	23	Son of John Stewart and Mary Gibson Coates.	Panel 4 and 6.	Ypres (Menin Gate) Memorial	Ieper, West-Vlaanderen
COLEMAN, GEORGE	Lance Corporal	3221	1st/10th Bn.	The King's (Liverpool Regiment)	16-Jun-15	25	Son of Edward and Kate Elizabeth Coleman, of 6, St. Mary's Avenue, Liscard, Wallasey.	Panel 4 and 6.	Ypres (Menin Gate) Memorial	Ieper, West-Vlaanderen
CONSTANTINE, CHARLES	Corporal	2705	1st/10th Bn.	The King's (Liverpool Regiment)	16-Jun-15	unknown		Panel 4 and 6.	Ypres (Menin Gate) Memorial	Ieper, West-Vlaanderen
COOKE, THOMAS	Private	4278	1st/10th Bn.	The King's (Liverpool Regiment)	16-Jun-15	26	Son of Sarah Cooke, of Hillcrest Mines, Alberta, Canada, and the late John Cooke.	Panel 4 and 6.	Ypres (Menin Gate) Memorial	Ieper, West-Vlaanderen
COOPER, HERBERT	Private	3227	1st/10th Bn.	The King's (Liverpool Regiment)	16-Jun-15	unknown		Panel 4 and 6.	Ypres (Menin Gate) Memorial	Ieper, West-Vlaanderen
CORSON, DONALD	Private	3806	1st/10th Bn.	The King's (Liverpool Regiment)	16-Jun-15	20	Son of Alexander and Florence Corson, of 45, Granby St, Liverpool.	Panel 4 and 6.	Ypres (Menin Gate) Memorial	Ieper, West-Vlaanderen
DAWKINS, RICHARD	Sergeant	1829	1st/10th Bn.	The King's (Liverpool Regiment)	16-Jun-15	unknown		Panel 4 and 6.	Ypres (Menin Gate) Memorial	Ieper, West-Vlaanderen

Name	Rank	Number	Battalion	Regiment	Date	Age	Family	Panel	Memorial	Location
DAWSON, THOMAS	Private	4141	1st/10th Bn.	The King's (Liverpool Regiment)	16-Jun-15	unknown	Son of the late William and Anne Dawson.	Panel 4 and 6.	Ypres (Menin Gate) Memorial	Ieper, West-Vlaanderen
DICKINSON, RONALD FRANCIS BICKERSTETH	Captain		"C" Coy. 10th Bn.	The King's (Liverpool Regiment)	16-Jun-15	27	Son of George and Mary Florence Dickinson, of Red How, Lamplugh, Cumberland.	Panel 4 and 6.	Ypres (Menin Gate) Memorial	Ieper, West-Vlaanderen
DICKSON, RONALD ARTHUR CAMPBELL	Private	3243	1st/10th Bn.	The King's (Liverpool Regiment)	16-Jun-15	23	Son of Capt. A. W. Dickson.	Panel 4 and 6.	Ypres (Menin Gate) Memorial	Ieper, West-Vlaanderen
DICKSON, THOMAS AUGUSTUS	Private	4292	1st/10th Bn.	The King's (Liverpool Regiment)	16-Jun-15	unknown		Panel 4 and 6.	Ypres (Menin Gate) Memorial	Ieper, West-Vlaanderen
DUNLOP, CHRISTIAN DALRYMPLE	Second Lieutenant		10th Bn.	The King's (Liverpool Regiment)	16-Jun-15	34	Son of Mrs. Julia R. Dunlop, of 23, Murrayfield Avenue, Edinburgh, and the late Capt. Hamilton Dunlop, R.N.	Panel 4 and 6.	Ypres (Menin Gate) Memorial	Ieper, West-Vlaanderen
ELLWOOD, CHARLES HASSALL	Private	4103	1st/10th Bn.	The King's (Liverpool Regiment)	16-Jun-15	23	Son of John Hassall Ellwood and Prudence H. Ellwood, of Lowwood House, Ulverston, Lancs.	Panel 4 and 6.	Ypres (Menin Gate) Memorial	Ieper, West-Vlaanderen
EVANS, JAMES COLLINGWOOD	Private	2988	1st/10th Bn.	The King's (Liverpool Regiment)	16-Jun-15	23	Son of Samuel and Gertrude Evans, of "Hardwick," Carpenter's Lane, West Kirby, Birkenhead.	Panel 4 and 6.	Ypres (Menin Gate) Memorial	Ieper, West-Vlaanderen
EVANS, OSWALD	Private	3259	1st/10th Bn.	The King's (Liverpool Regiment)	16-Jun-15	20	Son of John and Harriet Evans, of 9, Pagefield Rd., Wavertree, Liverpool.	Panel 4 and 6.	Ypres (Menin Gate) Memorial	Ieper, West-Vlaanderen
FLETT, DAVID	Company Sergeant Major	1033	1st/10th Bn.	The King's (Liverpool Regiment)	16-Jun-15	27	Son of James and Jane Flett, of 33, Lyttelton Rd., Aigburth, Liverpool.	Panel 4 and 6.	Ypres (Menin Gate) Memorial	Ieper, West-Vlaanderen

Full name	Rank	Service	Unit	Regiment	Date	Age	Additional	Grave	Cemetery	Locality
FOSTER, JAMES	Corporal	2554	1st/10th Bn.	The King's (Liverpool Regiment)	16-Jun-15	unknown		Panel 4 and 6.	Ypres (Menin Gate) Memorial	Ieper, West-Vlaanderen
FOTHERGILL, JAMES LESLIE	Private	2637	1st/10th Bn.	The King's (Liverpool Regiment)	16-Jun-15	unknown	Born at Highfields, Lenton, Notts., 30th Sept., 1886. Younger son of Ada Alice Fothergill, of Blundel lsands, Liverpool.	Panel 4 and 6.	Ypres (Menin Gate) Memorial	Ieper, West-Vlaanderen
GEMMELL, KENNETH ALEXANDER	Lieutenant		10th Bn.	The King's (Liverpool Regiment)	16-Jun-15	20	Son of John Edward and Margaret Ann Gemmell, of "Beechlands," Mossley Hill, Liverpool.	Panel 4 and 6.	Ypres (Menin Gate) Memorial	Ieper, West-Vlaanderen
GIBBONS, HENRY	Private	3286	1st/10th Bn.	The King's (Liverpool Regiment)	16-Jun-15	unknown		Panel 4 and 6.	Ypres (Menin Gate) Memorial	Ieper, West-Vlaanderen
GILLANDERS, HARVEY SISSON	Company Serjeant Major	85	1st/10th Bn.	The King's (Liverpool Regiment)	16-Jun-15	35	Son of the late George and Anna Gillanders, of 7, Harlech Rd., Blundelsands, Liverpool.	Panel 4 and 6.	Ypres (Menin Gate) Memorial	Ieper, West-Vlaanderen
GRAHAM, JOHN	Captain		10th Bn.	The King's (Liverpool Regiment)	16-Jun-15	38	Son of the late John and Mary Gilkison Graham.	Panel 4 and 6.	Ypres (Menin Gate) Memorial	Ieper, West-Vlaanderen
GRAVE, LAMONT	Private	3969	1st/10th Bn.	The King's (Liverpool Regiment)	16-Jun-15	23	Son of the late William and Margaret Ann Grave.	Panel 4 and 6.	Ypres (Menin Gate) Memorial	Ieper, West-Vlaanderen
GRIFFITHS, STANLEY THOMAS	Private	3921	"Y" Coy. 1st/10th Bn.	The King's (Liverpool Regiment)	16-Jun-15	24	Son of Mrs. Elizabeth J. Griffiths, of 249, County Rd., Walton, Liverpool.	Panel 4 and 6.	Ypres (Menin Gate) Memorial	Ieper, West-Vlaanderen
GRIFFITHS, WILLIAM MADOC	Lance Corporal	2818	1st/10th Bn.	The King's (Liverpool Regiment)	16-Jun-15	20	Son of William and Margaret Griffiths, of 16, Garmoyle Rd., Sefton Park, Liverpool.	Panel 4 and 6.	Ypres (Menin Gate) Memorial	Ieper, West-Vlaanderen
GROSSART, DOUGLAS	Private	3770	10th Bn.	The King's (Liverpool Regiment)	16-Jun-15	19	Son of Alexander and Mary Stuart Grossart, of 36, College Rd., Great Crosby, Liverpool. One of three	Panel 4 and 6.	Ypres (Menin Gate) Memorial	Ieper, West-Vlaanderen

Name	Rank	Service No.	Battalion	Regiment	Date	Age	Details	Panel	Memorial	Location
ERIC			Bn.	(Liverpool Regiment)				Panel 4 and 6.	Ypres (Menin Gate) Memorial	Ieper, West-Vlaanderen
HENERY, GRAHAM THORNTON	Private	3305	1st/10th Bn.	The King's (Liverpool Regiment)	16-Jun-15	27	Son of Percival Jeffery Thornton Henery and Maria Henery (nee Bullock). Educated at Cothill House, Abingdon, and Harrow School. Enlisted Aug, 1914.	Panel 4 and 6.	Ypres (Menin Gate) Memorial	Ieper, West-Vlaanderen
HEYWOOD, JOHN	Private	3112	1st/10th Bn.	The King's (Liverpool Regiment)	16-Jun-15	30	Son of the late John and Caroline Heywood, of 16, Dove Rd., Orrell Park, Liverpool.	Panel 4 and 6.	Ypres (Menin Gate) Memorial	Ieper, West-Vlaanderen
HIGGINS, GEOFFREY LEA	Private	3847	10th Bn.	The King's (Liverpool Regiment)	16-Jun-15	0		Panel 4 and 6.	Ypres (Menin Gate) Memorial	Ieper, West-Vlaanderen
HILL, GEOFFREY HAWKSLEY	Private	3299	1st/10th Bn.	The King's (Liverpool Regiment)	16-Jun-15	19	Son of Mr. W. F. and Mrs. M. A. Hawksley Hill, of "Edenholme," 3, St. George's Rd., Freshfield, Formby, Liverpool.	Panel 4 and 6.	Ypres (Menin Gate) Memorial	Ieper, West-Vlaanderen
HILL, ROLAND EDWIN	Private	2882	1st/10th Bn.	The King's (Liverpool Regiment)	16-Jun-15	18	Son of Edwin Henry and Anna Elizabeth Hill.	Panel 4 and 6.	Ypres (Menin Gate) Memorial	Ieper, West-Vlaanderen
HILLIS, SAMUEL DENYS	Private	3583	1st/10th Bn.	The King's (Liverpool Regiment)	16-Jun-15	0		Panel 4 and 6.	Ypres (Menin Gate) Memorial	Ieper, West-Vlaanderen
HOLMES, WILLIAM ARTHUR	Lance Corporal	2806	1st/10th Bn.	The King's (Liverpool Regiment)	16-Jun-15	0		Panel 4 and 6.	Ypres (Menin Gate) Memorial	Ieper, West-Vlaanderen
HORSLEY, JOHN HENRY	Private	3989	1st/10th Bn.	The King's (Liverpool Regiment)	16-Jun-15	25	Son of Bernard and Mary Horsley, of 58, Redston Rd., Hornsey, London.	Panel 4 and 6.	Ypres (Menin Gate) Memorial	Ieper, West-Vlaanderen
HUGHES, DAVID GEIRIONYDD	Private	4238	1st/10th Bn.	The King's (Liverpool Regiment)	16-Jun-15	21	Son of David S. and Helen Jane Hughes, of 44, Gainsborough Rd., Sefton Park, Liverpool.	Panel 4 and 6.	Ypres (Menin Gate) Memorial	Ieper, West-Vlaanderen

Full name	Rank	Service	Unit	Regiment	Date	Age	Additional	Grave	Cemetery	Locality
HUGHES, WILLIAM ROBERT	Private	2491	1st/10th Bn.	The King's (Liverpool Regiment)	16-Jun-15	20	Son of Cuthbert and Grace Hughes, of 171, Poulton Rd., Wallasey.	Panel 4 and 6.	Ypres (Menin Gate) Memorial	Ieper, West-Vlaanderen
IRVINE, WILLIAM HAROLD	Private	1682	"X" Coy. 1st/10th Bn.	The King's (Liverpool Regiment)	16-Jun-15	23	Son of John Bannatyne Irvine and Frances Ada Irvine, of 101, Blantyre Rd., Wavertree, Liverpool.	Panel 4 and 6.	Ypres (Menin Gate) Memorial	Ieper, West-Vlaanderen
JOHNSTON, GEORGE	Private	3092	1st/10th Bn.	The King's (Liverpool Regiment)	16-Jun-15	25	Son of Catherine Johnston, of 17, South Rd., Waterloo, Liverpool, and the late Lewis P. Johnston.	Panel 4 and 6.	Ypres (Menin Gate) Memorial	Ieper, West-Vlaanderen
JOHNSTONE, JAMES THOMAS	Private	3324	1st/10th Bn.	The King's (Liverpool Regiment)	16-Jun-15	unknown		Panel 4 and 6.	Ypres (Menin Gate) Memorial	Ieper, West-Vlaanderen
JONES, JOHN BLAKE	Sergeant	1538	"D" Coy. 1st/10th Bn.	The King's (Liverpool Regiment)	16-Jun-15	28	Son of Mr. and Mrs. J. H. Jones, of 8, Windsor Rd., Tue Brook, Liverpool.	Panel 4 and 6.	Ypres (Menin Gate) Memorial	Ieper, West-Vlaanderen
JONES, THOMAS FREDERICK	Sergeant	3326	1st/10th Bn.	The King's (Liverpool Regiment)	16-Jun-15	26	Son of Thomas Arrowsmith Jones and Edith Laura Jones, of 29, Horringford Rd., Aigburth, Liverpool. Born at Garston, Lancashire.	Panel 4 and 6.	Ypres (Menin Gate) Memorial	Ieper, West-Vlaanderen
JONES, WILLIAM	Private	2507	10th Bn.	The King's (Liverpool Regiment)	16-Jun-15	23	Son of Ann Jones, of Tanrallt Farm, Hoe, Holywell, Flints.	Panel 4 and 6.	Ypres (Menin Gate) Memorial	Ieper, West-Vlaanderen
KINCAID, HUGH	Private	3775	1st/10th Bn.	The King's (Liverpool Regiment)	16-Jun-15	unknown		Panel 4 and 6.	Ypres (Menin Gate) Memorial	Ieper, West-Vlaanderen
LARGE, VICTOR	Private	2872	"Z" Coy. 1st/10th Bn.	The King's (Liverpool Regiment)	16-Jun-15	19	Son of William Henry and Lassie Large, of 7, Oakfield Rd., Anfield, Liverpool.	Panel 4 and 6.	Ypres (Menin Gate) Memorial	Ieper, West-Vlaanderen

LAWSON, ROBERT	Private	3014	1st/10th Bn.	The King's (Liverpool Regiment)	16-Jun-15	unknown		Panel 4 and 6.	Ypres (Menin Gate) Memorial	Ieper, West-Vlaanderen
LAWSON, EDWARD GEMMELL	Corporal	1282	1st/10th Bn.	The King's (Liverpool Regiment)	16-Jun-15	25	Son of the late Thomas and Eleanor Margaret Lawson.	Panel 4 and 6.	Ypres (Menin Gate) Memorial	Ieper, West-Vlaanderen
LITTLE, ROLAND	Private	2332	1st/10th Bn.	The King's (Liverpool Regiment)	16-Jun-15	21	Son of Robert and Jessie Little, of 20, Thorburn Rd., New Ferry, Birkenhead.	Panel 4 and 6.	Ypres (Menin Gate) Memorial	Ieper, West-Vlaanderen
LORIMER, DAVID	Private	2711	1st/10th Bn.	The King's (Liverpool Regiment)	16-Jun-15	20	Son of Mr. and Mrs. David Lorimer, of 60, Lodge Lane, Liverpool.	Panel 4 and 6.	Ypres (Menin Gate) Memorial	Ieper, West-Vlaanderen
MACDONALD, DOUGLAS	Private	2675	1st/10th Bn.	The King's (Liverpool Regiment)	16-Jun-15	unknown		Panel 4 and 6.	Ypres (Menin Gate) Memorial	Ieper, West-Vlaanderen
MACKENZIE, WILLIAM ROBERT	Private	4260	1st/10th Bn.	The King's (Liverpool Regiment)	16-Jun-15	unknown		Panel 4 and 6.	Ypres (Menin Gate) Memorial	Ieper, West-Vlaanderen
MACKIE, CHARLES BODDINGTON	Private	4071	1st/10th Bn.	The King's (Liverpool Regiment)	16-Jun-15	23	Son of Alexander Boddington Mackie and Sarah Mackie.	Panel 4 and 6.	Ypres (Menin Gate) Memorial	Ieper, West-Vlaanderen
MacSWINEY, BRISCO FRANCIS	Private	3076	1st/10th Bn.	The King's (Liverpool Regiment)	16-Jun-15	30	Son of Lt. Col. Eugene Valentine MacSwiney (R.A.M.C.) and Florence Mary MacSwiney, of 7, Arnside Rd., Oxton, Birkenhead.	Panel 4 and 6.	Ypres (Menin Gate) Memorial	Ieper, West-Vlaanderen
MALCOLM, HAMILTON WILLIAM	Private	4075	1st/10th Bn.	The King's (Liverpool Regiment)	16-Jun-15	28	Son of Andrew Robert Hamilton Malcolm and Elizabeth Malcolm, of 63, Dacy Rd., Breakfield Rd. North, Liverpool.	Panel 4 and 6.	Ypres (Menin Gate) Memorial	Ieper, West-Vlaanderen
MARTIN, EDWARD	Private	3365	1st/10th Bn.	The King's (Liverpool Regiment)	16-Jun-15	unknown		Panel 4 and 6.	Ypres (Menin Gate) Memorial	Ieper, West-Vlaanderen

Full name	Rank	Service	Unit	Regiment	Date	Age	Additional	Grave	Cemetery	Locality
MASSEY, HUBERT HAMMOND	Sergeant	1766	1st/10th Bn.	The King's (Liverpool Regiment)	16-Jun-15	33	Son of George and Sarah Anne Massey, of "The Haven," 41, Stanley Avenue, Wallasey, Cheshire.	Panel 4 and 6.	Ypres (Menin Gate) Memorial	Ieper, West-Vlaanderen
MATTHEWS, HERBERT JAMES	Private	3950	1st/10th Bn.	The King's (Liverpool Regiment)	16-Jun-15	23	Son of Mr. E. J. and Alice Jane Matthews, of 258, Bedford Rd., Bootle, Liverpool.	Panel 4 and 6.	Ypres (Menin Gate) Memorial	Ieper, West-Vlaanderen
McADAM, JAMES CAMERON	Private	3028	1st/10th Bn.	The King's (Liverpool Regiment)	16-Jun-15	unknown		Panel 4 and 6.	Ypres (Menin Gate) Memorial	Ieper, West-Vlaanderen
McATEER, THOMAS	Private	4097	1st/10th Bn.	The King's (Liverpool Regiment)	16-Jun-15	23	Son of Thomas and Annie McAteer, of 43, Lenthall St., Walton, Liverpool.	Panel 4 and 6.	Ypres (Menin Gate) Memorial	Ieper, West-Vlaanderen
McGREGOR, ADAM	Private	4249	1st/10th Bn.	The King's (Liverpool Regiment)	16-Jun-15	23	Son of Adam and Mary McGregor, of 23, Ellis St., Kilmarnock.	Panel 4 and 6.	Ypres (Menin Gate) Memorial	Ieper, West-Vlaanderen
McKINNELL, BRYDEN	Captain		10th Bn.	The King's (Liverpool Regiment)	16-Jun-15	unknown		Panel 4 and 6.	Ypres (Menin Gate) Memorial	Ieper, West-Vlaanderen
McLACHLAN, JAMES	Corporal	3892	1st/10th Bn.	The King's (Liverpool Regiment)	16-Jun-15	36	Husband of Agnes Kirk McLachlan, of 92, Fazakerley Rd., Rice Lane, Liverpool.	Panel 4 and 6.	Ypres (Menin Gate) Memorial	Ieper, West-Vlaanderen
McNAB, DAVID GEORGE	Private	3098	1st/10th Bn.	The King's (Liverpool Regiment)	16-Jun-15	21	Son of David and Elizabeth McNab, of 47, Kensington, Liverpool.	Panel 4 and 6.	Ypres (Menin Gate) Memorial	Ieper, West-Vlaanderen
MEYER, STANLEY	Lance Corporal	3359	1st/10th Bn.	The King's (Liverpool Regiment)	16-Jun-15	unknown		Panel 4 and 6.	Ypres (Menin Gate) Memorial	Ieper, West-Vlaanderen
MONTEATH, FRANK	Private	4201	1st/10th Bn.	The King's (Liverpool	16-Jun-15	unknown		Panel 4 and 6.	Ypres (Menin Gate) Memorial	Ieper, West-Vlaanderen

Name	Rank	Service No.	Battalion	Regiment	Date	Age	Notes	Panel	Memorial	Location
MORRIS, CLEMENT	Corporal	2369	1st/10th Bn.	The King's (Liverpool Regiment)	16-Jun-15	unknown		Panel 4 and 6.	Ypres (Menin Gate) Memorial	Ieper, West-Vlaanderen
MORRIS, JOHN REGINALD	Private	3357	1st/10th Bn.	The King's (Liverpool Regiment)	16-Jun-15	30	Son of William and Margery Ellen Morris, of Ellesmere House, Denton's Green, St. Helens, Lancs.	Panel 4 and 6.	Ypres (Menin Gate) Memorial	Ieper, West-Vlaanderen
MORRIS, WILLIAM GEORGE	Private	3651	1st/10th Bn.	The King's (Liverpool Regiment)	16-Jun-15	unknown		Panel 4 and 6.	Ypres (Menin Gate) Memorial	Ieper, West-Vlaanderen
MUSKER, ARTHUR WOOD	Private	3951	1st/10th Bn.	The King's (Liverpool Regiment)	16-Jun-15	20	Son of George and Alice Ann Musker, of 5, Trevelyan St., Walton, Liverpool.	Panel 4 and 6.	Ypres (Menin Gate) Memorial	Ieper, West-Vlaanderen
NICOL, WILLIAM	Private	2487	"H" Coy. 1st/10th Bn.	The King's (Liverpool Regiment)	16-Jun-15	22	Reported missing after being in action at Hooge. Son of Alexander and Louisa Nicol, of 133, Wistaston Rd., Crewe.	Panel 4 and 6.	Ypres (Menin Gate) Memorial	Ieper, West-Vlaanderen
O'CONNOR, JACK	Private	4253	1st/10th Bn.	The King's (Liverpool Regiment)	16-Jun-15	20	Son of M. O'Connor, of Yambo Mantua, Castlerea, Co. Roscommon.	Panel 4 and 6.	Ypres (Menin Gate) Memorial	Ieper, West-Vlaanderen
ORCHARDSON, CHARLES	Private	4178	1st/10th Bn.	The King's (Liverpool Regiment)	16-Jun-15	unknown		Panel 4 and 6.	Ypres (Menin Gate) Memorial	Ieper, West-Vlaanderen
ORMESHER, CHARLES WILLIAM	Sergeant	1294	10th Bn.	The King's (Liverpool Regiment)	16-Jun-15	27	Son of James and Catherine Jane Ormesher of Clock Hotel, 93a Great George Street, Liverpool.	Addenda Panel 60.	Ypres (Menin Gate) Memorial	Ieper, West-Vlaanderen
PATERSON, JOHN SUTTON	Private	2725	1st/10th Bn.	The King's (Liverpool Regiment)	16-Jun-15	24	Son of Stephen Alexander and Annie Paterson, of 8, Dewlands Rd., Seaforth, Liverpool.	Panel 4 and 6.	Ypres (Menin Gate) Memorial	Ieper, West-Vlaanderen

Full name	Rank	Service	Unit	Regiment	Date	Age	Additional	Grave	Cemetery	Locality
PENDLETON, WILLIAM	Private	2779	1st/10th Bn.	The King's (Liverpool Regiment)	16-Jun-15	20	Son of John and Louisa Pendleton.	Panel 4 and 6.	Ypres (Menin Gate) Memorial	Ieper, West-Vlaanderen
PLEVIN, NORMAN	Private	3401	1st/10th Bn.	The King's (Liverpool Regiment)	16-Jun-15	20	Only son of John and Helena Plevin, of 23, Church Rd., Wavertree, Liverpool.	Panel 4 and 6.	Ypres (Menin Gate) Memorial	Ieper, West-Vlaanderen
POSTLETHWAITE, JOHN ARTHUR	Private	4194	1st/19th Bn.	The King's (Liverpool Regiment)	16-Jun-15	28	Son of Louisa Postlethwaite, of 2, Bowring St., Dingle, Liverpool, and the late John Postlethwaite.	Panel 4 and 6.	Ypres (Menin Gate) Memorial	Ieper, West-Vlaanderen
PRESTON, JOHN SYDNEY	Corporal	2395	1st/10th Bn.	The King's (Liverpool Regiment)	16-Jun-15	26	Son of John William and Marian Preston, of 5, Stratford Terrace, Dewsbury Rd., Leeds.	Panel 4 and 6.	Ypres (Menin Gate) Memorial	Ieper, West-Vlaanderen
PURTON, GODFREY LAWRENCE	Lance Corporal	3400	1st/10th Bn.	The King's (Liverpool Regiment)	16-Jun-15	28	Son of the late Rev. and Mrs. H. B. Purton, of Kinwarton, Alcester, Warwickshire.	Panel 4 and 6.	Ypres (Menin Gate) Memorial	Ieper, West-Vlaanderen
RASCHEN, JOHN GODWIN	Private	4040	1st/10th Bn.	The King's (Liverpool Regiment)	16-Jun-15	19	Son of John and Eleanor Raschen, of 44, Beresford Rd., Oxton, Birkenhead.	Panel 4 and 6.	Ypres (Menin Gate) Memorial	Ieper, West-Vlaanderen
REPPKE, JOHN	Lance Sergeant	2423	1st/10th Bn.	The King's (Liverpool Regiment)	16-Jun-15	21	Son of Mrs. Margaret Reppke, of 30, Pluto St., Kirkdale, Liverpool.	Panel 4 and 6.	Ypres (Menin Gate) Memorial	Ieper, West-Vlaanderen
RIDDOCH, DONALD ALEXANDER	Private	2468	1st/10th Bn.	The King's (Liverpool Regiment)	16-Jun-15	22	Son of Alexander and Annie Riddoch, of 113, Walton Lane, Kirkdale, Liverpool.	Panel 4 and 6.	Ypres (Menin Gate) Memorial	Ieper, West-Vlaanderen
RIGBY, NORMAN OGILVIE	Private	4274	1st/10th Bn.	The King's (Liverpool Regiment)	16-Jun-15	26	Son of Mrs. E. Rigby, of 9, Avenham Rd., Preston, Lancs., and the late Mr. J. W. E. Rigby.	Panel 4 and 6.	Ypres (Menin Gate) Memorial	Ieper, West-Vlaanderen

Name	Rank	Service No.	Battalion	Regiment	Date	Age	Family	Panel	Memorial	Location
RIMMER, FREDERICK	Corporal	3896	1st/10th Bn.	The King's (Liverpool Regiment)	16-Jun-15	30	Son of John S. and Catherine Rimmer, of 9, Danehurst Rd., Aintree, Liverpool.	Panel 4 and 6.	Ypres (Menin Gate) Memorial	Ieper, West-Vlaanderen
RIMMER, GEORGE FREDERIC	Private	3128	1st/10th Bn.	The King's (Liverpool Regiment)	16-Jun-15	21	Son of Henry and Fanny Rimmer, of 52, Wembley Rd., Mossley Hill, Liverpool.	Panel 4 and 6.	Ypres (Menin Gate) Memorial	Ieper, West-Vlaanderen
ROBERTS, ARCHIBALD YOUNGER	Private	1422	1st/10th Bn.	The King's (Liverpool Regiment)	16-Jun-15	24	Son of Archibald John and Flora Roberts, of 36, Camden St., Birkenhead.	Panel 4 and 6.	Ypres (Menin Gate) Memorial	Ieper, West-Vlaanderen
ROBERTS, PERCY ELWYN	Private	4010	1st/10th Bn.	The King's (Liverpool Regiment)	16-Jun-15	21	Son of David E. and Annie Roberts, of "Walton," 437, Breck Rd., Liverpool.	Panel 4 and 6.	Ypres (Menin Gate) Memorial	Ieper, West-Vlaanderen
ROBINSON, GEORGE	Private	4298	1st/10th Bn.	The King's (Liverpool Regiment)	16-Jun-15	unknown		Panel 4 and 6.	Ypres (Menin Gate) Memorial	Ieper, West-Vlaanderen
ROBINSON, RICHARD ALAN	Private	3555	1st/10th Bn.	The King's (Liverpool Regiment)	16-Jun-15	26	Son of Allen Hugh and Martha Robinson, of 319, Old Chester Rd., Rock Ferry, Birkenhead.	Panel 4 and 6.	Ypres (Menin Gate) Memorial	Ieper, West-Vlaanderen
ROGERSON, WILLIAM GEORGE	Private	3830	1st/10th Bn.	The King's (Liverpool Regiment)	16-Jun-15	21	Son of James and Marion Rogerson, of 42, Balliol Rd., Bootle, Liverpool.	Panel 4 and 6.	Ypres (Menin Gate) Memorial	Ieper, West-Vlaanderen
ROSS, JOHN CASSELLS	Private	2852	1st/10th Bn.	The King's (Liverpool Regiment)	16-Jun-15	18	Son of Alexander and Marion Ross, Of West Point, Colwyn Bay, Denbighshire.	Panel 4 and 6.	Ypres (Menin Gate) Memorial	Ieper, West-Vlaanderen
ROWE, THOMAS FREDERICK MORVIA	Private	3638	1st/10th Bn.	The King's (Liverpool Regiment)	16-Jun-15	24	Son of Miriam Annie Rowe, of Packet Lane, Perrin Downs, Marazion, Cornwall, and the late Thomas Rowe.	Panel 4 and 6.	Ypres (Menin Gate) Memorial	Ieper, West-Vlaanderen

Full name	Rank	Service	Unit	Regiment	Date	Age	Additional	Grave	Cemetery	Locality
RULE, STANLEY HERBERT	Private	3552	1st/10th Bn.	The King's (Liverpool Regiment)	16-Jun-15	unknown		Panel 4 and 6.	Ypres (Menin Gate) Memorial	Ieper, West-Vlaanderen
SANDS, EDWARD	Private	3879	1st/10th Bn.	The King's (Liverpool Regiment)	16-Jun-15	unknown		Panel 4 and 6.	Ypres (Menin Gate) Memorial	Ieper, West-Vlaanderen
SAVAGE, NORMAN BARNEWALL	Lance Corporal	2436	"A" Coy. 1st/10th Bn.	The King's (Liverpool Regiment)	16-Jun-15	20	Son of George William and Mary Elizabeth Savage, of 18, Brookfield Avenue, Great Crosby, Liverpool.	Panel 4 and 6.	Ypres (Menin Gate) Memorial	Ieper, West-Vlaanderen
SCHOFIELD, CLIFFORD	Private	4050	1st/10th Bn.	The King's (Liverpool Regiment)	16-Jun-15	19	Son of Mr. W. M. and Mrs. S. Schofield, of 48, Greenheys Rd., Wallasey, Cheshire.	Panel 4 and 6.	Ypres (Menin Gate) Memorial	Ieper, West-Vlaanderen
SHARP, THOMAS	Lance Corporal	1744	1st/10th Bn.	The King's (Liverpool Regiment)	16-Jun-15	24	Son of Thomas and Jane Sharp, of 106, Robson St., Liverpool.	Panel 4 and 6.	Ypres (Menin Gate) Memorial	Ieper, West-Vlaanderen
SIMPSON, ARTHUR NEIL	Corporal	3456	1st/10th Bn.	The King's (Liverpool Regiment)	16-Jun-15	22	Son of Joseph and Jessie Simpson, of School House, Cousland, Dalkeith, Midlothian.	Panel 4 and 6.	Ypres (Menin Gate) Memorial	Ieper, West-Vlaanderen
SIMPSON, WILLIAM ALEXANDER	Private	3515	1st/10th. Bn.	The King's (Liverpool Regiment)	16-Jun-15	27	Son of Janet and the late John Simpson. His brother Murray also fell.	Panel 4 and 6.	Ypres (Menin Gate) Memorial	Ieper, West-Vlaanderen
SINCLAIR, DAVID MCDONALD	Private	2670	10th Bn.	The King's (Liverpool Regiment)	16-Jun-15	20	Son of William and Johanna Sinclair, of 88, Langton Rd., Wavertree, Liverpool.	Panel 4 and 6.	Ypres (Menin Gate) Memorial	Ieper, West-Vlaanderen
SLADE, CHARLES	Private	3050	1st/10th Bn.	The King's (Liverpool Regiment)	16-Jun-15	22	Son of David and Ada J. Slade, of 4, Greasby Rd., Wallasey, Cheshire.	Panel 4 and 6.	Ypres (Menin Gate) Memorial	Ieper, West-Vlaanderen

Name	Rank	Number	Battalion	Regiment	Date	Age	Family	Panel	Memorial	Location
SLOAN, THOMAS ALEXANDER	Private	2582	1st/10th Bn.	The King's (Liverpool Regiment)	16-Jun-15	22	Son of John and Jane Ann Sloan, of 24, Rocky Bank Rd., Birkenhead.	Panel 4 and 6.	Ypres (Menin Gate) Memorial	Ieper, West-Vlaanderen
SMITH, JOSHUA	Private	2294	1st/10th Bn.	The King's (Liverpool Regiment)	16-Jun-15	23	Son of James and Jane Smith, of Erw Nant, Llanarmon-yn-Yale, Mold, Flints.	Panel 4 and 6.	Ypres (Menin Gate) Memorial	Ieper, West-Vlaanderen
SPEERS, JOHN GREGG	Lance Corporal	3737	1st/10th Bn.	The King's (Liverpool Regiment)	16-Jun-15	31	Son of John Reid Speers, of 30, Elizabeth St., Liverpool, and the late Amy Speers.	Panel 4 and 6.	Ypres (Menin Gate) Memorial	Ieper, West-Vlaanderen
STARK, WILLIAM WEBSTER	Private	2475	1st/10th Bn.	The King's (Liverpool Regiment)	16-Jun-15	21	Son of Margaret Stark, of 400, Edge Lane, Fairfield, Liverpool, and the late John S. Stark.	Panel 4 and 6.	Ypres (Menin Gate) Memorial	Ieper, West-Vlaanderen
STEPHENSON, HAROLD	Private	4020	1st/10th Bn.	The King's (Liverpool Regiment)	16-Jun-15	22	Son of Mrs. I. Stephenson, of 18, Shepston Avenue, Walton, Liverpool.	Panel 4 and 6.	Ypres (Menin Gate) Memorial	Ieper, West-Vlaanderen
THOMAS, FREDERICK	Private	3873	1st/10th Bn.	The King's (Liverpool Regiment)	16-Jun-15	26	Son of Philip and Elizabeth Thomas, of 2, Victoria Mount, Oxton, Birkenhead.	Panel 4 and 6.	Ypres (Menin Gate) Memorial	Ieper, West-Vlaanderen
THOMAS, HARRY EDWARD	Private	1563	1st/10th Bn.	The King's (Liverpool Regiment)	16-Jun-15	27	Son of Henry Edwin and Martha Thomas, of 10, Alverstone Avenue, Birkenhead.	Panel 4 and 6.	Ypres (Menin Gate) Memorial	Ieper, West-Vlaanderen
THORNE, HARRY	Lance Corporal	3477	1st/10th Bn.	The King's (Liverpool Regiment)	16-Jun-15	unknown		Panel 4 and 6.	Ypres (Menin Gate) Memorial	Ieper, West-Vlaanderen
TINSLEY, THOMAS SYDNEY	Private	2732	1st/10th Bn.	The King's (Liverpool Regiment)	16-Jun-15	20	Son of Thomas and Annie Tinsley; husband of Elsie Tinsley, of 96, Boswell St., Liverpool.	Panel 4 and 6.	Ypres (Menin Gate) Memorial	Ieper, West-Vlaanderen
TROTTER, HAROLD	Private	2865	1st/10th Bn.	The King's (Liverpool Regiment)	16-Jun-15	18	Son of Walter and Agnes Trotter, of 397, Edge Lane, Liverpool.	Panel 4 and 6.	Ypres (Menin Gate) Memorial	Ieper, West-Vlaanderen

Full name	Rank	Service	Unit	Regiment	Date	Age	Additional	Grave	Cemetery	Locality
TURNER, WILLIAM STEWART	Lieutenant		10th Bn.	The King's (Liverpool Regiment)	16-Jun-15	32	Son of Mr. W. N. Turner, of Mossley Hill Drive, Sefton Park, Liverpool. His brother Frederick also fell.	Panel 4 and 6.	Ypres (Menin Gate) Memorial	Ieper, West-Vlaanderen
TYNAN, JOHN	Private	4263	1st/10th Bn.	The King's (Liverpool Regiment)	16-Jun-15	unknown		Panel 4 and 6.	Ypres (Menin Gate) Memorial	Ieper, West-Vlaanderen
WATERHOUSE, FRANK	Private	3481	1st/10th Bn.	The King's (Liverpool Regiment)	16-Jun-15	20	Son of the Rev. George E. and Annie Waterhouse, of "Eads Heaton," Whitby, Yorks.	Panel 4 and 6.	Ypres (Menin Gate) Memorial	Ieper, West-Vlaanderen
WAUGH, WILLIAM JOHN JENKINS	Private	2671	"Y" Coy. 1st/10th Bn.	The King's (Liverpool Regiment)	16-Jun-15	19	Son of John and the late Mary A. Waugh.	Panel 4 and 6.	Ypres (Menin Gate) Memorial	Ieper, West-Vlaanderen
WHITE, JAMES PRINGLE	Second Lieutenant		10th Bn.	The King's (Liverpool Regiment)	16-Jun-15	35	Son of Mary Pringle White, of 77, Great King St., Edinburgh, and the late Hugh White.	Panel 4 and 6.	Ypres (Menin Gate) Memorial	Ieper, West-Vlaanderen
WHITTLE, THOMAS	Private	3957	1st/10th Bn.	The King's (Liverpool Regiment)	16-Jun-15	24	Son of William and Mary Whittle, of 10, Elmswood Rd., Aigburth, Liverpool.	Panel 4 and 6.	Ypres (Menin Gate) Memorial	Ieper, West-Vlaanderen
WILCOX, HENRY	Private	4057	1st/10th Bn.	The King's (Liverpool Regiment)	16-Jun-15	28	Son of Charles E. and Elizabeth A. Wilcox, of "Home Lea," Manor Lane, Liscard, Wallasey, Cheshire.	Panel 4 and 6.	Ypres (Menin Gate) Memorial	Ieper, West-Vlaanderen
WILSON, GEORGE ALBERT	Private	4056	1st/10th Bn.	The King's (Liverpool Regiment)	16-Jun-15	unknown		Panel 4 and 6.	Ypres (Menin Gate) Memorial	Ieper, West-Vlaanderen
WILSON, WILLIAM DENIS	Private	3483	1st/10th Bn.	The King's (Liverpool Regiment)	16-Jun-15	21	Son of John and Helen Wilson, of 41, Leece St., Liverpool.	Panel 4 and 6.	Ypres (Menin Gate) Memorial	Ieper, West-Vlaanderen

Name	Rank	Service No.	Battalion	Regiment	Date of Death	Age	Details	Memorial	Location
..., ROBERT	...	...	...	The King's (Liverpool) Regiment	16-Jun-15	unknown		Ypres (Menin Gate) Memorial	Ieper, West-Vlaanderen
WOOD, ROBERT ALLAN	Private	4166	1st/10th Bn.	The King's (Liverpool) Regiment	16-Jun-15	26	Son of Frederick and Hannah Wood, of 67, Marlborough Rd., Tue Brook, Liverpool.	Ypres (Menin Gate) Memorial Panel 4 and 6.	Ieper, West-Vlaanderen
WOODBURN, JAMES	Private	2321	1st/10th Bn.	The King's (Liverpool) Regiment	16-Jun-15	20	Son of William and Catherine Woodburn of 71, Lowther St., Crown St., Liverpool.	Ypres (Menin Gate) Memorial Panel 4 and 6.	Ieper, West-Vlaanderen
WRAY, ALFRED	Private	4300	1st/10th Bn.	The King's (Liverpool) Regiment	16-Jun-15	28	Son of Mr. W. H. and Mrs. E. Wray, of 16, Laburnham Grove, Bridge Rd., Litherland, Liverpool.	Ypres (Menin Gate) Memorial Panel 4 and 6.	Ieper, West-Vlaanderen
WRIGHT, GEORGE ANDERSON	Private	3502	1st/10th Bn.	The King's (Liverpool) Regiment	16-Jun-15	22	Son of James A. Wright, of 13, Imrie St., Walton, Liverpool. Employee of Messrs. Heinz, Ltd., Manchester.	Ypres (Menin Gate) Memorial Panel 4 and 6.	Ieper, West-Vlaanderen
WYATT, FRANCIS EDWARD	Lance Sergeant	2327	1st/10th Bn.	The King's (Liverpool) Regiment	16-Jun-15	23	Third son of Henry Wyatt, of Liverpool, and of Eleanor I. Wyatt, of 17, Dovedale Rd., New Brighton, Wallasey, Cheshire.	Ypres (Menin Gate) Memorial Panel 4 and 6.	Ieper, West-Vlaanderen
YATES, EVERARD	Private	4246	1st/10th Bn.	The King's (Liverpool) Regiment	16-Jun-15	unknown		Ypres (Menin Gate) Memorial Panel 4 and 6.	Ieper, West-Vlaanderen
GILLIES, HARRY	Private	9797	1st Bn	West Yorkshire Regiment (Prince of Wales's Own)	16-Jun-15	unknown		Ypres (Menin Gate) Memorial	Ieper, West-Vlaanderen
HETHERINGTON, MILTON	Private	Mar-90	1st Bn	West Yorkshire Regiment (Prince of Wales's Own)	16-Jun-15	unknown		Ypres (Menin Gate) Memorial	Ieper, West-Vlaanderen

Full name	Rank	Service	Unit	Regiment	Date	Age	Additional	Grave	Cemetery	Locality
HILTON, GEORGE HENRY	Private	9711	1st Bn	West Yorkshire Regiment (Prince of Wales's Own)	16-Jun-15	unknown	Son of John W. Hilton, of 57, Falcon St., Plaistow, London.		Ypres (Menin Gate) Memorial	Ieper, West-Vlaanderen
KAYE, J	Private	Mar-81	1st Bn	West Yorkshire Regiment (Prince of Wales's Own)	16-Jun-15	unknown			Ypres Town Cemetary Extension	Ieper, West-Vlaanderen
NEARY, WILLIAM JOSEPH	Private	Mar-36	1st Bn	West Yorkshire Regiment (Prince of Wales's Own)	16-Jun-15	unknown			Ypres (Menin Gate) Memorial	Ieper, West-Vlaanderen
RAW, ROBERT	Private	5440	1st Bn	West Yorkshire Regiment (Prince of Wales's Own)	16-Jun-15	unknown			Ypres (Menin Gate) Memorial	Ieper, West-Vlaanderen
SMITH, WILLIAM HENRY	Private	7136	1st Bn	West Yorkshire Regiment (Prince of Wales's Own)	16-Jun-15	unknown			Ypres (Menin Gate) Memorial	Ieper, West-Vlaanderen
TENNENT, OSWALD MONCRIEFF	2nd Lieutenant		1st Bn	West Yorkshire Regiment (Prince of Wales's Own)	16-Jun-15	unknown	Son of the Rev. R. P. T. Tennent, Vicar of Acomb. Yorks.		Ypres Town Cemetary Extension	Ieper, West-Vlaanderen
BAKER, HARRY	Private	19667	1st Bn	Wiltshire Regiment	16-Jun-15	unknown		Panel 53.	Ypres (Menin Gate) Memorial	Ieper, West-Vlaanderen
BARRADELL, ALBERT	Private	10089	1st Bn	Wiltshire Regiment	16-Jun-15	unknown		Panel 53.	Ypres (Menin Gate) Memorial	Ieper, West-Vlaanderen
BARTHOLOMEW, HENRY GEORGE	Lance Corporal	18307	1st Bn	Wiltshire Regiment	16-Jun-15	19	Son of Percival and Fanny Bartholomew, of Neston Lodge,	Panel 53.	Ypres (Menin Gate) Memorial	Ieper, West-Vlaanderen

					of 43, Sebright Avenue, London Rd., Worcester.			Ieper, West-Vlaanderen
BRAIN, WILLIAM THOMAS	Private	10402	1st Bn	Wiltshire Regiment	16-Jun-15	unknown		Panel 53.	Ypres (Menin Gate) Memorial	Ieper, West-Vlaanderen
BUSE, JAMES	Private	10428	1st Bn	Wiltshire Regiment	16-Jun-15	21	Son of John Buse.	Panel 53.	Ypres (Menin Gate) Memorial	Ieper, West-Vlaanderen
CHESTERMAN, HENRY JOHN	Private	Mar-32	1st Bn	Wiltshire Regiment	16-Jun-15	unknown		Panel 53.	Ypres (Menin Gate) Memorial	Ieper, West-Vlaanderen
CHIVERS, ALBERT VICTOR	Private	10417	"C" Coy.1st Bn.	Wiltshire Regiment	16-Jun-15	23	Son of George and Charlotte Chivers, of Stanton St. Bernard, Marlborough, Wilts.	Panel 53.	Ypres (Menin Gate) Memorial	Ieper, West-Vlaanderen
CHIVERS, WILLIAM JOSEPH	Private	8755	1st Bn	Wiltshire Regiment	16-Jun-15	unknown		Panel 53.	Ypres (Menin Gate) Memorial	Ieper, West-Vlaanderen
CLARK, SIDNEY WALTER	Private	10913	1st Bn	Wiltshire Regiment	16-Jun-15	31	Son of Fanny Clark, of 69, Derby Rd., South Woodford, Essex, and the late Donald Clark. Draughtsman, L. B. and S. C. Rly.	Panel 53.	Ypres (Menin Gate) Memorial	Ieper, West-Vlaanderen
COLE, JAMES	Private	3/824	1st Bn	Wiltshire Regiment	16-Jun-15	unknown	Husband of Daisy Sarah Cole, of 101, Bright St., Gorse Hill, Swindon.	Panel 53.	Ypres (Menin Gate) Memorial	Ieper, West-Vlaanderen
COLLARD, PERCY EDWARD	Private	10497	1st Bn	Wiltshire Regiment	16-Jun-15	unknown		Panel 53.	Ypres (Menin Gate) Memorial	Ieper, West-Vlaanderen
COOK, GEORGE	Private	10846	"D" Coy. 1st Bn.	Wiltshire Regiment	16-Jun-15	19	Son of Albert John and Agnes Ann Cook, of 25, The Street, All Cannings, Devizes, Wilts.	Addenda Panel 59.	Ypres (Menin Gate) Memorial	Ieper, West-Vlaanderen
COOK, WALTER JAMES	Private	8966	1st Bn	Wiltshire Regiment	16-Jun-15	21	Son of William and Emely Blanch Cook, of 8, John St., Swindon.	Panel 53.	Ypres (Menin Gate) Memorial	Ieper, West-Vlaanderen
COWTON, GEORGE	Private	19625	1st Bn	Wiltshire Regiment	16-Jun-15	22	Son of the late Joseph Arthur and Mary Cowton.	Panel 53.	Ypres (Menin Gate) Memorial	Ieper, West-Vlaanderen

Full name	Rank	Service	Unit	Regiment	Date	Age	Additional	Grave	Cemetery	Locality
CREW, HERBERT	Private	10628	"D" Coy. 1st Bn.	Wiltshire Regiment	16-Jun-15	19	Son of Mrs. Vines, of Showell Cottage, Lacock, Chippenham.	Panel 53.	Ypres (Menin Gate) Memorial	Ieper, West-Vlaanderen
CULLEY, PERCY SAMUEL	Serjeant	31579	1st Bn	Wiltshire Regiment	16-Jun-15	unknown		Panel 53.	Ypres (Menin Gate) Memorial	Ieper, West-Vlaanderen
DRAYTON, CHARLES HINDON	Private	19646	1st Bn	Wiltshire Regiment	16-Jun-15	19	Son of Mr. and Mrs. Hindon, of 4, Leicester St., Coventry.	Panel 53.	Ypres (Menin Gate) Memorial	Ieper, West-Vlaanderen
EMM, F	Private	9044	1st Bn	Wiltshire Regiment	16-Jun-15	unknown		Panel 53.	Ypres (Menin Gate) Memorial	Ieper, West-Vlaanderen
FARMER, WILLIAM	Private	10256	1st Bn	Wiltshire Regiment	16-Jun-15	unknown		Panel 53.	Ypres (Menin Gate) Memorial	Ieper, West-Vlaanderen
FERRIS, FRANK	Private	19737	1st Bn	Wiltshire Regiment	16-Jun-15	19	Son of James Ferris, of Marshall Lake Rd., Shirley, Birmingham.	Panel 53.	Ypres (Menin Gate) Memorial	Ieper, West-Vlaanderen
GIPSON, JOSEPH	Private	11893	1st Bn	Wiltshire Regiment	16-Jun-15	unknown		Panel 53.	Ypres (Menin Gate) Memorial	Ieper, West-Vlaanderen
GOODE, HARRY	Private	19633	1st Bn	Wiltshire Regiment	16-Jun-15	19	Son of Amy Goode, of II, Tunnel Cottages, Galley Common, Nuneaton, Warwickshire, and the late Henry Goode.	Panel 53.	Ypres (Menin Gate) Memorial	Ieper, West-Vlaanderen
GOULDEN, FRANK	Private	19692	1st Bn	Wiltshire Regiment	16-Jun-15	17	Son of James and Maria Goulden, of 7, Lansdowne St., Coventry.	Panel 53.	Ypres (Menin Gate) Memorial	Ieper, West-Vlaanderen
HAINES, EDWIN FELIX	Corporal	10332	1st Bn	Wiltshire Regiment	16-Jun-15	30	Son of the late Edwin and Emilie Haines.	Panel 53.	Ypres (Menin Gate) Memorial	Ieper, West-Vlaanderen
HARVEY, EDWARD GEORGE	Captain			Wiltshire Regiment	16-Jun-15	unknown		Panel 53.	Ypres (Menin Gate) Memorial	Ieper, West-Vlaanderen
HOBBS, JONATHAN	Private	4744	1st Bn	Wiltshire Regiment	16-Jun-15	37	Son of James Biggs Hobbs and Jane Hobbs.	VI. E. 13.	Aeroplane Cemetery	Ieper, West-Vlaanderen

Name	Rank	Number	Unit	Regiment	Date	Age	Details	Panel	Cemetery	Location
JOSEPH							Holliday; husband of the late Florence Emily Holliday.			
HUNT, JOHN	Private	11051	1st Bn	Wiltshire Regiment	16-Jun-15	unknown		Panel 53.	Ypres (Menin Gate) Memorial	Ieper, West-Vlaanderen
JAMES, HAROLD	Private	10587	1st Bn	Wiltshire Regiment	16-Jun-15	19	Brother of Alfred James.	Panel 53.	Ypres (Menin Gate) Memorial	Ieper, West-Vlaanderen
JOYCE, WILLIAM EDWARD	Lance Corporal	18309	1st Bn	Wiltshire Regiment	16-Jun-15	23	Son of Edward Archibald and Edith Anne Joyce, of The Greyhound, Broughton, Hants.	Panel 53.	Ypres (Menin Gate) Memorial	Ieper, West-Vlaanderen
JUDD, PERCY	Private	10574	1st Bn	Wiltshire Regiment	16-Jun-15	20	Son of Mr. H. and Mrs. A. Judd, of 119, Bynes Rd., South Croydon.	Panel 53.	Ypres (Menin Gate) Memorial	Ieper, West-Vlaanderen
LANG, CECIL	Private	10573	1st Bn	Wiltshire Regiment	16-Jun-15	26	Son of Mrs. Mercy Lang, of 46, Havelock St., Swindon.	Panel 53.	Ypres (Menin Gate) Memorial	Ieper, West-Vlaanderen
LANGFORD, WILLIAM	Lance Corporal	10345	1st Bn	Wiltshire Regiment	16-Jun-15	20	Son of Robert E. and Elizabeth Langford, of 48, Shillington St., Battersea, London.	Panel 53.	Ypres (Menin Gate) Memorial	Ieper, West-Vlaanderen
LATHAM, WILLIAM	Private	19641	1st Bn	Wiltshire Regiment	16-Jun-15	unknown		Panel 53.	Ypres (Menin Gate) Memorial	Ieper, West-Vlaanderen
LEGG, SEPTIMUS HENRY	Private	10435	1st Bn	Wiltshire Regiment	16-Jun-15	35	Husband of Lily L. K. Edwards (formerly Legg), of 29, Drew St., Swindon.	Panel 53.	Ypres (Menin Gate) Memorial	Ieper, West-Vlaanderen
LEGGETT, WILLIAM STEPHEN	Lance Corporal	10981	1st Bn	Wiltshire Regiment	16-Jun-15	22	Son of Mr. W. and Mrs. I. Leggett, of 282, Ferndale Rd., Swindon.	Panel 53.	Ypres (Menin Gate) Memorial	Ieper, West-Vlaanderen
LONG, THOMAS	Private	10521	1st Bn	Wiltshire Regiment	16-Jun-15	29	Son of Minnie Elizabeth Long, of South Cerney, Cirencester, Glos., and the late Worthy Long.	Panel 53.	Ypres (Menin Gate) Memorial	Ieper, West-Vlaanderen
MATTHEWS, STANLEY WELCOME	Private	10465	1st Bn	Wiltshire Regiment	16-Jun-15	unknown		Panel 53.	Ypres (Menin Gate) Memorial	Ieper, West-Vlaanderen

Full name	Rank	Service	Unit	Regiment	Date	Age	Additional	Grave	Cemetery	Locality
McCLENAGHAN, ARTHUR BRYANT PHELPS	Second Lieutenant		1st Bn	Wiltshire Regiment	16-Jun-15	unknown		Panel 53.	Ypres (Menin Gate) Memorial	Ieper, West-Vlaanderen
MILES, EDWARD	Sergeant	7957	1st Bn	Wiltshire Regiment	16-Jun-15	25	Son of Stanley and Emily Miles; husband of Kate Miles, of 48, Prince Alfred St., Gosport, Hants.	Panel 53.	Ypres (Menin Gate) Memorial	Ieper, West-Vlaanderen
MITCHELL, JOHN EDWARD	Private	9033	1st Bn	Wiltshire Regiment	16-Jun-15	22	Son of the late Mark Mitchell, of Countess Farm, Amesbury, Wilts.	Panel 53.	Ypres (Menin Gate) Memorial	Ieper, West-Vlaanderen
PHILLIMORE, FRANCIS WILLIAM	Sergeant	7166	1st Bn	Wiltshire Regiment	16-Jun-15	unknown		Panel 53.	Ypres (Menin Gate) Memorial	Ieper, West-Vlaanderen
PIKE, CHARLES	Private	18393	1st Bn	Wiltshire Regiment	16-Jun-15	28	Son of Eliza Pike, of Eastcott Hill, Swindon; husband of Frances A. Pike, of 63, Providence Row, Regent Place, Swindon.	Panel 53.	Ypres (Menin Gate) Memorial	Ieper, West-Vlaanderen
READ, F	Private	19724	1st Bn	Wiltshire Regiment	16-Jun-15	unknown		Panel 53.	Ypres (Menin Gate) Memorial	Ieper, West-Vlaanderen
ROWDEN, STANLEY CHARLES	Private	10302	1st Bn	Wiltshire Regiment	16-Jun-15	21	Son of Harry Rowden, of The Dairy, Croucheston Farm, Bishopstone, Salisbury.	Panel 53.	Ypres (Menin Gate) Memorial	Ieper, West-Vlaanderen
SAFE, FRANK REGINALD	Corporal	5815	1st Bn	Wiltshire Regiment	16-Jun-15	32	Son of Mrs. Martin.	Panel 53.	Ypres (Menin Gate) Memorial	Ieper, West-Vlaanderen
SHARPS, CHARLES	Private	9055	1st Bn	Wiltshire Regiment	16-Jun-15	unknown		Panel 53.	Ypres (Menin Gate) Memorial	Ieper, West-Vlaanderen
SILVERWOOD, HORACE	Private	19716	1st Bn	Wiltshire Regiment	16-Jun-15	22	Son of Uriah Silverwood, of 5, Moorwood Cottages, Chapel End, Nuneaton.	Panel 53.	Ypres (Menin Gate) Memorial	Ieper, West-Vlaanderen
STROUD, STEPHEN	Private	7884	1st Bn	Wiltshire Regiment	16-Jun-15	33	Son of Stephen and Elizabeth Stroud, of 34, Marlborough Rd.,	Panel 53.	Ypres (Menin Gate) Memorial	Ieper, West-Vlaanderen

Name	Rank	Number	Battalion	Regiment	Date	Age	Notes	Panel	Cemetery	Location
THOMAS				Regiment			Son of the late George and Ann Tomlin. Served in the South African Campaign.	Panel 53.	Ypres (Menin Gate) Memorial	Ieper, West-Vlaanderen
WASHBROOK, THOMAS	Private	19877	1st Bn	Wiltshire Regiment	16-Jun-15	unknown		Panel 53.	Ypres (Menin Gate) Memorial	Ieper, West-Vlaanderen
WEST, JAMES	Private	10180	1st Bn	Wiltshire Regiment	16-Jun-15	26	Husband of Maud Elizabeth Georgina West, of "Ideal," Cavendish Rd., Collier's Wood, Merton, London.	Panel 53.	Ypres (Menin Gate) Memorial	Ieper, West-Vlaanderen
WEST, WILLIAM WALTER	Private	9068	1st Bn	Wiltshire Regiment	16-Jun-15	20	Son of Margaret Mary West, of 23, Craven St., Kingsland St. Mary'S, Southampton.	Panel 53.	Ypres (Menin Gate) Memorial	Ieper, West-Vlaanderen
WHALE, ARTHUR	Lance Corporal	10582	1st Bn	Wiltshire Regiment	16-Jun-15	unknown		Panel 53.	Ypres (Menin Gate) Memorial	Ieper, West-Vlaanderen
WHITE, ALBERT	Private	19613	1st Bn	Wiltshire Regiment	16-Jun-15	unknown		Panel 53.	Ypres (Menin Gate) Memorial	Ieper, West-Vlaanderen
WHITE, HENRY ROBERT	Private	5937	"D" Coy. 1st Bn.	Wiltshire Regiment	16-Jun-15	32	Son of Harry and Emma White, of 152, Leaf Lane, Crockerton, Warminster; husband of Gertrude Mabel White, of 127, Shear Cross, Crockerton, Warminster, Wilts. Served in the South African Campaign.	Panel 53.	Ypres (Menin Gate) Memorial	Ieper, West-Vlaanderen
WHITE, ROBERT HENRY	Private	7382	1st Bn	Wiltshire Regiment	16-Jun-15	unknown		Panel 53.	Ypres (Menin Gate) Memorial	Ieper, West-Vlaanderen
WOOD, GEORGE THOMAS	Private	19882	1st Bn	Wiltshire Regiment	16-Jun-15	unknown	Son of the late Thomas John and Mary Wood.	Panel 53.	Ypres (Menin Gate) Memorial	Ieper, West-Vlaanderen
AINSWORTH, THOMAS WILLIAM	Sergeant	7904	"A" Coy. 3rd Bn.	Worcestershire Regiment	16-Jun-15	28	Son of Thomas William Ainsworth, of 96, Vicarage Rd., Aston; husband of Elizabeth Ainsworth, of 13, Montague St., Aston, Birmingham.	Panel 34.	Ypres (Menin Gate) Memorial	Ieper, West-Vlaanderen

Full name	Rank	Service	Unit	Regiment	Date	Age	Additional	Grave	Cemetery	Locality
BERESFORD, CHARLIE	Private	9255	3rd Bn.	Worcestershire Regiment	16-Jun-15	unknown		Panel 34.	Ypres (Menin Gate) Memorial	Ieper, West-Vlaanderen
BLACKFORD, SAMUEL	Private	8280	3rd Bn.	Worcestershire Regiment	16-Jun-15	25	Son of Samuel and Eliza Blackford; husband of Ada Elizabeth Rhodes (formerly Blackford), of 8, Bloomfield Rd., Tipton, Staffs.	Panel 34.	Ypres (Menin Gate) Memorial	Ieper, West-Vlaanderen
BOULTON, ALBERT	Lance Corporal	7525	3rd Bn.	Worcestershire Regiment	16-Jun-15	unknown		Panel 34.	Ypres (Menin Gate) Memorial	Ieper, West-Vlaanderen
BOWRON, HENRY	Private	8521	3rd Bn.	Worcestershire Regiment	16-Jun-15	unknown		Panel 34.	Ypres (Menin Gate) Memorial	Ieper, West-Vlaanderen
BUCKLER, ERIC WILSON	Captain		6th Bn. attd. 3rd Bn.	Worcestershire Regiment	16-Jun-15	30	Son of Adelaide Maud Ashwin (formerly Buckler), of Brackleys, Wickham Bishops, Essex, and the late John Henry Buckler (Capt. R.M.S.S.); husband of Muriel Irene Buckler, of Canada.	Panel 34.	Ypres (Menin Gate) Memorial	Ieper, West-Vlaanderen
COLE, ROBERT	Private	8984	3rd Bn.	Worcestershire Regiment	16-Jun-15	32	Husband of Elizabeth Lee Cole, of 21, Ulleswater Rd., Freehold, Lancaster.	Panel 34.	Ypres (Menin Gate) Memorial	Ieper, West-Vlaanderen
COLLINS, SYDNEY ALFRED	Private	6985	3rd Bn.	Worcestershire Regiment	16-Jun-15	31	Son of Henry and Emily Collins, of Shakespear Rd., Ladywood; husband of Florence Collins, of 58, Garbett St., Ladywood, Birmingham.	Panel 34.	Ypres (Menin Gate) Memorial	Ieper, West-Vlaanderen
CUMMINGS, FREDERICK	Private	20434	3rd Bn.	Worcestershire Regiment	16-Jun-15	36	Husband of Minnie J. Cummings, of 37, Arley Rd., Saltley, Birmingham.	Panel 34.	Ypres (Menin Gate) Memorial	Ieper, West-Vlaanderen
DAVIES, WILLIAM	Private	21285	3rd Bn.	Worcestershire Regiment	16-Jun-15	18	Son of Mrs. Margaret Davies, of 13, Furness Lane, Halesowen,	Panel 34.	Ypres (Menin Gate) Memorial	Ieper, West-Vlaanderen

Name	Rank	Service No.	Battalion	Regiment	Date	Age	Details	Panel	Memorial	Location
DAWES, RICHARD	Private	10961	3rd Bn.	Worcestershire Regiment	16-Jun-15	24	Son of the late William and Sarah Dawes, of 227, Bell Barn Rd., Birmingham.	Panel 34.	Ypres (Menin Gate) Memorial	Ieper, West-Vlaanderen
DENCH, JACK	Sergeant	11170	3rd Bn.	Worcestershire Regiment	16-Jun-15	27	Son of Alfred and Sophia Dench, of 13, Sharrocks St., Wolverhampton; husband of Nellie Dench, of 33, St. Alban's Square, Copenhagen St., Worcester.	Panel 34.	Ypres (Menin Gate) Memorial	Ieper, West-Vlaanderen
DUDLEY, CHARLES	Private	15985	3rd Bn.	Worcestershire Regiment	16-Jun-15	unknown		Panel 34.	Ypres (Menin Gate) Memorial	Ieper, West-Vlaanderen
DUNN, WILFRED	Private	19924	3rd Bn.	Worcestershire Regiment	16-Jun-15	25	Son of David Dunn, of 14, Dudley Field, Dudley Wood, Cradley Heath, Staffs.	Panel 34.	Ypres (Menin Gate) Memorial	Ieper, West-Vlaanderen
FREEMAN, HENRY	Serjeant	13202	3rd Bn.	Worcestershire Regiment	16-Jun-15	unknown		Panel 34.	Ypres (Menin Gate) Memorial	Ieper, West-Vlaanderen
GOULD, JOHN WILLIAM ROBERT	Private	16365	3rd Bn.	Worcestershire Regiment	16-Jun-15	22	Son of Robert and Ellen Gould, of 30, Hinton, Evesham, Worcs.	Panel 34.	Ypres (Menin Gate) Memorial	Ieper, West-Vlaanderen
GRIFFITHS, WILLIAM PERCY	Lance Corporal	11761	3rd Bn.	Worcestershire Regiment	16-Jun-15	23	Son of Mrs. Rosey Griffiths, of 3, Beaumont Terrace, Beach St., Ladywood, Birmingham.	Panel 34.	Ypres (Menin Gate) Memorial	Ieper, West-Vlaanderen
GRINNELL, JOHN	Private	8033	3rd Bn.	Worcestershire Regiment	16-Jun-15	28	Son of Charles and Cecilia Grinnell; husband of Rosina D. Steele (formerly Grinnell), of Ragley Park, Alcester, Warwickshire. Native of Birmingham.	Panel 34.	Ypres (Menin Gate) Memorial	Ieper, West-Vlaanderen
HANLEY, FRANCIS	Private	8940	"B" Coy. 3rd Bn.	Worcestershire Regiment	16-Jun-15	39	Husband of Ann Maria Hanley, of 4, George St., Dudley, Worcs.	Panel 34.	Ypres (Menin Gate) Memorial	Ieper, West-Vlaanderen
HARRIS, WILLIAM	Corporal	3098	3rd Bn.	Worcestershire Regiment	16-Jun-15	unknown		Panel 34.	Ypres (Menin Gate) Memorial	Ieper, West-Vlaanderen

Full name	Rank	Service	Unit	Regiment	Date	Age	Additional	Grave	Cemetery	Locality
HAYCOX, JOHN	Private	15064	3rd Bn.	Worcestershire Regiment	16-Jun-15	35	Husband of Mary Elizabeth Haycox, of 15, Coppice Lane, Cheslyn Hay, Walsall, Staffs.	Panel 34.	Ypres (Menin Gate) Memorial	Ieper, West-Vlaanderen
HAYLCR, GEORGE	Private	8490	3rd Bn.	Worcestershire Regiment	16-Jun-15	unknown	Son of Charles Haylor, of 76, Lily Rd., Yardley, Birmingham; husband of Alice Haylor, of 7 Back, 44, Ichnield Port Rd., Ladywood, Birmingham.	Panel 34.	Ypres (Menin Gate) Memorial	Ieper, West-Vlaanderen
HEATH, WILLIAM	Private	12141	3rd Bn.	Worcestershire Regiment	16-Jun-15	unknown		Panel 34.	Ypres (Menin Gate) Memorial	Ieper, West-Vlaanderen
HOMER, CALEB	Private	8888	3rd Bn.	Worcestershire Regiment	16-Jun-15	22	Son of Caleb Homer, of Stone St., Dudley, Worcs.	Panel 34.	Ypres (Menin Gate) Memorial	Ieper, West-Vlaanderen
JARVIS, THOMAS	Private	7299	3rd Bn.	Worcestershire Regiment	16-Jun-15	unknown		Panel 34.	Ypres (Menin Gate) Memorial	Ieper, West-Vlaanderen
JEFFERSON, WILLIAM	Private	14543	3rd Bn.	Worcestershire Regiment	16-Jun-15	21	Son of William and Elizabeth Jefferson, of 6/185, Ichnield Port Rd., Birmingham.	Panel 34.	Ypres (Menin Gate) Memorial	Ieper, West-Vlaanderen
JONES, ALBERT JAMES	Private	20217	3rd Bn.	Worcestershire Regiment	16-Jun-15	32	Son of Thomas and Emma Jones; husband of Minnie Jones, of Woodgreen, Worcester.	Panel 34.	Ypres (Menin Gate) Memorial	Ieper, West-Vlaanderen
JORDAN, HENRY	Lance Corporal	16379	"C" Coy. 3rd Bn.	Worcestershire Regiment	16-Jun-15	23	Son of William and Annie M. Jordan, of 7, Merstow Green, Evesham, Worcs.	Panel 34.	Ypres (Menin Gate) Memorial	Ieper, West-Vlaanderen
LACEY, FRANCIS JOHN	Private	8832	3rd Bn.	Worcestershire Regiment	16-Jun-15	unknown		Panel 34.	Ypres (Menin Gate) Memorial	Ieper, West-Vlaanderen
LORING, ROBERT NELE	Second Lieutenant		5th Bn.	Worcestershire Regiment	16-Jun-15	27	Son of Mr. John and Mrs. A. J. Loring, of "Longstile," Connaught Rd., Fleet, Hants.	Panel 34.	Ypres (Menin Gate) Memorial	Ieper, West-Vlaanderen

LUNNON, HARRY	Private	15393	3rd Bn.	Worcestershire Regiment	16-Jun-15	27	Son of Mrs. Elizabeth Lunnon, of Tredington, Shipston-on-Stour, Worcs.	Panel 34. Ypres (Menin Gate) Memorial	Ieper, West-Vlaanderen
MAISEY, HOWARD JAMES	Private	17411	3rd Bn.	Worcestershire Regiment	16-Jun-15	unknown		Panel 34. Ypres (Menin Gate) Memorial	Ieper, West-Vlaanderen
MASON, SAM	Private	18191	3rd Bn.	Worcestershire Regiment	16-Jun-15	unknown		Panel 34. Ypres (Menin Gate) Memorial	Ieper, West-Vlaanderen
MATTHEWS, JOHN HENRY	Private	14585	3rd Bn.	Worcestershire Regiment	16-Jun-15	23	Son of the late Mr. and Mrs. Frank Matthews, of 7, Lowesmoor Terrace, Lowesmoor, Worcester.	Panel 34. Ypres (Menin Gate) Memorial	Ieper, West-Vlaanderen
MILLERSHIP, THOMAS	Private	19962	3rd Bn.	Worcestershire Regiment	16-Jun-15	31	Son of the late Samuel and Hannah Millership; husband of Mary Ann Millership, of 262, Birchfield Lane, Oldbury, Birmingham.	Panel 34. Ypres (Menin Gate) Memorial	Ieper, West-Vlaanderen
MOULSON, WILLIAM JAMES	Private	8535	3rd Bn.	Worcestershire Regiment	16-Jun-15	unknown		Panel 34. Ypres (Menin Gate) Memorial	Ieper, West-Vlaanderen
MUIR, BASIL	Second Lieutenant		6th Bn. attd. 3rd Bn.	Worcestershire Regiment	16-Jun-15	unknown		Panel 34. Ypres (Menin Gate) Memorial	Ieper, West-Vlaanderen
MYRING, CHARLES SEYMOUR	Private	16382	"C" Coy. 3rd Bn.	Worcestershire Regiment	16-Jun-15	24	Son of Charles William and Margaret Myring, of 54, Lower Dartmouth St., Small Heath, Birmingham.	Panel 34. Ypres (Menin Gate) Memorial	Ieper, West-Vlaanderen
PERRY, ARTHUR JOHN MEWIS	Private	8330	3rd Bn.	Worcestershire Regiment	16-Jun-15	unknown		Panel 34. Ypres (Menin Gate) Memorial	Ieper, West-Vlaanderen
PINFOLD, ALFRED FREDERICK	Private	13413	3rd Bn.	Worcestershire Regiment	16-Jun-15	unknown		Panel 34. Ypres (Menin Gate) Memorial	Ieper, West-Vlaanderen
PITT, WILLIAM	Private	8942	3rd Bn.	Worcestershire Regiment	16-Jun-15	unknown		Panel 34. Ypres (Menin Gate) Memorial	Ieper, West-Vlaanderen

Full name	Rank	Service	Unit	Regiment	Date	Age	Additional	Grave	Cemetery	Locality
POLLARD, GEORGE WILLIAM	Private	13565	3rd Bn.	Worcestershire Regiment	16-Jun-15	20	Son of Mrs. M. Pollard, of 68, Chesterton Terrace, Plaistow, London, and of Serjt. G. W. J. Pollard, 9th Bn. Royal Warwickshire Regt.	Panel 34.	Ypres (Menin Gate) Memorial	Ieper, West-Vlaanderen
PRIEST, JOSEPH	Lance Corporal	8491	3rd Bn.	Worcestershire Regiment	16-Jun-15	24	Son of Josiah and Mira Priest, of 32 Newtown, Cradley Heath, Staffs.; husband of Anne Pearsall (formerly Priest), of 2, Elbow St., Old Hill, Staffs.	Panel 34.	Ypres (Menin Gate) Memorial	Ieper, West-Vlaanderen
REEVES, THOMAS	Private	9304	3rd Bn.	Worcestershire Regiment	16-Jun-15	unknown		Panel 34.	Ypres (Menin Gate) Memorial	Ieper, West-Vlaanderen
REYNOLDS, GEORGE	Private	12059	3rd Bn.	Worcestershire Regiment	16-Jun-15	unknown		Panel 34.	Ypres (Menin Gate) Memorial	Ieper, West-Vlaanderen
REYNOLDS, SIDNEY ROBERT	Lance Corporal	13441	3rd Bn.	Worcestershire Regiment	16-Jun-15	20	Son of Robert Reynolds, of 46A Renmuir St., Tooting Junction, London, and the late Alice Reynolds.	Panel 34.	Ypres (Menin Gate) Memorial	Ieper, West-Vlaanderen
RODEN, JOSEPH WILLIAM	Private	5422	3rd Bn.	Worcestershire Regiment	16-Jun-15	36	Son of Charles Henry and Elizabeth Roden, of 1 Back, 98, Ledsam St., Ladywood, Birmingham. One of three brothers who fell.	Panel 34.	Ypres (Menin Gate) Memorial	Ieper, West-Vlaanderen
SAVAGE, ALLEN	Lance Corporal	19074	3rd Bn.	Worcestershire Regiment	16-Jun-15	25	Son of Fanny Savage, of 81, Sidney Rd., Southport, and the late Robert Savage.	Panel 34.	Ypres (Menin Gate) Memorial	Ieper, West-Vlaanderen
SHAKESPEARE, JOHN	Private	19957	3rd Bn.	Worcestershire Regiment	16-Jun-15	32	Son of Edward Shakespeare; husband of Blanch Shakespeare, of 20, Hill St., Dudley, Worcs.	Panel 34.	Ypres (Menin Gate) Memorial	Ieper, West-Vlaanderen

Name	Rank	Number	Battalion	Regiment	Date	Age	Details	Panel	Memorial	Location
SPRAGG, GEORGE HENRY	Private	19710	3rd Bn.	Worcestershire Regiment	16-Jun-15	unknown		Panel 34.	Ypres (Menin Gate) Memorial	Ieper, West-Vlaanderen
STANTON, DONALD	Private	17825	3rd Bn.	Worcestershire Regiment	16-Jun-15	18	Son of George and Elizabeth Stanton, of 12, York Rd., Sidemoor, Bromsgrove, Worcs.	Panel 34.	Ypres (Menin Gate) Memorial	Ieper, West-Vlaanderen
STOKES, WILLIAM HENRY	Lance Corporal	10469	3rd Bn.	Worcestershire Regiment	16-Jun-15	unknown		Panel 34.	Ypres (Menin Gate) Memorial	Ieper, West-Vlaanderen
STONES, ENOCH	Corporal	8056	3rd Bn.	Worcestershire Regiment	16-Jun-15	unknown		Panel 34.	Ypres (Menin Gate) Memorial	Ieper, West-Vlaanderen
STUBBS, JAMES	Private	13046	3rd Bn.	Worcestershire Regiment	16-Jun-15	22	Son of Thomas G. and Elizabeth Stubbs, of 24, Alma Rd., Bethnal Green, London.	Panel 34.	Ypres (Menin Gate) Memorial	Ieper, West-Vlaanderen
SUMMERS, ISAAC	Private	8215	3rd Bn.	Worcestershire Regiment	16-Jun-15	28	Son of Isaac and Phoebe Summers, of 121, Oldbury Rd., West Smethwick. Staffs.; husband of Emily Summers, of 4, Woodgreen Villas, Camden St., Birmingham.	Panel 34.	Ypres (Menin Gate) Memorial	Ieper, West-Vlaanderen
TAYLOR, GEORGE	Lance Corporal	7832	3rd Bn.	Worcestershire Regiment	16-Jun-15	unknown		Panel 34.	Ypres (Menin Gate) Memorial	Ieper, West-Vlaanderen
TAYLOR, OSWIN	Private	15349	3rd Bn.	Worcestershire Regiment	16-Jun-15	unknown		Panel 34.	Ypres (Menin Gate) Memorial	Ieper, West-Vlaanderen
WALL, JOHN	Lance Corporal	9857	3rd Bn.	Worcestershire Regiment	16-Jun-15	25	Son of the late Mr. and Mrs. John Wall. Seven years' service in Malta and India.	Panel 34.	Ypres (Menin Gate) Memorial	Ieper, West-Vlaanderen
WIGGAN, JOSEPH	Private	7614	3rd Bn.	Worcestershire Regiment	16-Jun-15	unknown		Panel 34.	Ypres (Menin Gate) Memorial	Ieper, West-Vlaanderen
WIGGINS, ROY GAFFNEY ARGYLE	Corporal	13228	3rd Bn.	Worcestershire Regiment	16-Jun-15	unknown		Panel 34.	Ypres (Menin Gate) Memorial	Ieper, West-Vlaanderen

Full name	Rank	Service	Unit	Regiment	Date	Age	Additional	Grave	Cemetery	Locality
WILLIAMS, ADAM	Private	16489	3rd Bn.	Worcestershire Regiment	16-Jun-15	22	Son of the late Isaiah and Elizabeth Williams, of Holly Bush St., Cradley Heath, Staffs.	Panel 34.	Ypres (Menin Gate) Memorial	Ieper, West-Vlaanderen
WOOLLEY, JOE	Sergeant	11054	3rd Bn.	Worcestershire Regiment	16-Jun-15	25	Son of Leah Woolley, of 12, Beechlyn Beech Rd., Norton, Stourbridge, Worcs., and the late Samuel Woolley; husband of Mrs. E. Woolley, of Stratton Mill, Cirencester, Glos.	Panel 34.	Ypres (Menin Gate) Memorial	Ieper, West-Vlaanderen
WORKMAN, FREDERICK	Company Sergeant Major	5610	3rd Bn.	Worcestershire Regiment	16-Jun-15	34	Son of Thomas and Charlotte Workman, of Kortright House, Les Blanche, St. Martins, Guernsey, Channel Islands.	Panel 34.	Ypres (Menin Gate) Memorial	Ieper, West-Vlaanderen
JOHN, HUGH GRAHAM	2nd Lieutenant		3rd Bn.	York and Lancaster Regiment	16-Jun-15		Son of Dr. Hugh John and Margaret John, of Bronygarth, Llangennech, Carmarthenshire.	Panel 36 & 55	Ypres (Menin Gate) Memorial	Ieper, West-Vlaanderen

Appendix B

The Fallen German

RIR 246

Dienstgrad	Nachname	Vorname	Kompanie	Geburtsstadt und Bezirksstadt	Typ des Unfalls
Leutnant	Burry	Adolf R	2	Rottweil	Gefallen
Unteroffizer	Sing	Josef	2	Eglingen, Neresheim	Gefallen
Soldat	Dengler	Herman	2	Dunajewski, Rusland	Gefallen
Soldat	Geywitz	Christof	2	Temmenhausen, Blaubeuren	Gefallen
Soldat	Schepperle	Karl	2	Göppingen	Gefallen
Soldat	Striegel	Wilhelm	2	Tübingen	Gefallen
Soldat	Baier	Albert	2	Steinberg, Laupheim	Gefallen
Soldat	Gneiting	Ludwig	2	Fridenhausen, Nürtingen	Gefallen
Soldat	Käsz	Wilhelm	2	Oszweil, Ludwigsburg	Gefallen
Soldat	Kettenmann	Eugen	2	Stuttgart	Gefallen
Soldat	Müller	Daniel	2	Dettingen, Urach	Gefallen
Soldat	Rödl	Alois	2	Entschenreuth, Grafenau	Gefallen
Soldat	Stoll	Wilhelm	2	Alpirsbach, Oberndorf	Gefallen
Soldat	Weber	Ulrich	2	Neuweiler, Calro	Gefallen
Leutnant	Schellhorn	Karl	3	Waldsee, Ravensburg	Gefallen
Vzfeldw	Kircher	Heinrich	3	Bubenorbis, Hall	Gefallen
Unteroffizer	Raible	Josef	3	Nordstetten, Horb	Gefallen
Soldat	Allmendinger	Vaihingen	3	Horrheim, Baihingen	Gefallen
Soldat	Herrlinger,	Georg	3	Geislingen, Altenstadt	Gefallen
Soldat	Hirshmüller	Gottfried	3	Laussen, Besigheim	Gefallen
Soldat	Mann	Gottlieb	3	Kleinsachsenheim, Baibingen	inf. Verw. Gestorben
Soldat	Mann	Johannes	3	Erfingen, Ebingen	Gefallen

Rank	Surname	First Name		Place	Status
Soldat	Sauerzaps	Karl	3	Hobened, Ludwigsburg	Gefallen
Soldat	Elsässer	Karl	3	Baibingen a. Y.	Gefallen
Soldat	Schwab	Albert	3	Stuttgart	Gefallen
Soldat	Alt	Emil	4	Stuttgart	Gefallen
Soldat	Dibra	Adolf	4	Balingen	Gefallen
Soldat	Gaul	Emil	4	Bielefeld	Gefallen
Soldat	Grokmann	Christian	4	Emberg, Calw	Gefallen
Soldat	Hamburger	Josef	4	Nördlingen	Gefallen
Soldat	Kappler	Karl	4	Dobel, Neuenbürg	Gefallen
Soldat	Kuhnle	Eugen	4	Endersbach, Waiblingen	Gefallen
Soldat	Link	Hans	4	Grasbeuren, Baden	Gefallen
Soldat	Thumm	Wilhelm	4	Altenburg, Tübingen	Gefallen
Soldat	Trefz	Wilhelm	4	Ohmenhausen, Reutlingen	Gefallen
Vzfeldw	Harm	Hans	4	Winnenden, Waiblingen	Gefallen
Soldat	Braun	Alfred	4	Reutlingen	Gefallen
Soldat	Horrer	Karl	4	Reutlingen	Gefallen
Sergt	Metzger	Wilhelm	4	Saarbrüden	Gefallen
Soldat	Niebling	Emil	4	Reutlingen	Gefallen
Leutnant	Häussler	Eduard	5	Stuttgart, Cannstatt	Gefallen
Soldat	Hafner	Otto	5	Stuttgart	Gefallen
Unteroffizer	Flurer	Wilhelm	5	Eberbach, Küntzelsau	Gefallen
Gefreiter	Buntz	Georg	5	Niederstozingen, Ulm	Gefallen
Soldat	Dengler	Wilh	5	Mötzingen, Herrenberg	Gefallen
Soldat	Haist	Otto	5	Hirchauerwald, Freubenstadt	Gefallen
Soldat	Hutter	Paul	5	Stuttgart	Gefallen

Dienstgrad	Nachname	Vorname	Kompanie	Geburtstadt und Bezirksstadt	Typ des Unfalls
Soldat	Kunst	Willy	5	Elsteberg, Zwichau	Gefallen
Soldat	Leidig	Ernst	5	Steinbächle, Hall	Gefallen
Soldat	Müller	Christ	5	Denkendorf, Etzlingen	Gefallen
Soldat	Paule	Julius	5	Stuttgart, Unterfürkheim	Gefallen
Soldat	Siegle	Kuno	5	Enzrueihingen, Baihingen	Gefallen
Soldat	Streicher	Josef	5	Aalen	Gefallen
Soldat	Zwitzler	Wolf	5	Stuttgart	Gefallen
Unteroffizer	Berner	Paul	6	Rotenberg, Cannstatt	Gefallen
Unteroffizer	Blümle	Josef	6	Lippach,	Gefallen
Gefreiter	Horn	Karl Leibold	6	Höpfigheim, Marbach	inf. Verw. Gestorben
Soldat	Doster	Wilhelm	6	Neussen, Nürtingen	Gefallen
Soldat	Geiger	Eugen	6	Gmünd	Gefallen
Soldat	Gruner	Johannes	6	Obmenhausen, Reutlingen	Gefallen
Soldat	Hansal	Alois	6	Trauchgau, Füssen	Gefallen
Soldat	Huber	Friedrich	6	Böttingen, Spaichingen	Gefallen
Soldat	Obenaus	Willy	6	Gera	Gefallen
Soldat	Schlotz	Karl	6	Börtlingen, Göppingen	Gefallen
Soldat	Schrepper,	Herman	6	Hauteroda, Edartsberga	Gefallen
Soldat	Stoll	Gustav	6	Stammheim, Ludwigsburg	Gefallen
Soldat	Tretbar	Kurt	6	Teuritz, Lucka	Gefallen
Soldat	Schnatterer	Friedrich	7	Bönnigheim, Besigheim	inf. Verw. Gestorben
Gefreiter	Horn	Fritz Kurtz	8	Pfullingen, Reutlingen	Gefallen
Vzfeldw	Grathwohl	Hugo	8	Airheim, Spaichingen	Gefallen
Unteroffizer	Durst	Eugen	8	Stuttgart, Cannstatt	Gefallen

Unteroffizier	Kabe	Eduard	8	Friedrichsthal, Freubenstadt	Gefallen
Unteroffizier	Waller	Bernhard	8	Hirrlingen, Rottenburg	Gefallen
Gefreiter	Behringer	Otto	8	Wittenschwandt, St. Blasien	Gefallen
Gefreiter	Dengler	Jakob	8	Affstätt, Herrenberg	Gefallen
Soldat	Bauer	Paul	8	Stuttgart, Cannstatt	Gefallen
Soldat	Fischer	Albin	8	Pobershau, Marienberg	Gefallen
Soldat	Greitens	Georg	8	Ostenland, Paderborn	Gefallen
Soldat	Hauser	August	8	Hanweiler, Waiblingen	Gefallen
Soldat	Hettrich	Michael	8	Ennabeuren, Wünsingen	Gefallen
Soldat	Mundling	Josef	8	Feuerbach	Gefallen
Soldat	Nasz	Johann	8	Stratzburg	Gefallen
Soldat	Oppenländer	Albert	8	Hertmannsweiler, Waiblingen	Gestorben
Soldat	Schönleb	Karl	8	Gönningen, Tübingen	inf. Verw. Gestorben
Soldat	Vogel	Patrizius	8	Altmannsweiler, Ellwangen	Gefallen
Unteroffizier	Konz	Georg	9	Simmozheim	Gefallen
Gefreiter	Berger	Anton	9	Wollenbronn, Ravensburg	Gefallen
Soldat	Alt	Karl	9	Schlierbach, Göppingen	Gefallen
Soldat	Christens	Rudolf	9	Stuttgart	Gefallen
Soldat	Ehnis	Friedrich	9	Nagold	Gefallen
Soldat	Häbe	Hans	9	Upfingen, Urach	Gefallen
Soldat	Haas	Franz	9	Urlau, bish.	inf. Verw. Gestorben
Soldat	Heugel	Gottlob	9	Schmie, Maulbronn	Gefallen
Soldat	Igel	Mathäus	9	Grünkraut, Ravensburg	Gefallen
Soldat	Klauer	Christian	9	Herbrechtingen, Heidenheim	Gefallen
Soldat	Locher	Mathäus	9	Feuerbach, Stuttgart	Gefallen
Soldat	Maser	Ernst	9	Bergfelden, Sulz	Gefallen

Dienstgrad	Nachname	Vorname	Kompanie	Geburtsstadt und Bezirksstadt	Typ des Unfalls
Soldat	Steiniger	Ernst	9	Börnchen~Gummersbach	Gefallen
Soldat	Mittrupp	Ferdinand	9	Münster, Wests	Gefallen
Soldat	Brennenstuhl	Karl	10	Weil im Schönbuch	Gefallen
Soldat	Herold	Wilhelm	10	Unterbüden, Backnang	Gefallen
Soldat	Heinz	Gottlieb	10	Willmandingen, Raulbronn	Gefallen
Soldat	Seiber	Wilh.	10	Oberreute, Wangen	Gefallen
Soldat	Walter	Karl	10	Stuttgart	Gefallen
Unteroffizier	Gaiser	Franz	11	Göszlingen, Rottweil	Gefallen
Gefreiter	Johann	Kübler	11	Heitenheim	inf. Verw. Gestorben
Gefreiter	Michael	Küchle	11	Herlazhofen, Leutkirch	Gefallen
Soldat	Feile	Anton	11	Killingen, Ellwangen	inf. Verw. Gestorben
Soldat	Kretschmer	Martin	11	Winnenden, Waiblingen	Gefallen
Soldat	König	Georg	11	Haubach, Wangen	Gefallen
Soldat	Pfitzenmaier	Alfred	11	Berkheim, Eszlingen	Gefallen
Soldat	Beck	Emil	11	Rommelsbach, Tübingen	Gefallen
Soldat	Uttenweiler	Heinrich	11	Rottenburg	Gefallen
Unteroffizier	Rubach	Christian	12	Rochersteinsfeld, Neckarsulm	Gefallen
Soldat	Friesinger	Adam	12	Böttingen, Münsingen	Gefallen
Soldat	Hehl	Engelbert	12	Riedhausen, Saulgau	Gefallen
Soldat	Kugler	Karl	12	Cronbütte, Welzheim	Gefallen
Soldat	Lang	Gustav	12	Heumaden, Stuttgart	inf. Verw. Gestorben
Soldat	Rahm	Christian	12	Goldburghausen, Neresheim	Gefallen
Soldat	Schmohl	Richard	12	Biberach	Gefallen
Soldat	Schaich	Josef	12	Maselheim, Biberach	Gefallen
Soldat	Renz	Herman	12	Stuttgart~Gaisburg	Gefallen

Dienstgrad	Name	Vorname	Kompanie	Geburtsdatum & Ort	Todesdatum & Ort	Bemerkungen
Kriegsfreiw.	MÖGLE	Heinrich	1 Maschinengewehr	08.10.1894 Stuttgart-Gablenberg	16.06.1915 Bellewaarde	Gefallen
Ersatzreservist	BÖHM	Johannes	2 Kompanie	31.03.1882 Trochtelfingen (Neresheim)	16.06.1915 Bellewaarde	Gefallen
Ersatzreservist	HÄFNER	Georg	2 Kompanie	15.11.1888 Ilshofen (Hall)	16.06.1915 Bellewaarde	Gefallen
Unteroffizier	KIEFER	Karl	2 Kompanie	28.03.1878 Calmbach (Neuenbürg)	16.06.1915 Bellewaarde	Gefallen
Leutnant d. R.	SEEGER	Wilhelm	2 Kompanie	14.01.1890 Ravensburg	16.06.1915 Bellewaarde	Gefallen
Unteroffizier	KIRCHER	Ludwig	4 Kompanie	02.06.1882 Neulautern (Weinsberg)	16.06.1915 Bellewaarde	Gefallen
Landsturmm.	FAIST	Matthäus	5 Kompanie	30.03.1891 Glatten (Freudenstadt)	16.06.1915 Bellewaarde	vermisst, für tot erklärt
Landsturmm.	FRITZ	Adolf	5 Kompanie	29.11.1892 Böckingen (Heilbronn)	16.06.1915 Bellewaarde	Gefallen
Gefreiter	FRITZSCHE	Karl	5 Kompanie	28.10.1893 Offenbach (Hessen)	16.06.1915 Bellewaarde	Gefallen
Ersatzreservist	GEILE	Eugen	5 Kompanie	04.10.1888 Gmünd	16.06.1915 Bellewaarde	vermisst, für tot erklärt
Landsturmm.	GULDEN	Karl	5 Kompanie	12.05.1891 Ulm	16.06.1915 Bellewaarde	Gefallen

Dienstgrad	Name	Vorname	Kompanie	Geburtsdatum & Ort	Todesdatum & Ort	Bemerkungen
Gefreiter	HALLER	Erhardt	5 Kompanie	25.05.1890 Schwenningen (Tuttlingen)	16.06.1915 Bellewaarde	Gefallen
Wehrmann	HÜSSER	Alfons	5 Kompanie	13.05.1880 Wittelsheim (Elsaß)	16.06.1915 Bellewaarde	vermisst, für tot erklärt
Landsturmm.	LINDNER	Ernst	5 Kompanie	06.07.1883 Suhl (Schleusingen-Pr.)	16.06.1915 Bellewaarde	Gefallen
Landsturmm.	MAIER	Karl	5 Kompanie	07.08.1890 Alfdorf (Welzheim)	16.06.1915 Bellewaarde	Gefallen
Ersatzreservist	RÖTTER	Johann	5 Kompanie	01.07.1888 Treffelhausen (Geislingen)	16.06.1915 Bellewaarde	Gefallen
Ersatzreservist	RÜHLE	Otto	5 Kompanie	20.05.1893 Gmünd	16.06.1915 Bellewaarde	Gefallen
Ersatzreservist	SCHWARZ	Christian	5 Kompanie	19.09.1883 Korb (Waiblingen)	16.06.1915 Bellewaarde	Gefallen
Landsturmm.	ZIEGENHARDT	August	5 Kompanie	08.12.1884 Mühlhausen (Thüringen)	16.06.1915 Bellewaarde	Gefallen
Landsturmm.	BRODBECK	Hermann	7 Kompanie	03.04.1891 Haberschlacht (Brackenheim)	16.06.1915 Bellewaarde	Gefallen
Musketier	BRUNS	Enno	7 Kompanie	12.06.1894 Westlindel (Norden–Preußen)	16.06.1915 Bellewaarde	Gefallen
Ersatzreservist	BURGER	Wendelin	7 Kompanie	20.10.1887 Rieden	16.06.1915	Gefallen

Ersatzreservist	EBENHOCH	Johannes	7 Kompanie	08.01.1887 Aigeltshofen (Wangen)	16.06.1915 Bellewaarde	Gefallen
Ersatzreservist	FISCHER	Friedrich	7 Kompanie	24.07.1886 Ellrichshausen (Crailsheim)	16.06.1915 Bellewaarde	Gefallen
Landsturmm.	FISCHER	Karl	7 Kompanie	22.04.1890 Morbach (Backnang)	16.06.1915 Bellewaarde	Gefallen
Musketier	GLÄSSNER	Karl	7 Kompanie	01.10.1894 Herzberg (Osterode-Preuß.)	16.06.1915 Bellewaarde	Gefallen
Musketier	OLTMANNS	Johann	7 Kompanie	21.09.1894 Walle (Hannover-Preußen)	17.06.1915 Bellewaarde	Gefallen
Musketier	RAPP	Robert	7 Kompanie	07.05.1897 Eisenach (Thüringen)	16.06.1915 Bellewaarde	Gefallen
Musketier	ROSENBOOM	Enno	7 Kompanie	31.03.1894 Aurich (Oldenburg)	16.06.1915 Bellewaarde	Gefallen
Landsturmm.	SCHECK	Friedrich	7 Kompanie	20.09.1883 Rutesheim (Leonberg)	16.06.1915 Bellewaarde	Gefallen
Wehrmann	SCHMEZER	Johann	7 Kompanie	24.10.1876 Niedernhall (Künzelsau)	16.06.1915 Bellewaarde	vermisst, für tot erklärt
Wehrmann	SCHÖNEMANN	Gottlieb	7 Kompanie	17.06.1876 Bruch (Backnang)	16.06.1915 Bellewaarde	Gefallen
Musketier	STEIN	Heinrich	7 Kompanie	10.09.1894 Eschach (Gaildorf)	16.06.1915 Bellewaarde	Gefallen

Dienstgrad	Name	Vorname	Kompanie	Geburtsdatum & Ort	Todesdatum & Ort	Bemerkungen
Landsturmm.	TREFZ	Josef	7 Kompanie	21.05.1884 Magolsheim (Münsingen)	16.06.1915 Bellewaarde	Gefallen
Landsturmm.	FIGEL	Engelbert	9 Kompanie	07.11.1880 Kirchen (Ehingen)	16.06.1916 Bellewaarde	Gefallen
Landsturmm.	BIHL	Eugen	10 Kompanie	18.06.1890 Zimmern (Rottweil)	16.06.1915 Bellewaarde	Gefallen
Ersatzreservist	BRÄU	Josef	10 Kompanie	08.12.1889 Schlammering (Bayern)	16.06.1915 Bellewaarde	Gefallen
Musketier	HELLER	Georg	10 Kompanie	17.02.1893 Gerstetten (Heidenheim)	16.06.1915 Bellewaarde	Gefallen
Unteroffizier	JÜLLY	Karl	10 Kompanie	29.06.1891 Heßheim (Franken-thal-Pfalz-Bayern)	16.06.1915 Bellewaarde	Gefallen
Landsturmm.	KLEPSER	Ernst	10 Kompanie	16.03.1891 Pleidelsheim (Marbach)	16.06.1915 Bellewaarde	Gefallen
Musketier	ZELLER	Josef	10 Kompanie	22.08.1894 Unterschwarzach (Waldsee)	16.06.1915 Bellewaarde	Gefallen

Index

Ainslie, Lt Col 22
Aisne/River xv, 8, 30, 59, 62, 66, 74, 79, 80, 86, 102
Albrecht, Generalfeldmarschall 14
Allenby, Lt General Sir E xvi, 7, 8
Alsace 11, 18
Amiens 6, 11, 106
Armentieres 8, 59, 64, 115, 120
Army Cyclists Corps, 3rd Co 10
Army Group, 2 xvi
Army Order 324 10
Army Service Corps 106, 107
Artois 80
Aubers 39
Aubers Ridge 77, 102, 103
Augy 80
Aulnoye 100

Battery 23 xv
Bailleul 44, 45, 91, 110, 115, 120, 125
Baumann, Maj 18
Beauvois 73
Bedfordshire Regt 105
BEF 4, 6, 7, 8, 13, 23, 30, 57, 58, 59, 60, 62, 66, 67, 70, 71, 72, 74, 78, 79 80, 86, 100, 106, 107
Bellewaarde x, xi, xv, xvi, 9, 21, 60, 69, 77, 82, 105, 193
Bellewarde Farm 128, 135, 137, 138, 139, 142, 143, 159, 161, 164, 170, 172, 173, 180, 186, 187, 188, 198
Bellewaarde Lake v, 40, 127, 135, 145, 154, 168, 179, 181, 190
Bellewaarde Ridge v, xvi, 3, 19, 41, 127, 135, 193, 198
Berlin 45
Bethune 4
Birr Cross Road xvi, 98,127,153, 197
Blendecques 44
Bleu-Haute Maison 64
Bluff, The 9
Bois de Baudour 26

Boulogne 124
Brandhoek 60
Brenelle 59, 86
Brigade, 4 114
Brigade, 5 28, 29, 71
Brigade, 7 xvi, 10, 29, 67, 71, 72, 74, 76, 78, 83, 85, 88, 98, 101, 111, 127, 135, 137, 148, 149, 156, 169, 171, 172, 179, 181, 211
Brigade, 8 9, 29, 30, 68, 77, 79, 86, 91, 110, 135, 156, 192, 193, 212
Brigade, 9 xvi, 10, 24, 25, 26, 28, 33, 34, 41, 45, 50, 51, 52, 53, 54, 57, 66, 67, 69, 77, 79, 86, 98, 127, 128, 136, 137, 138, 148, 149, 156, 160, 161, 171, 172, 212
Brigade, Infantry 10 v
Brigade, 16 30, 74
Brigade, Infantry, 18 61, 64, 116, 117
Brigade 40 xv
Brigade, 41 10
Brigade, 42 10, 120, 183, 212
Brigade, 43 10
Brigade, 61 18
Brigade, 82 18
Brigade, 83 54
Brigade, 85 50, 69
Brigade, 150 55
Brigade, Cavalry, 4 32
Brigade, Cavalry 6 39
Brussels 11, 13, 78
Burgundy, Maj 18
Busseboom 50, 77, 130, 149

Calais 106, 107, 115
Calvart Farm 116
Cambridge Road xvi, 41, 127, 135, 146, 150, 151, 179
Cameron Highlanders, 1st Bn 8
Canadian Reg 3rd (Toronto) 119
Cassel 121
Caudry 73, 79, 86, 100, 101
Cavalry, 9th 100

Cavalry Regiment, 53 82
Chartres 30
Chassemy 80, 86
Chaulnes 4
Chasseurs 17
Chateau Wood 127
Chemin des Dames 79
Cherbourg 106
Cloth Hall 53, 97
Ciply 25, 57, 71, 78, 85, 100
Conde Canal 24, 66
Congreve VC, Brigadier-General 64
Corps, 1 28, 29, 67
Corps, 2 v, 6, 8, 29, 62, 64, 66, 67, 69, 100
Corps, 5 v, xvi, 93
Corps, 6 v
Corps, XV 14, 18
Courcelles 39
Coyelles 86
Croix Barbee 102, 103, 110
Cuesmes 24, 25, 57, 71
Curragh 6

de Castelnau, General 4
Devonshire Regt. 105
Dickebusch 32, 33, 40, 41, 53, 82, 84, 89, 105, 111, 122, 123
Division, 2 28, 74
Division, 3 xv, xvi, 8, 9, 21, 24, 28, 29, 34, 55, 57, 66, 69, 71, 74, 75, 77, 80, 83, 100, 111, 112, 211
Division, 5 xv, 28, 30, 75
Division, 6 61, 64, 136, 153, 179
Division, 7 68, 104, 136
Division, 14 125, 181, 198, 212
Division, 27 69
Division, 28 33, 50, 69
Divisional Artillery 10
Divisional Motor Ambulance Workshop Unit 10
Division, Infantry, 39 18
Division, Light 8 10
Division, Light 14 10
Divisional Troops, 76 9
Dormey House 104
Dragoon Guard, 3rd 112
Dranoutre 76
Dublin xv
Duke of Cornwall's LI, 1st Bn 60, 75
Dunkirk 4

Durham Light Infantry, 5 Bn 55, 64, 115, 116, 118

East Yorkshire Regt. 64, 116, 117, 120
Eecke 122
Elouges 72
Elzenwalle Chateau 84, 111
Ennetiers 64
Epremesnil 23
Erkelsbrugge 122
Escobecues 64
Estaires 31, 68
Etaples 106

Faremoutieres 74
Festubert 68
Field Ambulance, 7 10
Field Ambulance, 8 10
Field Ambulance, 9 10
Flanders 80
Forest of Crecy 74
Frameries 28, 29, 57, 66, 71, 78
Franco-Prussian War 11
French Army, 4 13
French Army, 5 13, 28, 57, 58, 78
French Army, 6 13, 58, 74
French Army, 10 4
French Corps, 36 v
French, Sir John v, 3, 4, 5, 6, 7, 28, 78, 109, 110, 120

Genly 72
German Army, 1 13, 36, 58
German Army, 2 13, 58
German Army, 4 14, 18
German Army, 6 67
Ghlin 36, 67
Givenchy 68, 75
Gordon, General 5
Gordon Highlanders, 1st Bn 82, 91, 92, 192
Gordon Highlanders, 1 / 4 90, 143, 161, 169, 170, 175, 177, 183, 187, 197, 210
Grapperies 83, 91
Gris-Pot 116
Guard Grenadiers (Queen Augusta's), 4th 40

Hagicourt 86
Haig, Sir Douglas 6
Haldane, Maj J A L xvi, 8, 9, 69
Ham 86

Index 325

Hamilton, Maj Gen Hubert I W 8
Harfleur 36, 57
Harmignies 100
Hauteville 74
Hazebrouck 8, 44, 64, 115
Hebuterne 4
Hell Fire Corner 98, 128, 140, 183, 193
Herlies 39, 67
Hess, Rudolf 67
Hill 60 v, 50, 51, 82, 93, 104, 183
Hill 62 x
Hitler, Adolf 67
Hollendischur Spur 111
Home Rule Ireland 99
Honourable Artillery Company, 1st Bn xvi, 10, 48, 68, 89, 108, 111, 127, 128, 130, 137, 154, 155, 156, 157, 161, 175, 187, 188, 191, 211
Hooge x, xvi, xvii, 9, 21, 39, 60, 77, 81, 82, 83, 88, 89, 98, 104, 112, 127, 128, 129, 130, 143, 156, 157, 198
Hooge Chateau 19, 127, 137, 153
Houpelines 119, 120
Hussars, 8 5, 84
Hussars, 15th 100
Hussars, 18 62
Hussars, 19 5, 87
Hyon 71

India 22
Infantry Regiment, 105 82
Infantry Regiment, 117 82
Infantry Regiment, 139 82
Irish Home Rule 6

Jaeger Division, 18 36
Jernappes 67
Joffre, General 4, 13, 58
Jordan, Maj 18

Kemmel 31, 32, 33, 40, 45, 48, 60, 81, 88, 93, 109, 110, 111, 122
Kensingtons, The 114
Kings Liverpool Regiment, 1/10 x, xvi, 10, 42, 53, 54, 55, 128, 130, 137, 208
Kings Own Yorkshire LI 103, 105, 124
Kings Royal Rifle Corps 113
Kings Royal Rifle Corps, 3rd Bn 93
Kings Royal Rifle Corps, 7th Bn 182, 187
King's Royal Rifle Corps, 9th Bn 10, 121, 123, 182, 184, 187, 210

King's Shropshire LI 10
Kings Shropshire LI, 2nd Bn 93
Kings Shropshire LI, 5th Bn 121, 123, 183, 184, 187, 210
Kitchener, Lord 6, 124

La Basse 68, 102, 103
Laclytte 83, 84, 91, 93
Lacoutre 80, 81, 102
La Longueville 24
Lancers, 12 87
Landrecies 57, 67
La Tourelle 75
La Verrier 64
La Vesse 116
Le Cateau 6, 28, 57, 73, 100
Le Havre 23, 43, 56, 57, 67, 70, 78, 83, 91, 99, 100, 115
Le Hue 74
Le Mans 106, 109
Leman, General Gerard 11
Le Touquet 65
Les Chapelles Bourbon 74
Liege 12
Life Guards, 2nd Bn 84
Lille 11
Lille Gate 50, 111, 128, 130, 182
Lincolnshire Regiment, 1st xvi, 10, 24, 29, 31, 32, 40, 48, 51, 56, 57, 58, 67, 89, 129, 130, 135, 137, 138, 147, 148, 149, 151, 152, 153, 164, 179, 192, 204, 208
Lindenhoek 31, 81
'List' Regiment 67
Liverpool Rifles 51
Liverpool Scottish x, 34, 49, 50, 52, 111, 129, 135, 138, 148, 149, 158, 159, 161, 164, 166, 167, 171, 176, 177, 178, 179, 180, 192
Locre 33, 60, 76, 88, 89, 92, 122
London Scottish 42, 114
Lorraine 11
Ludwigsburg 18
Lumigny 30
Lys 59, 75

Mackenzie, General 8
Maison Rouge Spur 38
Manchester Regt 75
Mariette 24, 25, 26, 57, 66
Markham, Brigadier-General CJ 10
Marne xv, 38, 58

Marne, River 13, 79
Maubeuge 57, 78
Maunory, General 13, 58
Maurois 100
McMahon, Brigadier-General NR 36
Menin Gate 50, 76, 98, 140
Menin Road x, xi, xvi, 3, 9, 59, 68, 77, 81, 89, 98, 112, 127, 129, 135, 136, 140, 143, 153, 154, 157, 182, 183, 184, 185, 191, 193
Messines Ridge 9, 59, 76, 81, 83, 88
Messines-Wytschaete Ridge 30
Meuse, River 11
Middlesex, 1st Bn 36
Middlesex, 4 Bn 36, 91, 92, 128
Missy 66
Mons xv, 6, 8, 10, 13, 24, 25, 26, 29, 36, 37, 38, 57, 71, 78, 79, 85, 100
Montigny 73, 100, 101
Mont St Aignon 85, 100
Mount Erebus 71, 72
Muensingen Camp 18

Namur 13
Neuve Chapelle 65, 80, 81, 87, 103
Nieuport 4, 18
Nimy 24, 36, 57
Nimy Bridge 36, 66
Norfolk Regiment 87
North Irish Horse, C Squadron 8
Northumberland Fusiliers, 1st xvi, 10, 22, 24, 29, 31, 32, 51, 52, 56, 57, 66, 67, 68, 80, 106, 111, 130, 135, 136, 137, 139, 140, 148, 149, 158, 159, 164, 171, 177, 179, 180, 192, 206
North Staffordshire Regt, 1/5 125
Nottingham and Derbyshire Regt 93, 116, 119, 120
Nouvelles 71, 100
Noyelles 24, 36

Oxford and Buckinghamshire LI, 5Bn 10, 121, 125, 182, 184, 185, 210
Ostrohove 124
Ouderdoom 40, 50, 111

Pargnan 63
Paris 11, 13, 58, 106
Parkhurst 36
Pataurages 28
Pilkem v
Pilly 39

Ploegsteert Wood 75, 76
Poperinghe 8, 77
Plumer, General Herbert xvi, 69
Plan XVII 11
Pont Logy 103
Portsmouth 22, 56
Presles 86
Prince of Wales Own Civil Service Rifles 114
Prussia 11

Quaregnon 25
Queen Victoria Rifles 53
Queen Westminster Rifles 43, 113, 114, 117, 120, 130, 138, 152, 154, 163, 176, 188, 193, 203, 211

Railway Wood xv, xvi, xvii, 127, 130, 136, 139, 140, 152, 158, 160, 164, 172, 179, 198
RAMC, Field Ambulance, 9th 10, 202
RAMC, No 19 Field Ambulance 8
Reserve Corps, XIII 14
Reserve Corps, XXVI 14
Reserve Corps, XVII 14, 17
Reserve Division, 53 16, 126
Reserve Division, 54 16, 17, 126, 218
Reserve Infantry Brigade, 107 17, 18
Reserve Infantry Brigade, 108 17, 18
Reserve Infantry Regiment, 245 17, 18
Reserve Infanterie Regiment 246 xv, xvii, 17,18,131, 137, 138, 144, 147, 154, 163, 165, 168, 174, 176, 186, 187, 190, 214
Reserve Infantry Regiment, 247 17, 18
Reserve Infanterie Regiment 248 xv, 17, 18, 126, 137, 162, 168, 179, 190, 217
Reserve Jaeger Battalion 26 xv, 17, 163, 176, 186, 187, 190, 191
Richebourg 81
Rifle Brigade, 1st Bn 93
Rifle Brigade, 9Bn 10, 121, 124, 182, 184, 185, 187, 210
Rouge Croix 110
Rouge Maison 101
Royal Field Artillery, 41st Battery 100
Royal Field Artillery, Cheshire Field Company xvi, 10, 20, 21, 75, 129, 136, 138, 151, 181, 206
Royal Field Artillery, Mortar Batteries 10
Royal Field Artillery, 23rd Brigade 57
Field Company, RE, 57 27
Royal Engineers x, 10, 55, 66, 87, 89, 181

Index 327

RE, (E(Air Line) Section 8
RE, Bridging Train No 2 8
RE, MN&O (Cable Sections) 8
Rouen 70, 99, 100, 106, 107, 115
Royal Dragoons 77
Royal Flying Corps, No 6 Squadron xvi, 127
Royal Fusiliers, 4th xvi, 24, 36, 39, 40, 41, 48, 56, 57, 67, 68 77, 80, 88, 130, 135, 136, 137, 146, 148, 149, 153, 164, 169, 177, 179, 181, 208
Royal Horse Artillery 73
Royal Horse Guards 77
Royal Irish Rifles, 2nd Bn 10, 39, 67, 71, 73, 74, 77, 79, 86, 88, 99, 101, 102, 103, 104, 105, 129, 137, 159, 171, 173, 178, 179, 181, 185, 193, 198, 211
Royal Medical Corps 10
Royal Navy 5
Royal Saxon Reserve Jaeger Bn, 26 126
Royal Scots, 2nd Bn 110, 192, 193
Royal Scots Fusiliers, 1st xvi, 10, 24, 40, 51, 54, 56, 57, 66, 67, 91, 100, 110, 111, 130, 135, 137, 143, 146, 148, 149, 159, 161, 164, 179, 186, 209
Royal Sussex 40, 62
Royal West Kents 74
Rozenhill Huts 93
Rue du Marais 75

Salle Port 112
Sanctuary Wood x, 54, 77, 82
Sanitary Section, 4a 10
Sars La Bruyere 29
Saxon/y 14, 17
Saxon Regt, 107 119
Schlieffen Plan 11, 13
Signal Company, 2nd Army HQ 8
Shaw, Brigadier-General FC 10, 31, 32
Shell Trap Farm 40
Shrapnell Corner 104
Shrapnell Farm 110
Siege Farm 92
Slaughter Hill 51, 52
Smith-Dorien, Sir Horace 6, 7, 30, 45, 87,110
Solesmes 72, 79
Somme 11
Southampton 23, 43, 56, 61
South Irish Horse, C Squadron 10
South Lancashire Regiment, 1/4th Bn 10, 50, 83, 137, 163, 164, 187, 199

South Lancashire Regiment, 2nd Bn 10, 71, 75, 76, 78, 79, 83, 87, 88, 100, 102, 104, 105, 128, 156, 192, 209
South Staffordshire Reg, 1/5 125
Spanbroekmolen 76, 81, 88, 110
Spur of Spanbroekmolen 111
St Aignan 100
St Eloi 9, 35, 52, 53, 81, 82, 111
Stewart, Sir Herbert 5
St Julien Front 34
St Nazaire 61, 109
St Omer 43, 63, 64, 109, 115
St Valery 106
St Waast 72, 85
Strasburg 18
Stuttgart 18
Sudan Campaign 5
Suffolk Regiment, 2nd Bn 91, 92

Tannenburg 13

UDF 99
Uhlans 72, 86
Ulster 6, 99
Unter-Elsässisches Infanterie-Regiment Nr. 132 14, 18, 137, 138, 142, 145, 162, 168, 170, 174, 176, 190, 213

Vailly 66, 67, 74, 79, 80, 86
Varenne 86
Varnbuler und Hemmingen, Maj (Rtd) 18
Vauxelles 67
Vermand 86
Veuilly 38
Vic Sur Aisne 86
Vieille Chapelle 39
Vieux Berquin 64
Vlamertinghe 53, 55, 93, 122, 123, 124, 140, 182, 192, 193
von Bulow, General 13, 58
von Carlowitz, Generalleutnant Adolf 14, 15
von der Holzhausen, Maj 18
von Falkenhayn, Erich George Sebastian 14
von Hill, Baron 18
von Kluck, General 13, 58
von Lutzow, Maj 18
von Roschman, Baron, Col D 18
von Schubert, General der Artillerie, Richard 14, 16
Voormezeele 82

War Office 4, 42
Wargnies 72
West Kents 124
Westoutre 32, 40, 59, 104
West Yorkshire Regiment, 1st Bn 10, 61, 62, 63, 64, 116, 120, 138, 148, 157, 179, 204, 209
West Ridings 39
Wiltshire Regiment, 1st Bn 10, 67, 72, 73, 74, 76, 79, 85, 86, 87, 88, 100, 102, 112, 137, 139, 148, 153, 156, 170, 171, 191, 210
Wing, Brigadier General 8
Witteport Farm 105, 130, 182, 197
Worcester Regt, 2nd Bn 28
Worcestershire Regiment, 3rd Bn 10, 70, 74, 76, 77, 78, 86, 87, 88, 89, 100, 101, 105, 130, 137, 170, 173, 175, 181, 185, 186, 192, 209
Wright, Lt 27
Wurttemberg, Duke of 14
Wurttemberg 14, 17, 144
Wytschaete 31, 64, 81

Yatman, Maj 25, 26

Ypres v, xi, xv, xvi, 3, 4, 10, 30, 31, 33, 34, 50, 51, 53. 60, 65, 68, 75, 77, 82, 88, 89, 93, 96, 104, 109, 111, 120, 122, 123, 128, 129, 140, 156, 182, 192, 193, 200, 201
Ypres, First Battle of 3, 35, 39, 67, 68, 69, 81, 109
Ypres-Menin Road v, xvii, 39, 40
Ypres-Roulers xvi
Ypres Salient xvi, 4, 9, 32, 34, 68, 83, 84, 105, 111, 120, 141, 186
Ypres, Second Battle of xv, 18, 19, 60, 69, 77, 82, 111, 127
Yser, Battle of 18
Yser Canal 120
Y Wood 127, 130, 143, 157, 170, 172, 181, 197

Zandvoorte 31
Zevecoten 125
Zillebeke 50, 54, 93, 104
Zouaves 39
Zouave Wood 60, 89, 112
Zwarteleen 81